The International Law of Environmental Impact Assessment

The central idea animating environmental impact assessment (EIA) is that decisions affecting the environment should be made through a comprehensive evaluation of predicted impacts. Notwithstanding their evaluative mandate, EIA processes do not impose specific environmental standards, but rely on the creation of open, participatory and information-rich decision-making settings to bring about environmentally benign outcomes.

In light of this tension between process and substance, Neil Craik assesses whether EIA, as a method of implementing international environmental law, is a sound policy strategy, and how international EIA commitments structure transnational interactions in order to influence decisions affecting the international environment.

Through a comprehensive description of international EIA commitments and their implementation within domestic and transnational governance structures, and drawing on specific examples of transnational EIA processes, the author examines how international EIA commitments can facilitate interest coordination, and provide opportunities for persuasion and for the internalization of international environmental norms.

NEIL CRAIK is an associate professor at the Faculty of Law, University of New Brunswick, where he teaches and researches in the fields of international environmental law and domestic (Canadian) environmental law. Prior to his academic appointment, Professor Craik practised environmental and land use law with a major Canadian law firm.

CAMBRIDGE STUDIES IN INTERNATIONAL AND COMPARATIVE LAW

Established in 1946, this series produces high quality scholarship in the fields of public and private international law and comparative law. Although these are distinct legal sub-disciplines, developments since 1946 confirm their interrelation.

Comparative law is increasingly used as a tool in the making of law at national, regional and international levels. Private international law is now often affected by international conventions, and the issues faced by classical conflicts rules are frequently dealt with by substantive harmonisation of law under international auspices. Mixed international arbitrations, especially those involving state economic activity, raise mixed questions of public and private international law, while in many fields (such as the protection of human rights and democratic standards, investment guarantees and international criminal law) international and national systems interact. National constitutional arrangements relating to 'foreign affairs', and to the implementation of international norms, are a focus of attention.

The Board welcomes works of a theoretical or interdisciplinary character, and those focusing on the new approaches to international or comparative law or conflicts of law. Studies of particular institutions or problems are equally welcome, as are translations of the best work published in other languages.

General Editors James Crawford SC FBA
Whewell Professor of International Law, Faculty of Law, and Director, Lauterpacht Research Centre for International Law, University of Cambridge
John S. Bell FBA
Professor of Law, Faculty of Law, University of Cambridge

Editorial Board Professor Hilary Charlesworth *Australian National University*
Professor Lori Damrosch *Columbia University Law School*
Professor John Dugard *Universiteit Leiden*
Professor Mary-Ann Glendon *Harvard Law School*
Professor Christopher Greenwood *London School of Economics*
Professor David Johnston *University of Edinburgh*
Professor Hein Kötz *Max-Planck-Institut, Hamburg*
Professor Donald McRae *University of Ottawa*
Professor Onuma Yasuaki *University of Tokyo*
Professor Reinhard Zimmermann *Universität Regensburg*

Advisory Committee Professor D. W. Bowett QC
Judge Rosalyn Higgins QC
Professor J. A. Jolowicz QC
Professor Sir Elihu Lauterpacht CBE QC
Professor Kurt Lipstein
Judge Stephen Schwebel

A list of books in the series can be found at the end of this volume.

The International Law of Environmental Impact Assessment

Process, Substance and Integration

Neil Craik

University of New Brunswick

CAMBRIDGE UNIVERSITY PRESS
Cambridge, New York, Melbourne, Madrid, Cape Town, Singapore, São Paulo, Delhi

Cambridge University Press
The Edinburgh Building, Cambridge CB2 8RU, UK

Published in the United States of America by Cambridge University Press, New York

www.cambridge.org
Information on this title: www.cambridge.org/9780521879453

© Neil Craik 2008

This publication is in copyright. Subject to statutory exception
and to the provisions of relevant collective licensing agreements,
no reproduction of any part may take place without
the written permission of Cambridge University Press.

First published 2008

Printed in the United Kingdom at the University Press, Cambridge

A catalogue record for this publication is available from the British Library

ISBN 978-0-521-87945-3 hardback

Cambridge University Press has no responsibility for the persistence or accuracy of URLs for external or third-party internet websites referred to in this publication, and does not guarantee that any content on such websites is, or will remain, accurate or appropriate.

Contents

Acknowledgments

I am grateful to a large number of colleagues, friends and family for their encouragement, support and guidance during the preparation and drafting (and redrafting) of this book. Foremost among those are the members of my doctoral dissertation (upon which this book is based) committee at the University of Toronto, consisting of my supervisor, Jutta Brunnée of the Faculty of Law, as well as Steven Bernstein of the Political Science Department, and Karen Knop and Lorne Sossin, both of the Faculty of Law. The committee's comments on earlier drafts and their critical questioning over the course of our many meetings improved the completed project immeasurably, and their encouragement and intellectual generosity were appreciated more than they know. I cannot adequately express the debt of gratitude I owe Jutta Brunnée. Not only did she expertly guide me through the project, she has provided me with the very best example of the kind of scholar I strive to become. Professor Ellen Hey of Erasmus University Rotterdam acted as the external appraiser of the thesis. Her constructive comments and insights were of great assistance to me in the subsequent revision of the draft manuscript. I also benefited from the comments of three anonymous reviewers for Cambridge University Press.

This book profited from my participation in the 2002 Academic Council of the United Nations System/American Society of International Law Summer Workshop in Windhoek, Namibia, where I presented a very early version of the ideas contained in the book, and I am grateful to the participants of that workshop for their helpful input. I would also acknowledge the kind assistance of officials from the Canadian Environmental Assessment Agency, the Canadian Department of Foreign Affairs and the Espoo Convention Secretariat, who shared their insights and answered my inquiries.

During my three years in residence at the Faculty of Law at the University of Toronto, I received generous financial support from both the Faculty and the University.

I have also benefited from the support of my colleagues at the University of New Brunswick Faculty of Law, and particularly Dean Philip Bryden, who ensured that I had sufficient time and resources to complete the book. Tracey Pennell (LLB, 2005) and David Yarwood (LLB, 2007) provided excellent editorial assistance in the latter stages of the project.

Although he was not involved in this project, Alan Boyle of the Edinburgh University Faculty of Law inspired my interest in international environmental law during my LLM studies under his supervision and continued in his support of my academic career long after I left Edinburgh.

I am grateful to the editorial and production staff at Cambridge University Press, particularly Finola O'Sullivan and Richard Woodham.

Finally, I would like to thank my family, particularly my parents, Fergus and Anne Craik, and my children, Lauren and William, for their support and forbearance. But my greatest thanks go to my spouse, Janet Craik. She was often the sounding board for many of the ideas in this thesis, and without question the quality of this project was greatly improved by my many discussions with her. Without her support, this project would never have been started, let alone completed. I am entirely indebted to her.

This book is dedicated to my parents.

Table of cases

Canada

United States

United Kingdom

European Community

International courts and tribunals

Table of international instruments

Treaties

Other international instruments

European Community documents

Part I Introduction

1 Introduction and overview

1.1 EIAs and the process and substance of international law

Government officials, when required to make a decision that has potential consequences for the natural environment, are faced with the daunting task of having to integrate political, scientific and normative considerations into a unified decision-making process. Where the decision in question has the potential to impact the environment of another state, or where the possible impact is to a resource of global common concern, decision-makers may have to account for the political, scientific and normative views of affected states, affected persons within other states, and the wider international community, including international organizations and nongovernmental actors. How decision-makers account for these considerations, the conditions under which they are required to account for them and the modalities by which these considerations are brought into domestic decision-making processes, are among the questions this book seeks to address. My interest is with the operation of a set of institutionalized decision-making arrangements commonly referred to as environmental impact assessment (EIA).[1] In particular, this book is concerned with the employment of EIA processes in domestic decision-making processes to address environmental issues that have international dimensions.

[1] Throughout this book, I refer to the term "EIA," by which I mean the broader process of environmental impact assessment, including specified ways of determining the applicability of the process, the assessment itself, its dissemination, the participatory processes that occur through the process and any post-project monitoring process directly related to the EIA process. The term "EIA," as used here, also captures "strategic environmental assessment" (SEA), which is the application of assessment methodology to policies, plans and programs.

The central idea that animates the EIA process, that decisions affecting the environment should be made in light of a comprehensive understanding of their effects, is straightforward enough. Yet, when EIA was introduced in the United States in 1969,[2] it was considered a significant innovation to the domestic policy-making landscape.[3] Not only did EIA commitments require the *ex ante* consideration of the environmental consequences of proposed activities, but they opened up decision-making processes to affected members of the public, environmental interest groups and interested government agencies by providing for an information-rich and participatory environment for agency decision-making. Despite its evaluative mandate, domestic EIA legislation does not impose specific environmental standards on the decision-making process. Moreover, even where an EIA discloses that a proposed activity is likely to have a significant adverse impact on the natural environment, the proponent of that activity is not necessarily required to abandon the activity or mitigate its adverse environmental affects. It is this absence of required substantive outcomes that has led EIA supporters to herald it as creative and efficient, but has similarly led to critiques of the process as being costly, ineffective and hopelessly naive.[4]

Notwithstanding the controversy surrounding EIA in domestic legal settings, EIA commitments have been rapidly adopted by countries, both developed and developing, throughout the globe. It is now estimated that in excess of 100 countries have EIA legislation.[5] EIAs have been similarly embraced by international policy-makers. EIA processes at the international level were considered as early as the Stockholm Conference, a scant two years after their adoption by the US federal government in the National Environmental Policy Act. EIA commitments are now contained in international instruments addressing a broad array of environmental issues and geographical contexts.[6] So, for example, international EIA commitments relate to transboundary impacts, impacts to areas of the

[2] National Environmental Policy Act, 42 USC §§ 4321–4370(f) (NEPA).

[3] Robert Bartlett, "Impact Assessment as a Policy Strategy" in R. V. Bartlett, ed., *Policy Through Impact Assessment: Institutionalized Analysis as a Policy Strategy* (Westport, CT: Greenwood Press, 1986) 1 at 1.

[4] Ibid. at 3.

[5] *Indicators and Environmental Impact Assessment*, UNEP CBD SBSTTA, 7th Meeting, UNEP/CBD/SBSTTA/7/13 (2001); B. Sadler, *Environmental Assessment in a Changing World: Final Report of the International Book of the Effectiveness of Environmental Assessment* (Ottawa: CEAA, 1996).

[6] See the list of instruments in Appendix 1 below.

global commons, as well as to impacts that may occur wholly within a state, but have an element of common concern to the international community, such as biodiversity and climate change.

Despite the wide-ranging incorporation of EIA commitments into international instruments,[7] there has been little critical consideration of the role that EIA commitments are intended to play within international environmental governance structures.[8] As an ostensibly procedural commitment, EIA does not require, as a matter of legal obligation, decision-makers to reach outcomes that reflect the substantive rules and values of the international instrument in which the EIA commitment is found. In light of its apparent ambivalence toward outcomes, EIA has been understood as a planning tool, rather than as a means to promote outcomes consonant with particular environmental norms. This purely procedural view of EIA was succinctly captured in the domestic context by the US Supreme Court when it noted that US federal EIA legislation "merely prohibits uninformed – rather than unwise – agency action."[9] The US Supreme Court was right, of course, in the sense that EIA commitments do not require decision-makers to adhere to particularized environmental standards. Yet, there is a difficulty in conceiving of EIA commitments, whether in a domestic or international context, in entirely procedural terms in that such an understanding conflicts with the stated environmental objectives of EIA.[10] In light of this tension between the substantive ambitions and the procedural orientation of EIA commitments, the central objective of this book is to assess whether EIA, as a method of implementing international environmental objectives, is a sound policy strategy, and how EIA commitments may structure scientific, political and normative considerations in such a way as to influence substantive outcomes.

[7] Throughout this book, I refer to EIA "commitments," as opposed to obligations. The significance of this distinction is that the term "obligation" may denote that the instrument in question has a formally binding character. This book has a broader focus, as it includes international instruments beyond treaties, such as guidelines and declarations of international institutions. This approach is consistent with other studies of international environmental law. See, for example, David G. Victor, Kal Raustiala and Eugene B. Skolnikoff, eds., *The Implementation and Effectiveness of International Environmental Commitments* (Cambridge, MA: MIT Press, 1998).

[8] A notable exception is Timo Koivurova, *Environmental Impact Assessment in the Arctic: A Book of International Legal Norms* (Aldershot: Ashgate Publishing, 2002).

[9] *Robertson* v. *Methow Valley Citizens Council*, 490 US 332 at 350–351 (1989).

[10] See, for example, NEPA, at § 4331.

1.2 Proceduralism, transnationalism and integration

It may be helpful at this early stage to draw out some characteristics that EIA commitments share with international environmental law more generally, as a way to situate this book within the broader framework of international environmental governance. Consider, for example, the dispute between the United Kingdom and Ireland respecting the authorization by the United Kingdom of a plant to manufacture mixed oxide (MOX) fuel as part of an existing nuclear facility located at Sellafield, England, on the Irish Sea.[11] The activity in dispute uses spent fuel elements from nuclear reactors located outside the United Kingdom and transported to Sellafield chiefly via the Irish Sea. The spent fuel is reprocessed, producing, among other things, plutonium oxide. The plutonium oxide is then mixed with uranium oxide in the MOX plant, producing MOX pellets, which can then be placed in fuel rods for use in nuclear power reactors. Ireland's principal concerns with the proposal revolve around the potential for harm to the marine environment that may arise as a result of the transportation of radioactive materials in and out of Sellafield and by virtue of the release of radioactive isotopes into the Irish Sea from the MOX plant and related activities through either liquid or aerial discharges. As a result of its concerns, Ireland objected to the establishment of the MOX plant, and, when its diplomatic efforts failed, the Irish government commenced litigation against the United Kingdom under the Convention for the Protection of the Marine Environment of the North-East Atlantic, 1992[12] and under the United Nations Convention on the Law of the Sea (UNCLOS).

In objecting to the project, the Irish government is faced with a number of complications. First of all, while Ireland maintains that the authorization of the MOX plant by UK authorities contravenes the United Kingdom's obligation to prevent harm to the marine environment, the existing customary and treaty-based obligations respecting marine pollution contain few quantifiable standards by which permissible discharges can be distinguished from impermissible ones. For example, UNCLOS includes an obligation requiring states "to protect and preserve the marine environment"[13] and to take all measures necessary to prevent

[11] For a description of the MOX plant litigation, see Robin Churchill and Joanne Scott, "The MOX Plant Litigation: The First Half-Life" (2004) 53 ICLQ 643.

[12] Paris, September 22, 1992, 32 ILM 1072, in force March 25, 1998 (the OSPAR Convention).

[13] UNCLOS, Montego Bay, December 10, 1982, 21 ILM 1261 (1982), entered into force November 16, 1984, Art. 192.

pollution of the marine environment from land-based sources and activities under their jurisdiction,[14] but these prohibitions are not elaborated upon. In the place of clearly discernible standards as to what constitutes illegal pollution, UNCLOS turns to process, requiring parties to cooperate with one another through requirements for notification, disclosure and consultation.[15] The point here is not that there is no substantive obligation to avoid marine pollution, but rather that the obligation is couched in such abstract terms that a determination as to legality can only be made with reference to a known context. As a result, many of Ireland's arguments in the proceedings under UNCLOS relate to the failure of the UK government to comply with its procedural obligations, including the duty to conduct an EIA in accordance with international standards.[16]

Secondly, the dispute itself is not exclusively an international one, at least not in a formal sense. For example, the actual proponent of the MOX plant is a private commercial enterprise (albeit with close ties to the UK government), and as such is not recognized as properly subject to international law. Moreover, it is not clear that the interests being protected by the Irish government, such as the protection of the economic rights of the Irish fishing and tourism industries that would be affected by the release of radioactive material into the Irish Sea, are exclusively state interests. The non-state dimension of the dispute is evident by the involvement in the dispute of a number of environmental nongovernmental organizations, such as Greenpeace and Friends of the Earth, who brought proceedings of their own.[17] In addition, while the United Kingdom's adherence to its international legal responsibilities lies at the center of the dispute, the boundaries between national, regional and international law are blurred. The EIA process that Ireland views as insufficient is a process constituted under the domestic law of the United Kingdom. Ireland, in fact, participated in parts of the process

[14] Ibid., Art. 194.

[15] Ibid., Arts. 123, 197 and 206.

[16] The obligation to conduct an EIA is found in Art. 206 of UNCLOS, but Ireland also draws on the EIA requirements found in other international and European Community instruments, chiefly the Convention on Environmental Impact Assessment in a Transboundary Context, 30 ILM 802, Espoo, Finland, February 25, 1991, in force January 14, 1998 (the "Espoo Convention"), and the EC EIA Directive, EC, Council Directive 85/337, OJ 1985 L175/40, amended by EC, Council Directive 97/11, OJ 1997 L73/5, and by EC, Council Directive 03/35 (the "EIA Directive").

[17] *R. (on the application of Friends of the Earth Ltd and Greenpeace Ltd)* v. *Secretary of State for Environment, Food and Rural Affairs and the Secretary of State for Health* [2001] EWCA Civ 1847; [2002] 1 CMLR 21; [2001] 50 EGCS 91; [2002] Env LR 24; [2001] NPC 181.

in much the same manner as other private parties.[18] In maintaining that the EIA process was inadequate, the Irish government not only points to the requirements for EIAs contained in international instruments, but also raises European Community law.[19] There were even comparisons of the MOX plant approvals process with a similar approvals process in the United States. The point being that a domestic environmental regulatory process may be subject to normative influences that cross the national/international divide, the public/private divide, as well as the binding/non-binding divide. It is perhaps telling that the controversy over the MOX plant has generated legal proceedings in the domestic courts of the United Kingdom,[20] before the International Tribunal for the Law of the Sea,[21] two separate international arbitrations[22] and before the European Court of Justice.[23]

Finally, the dispute is further complicated by questions of a scientific nature and by questions that implicate a broader range of economic and security considerations. So, for example, a central issue is whether the potential environmental impacts of the MOX plant proposal, chiefly the release of radioactive isotopes, are likely to cause "substantial pollution" – a determination that acts as a legal threshold to trigger certain procedural obligations, including those relating to EIA. Such an assessment requires both a technical understanding of the potential for intended and unintended releases and a scientific understanding of the environmental impacts of the potential releases over time. Moreover, the determination of impacts cannot be separated from social and economic considerations. The transportation of spent nuclear fuels through the Irish Sea has raised issues linking national security with marine pollution. Concerns have also been raised in respect of the inadequacy of

[18] Discussed in Churchill and Scott, "The MOX Plant Litigation" at 644–645.

[19] EIA Directive.

[20] *Friends of the Earth* v. *Secretary of State for the Environment.*

[21] *MOX Plant Case (Ireland* v. *United Kingdom)*, Provisional Measures, 41 ILM 405 (2002).

[22] The two separate arbitration cases were commenced in the Permanent Court of Arbitration in relation to alleged breaches of the OSPAR Convention and UNCLOS, respectively. The OSPAR proceedings related to access to information requested by Ireland. A final award, rejecting Ireland's claim, was made in July 2003: *Ireland* v. *United Kingdom* (OSPAR Arbitration), Final Award July 2, 2003, www.pca-cpa.org. The proceedings under UNCLOS (the provisional measures were heard by the ITLOS) were suspended pending a determination by the European Court of Justice as to whether the European Court of Justice has exclusive jurisdiction over the dispute: *Ireland* v. *United Kingdom (MOX Plant Case)*, Order No. 4, November 14, 2003, www.pca-cpa.org.

[23] Case C-459/03, *Commission* v. *Ireland*, Judgment, May 30, 2006, finding that the European Court of Justice has exclusive jurisdiction.

the economic justification for the MOX plant itself, a requirement of the European nuclear regulatory authorities linked to domestic EIA requirements.[24] In light of the overlapping of environmental issues with economic and political policy objectives, decision-making processes must be designed to integrate these different and often competing considerations.

EIA obligations, which are at the center of the MOX plant litigation, respond to these complications by providing a procedural mechanism that allows decision-makers to consider the environmental consequences of their proposed activities within a highly contextualized framework. The result is a mechanism that brings together scientific, political and normative considerations in a decision-making process that is directed toward a range of transnational actors, whose inclusion in the process is determined not so much by their formal status, as by their potential to be impacted by the decision being made. If one accepts that the turn toward proceduralism, transnationalism and integration is not confined to the MOX plant dispute, but represents a broader trend in international environmental law, then international EIA requirements, which respond to these characteristics, are at the very least deserving of our attention.

As these characteristics and their relationship to EIA commitments underlie much of the discussion that follows, some elaboration of the significance of these characteristics for this book is warranted. First, by examining procedural commitments, I do not mean to marginalize or subordinate the role of substantive obligations and principles in international environmental law. Quite to the contrary, much of the analysis of international EIA commitments looks beyond the procedural requirements of EIA commitments to the relationship between EIA process and the substantive environmental goals of the international community. Since much of the focus of this book is on how the procedural requirements of EIA commitments structure interactions between interested actors and operationalize substantive norms and scientific findings, this book also looks in detail at the relationship between EIA requirements and other general principles of international environmental law, such as the harm principle, the duty to cooperate and the relationship of EIAs to the concept of sustainable development. In addition, I examine the development and structure of EIA processes in domestic law, which has clearly influenced the international obligations in both their development and implementation.

[24] Directive 96/27/Euratom, OJ 1996 L159/1.

The relationship between international EIA commitments and domestic EIA systems points to the transnationalism of EIA commitments.[25] As the MOX plant litigation indicates, while obligations to conduct EIAs may arise as an international commitment, the process itself is carried out in a domestic setting. The transnational nature of the process impacts who can participate, and it also provides an avenue for the projection of international norms into domestic decision-making processes. For example, part of Ireland's concern is to ensure that the geographic scope of the EIA includes environmental impacts to areas, such as the Irish Sea, that are beyond the territory of the United Kingdom, but also to ensure that the domestic EIA process accounts for substantive principles and standards of international law, such as the duty to prevent pollution to the marine environment.[26] In some cases the distinction between domestic and international norms within EIA processes is difficult to discern. Biological diversity and climate change norms, for example, are matters affecting the domestic environment, but have implications for the health of the global environment, and as such are considered as part of this book. It follows from this that there is a broad range of interactions that are germane to this book, including traditional (for international law) state-to-state interactions, interactions between the agencies of one state and the agencies of another, and interactions between non-governmental organizations and decision-makers where international environmental norms are being projected into domestic EIA processes.

Finally, the trend toward greater integration points to one of the central tensions within international environmental governance. Environmental decision-making inevitably requires choices to be made between competing values, often pitting economic goals against environmental considerations. The driving motivation behind the development of EIA processes was the recognition that environmental considerations were

[25] The term "transnational," as used in this book, adopts the definition as first put forward by Philip Jessup, who used the term "transnational law" to indicate those laws that regulate actions or events that transcend national boundaries, including interactions between both public and private actors. Transnational law in this regard has a broader scope than international law (at least as formally understood), which operates only between states. See Philip Jessup, *Transnational Law* (New Haven, CT: Yale University Press, 1956) at 2.

[26] *MOX Plant Case* (Annex VII Arbitration), Memorial of Ireland, paras. 7.50–7.57 (noting, for example, in para. 7.54, Ireland's concerns that the EIA was "deficient by reason of the fact that it failed to take *any* account of the material developments in English, EC and international law which occurred since 1993 for the protection of the marine environment of the Irish Sea").

far too often marginalized by agency decision-makers, who viewed environmental objectives as peripheral to their policy objectives. At a minimum, domestic EIA legislation requires agency decision-makers not to ignore the environmental consequences of their proposed activities. Consequently, EIA requirements were developed as a strategy for bureaucratic reform. While some view the process of evaluating environmental consequences as a value-free and technical exercise, it is evident that domestic EIA processes in their operation are more political, requiring decision-makers to choose between environmental and economic goals. At the international level, the division between development goals and environmental goals is further complicated by the demands of sovereignty, since the state of origin (that state in which the proposed activity is to be located) claims a sovereign right to economic development within its territory without interference, while the affected state claims a sovereign right to not be subjected to environmental harm. A similar, although less stark, division arises in relation to impacts to areas of the global commons (which states have a sovereign right to utilize) and to issues of global common concern. Fundamental to the operation of EIA processes as a means to mediate this tension is that neither side can ignore the reasonable claims of the other. Because neither proponent may claim a superior right, the reconciliation of these competing claims is inherently political. However, this book proceeds from the understanding that these political interactions are constrained by legal and scientific norms. The central argument that is presented in this book is that the way in which EIA commitments structure interactions, who can participate in those interactions, and how those commitments influence the scientific and normative inputs will shape the political processes in such a way that decision-makers will be drawn toward outcomes that are reflective of international environmental norms.

1.3 EIAs and compliance

Many of the claims that this book develops in relation to the role and operation of EIA commitments are framed with reference to explanations developed by international legal and international relations scholars of state compliance with international law. More precisely, I draw upon process-oriented approaches to international law and compliance, which emphasize the role of legal norms in interactions that are oriented toward persuasion rather than coercion.[27] The common thread

[27] Discussed below at ch. 6.3.

to process-oriented explanations of compliance is the belief that compliant behavior depends less on the enforceability of the norm invoked and more upon process values, such as transparency, access to information and broad public participation, all of which are geared toward bringing about reasoned communication between interested parties. These explanations do not suggest that state interests do not influence state behavior, but unlike some rationalist (interest-based) explanations, process-oriented scholarship tends not to reduce state behavior to interest maximization alone.[28]

Comparing EIA processes with the features of legal processes that promote compliance with international law, it is argued that international EIA commitments are well suited to integrate international environmental norms into decision-making processes and to promote outcomes that reflect prevailing international environmental norms. For example, EIAs institutionalize process values such as transparency, access to information and public participation. Additionally, the EIA process itself is largely discursive, requiring the proponent to interact with potential objectors and to justify its environmental decisions in a public forum and in light of prevailing environmental norms. In the context of international environmental law, it is particularly germane that the contextualized nature of the EIA process lends itself to the implementation of abstract principles. Given the normative landscape of international environmental law, which is characterized by open-textured principles, such as sustainable development and the duty to prevent transboundary harm, one may expect EIAs to play a prominent role in the implementation and compliance structures of various international environmental regimes.

To avoid confusion, two immediate points of clarification are helpful. First, my interest in compliance is not oriented toward providing a detailed examination or explanation of the circumstances under which states comply with their obligations to conduct EIAs. This issue is not unimportant in my view, but the intent here is to examine how international EIA commitments themselves influence state decision-making processes. Secondly, in drawing the parallel between EIA processes and compliance-promoting mechanisms, I do not mean to suggest that EIA processes produce outcomes that strictly adhere to normative prescriptions existing in international environmental law. Rather, compliance

[28] See Oona Hathaway, "Between Power and Principle: An Integrated Theory of International Law" (2005) 21 Chicago L. Rev. 469.

theory is used as a means to explain how certain features institutionalized by EIA commitments influence state decision-making processes. This book does, however, argue that EIA processes bring about compliance in the broad sense of pulling decision-makers toward outcomes that reflect international environmental values. The use of the term "compliance" in this sense differs from the conceptualization of compliance used by many international legal and international relations scholars, who view the process of compliance as being wholly distinct from the process of norm creation.[29] In contrast, this book examines the relationship between the process of elaborating upon norms through their contextual application and policy outcomes.

Flowing from this analysis, I describe two complementary roles that EIA processes play in international environmental governance structures. First, EIAs perform a broad interest-coordination function through the institutionalization of process values in domestic decision-making process where there is a likelihood of environmental impact. This characterization of EIA processes is consistent with explanations of the operation of EIA processes in relation to purely domestic environmental issues, and, as such, is unsurprising. However, framing the discussion in the context of theories of state compliance provides a more complete understanding of how the procedural elements of EIA operate in transnational settings. The second role of EIAs this book identifies, that EIAs provide opportunities for broad interest-transformation, is a less conventional understanding of EIA processes, as it emphasizes the substantive normativity of EIA processes. With reference to the projection of international environmental norms into specific domestic EIA processes, it is argued that through repeated interactions where norms are raised and considered in the context of specific project approvals, those norms can become internalized within the decision-making fabric of the domestic agencies. In this manner, EIA commitments, which require domestic decision-makers to account for international environmental norms, can produce domestic policy outcomes that are broadly reflective of the goals of international environmental law.

[29] For examples of studies of compliance with international environmental law using this narrower conception of compliance, see Edith Brown Weiss and Harold Jacobsen, eds., *Engaging Countries: Strengthening Compliance with International Environmental Accords* (Cambridge, MA: MIT Press, 1998) and Oran Young, ed., *The Effectiveness of International Environmental Regimes: Causal Connections and Behavioral Mechanisms* (Cambridge, MA: MIT Press, 1999).

1.4 Overview

The argument that is presented in this book proceeds in three principal parts. Chapters 2 and 3 describe the background norms that have influenced the development of international EIA commitments. These influences arise from domestic settings, where EIA processes were first developed, and international settings, particularly preexisting general principles of international environmental law. The discussion of domestic EIA systems is intended to provide an understanding of the basic features of EIA, and to consider the structure and role of EIA processes within domestic settings. As noted above, domestic EIA systems have added relevance as the mechanism by which international EIA commitments are implemented and as the process into which international environmental norms are projected into. As it is not uncommon for domestic EIA processes to consider the impacts of projects outside the territory of the state even in the absence of an international obligation to do so, the extent to which EIA has been applied extraterritorially and the limitations of the extraterritorial extension of EIA are considered. The extraterritorial application of domestic EIA is discussed in relation to the principle of nondiscrimination and equal access – which requires states to treat environmental impacts to other states in a manner similar to its treatment of domestic impacts. Finally, in this part there is a discussion of the relationship of EIA obligations to two foundational principles of international environmental law: the harm principle and the duty of cooperation. Here, it is argued that these principles provide a demand for a mechanism such as EIA in international law and provide the normative foundation for the development of the international EIA commitments described in Chapters 4 and 5.

Chapters 4 and 5 describe the major EIA commitments developed in multilateral environmental instruments. This discussion includes those EIA commitments that were developed as part of a broader substantive regime, such as the EIA commitments contained in UNCLOS and the Convention on Biological Diversity, and those that were developed as stand-alone procedural mechanisms, the most prominent being the Convention on Environmental Impact Assessment in a Transboundary Context.[30] The treatment of EIA commitments in interstate disputes and the question of the customary status of EIA commitments are also addressed

[30] Convention on Environmental Impact Assessment in a Transboundary Context, 30 ILM 802, Espoo, Finland, February 25, 1991, in force January 14, 1998 (the "Espoo Convention").

in Chapter 4. However, in light of the existence of a large number of treaty-based EIA commitments, the focus here is on the interrelationship of separate EIA commitments and how these sometimes overlapping commitments should be interpreted, and less on delineating the possible existence and scope of a formal customary obligation to perform EIAs.

The foremost intention of this part is to provide a comprehensive understanding of the structure of EIA commitments in international law. By structure, I mean to examine the particular requirements of the commitment, the kinds of environmental issues EIAs are called upon to consider, what actors the commitments contemplate being involved in the EIA process, how those commitments are to be implemented and the relationship of the EIA requirements to the substantive requirements of the regime or to substantive requirements existing in international environmental law more generally. Examining EIA commitments across a range of different environmental regimes and institutional contexts allows for some tentative conclusions to be drawn regarding the determinants of EIA commitments.

The discussion of the structure of EIA commitments in Chapters 4 and 5 provides, in turn, the basis for the analysis of the role of EIA commitments that follows in Chapters 6 and 7. As described above, the central arguments that are put forward in this part examine the role of EIA commitments in implementing and promoting compliance with substantive environment principles of international law. To this end, Chapter 6 identifies a set of governance features that are likely to have a positive influence on compliance with international law, namely, transparency, participation, discursiveness, contextuality and normativity. In order to provide a theoretical justification for these features, this chapter outlines what I identify as process-oriented approaches to compliance with international law. I then examine how international EIA commitments reflect these characteristics. This examination is evaluative in the sense that EIA commitments are assessed in light of their ability to generate open and discursive interactions between participants and to project normative considerations into those interactions.

The lynchpin of process-oriented compliance explanations is the role of legitimacy in promoting state behavior that reflects community values. The role of legitimacy as it relates specifically to EIAs is taken up in Chapter 7. Here, the concept of legitimacy is disaggregated into three related aspects: scientific legitimacy, political legitimacy and normative legitimacy. These three forms of legitimacy have each been recognized as playing an important function in EIA processes, but the interrelationship between them remains unsatisfactorily addressed. Through an examination of these different forms of legitimacy, Chapter 7 shows how EIA brings these different strands of legitimacy together in mutually reinforcing ways.

Chapter 8, which is the concluding chapter, discusses the findings of this book in the context of sustainable development, and considers the broader implications of the book for international environmental governance and for the concept of compliance. This book is not intended to be an empirical examination of the effectiveness of international EIA commitments. However, insofar as this book proposes to make sense of the relationship between process and substance, it is not indifferent to the issue of effectiveness. In this regard, this book seeks to contribute to the debate on the effectiveness of international environmental institutions by providing a model of how EIA processes may impact state decision-making. In other words, before we can assess *how well* international EIAs are working, it is necessary to understand *what* their function is and *how* they work.

1.5 Method

An examination of international obligations to conduct EIAs and their influence on environmental decision-making requires an understanding of both how legal meaning (of EIA obligations) is arrived at and of the relationship of normative influences to state behavior. These are questions of methodology in that they are analytically prior to the main inquiry. Most discussions about method, including the present one, involve a certain amount of labeling and compartmentalizing. The advantage of labeling methods is that it serves to situate a study within a broader analytical framework and a shared intellectual heritage. In the case of International Legal Process (ILP) scholarship, an approach closely related to the one adopted here, international lawyers have drawn inspiration from a set of ideas that have their origin in American public law scholarship that arose after the Second World War. This approach is most prominently associated with the ideas of Legal Process scholars, as well as more recent work by New Legal Process scholars.[31]

[31] The intellectual history of the Legal Process school is discussed in Neil Duxbury, *Patterns of American Jurisprudence* (New York: Oxford University Press, 1995) ch. 4. See also William Eskridge Jr. and Philip Frickey, "An Historical and Critical Introduction

The tendency toward compartmentalization may, however, leave the mistaken impression that different methodological approaches are mutually exclusive and in competition with each other, whereas in fact they are overlapping and often complementary.[32] For example, ILP scholarship shares many assumptions with both positivist and Policy Science (New Haven School) scholars, but it also draws, in its contemporary iterations, on feminist, civic republican and critical scholarship in both domestic and international law. Because of the diffuse range of influences in ILP scholarship, there is no contemporary school or a self-identified group of scholars who consider themselves to be working within a defined methodological context associated with Legal Process. In light of this, this study does not adopt the label of ILP or New ILP to describe the method outlined, but instead refers to process-oriented approaches to international law.[33]

Despite the diverse range of influences evident in process-oriented scholarship, there are a number of consistent themes that are threaded through process-oriented scholarship in international law that lend coherence to the idea of a distinct process-oriented methodology in international law. At the center is a desire to mediate law's relationship with politics and power. The evolution of process-oriented scholarship in both domestic and international legal settings is characterized by attempts to maintain for law a degree of autonomy from politics by emphasizing the unique role of reason within legal processes. Reason, in this context, is not the deductive logic of formalism, but rather stresses the purposive nature of legal norms and the dynamic and contextual nature of legal interpretation. This in turn points to the central role of process itself within a legal system. Process, because it is constitutive of substantive rules and governs their application, is viewed as being paramount.[34] By focusing on process and institutional arrangements, process-oriented scholars have come to see questions regarding

to the Legal Process" in Henry Hart Jr. and Albert Sacks, eds., *The Legal Process: Basic Problems in the Making and Application of Law*, prepared for publication from the 1958 tentative edition by Eskridge and Frickey (Westbury, NY: Foundation Press, 1994) li; and Edward Rubin, "The New Legal Process, the Synthesis of Discourse, and the Microanalysis of Institutions" (1996) 109 Harvard L. Rev. 1393.

[32] Steven Ratner and Anne-Marie Slaughter, "The Method Is the Message" (1999) 93 AJIL 410 at 410.

[33] The term "New ILP" has been used by Mary Ellen O'Connell to describe approaches to international law that build on the ideas contained in contemporary domestic Legal Process scholarship, often referred to as "New Legal Process" or "New Public Law": Mary Ellen O'Connell, "New International Legal Process" (1999) 93 AJIL 334 at 338.

[34] Hart and Sacks, *The Legal Process* at 3–4.

how law is made and who makes it as critical considerations in realizing social objectives. Consequently, the examination of institutional competences and their allocation within the legal system, choices regarding approaches to regulation and the interpretation of legal norms figure largely in process-oriented scholarship. Finally, process-oriented scholarship breaks from formal positivist conceptions of law in that it seeks to locate the legitimacy of law within law itself.[35] On this last point, process-oriented scholarship has progressively moved away from a purely procedural understanding of legitimacy based on right process toward a more substantive version resting on just outcomes.[36]

The publication that is most widely associated with ILP scholarship is a textbook prepared by international law professors Abram Chayes, Thomas Ehrlich and Andreas Lowenfeld entitled *International Legal Process: Materials for an Introductory Course*.[37] In the introduction to their casebook, Chayes, Ehrlich and Lowenfeld include an excerpt from the book *American Diplomacy* by political realist George Kennan, the gist of which is that international legal institutions are too inflexible and removed from the hard realities of international affairs to be of any real use to the practitioners of statecraft.[38] It is this understanding of international law as abstract and idealistic that Chayes, Ehrlich and Lowenfeld sought to challenge by demonstrating that international law does indeed shape and even constrain the interrelations of states.[39] The debate regarding the relationship between legal norms and legal institutions on the one hand, and state behavior on the other, has led many process-oriented scholars to draw on the work of international relations scholars, and much of their work sits comfortably within what Anne-Marie Slaughter and her colleagues have identified as a growing interdisciplinary (international relations (IR)/international law (IL)) body of scholarship.[40]

[35] See H. L. A. Hart, "Positivism and the Separation of Law and Morals" (1958) 71 Harvard L. Rev. 593; and L. Fuller, "Positivism and Fidelity to Law – A Reply to Professor Hart" (1958) 71 Harvard L. Rev. 630.

[36] William Eskridge Jr. and Gary Peller, "The New Public Law Movement: Moderation as a Postmodern Cultural Form" (1991) 89 Michigan L. Rev. 707 at 746–747.

[37] Abram Chayes, Thomas Ehrlich and Andreas Lowenfeld, *International Legal Process: Materials for an Introductory Course* (New York: Little, Brown and Co., 1968).

[38] Ibid. at xii, referencing George Kennan, *American Diplomacy, 1900–1950* (Chicago: University of Chicago Press, 1951) 98.

[39] See also Abram Chayes, *The Cuban Missile Crisis* (New York: Oxford University Press, 1974).

[40] Anne-Marie Slaughter, Andrew Tulumello and Stepan Wood, "International Law and International Relations Theory: A New Generation of Interdisciplinary Scholarship" (1998) 92 AJIL 367. See also Anne-Marie Slaughter Burley, "International Law and International Relations Theory: A Dual Agenda" (1993) 87 AJIL 205.

This book, through its examination of international EIA commitments, picks up on several of the key themes found in process-oriented scholarship in international law. As a point of departure, this book maintains that process can affect state behavior in important ways. Much of the research respecting compliance undertaken by IR scholars has tended to lump legal rules and principles under the broad and nebulous heading of "norms," without distinguishing between legal and non-legal norms, much less between different types of legal norms themselves. Not surprisingly, some international lawyers have criticized this tendency, arguing that legal obligations may operate to constrain state behavior in unique ways and must, therefore, be differentiated from other normative influences in compliance studies.[41] This book seeks to contribute to this debate by examining how procedural norms, as a distinct form of normative ordering, can structure interactions between states and between other transnational actors with consequences for environmental outcomes.

At the center of these discussions is the complex interrelationship between process and substance in international law. Unlike more cosmopolitan approaches to international law, process-oriented approaches reject the presence of a single "foundationalist" approach to legal meaning. Instead, process-oriented scholars have appealed to pragmatism or "practical reason" as underlying legal normativity. Practical reasoning posits that through deliberation and empathetic understanding of different points of view, common understandings may arise between states, which in turn provide a basis for further elaboration of norms.[42] The possibility that international legal norms can be created and sustained through deliberative interactions between transnational actors recognizes that state interests and state identities are not fixed, but may be transformed through interactions with other transnational actors.[43] From a process-oriented perspective, international EIA commitments,

[41] See Michael Byers, "Response: Taking the Law Out of International Law: A Critique of the 'Iterative Perspective'" (1997) 38 Harvard ILJ 201. See also Martha Finnemore, "Response: Are Legal Norms Distinctive" (2000) 32 NYU J. Int'l L & Pol'y 699; and Jutta Brunnée and Stephen Toope, "International Law and Constructivism: Elements of an Interactional Theory of International Law" (2000) 39 Columbia J. Transnat'l L. 19 at 24.

[42] Stephen Toope, "Emerging Patterns of Governance and International Law" in Michael Byers, ed., *The Role of Law in International Politics: Essays in International Relations and International Law* (New York: Oxford University Press, 2000) 91.

[43] The understanding of state interests and identities as being endogenous to interactions connects process-oriented scholars to constructivist IR theory, both of which draw on continental social theorists such as Foucault, Luhmann and Habermas. See Rubin, "The New Legal Process" at 1416–1426. See also Harold Koh, "Why Do Nations Obey International Law" (1997) 106 Yale LJ 2599.

which structure interactions, operate as both a means to arrive at legitimate environmental policy outcomes, and as an end in themselves since the process is constitutive of the participants' interests and identities and is an integral part of community membership. In this context, legitimacy is dependent upon adherence to both procedural and substantive requirements, neither of which have claims to neutrality, but will be assessed with reference to their congruence with broader social, scientific and political norms.

By bringing legitimacy into law, as opposed to maintaining the positivists' insistence on a separation of legality and legitimacy, contemporary process-oriented scholars acknowledge that law and politics, or, more pointedly in the international context, law and power, are inextricably linked. This places contemporary process-oriented scholars very much in the same position as their predecessors in trying to navigate the division between law as abstract and removed from state interaction and law as a pure reflection of state interests and state power.[44] This desire to find the middle ground between these poles reflects another often noted characteristic of process-oriented scholarship, the inclination for moderation and centrism in approaches to legal scholarship.[45] What moderation requires is that in the legal sphere the scope of politics be limited or cabined in such a way as to maximize the exercise of reasoned decision-making or, to use Friedrich Kratochwil's phrase, to maximize the ability "to gain assent to value judgments on reasoned rather than idiosyncratic grounds."[46] At its foundation, this book seeks to assess the capacity of international EIA commitments to achieve this end.

[44] Discussed in Martti Koskenniemi, "The Politics of International Law" (1990) 1 EJIL 4.

[45] See Eskridge and Peller, "The New Public Law Movement" at 787–790; see also Kent Roach, "What's New and Old About the Legal Process" (1997) 47 University of Toronto LJ 363at 392–393.

[46] Friedrich Kratochwil, *Rules, Norms, and Decisions on the Conditions of Practical and Legal Reasoning in International Relations and Domestic Affairs* (New York: Cambridge University Press, 1989) at 214.

Part II Background norms

2 Domestic origins of international EIA commitments

2.1 Introduction

The development of EIA commitments in international law has occurred against a backdrop of normative arrangements existing in domestic and international legal settings. EIA as a distinct form of public decision-making was first developed under US federal law as part of the National Environmental Policy Act (NEPA).[1] Subsequently, EIA processes were developed by a number of US states, and in the mid-1970s countries such as Canada, France, Australia and New Zealand developed their own EIA processes.[2] Since the 1970s, the adoption of EIA legislation has grown steadily throughout the world, and it is now estimated that over 100 countries have EIA legislation.[3] EIA norms have not only spread horizontally to other states, but they have also spread vertically, influencing the development of EIA norms in international law and within international organizations. The globalization of EIA commitments has not, however, been a one-way projection of domestic environmental policy into a transnational setting. The reception and development of EIA commitments by other states in both their domestic and international decision-making processes has also been influenced by general principles of international environmental law, such as the principle of nondiscrimination, the duty to prevent transboundary harm and the duty to

[1] 42 USC §§ 4321–4370(f) (2000) (NEPA).

[2] Nicholas Robinson, "International Trends in Environmental Impact Assessment" (1991–92) 19 Boston College Environmental Affairs L. Rev. 591 at 597. See also Christopher Wood, "What NEPA Has Wrought Abroad" in Larry Canter and Ray Clark, eds., *Environmental Policy and NEPA: Past, Present and Future* (Boca Raton, FL: St. Lucie Press, 1997), ch. 7.

[3] B. Sadler, *Environmental Assessment in a Changing World: Final Report of the International Study of the Effectiveness of Environmental Assessment* (Ottawa: Canadian Environmental Assessment Agency, 1996) § 2.2.2.

cooperate with other states to preserve and protect the natural environment. Latterly, the constellation of principles surrounding sustainable development that has become embedded in transnational environmental governance structures has also influenced the development of EIA processes in transnational legal settings.[4]

Mapping the relationship between these sets of background norms and the development of international EIA commitments provides an understanding of the structure and role of international EIA commitments. For example, the domestic EIA processes that were developed in the 1970s and 1980s form the template upon which the international commitments are based in terms of the elements of the process itself and in terms of the role that EIA performs within the broader regulatory framework of the state. Domestic EIA systems are also fundamentally a part of the international EIA framework in that the international commitments to conduct EIAs are implemented by incorporating the international requirements into the existing domestic EIA framework. In this regard, domestic EIA processes are themselves sites for the projection of international environmental norms into domestic policy decisions. Consequently, the receptiveness of domestic EIA to normative influences arising outside the state will impact the effectiveness of EIA processes in aiding the implementation of international environmental obligations.

In addition to influencing the form of international EIA commitments, background norms play a role in creating the conditions under which international cooperation in relation to EIAs is more or less likely to arise. In effect, background norms influence the demand by the international community for rules on EIA. To the extent that states can satisfactorily address extraterritorial environmental impacts unilaterally or with minimal cooperation from other states, then there will be less demand for detailed international rules on EIA. The extension of domestic EIA processes to environmental impacts beyond the territorial boundaries of the state should be viewed as a form of international environmental regulation, but with considerable limitations, not the least of which is the lack of reciprocity between states concerning the application of EIA processes outside the state. Examining the nature of these limitations and their relationship to existing international legal rules (principally those relating to jurisdiction) will also inform our understanding of the structure and role international EIA commitments.

[4] See Steven Bernstein, *The Compromise of Liberal Environmentalism* (New York: Columbia University Press, 2002).

While tracing the influence of domestic EIA processes on the development of their international counterparts is largely a descriptive effort, there are also normative aspects to this exercise that should be borne in mind. The procedural nature of EIA requirements and the relationship of process requirements to environmental goals has been the subject of considerable domestic controversy. This in turn has given rise to debates over the role that EIA processes play within the broader framework of environmental regulation in the state. Because these debates relate in part to the nature of decision-making structures and processes within the state, the appropriateness of adopting EIA processes in decision-making processes beyond the state depends on the extent to which these structures and processes are available in international settings.

The development of EIA process in international law and across different domestic settings worldwide is difficult to disentangle because of the mutual influences of each on the other. However, this fact is reflective of the increasingly blurred distinction between international and domestic law in the environmental field, where international commitments are equally oriented toward the behavior of states and individual actors within states and where domestic requirements and domestic agencies may look beyond the state without prompting from international instruments. That said, it remains helpful to treat domestic and international influences on the development of EIA commitments independently since they are conceptually and functionally distinct. For example, international legal norms operate vertically and involve some measure of legal obligation, while domestic EIA structures influence international law by providing exemplars and by influencing the update of international commitments by states. With this in mind, this chapter examines the form that EIAs have taken in domestic legal systems and the roles of domestic EIA in structuring decision-making processes in regards to both the domestic and the extraterritorial environmental impacts. Chapter 3 describes the impact that general principles of international law have had in the development of international EIA commitments, which are described in detail in the chapters that follow.

2.2 Elements of domestic EIA processes

The formation of EIA processes within domestic settings may best be understood as fulfilling the need for policy-makers to understand the environmental consequences of their decisions. Given the intuitive and fundamental nature of that need, the global diffusion of EIA norms reflects this increasingly shared starting point. In order for environmental information to be useful within decision-making processes, two basic components are required. First, policy-makers need to know what environmental objectives they should take into account, and, secondly, there is a need for a mechanism through which information that is responsive to those objectives can enter into decision-making processes. This basic structure is captured in embryonic form in section 101 of NEPA, which sets out both the US federal government's environmental policy objectives and requires federal government decision-makers to use "all practical means and measures" to fulfill these environmental objectives.[5] These means and measures are left unspecified in the legislation, except for the requirement that all federal government agencies prepare "a detailed statement" describing the potential environmental impacts of any proposed federal action where that proposed action may significantly affect the quality of the human environment.[6] This requirement for a detailed statement provides the legislative basis for the modern EIA system.

It is perhaps surprising, given its subsequent prominence, that the requirement to produce a "detailed statement," later referred to as an environmental impact study (EIS), arose fairly late in the legislative process and the impact of the inclusion of the requirement was most likely underestimated by Congress at the time of its passing.[7] Lynton Caldwell, a political scientist and one of NEPA's chief architects, explained the necessity to include the EIS requirement in the following terms:

> I would urge that in the shaping of such a policy, it have an action-forcing, operational aspect. When we speak of policy we ought to think of a statement which is so written that it is capable of implementation; that it is not merely a statement of things hoped for; not merely a statement of desirable goals or objectives; but that it is a statement which will compel or reinforce or assist all of these things, the executive agencies in particular, but going beyond this, the Nation as a whole, to take the kind of action which will protect and reinforce what I have called the life support system of the country.[8]

According to Caldwell, including the requirement for a "detailed statement" on the environmental impacts of a proposed action takes the statement of environmental policy objectives in NEPA beyond being merely

[5] NEPA, § 4331. [6] Ibid., § 4332.

[7] Michael Herz, "Parallel Universes: NEPA Lessons for the New Property" (1993) 93 Columbia L. Rev. 1668 at 1677–1678.

[8] Hearings on S. 1075, S. 237 and S. 1752 before Senate Comm., *On Interior and Insular Affairs*, 91 Cong., 1st Sess. 116 (1969).

aspirational or hortatory to being capable of affecting policy decisions by federal agencies.

The plain wording of the EIS requirement within NEPA does not betray the elaborate process of study, evaluation and consultation that has arisen from this straightforward and common-sense requirement, and, while the trajectory of this development has not followed the same path in all countries,[9] a generalized structure that is common to domestic EIA systems has arisen.[10] This structure is represented in Figure 1 and consists of the following components: (1) screening; (2) scoping; (3) impact analysis and report preparation; (4) public and agency participation; (5) final decision; and (6) follow up. Because this basic structure has been adopted in international EIA commitments, it is useful to briefly outline its components.

Screening. The threshold consideration for any EIA system is the extent of its application. The initial range of activities that is captured by EIA requirements has tended to be defined in extremely broad terms, requiring, in the case of NEPA, an EIS to be prepared for virtually all "major federal actions." Under NEPA, EIA was conceived of as a qualification to federal governmental decision-making and thus required some federal government action to trigger the application of the EIA process. The focus on governmental activity has the effect of excluding activities, such as purely private activities or those subject only to sub-state government oversight, that nevertheless have potential environmental impacts. In some jurisdictions, such as Canada, the gaps in federal coverage are supplemented by comprehensive EIA requirements at the sub-state level, but this is not always the case. The US, for example, has notable gaps in its coverage due to the absence of comprehensive EIA requirements in many states. In still other jurisdictions, the approach has been to identify areas of *prima facie* application without a requirement for a governmental trigger.[11] Instead, the legislation identifies industrial sectors

9 See Anne Hironaka, "The Globalization of Environmental Protection: The Case of Environmental Impact Assessment" (2002) 43(1) International Journal of Comparative Sociology 65, discussing the development of EIA in developing countries; see also D. Kobus *et al.*, "Comparison and Evaluation of EIA Systems in Countries in Transition" in E. Bellinger *et al.*, eds., *Environmental Assessment in Countries in Transition* (Budapest: CEU Press, 2000), discussing the development of EIA in Eastern Europe.

10 Jane Holder, *Environmental Assessment: The Regulation of Decision-Making* (New York: Oxford University Press, 2004) at 12.

11 This is the approach in most European Community countries, following the requirements of the European Council Directive 85/337 on the Assessment of the Effects of Certain Public and Private Projects on the Environment, OJ 1985 L175/40,

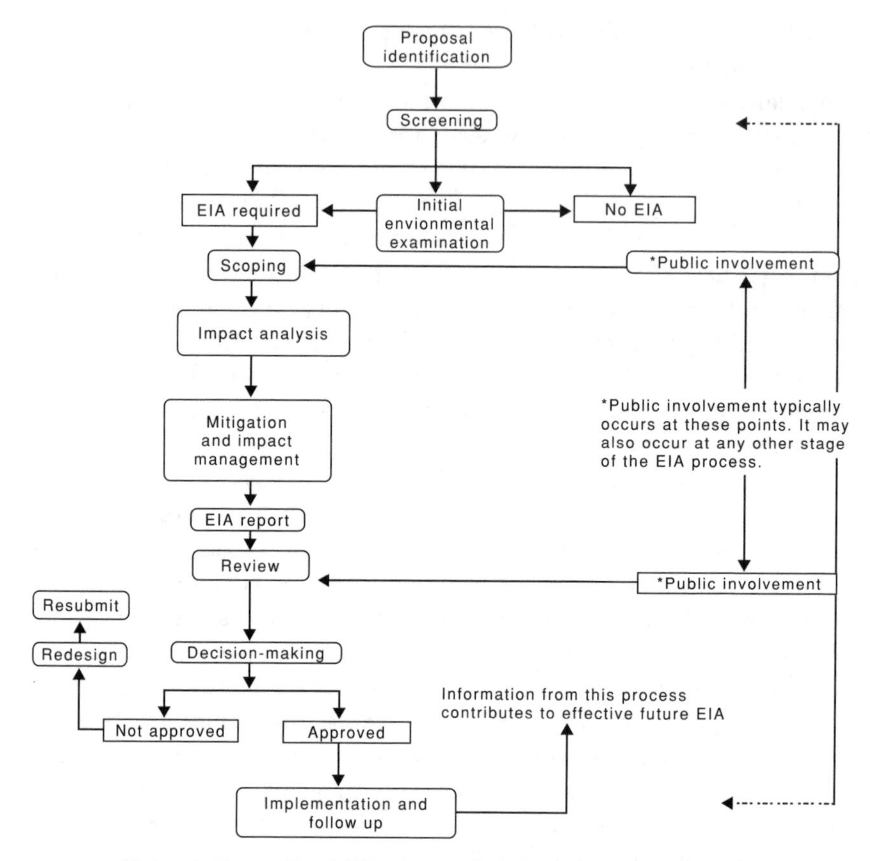

Figure 1. Generalized EIA process flowchart (United Nations Environment Programme, Environmental Impact Assessment Training Resource Manual (2nd edn, Nairobi: UNEP, 2002)

or categories of activities that are subject to *prima facie* EIA coverage. A second coverage issue upon which EIA systems differ is whether EIA processes will apply to physical undertakings only or whether they will apply to decisions respecting policies, plans and programs. Historically, EIAs were restricted to the former in practice, but in the last ten years there has been a trend toward requiring the assessment of the impacts of policies, plans and programs – often under separate legislation and

amended by EC, Council Directive 97/11, OJ 1997 L73/5, and by EC, Council Directive 03/35, Annex III ("EIA Directive"). See also Mexico, Regulation to the General Law of Ecological Equilibrium and Environmental Protection in Matters Pertaining to Environmental Impact Evaluation, issued May 23, 2000, reprinted online Westlaw ENFLEX 000463.

through a process, distinguished from EIA, referred to as strategic environmental assessment (SEA). While there are some signs of SEA gaining greater policy traction at the international level, the focus of the majority of international EIA commitments remains on project-level assessments.

Because the broad *prima facie* application of EIA legislation will capture a wide range of activities that have little potential to impact the environment, there is a further need to narrow the application of EIA to those activities that are likely to have some possible adverse consequences for the environment. As a result, it is only those projects that may potentially cause a "significant environmental effect" that are subject to the requirements of preparing an environmental impact analysis. Despite being fraught with ambiguity, the use of "significant impact" has remained the near-exclusive threshold for triggering EIA processes. Part of the difficulty is that there is an inevitable circularity in making this determination because it requires the decision-maker to arrive at a conclusion about the nature of the environmental effects as a precondition to preparing a study that is aimed at that precise determination. To mitigate this problem, most jurisdictions require that the responsible authority conduct a preliminary assessment, which has as its purpose to determine whether a full EIA is required. In an effort to reduce uncertainty around the determination of "significance," some domestic EIA legislation includes criteria or factors to be used in the screening process.[12] In some jurisdictions, it is becoming common for significance to be determined through the *ex ante* classification of projects into those where a likely significance effect is assumed, and those whose effect is assumed to fall below the required threshold (sometimes referred to as "categorical" exclusions and inclusions).[13]

Scoping. As a result of the open-ended nature of the EIA process, the tendency for agencies to produce excessively long, expensive and time-consuming studies has been an ongoing criticism of the EIA process since its inception.[14] This tendency is amplified in some cases by the

12 EIA Directive, Annex III. See also Council on Environmental Quality (CEQ) Regulations, 40 CFR § 1508.27.

13 Under NEPA, categorical exclusions are identified in various agency regulations implementing NEPA: see, for example, Department of Energy, 10 CFR § 1021, Appendices A and B. In Canada, see SOR/94–639 ("Exclusion List Regulation"), enacted under the Canadian Environmental Assessment Act, SC 1992, c. 37, as amended, (CEAA).

14 Bradley Karkkainen, "Towards a Smarter NEPA: Monitoring and Managing Government's Environmental Performance" (2002) 102 Columbia L. Rev. 903 at 917–923.

threat of litigation challenging the validity of EIA documents on the basis of a failure to consider some aspect of potential environmental harm.[15] Scoping seeks to address this problem by focusing the study as much as possible on the environmental issues that are truly likely to have a significant impact on the environment in order to enhance the efficiency of the process. The ideal sought in all scoping procedures is to match the level of study with the potential for harm and to focus the study process on those issues which are most likely to cause harm and are of the greatest concern. Again, the ideal is that the process is iterative and reflexive, which suggests that scoping is an ongoing, consultative exercise that leads to a narrowing of issues, as unfounded concerns are taken off the table, while issues that suggest greater potential for harm are given greater attention. The ideal is rarely, if ever achieved, because determining "significance" is highly subjective and environmental groups are often reluctant to eliminate issues.[16] Maintaining a balance between comprehensiveness and efficiency is further complicated by the presence of high levels of scientific uncertainty regarding environmental outcomes.

Impact analysis and report preparation. Once the scope of the EIA is determined, the focus of the process is the preparation of a detailed report outlining the substance of the assessment itself. In addition to identifying alternatives, an EIS should include a description of the purpose and need for the action, a description of the affected environment and a thorough examination of the environmental consequences of its action and of the alternatives to the action, including any mitigation measures.[17] Because the responsibility for preparing the report may be delegated to the project proponent, which will often be a private entity, specifying the minimum content for inclusion in the report is particularly important, as is public review over the scope of the report. In limited instances, a coordinating agency may play a role in reviewing assessment reports.[18]

A fundamental requirement of EIA processes is that a responsible authority must also look at reasonable alternatives to its proposed undertaking in the course of preparing its environmental impact analysis. This requirement is described in the NEPA regulations as "the heart of the environmental impact statement . . . providing a clear basis for choice

[15] Particularly in the US: see Daniel Mendelkar, *NEPA Law and Litigation* (2nd edn, looseleaf, Deerfield, IL: Clark Boardman Callaghan, 1992).

[16] Alan Gilpin, *Environmental Impact Assessment: Cutting Edge for the Twenty-First Century* (Cambridge: Cambridge University Press, 1995) at 19.

[17] 40 CFR § 1502.13–18.

[18] See, for example, CEAA, s. 21.1.

among options by the decision-maker and the public."[19] The rationale behind the alternatives requirement is that placing alternatives side by side and examining the environmental impacts of each most clearly exposes the relative environmental, economic and social burdens and benefits of proceeding with an action – a process that is all the more important in the absence of explicit standards. The requirement to look at alternatives provides an evaluative substitute for quantitative standards in the sense that the acceptability of impacts can be measured against the potential impacts of alternative ways to carrying out the undertaking.[20] The potential range of reasonable alternatives is near infinite, and may include reasonable alternatives outside the mandate of the lead agency and the "no action" alternative.[21] To make the process more manageable, the scoping process also serves to identify reasonable alternatives that will be pursued in the EIA process. This determination can have profound effects on the outcome of the EIA process, as avoidance of more environmentally benign alternatives will place the proposal (the preferred alternative) in more favorable light.[22]

Public participation. If the identification of alternatives is the heart of the EIA process, then public participation is its soul. Almost every EIA system includes some form of public participation and consultation. There are, however, significant differences in terms of when consultation must occur in the process and the form of that consultation. For example, notwithstanding the importance of the screening and scoping processes in determining the substance of the final EIA, participation is rarely mandated in these stages. Instead, consultation tends to be voluntary until the completion of the EIA report, at which stage formal consultation with the public and with other affected agencies occurs. Thus, under NEPA, while there are opportunities for agency and public consultation at every major stage of the EIA process, and while lead agencies are required to make "diligent efforts" to involve the public in preparing and implementing their NEPA requirements,[23] consultation is only a formal requirement after the EIS is prepared in draft. The draft

[19] 40 CFR § 1502.14.

[20] This could mean alternative designs, or routes (if a linear facility), or alternative approaches to achieve similar ends, such as energy conservation, as an alternative to an electrical generating facility.

[21] Ibid., § 1502.14(c) and (d).

[22] Mendelkar, *NEPA Law and Litigation* at § 9.18. For judicial discussion, see *Calvert Cliffs' Co-ordinating Committee Inc.* v. *United States Atomic Energy Commission*, 449 F 2d 1109 at 1128 (DC Cir. 1971).

[23] 40 CFR § 1506.6.

is then circulated to other interested agencies, including state and local agencies, as well as to interested members of the public, for the purpose of soliciting comments on the draft EIS.[24] The form of consultation varies between jurisdictions and may depend upon the severity of the potential impacts, with potentially more harmful activities warranting more extensive and legalistic forms of consultation, such as hearings.[25] After the consultation is complete, the responsible authority may prepare the final EIS, in which it must respond to all of the comments received.[26] In this regard, the courts have imposed a so-called "rule of reason" whereby the agency's obligation to respond is related to the salience of the comments received.[27] The intended result is to promote a reasoned justification of the decision in light of the input received from other agencies and the public.

Final decision. The extent of integration of the EIA into the decision-making process also varies across domestic EIA systems. However, one consistent principle is that a formal decision respecting the project should not be made until the EIA process has been completed. This approach is exemplified by provisions in the Canadian Environmental Assessment Act (CEAA) that forbid responsible authorities from exercising any power or performing any duty or function in relation to a project until the EIA process has been completed.[28] To maintain otherwise would severely impact the credibility of the EIA process, as any steps taken in advance of the final decision would have the potential to prejudice the outcome.[29]

The EIA process is self-regulatory in that the responsible authority retains the discretion to move ahead with projects notwithstanding the results of the EIA and the results of the public participation. Instead, the bringing forth of information regarding environmental impacts and broad public and agency involvement is relied upon to influence decisions in favor of more environmentally benign outcomes. The premise of EIAs is that more and better information respecting the environment will, if subject to public scrutiny, result in better decisions. However, EIA processes themselves do not as a matter of law require that an agency adopt the most environmentally desirable alternative or that

[24] Ibid., § 1503. [25] See, for example, CEAA, ss. 25–36. [26] 40 CFR § 1503.4.

[27] See W. M. Tabb, "Environmental Impact Assessment in the European Community: Shaping International Norms" (1999) 73 Tulane L. Rev. 923 at 959.

[28] CEAA, ss. 11(2) and 13.

[29] See, for example, Canadian Wildlife Federation Inc. v. Canada (Minister of the Environment) [1991] 1 FC 641 (CA).

decision-makers avoid activities that are found to have a significant environmental impact, nor are lead agencies required to adopt any particular measures mitigating environmental impacts. EIAs mandate adherence to procedural requirements, but do not require outcomes to reflect substantive environmental norms or objectives. Fundamentally, the results of the EIA are meant to inform, even mold, the decision-making process, but there is always room for the exercise of political discretion.

Follow up. An element of emerging importance is the requirement for the project proponent to engage in post-construction environmental monitoring of impacts and other follow-up actions. The inclusion of monitoring is somewhat at odds with the traditional understanding of EIA processes as *ex ante* planning tools, but it responds to the criticism that EIA processes naively rely on the notion that impacts can be accurately predicted. In support of this argument, critics have put forward a number of convincing examples where *ex post* audits of impact predictions found in EIAs indicated poor predictive performance, resulting in some cases in dire environmental consequences.[30] In a similar vein, the Council on Environmental Quality (CEQ) notes, "our improved understanding of the functioning of ecosystems makes it clear that we often cannot predict with precision how components of an ecosystem will react to disturbance and stress over time. What little monitoring information exists seems to bear this out."[31] The criticism leveled against EIA in this regard is not so much that it relies on scientific knowledge that is often uncertain, a state of affairs that, for the most part, applies to all environmental regulation, but that in the face of this uncertainty EIA processes remain almost entirely *ex ante* in their posture.[32] Monitoring, which is a much more dynamic process, suggests that the EIA process may be used as a regulatory tool by which actual environmental impacts are determined after project completion and compared with predicted impacts. Where the approval is subject to terms and conditions, proponents may be required to make ongoing adjustments in their project in order to minimize unpredicted environmental impacts (an approach often referred to as "adaptive management"). In addition,

[30] See Karkkainen, "Smarter NEPA" at 928–929. A more optimistic picture emerges from Sadler, "Environmental Assessment" § 3.3.4.

[31] CEQ, *Considering Cumulative Impacts under the National Environmental Policy Act* (Washington DC: Council on Environmental Quality, 1997) at 31, http://ceq.eh.doe.gov/nepa/nepa25fn.pdf.

[32] Karkkainen, "Smarter NEPA" at 929.

follow-up programs can be used to identify areas where predictive capacities are lacking and may suggest ways of improving EIA methodology more generally. In the American context, at least one author has persuasively argued in favor of increased use of follow-up programs, which were not originally part of NEPA and are now only voluntary, as a way of increasing the efficiency of NEPA.[33] Identification of follow-up programs is an express requirement under CEAA, but is still not well developed in the sense that there are no institutional mechanisms by which follow-up programs can be implemented.[34]

The relevance of this generalized form of EIA is that it has served as a template for the development of international EIA commitments. But each element may raise unique issues in its adoption in an international context. For example, is the threshold of "significance" appropriate in the context of transboundary harm and harm to specific global resources? Who should be the beneficiary of notification and consultation requirements, states alone, affected individuals within states, or international organizations? However, the larger question around the suitability of EIA process to address international environmental issues relates to the procedural and self-regulatory nature of EIA. Because this is the defining feature of EIA and has been a matter of considerable controversy in domestic settings, it is instructive to look at the challenges that the procedural nature of EIA processes poses for environmental governance.

2.3 Domestic EIA structure: process and substance

In its procedural orientation, EIA is quite purposely distinct from other forms of environmental regulation, such as command and control regulation or market mechanisms, where the state sets standards to be complied with either individually or aggregately. In these cases, the process operates toward a defined outcome, but the outcome is exogenous to the process itself, whereas, with EIAs, the outcome is endogenous to the process.[35] While the EIA process does not involve substantive obligations in the sense that the process is geared toward some particular end, it would be inaccurate to view the EIA process as being entirely neutral. NEPA, for example, is not agnostic about the kinds of values and principles that

[33] Karkkanian, "Smarter NEPA." [34] CEAA, s. 16(2).

[35] Herz, "Parallel Universes" at 1692.

decision-makers should account for in arriving at their decisions,[36] as is clearly evident in opening sections of NEPA, which describe the purposes of NEPA and the values underlying it.[37] Most other EIA schemes, unlike NEPA, are not intended to be a general pronouncement of governmental environmental policy, and do not, as such, contain an express statement of environmental policy like NEPA. That said, there is often, within national EIA legislation, an affirmation of the government's commitment to environmental values and a clear acknowledgment of the link between EIA and environmental goals.[38]

The absence of formal substantive requirements has led to domestic EIA legislation being criticized for its procedural orientation.[39] However, such a view may depend too heavily on a radical separation of the ends of EIA processes from their means, where no such separation was intended. Moreover, such a view also equates the substantive content of EIAs with that which can be judicially enforced, leading to the common criticism that, by failing to enforce the underlying policy objectives of EIA processes, the courts have ignored their substantive intent.[40] There is an all-or-nothing quality about the debate as to whether EIA is procedural or substantive in nature. The substantive objectives are either seen as binding legal rules that should be enforced, resulting in calls for the substantive strengthening of EIA obligations, or they are viewed as lacking any normative value at all and, consequently, are ignored. Here, the response is to insist upon the purely procedural nature of EIA requirements and, as a result, the utility of EIA is assessed solely in terms of procedural outcomes.

However, leaving agencies with broad discretion to determine substantive outcomes recognizes that environmental decisions entail a complex

[36] R. V. Bartlett, "The Rationality and Logic of NEPA Revisited" in Larry Canter and Ray Clark, eds., *Environmental Policy and NEPA: Past, Present and Future* (Boca Raton, FL: St. Lucie Press, 1997) 51 at 56.

[37] NEPA, § 4321.

[38] See, for example, EC, Council Directive 97/11, OJ 1997 L73/5, preamble, para. 2, referencing Art. 130R of the Treaty Establishing the European Community, OJ C325. See also CEAA, preamble.

[39] Discussed in Philip Weinberg, "It's Time to Put NEPA Back on Course" (1994) 3 NYU Envt'l LJ 99 at 100–103; and in Philip Michael Ferester, "Revitalizing the National Environmental Policy Act: Substantive Law Adaptations from NEPA's Progeny" (1992) 16 Harvard Envt'l L. Rev. 207 at 211–217. See also James Boggs, "Procedural v. Substantive in NEPA Law: Cutting the Gordian Knot" (1993) 15 Environmental Professional 25.

[40] See Lynton Caldwell, "Beyond NEPA: Future Significance of the National Environmental Policy Act" (1998) 22 Harvard Envt'l L. Rev. 203 at 207. See also Weinberg, "It's Time" at 108–110.

trade-off between environmental values and other, often economic, values. Consequently, the determination of how to prioritize these competing values is most appropriately undertaken by the political branches of the government. This latter point is consistent with the doctrine of the separation of powers and the respective competences of the judicial and political branches, whereby decisions requiring a balancing of competing interests are more suitably made by institutions that are democratically responsive and better resourced to consider the broad range of issues presented.[41] This argument is bolstered by the open-ended nature of the substantive environmental objectives contained within EIA legislation, which do not lend themselves to judicial application given their highly abstracted nature. The self-regulatory nature of EIA also explains why consultation and participation are such an integral part of the EIA process. Broad public oversight is necessary to ensure that agency decisions are reflective of, or at least account for, public values and priorities. Given the policy discretion that agency officials exercise in respect of environmental decision-making, public consultation and participation through EIA processes provide democratic legitimacy to the decision-making process, by ensuring that unelected officials account for public views and public (environmental) values in their decisions.[42]

Because the central objective of EIA is to require agencies to deliberate in a genuine and thorough manner on environmental considerations, there is a concern that this intent may be easily frustrated where agencies engage in a kind of box-ticking exercise, paying lip-service to environmental issues, but not treating the issues in a serious or genuine fashion. To prevent this, the US courts have required that the EIS "contains sufficient discussion of the relevant issues and opposing viewpoints to enable the decision-maker to take a 'hard look' at environmental factors, and to make a 'reasoned decision'."[43] In another NEPA case, it was noted that agencies must provide "convincing reason" and not simply provide "bald conclusions."[44] The result of the "hard look" doctrine is a more exacting form of judicial review, which is aimed at ensuring that

[41] See L. Fuller, "The Forms and Limits of Adjudication" (1978) 92 Harvard L. Rev. 353.

[42] Richard B. Stewart, "The Reformation of American Administrative Law" (1975) 88 Harvard L. Rev. 1669. See also Richard B. Stewart, "A New Generation of Environmental Regulation" (2001) 29 Capital University L. Rev. 21.

[43] *Natural Resources Defense Council Inc.* v. *Hodel*, 865 F 2d 288 at 294 (DC Cir. 1988) (quoting *Izaak Walton League of America* v. *Marsh*, 655 F 2d 346 at 371 (DC Cir. 1981)). See also *All Indian Pueblo Council* v. *US*, 975 F 2d 1437 at 1445 (10th Cir. 1992), and *Marsh* v. *Oregon Natural Resources Council*, 490 US 360 at 378 (1988).

[44] *Maryland National Capital Park and Planning Commission* v. *United States Postal Service*, 487 F 2d 1029 at 1040 (DC Cir. 1973).

the agency's deliberations are carried in good faith and that the agency has turned its attention to relevant considerations.[45] Ostensibly, such a review addresses the procedural aspects of the decision and, so long as the agency can demonstrate that it considered a matter in good faith and that it was cognizant of the relevant issues, the agency decision will stand. However, a determination of a decision-maker's good faith requires an assessment of the reasons themselves, whether they support the decision, and whether they are arbitrary or otherwise unconvincing. As such, it is difficult to draw the line between procedural review and substantive review of NEPA decisions.

The distinction between process and substance is not formal, but is instead functional and relational. For example, NEPA's procedural requirements are substantive in the sense that they grant rights and dictate particular outcomes that are desirable in and of themselves, such as public participation and justificatory decision-making. Moreover, the "hard look" doctrine, which requires genuine sensitivity to environmental issues, is both means and end. It is a means to improve environmental decision-making by ensuring that agency decisions are in fact principled, but the requirement for rationality in agency decision-making is surely an end in itself.

The essential structure of EIA is a unique combination of well-defined procedural rules aimed at careful deliberation and public involvement coupled with a strong statement of environmental values, which despite its open-textured quality is clearly meant to be binding in the sense that decision-makers must publicly account for those values and justify their decisions in light of them. This structure has been described variously as process substituting for substance,[46] and the substantiation of procedure.[47] Both these descriptions capture the complex relationship between process and substance that lies at the heart of EIA processes. Procedural specificity is adopted in the absence of substantive specificity, but is employed to push decisions in a substantive direction.

2.4 The roles of domestic EIA processes

The structure of domestic EIA requirements informs and influences the roles that EIA assumes in domestic governance structures. On a

[45] Cass Sunstein, "In Defense of the Hard Look: Judicial Activism and Administrative Law" (1984) 7 Harvard J. L. & Pub. Pol'y 51 at 52.

[46] Herz, "Parallel Universes" at 1669.

[47] Eric Bregman and Arthur Jacobson, "Environmental Performance Review: Self Regulation in Environmental Law" (1994) 16 Cardozo L. Rev. 465 at 496.

superficial level, the role of EIA is to ensure that decision-makers understand and consider the environmental consequences of their planned activities. However, this understanding gives rise to an anterior question: to what end is this done? The answer to this question has proved to be much more elusive. Given this study's principal interest in international EIA obligations, a resolution of this question as it relates to different domestic EIA regimes goes beyond the scope of this study, although, at this stage, it may be helpful to review the range of possible answers.[48]

One approach, based on a comprehensive-rationality model of decision-making, views the role of EIAs in technical and apolitical terms.[49] EIAs have a purely instrumental function under this model. They are a systematic way of gathering information and subjecting that information to scientific and technical analysis, on the understanding that an optimal solution is possible. It is assumed that the ends to which the process is oriented are known and are uncontested. Here, the most important actors within the EIA process are the scientists and other experts whose role it is to dispassionately assess the evidence and determine the right course of action. The proponent and members of the public play a supporting role at best, providing supplemental information about the project or the affected environment – as such interaction between the participants is not likely to be dialogical or aimed at justification. Even accepting that environmental considerations may be outweighed by economic or social goals, the underlying assumption is that these determinations can be made objectively through technical exercises, such as cost/benefit analyses.

It is evident that much of the structure of EIAs contradicts a pure comprehensive-rationality model. First, such a model is premised on the substantive rationality of science and as such there would be no reason to allow decision-makers to depart from the outcomes of the EIA report. EIA processes are structured on the basis that there are not necessarily right or optimal solutions, but rather decisions will often involve the privileging of one set of interests over another – a circumstance that must be resolved through political, not scientific or technical means. In a related fashion, this model is at odds with the prominence given to transparency and participation in EIA processes, which are aimed, at least in part, at political legitimacy, not right answers.

[48] But, for an excellent consideration of this question in relation to EIA processes in the UK, see Jane Holder, *Environmental Assessment*, identifying "information" and "culture" theories as the principal approaches to explaining the role of EIA.

[49] See Bartlett, "NEPA Revisited." See also Karkkainen, "Smarter NEPA."

Despite these contradictions, comprehensive-rationality remains a powerful influence over EIA processes, particularly in relation to how assessments are conducted. Bradley Karkkainen has critically commented on this aspect of NEPA, noting that NEPA tends to proceed from an assumption that information respecting environmental consequences is "free, abundant and unerringly accurate," resulting in an emphasis on *ex ante* predictive analyses of environmental consequences.[50] This form of analysis remains the dominant approach to assessment within EIA systems, which give prominence to EIA reports and downplay post-project analysis and monitoring. This approach is also the preeminent understanding of EIAs among environmental professionals who tend to view their work in apolitical terms, with EIA processes itself taking on a highly instrumental role in facilitating the collection, organization and analysis of data.[51]

A second model of EIA accepts the political nature of the decisions being made, and, as a result, views the role of EIA to facilitate bargaining between competing societal interests. A pluralistic bargaining model fits more comfortably within the structural framework of EIA. The discretionary nature of decision-making aids political bargaining, as does the openness and transparency of the process. Different actors, with competing interests, will negotiate the final outcome of the EIA. Through this process, compromises may be arrived at for expedient reasons. For example, a proponent may agree to mitigation measures in order to secure the consent of an environmental group thereby avoiding costly litigation or delay. Political accountability is particularly important here to ensure that public agencies are exercising their authority in ways that are responsive to political influences. Unlike a comprehensive-rationality model, a pluralistic bargaining model accepts that decisions will reflect certain interests and, as such, the role of EIA is not to determine an optimal solution. Instead, its role is to find decisions that reflect public values and to confer democratic legitimacy on the decision-making process.[52]

The difficulty with this model is that it suggests that EIA systems are entirely indifferent to the outcome achieved. A pure bargaining model

[50] Karkkainen, "Smarter NEPA" at 925–926, noting that, in fact, scientific knowledge is "typically scarce, costly to assemble, highly uncertain and variable in quality."

[51] R. V. Bartlett and Priya Kurian, "The Theory of Environmental Impact Assessment: Implicit Models of Policy Making" (1999) 27 Policy and Politics 415 at 417–418.

[52] See R. V. Bartlett, "Rationality and the Logic of the National Environmental Policy Act" (1986) 8 Environmental Professional 105; see also Stewart, "Reformation."

is non-directive. It simply assumes the rationality of the actors involved, but the system as a whole is not oriented toward some particularized end. Such a perspective is difficult to reconcile with the overt environmental mandate of EIA systems. Cynics, of whom there are legion in relation to EIA, would suggest that, in the absence of substantive obligations, the environmental objectives are simply window-dressing. That is, the EIA process may make a pretense out of having environmental goals, but the structure of the obligations is in fact non-directive. Put another way, environmentally favorable outcomes are possible, but only as a result of underlying political conditions, and not as a result of the EIA process itself.

A less cynical view would be to see benign environmental outcomes developing out of enlightened self-interest and public-regarding agency action. Serge Taylor, in his study on NEPA, *Making Bureaucracies Think*, attributes the efficacy of NEPA to a combination of internal pressures, such as the increased hiring of environmental professionals within federal agencies, external pressures from the public and other agencies, as well as the presence of explicit substantive objectives.[53] The different sources of pressure reinforce one another to overcome NEPA's weak substantive mandate by creating strong informal "norms of analysis" that favor outcomes that reflect identified environmental ends.[54] Under this model, interests are recalculated in light of institutional characteristics, such as the need for actors involved in repeated interactions, for example agency officials and environmental advocates both within and outside the agency, to maintain credibility.

A third model of EIA attributes greater transformational possibilities to EIA processes. Instead of accepting that the interests of participants in EIA processes are fixed, this model suggests that the EIA process itself may affect interests and values. The role of EIA under a transformational model is to generate new interests, particularly within government agencies, that reflect broader environmental values. This model would emphasize the deliberative aspects of democracy, which require genuine attempts by participants to understand opposing viewpoints. This model makes the most sense out of the discursive and justificatory nature of EIA processes. Consequently, under a transformational model, the "hard look" doctrine, which emphasizes the need for officials to

[53] Serge Taylor, *Making Bureaucracies Think: The Environmental Impact Statement Strategy of Administrative Reform* (Stanford, CA: Stanford University Press, 1984); Bartlett and Kurian, "Implicit Models" at 421.

[54] Bartlett and Kurian, "Implicit Models" at 473.

consider assessment reports with a genuinely open mind, becomes central to the EIA process. R. V. Bartlett has presented a model of EIA along these lines, based on what he calls NEPA's "ecological rationality."[55] Ecological rationality, as opposed to other forms of substantive or formal rationality, accepts the dynamic and contingent nature of human systems and therefore stresses adaptive and contextual approaches to problem-solving. Under this model, follow-up measures and social learning through feedback mechanisms in EIA take on greater importance. Unlike the other models presented, ecological rationality is not purely instrumental in its form.[56] From a structural standpoint, this can be seen in the tendency of EIA processes to simultaneously define or elaborate upon environmental objectives and provide the means to achieve those objectives. Another policy theorist has referred to this transformational role as being one of "cognitive reform," by which it is meant that EIA processes can impact the interests and identities of the actors who are engaged in them, leading to greater alignment of agency objectives and attitudes with environmental values.[57]

Because there is a strong emphasis on the role of norms and principles in transformational models, it is surprising that domestic policy theorizing has made little attempt to explore the normative relationship between EIA processes and institutions and the broader legal and normative framework in which these processes and institutions are situated. Under NEPA, these links are, to some degree, made explicit. Most obviously, in this regard, is the link between NEPA's policy objectives and the preparation of an EIS. However, it is evident that EIA processes draw on other substantive environmental norms, such as domestic legal standards, in determining the significance of impacts.[58] For example, of particular importance in this book is the extent to which substantive environmental norms formulated at the international level form part of this broader set of normative influences. In a related fashion, the influence of normative arrangements on environmental decision-making suggests that the effectiveness of EIA processes depends upon broader political and institutional arrangements that may vary from

[55] See Bartlett, "Rationality," and Bartlett, "NEPA Revisited." Bartlett attributes the term "ecological rationality" to J. Dryzek, *Rational Ecology: Environment and Political Economy* (New York: Blackwell, 1987).

[56] Bartlett, "NEPA Revisited" at 52.

[57] Boggs, "Cutting the Gordian Knot."

[58] Lyndon Caldwell, "Understanding Impact Analysis: Technical Process, Administrative Reform, Policy Principle" in R. V. Bartlett, ed., *Policy Through Impact Assessment: Institutionalized Analysis as a Policy Strategy* (Westport, CT: Greenwood Press, 1989) 6 at 12.

one legal/normative setting to another. This possibility applies equally to the adoption of EIA processes in diverse domestic settings and in the international legal setting.

2.5 EIA in developing countries

As noted in the introduction, the practice of EIA within developing countries[59] will vary considerably from country to country depending upon the level of development, political and social conditions and the environmental problems that face the state.[60] The development of EIA in many developing countries differs from the origination of EIA in NEPA in that the impetus for the development of environmental laws in the US in the 1960s and 1970s was a broad-based, bottom-up call for greater environmental and democratic accountability. In many developing countries the motivation for the development of EIA has been the result of exogenous pressures from international institutions, particularly development banks,[61] but also, in the case of Eastern European countries, the desire to fall into line with common European standards.[62]

UNEP estimates that some seventy developing countries have EIA legislation in place.[63] Often the EIA requirements are incorporated into a broader environmental law and do not set out detailed process requirements.[64] The result is that the legal basis for EIA is often permissive and, as a result, it is difficult for third parties, such as environmental NGOs or indigenous groups, to require compliance with the domestic

[59] The term "developing countries" as used here also includes those countries, chiefly in Central and Eastern Europe, that are in the process of transitioning to a market economy.

[60] Various EIA systems of developing countries are discussed in N. Lee and C. George, eds., *Environmental Assessment in Developing and Transitional Countries* (Chichester: Wiley Publishers, 2000).

[61] Christopher Wood, *Environmental Impact Assessment: A Comparative Review* (Harlow: Longman Group Ltd, 1995) at 301 (discussing top-down influences). See also Ann Hironaka and Evan Schofer, "Decoupling in the Environmental Arena: The Case of Environmental Impact Assessments" in Andrew Hoffmann, ed., *Organizations, Policy and the Natural Environment: Institutional and Strategic Perspectives* (Palo Alto, CA: Stanford University Press, 2004) 214.

[62] Sadler, "International EA Study" § 2.2.4. See also Kobus, "Comparison and Evaluation" at 157.

[63] Marceil Yeater and Lal Kurukulasuriya, "Environmental Impact Assessment Legislation in Developing Countries" in Sun Lin and Lal Kurukulasuriya, eds., *UNEP's New Way Forward: Environmental Law and Sustainable Development* (Nairobi: UNEP, 1995) 257 at 259.

[64] Sadler, "International EA Study," § 2.2.4.

EIA process absent some external constraints.[65] The strong relationship between development assistance programs and EIA has tended to orient EIA systems toward grant-assisted projects and toward satisfying the requirements of development-assistance agencies.[66] A number of studies have indicated that developing countries apply EIA to a more narrow range of projects and that the EIAs themselves tend to be more limited in their focus.[67] For example, the treatment of alternatives is often perfunctory or non-existent, and scoping procedures that involve the public are also limited.[68]

The lack of capacity to undertake detailed and open EIAs on a full range of projects is a key limitation. For example, developing states often have few experts trained in EIA techniques and related scientific disciplines, environment ministries or other institutions responsible for implementing EIA requirements lack financial resources, and there is often a lack of baseline environmental data. Improving the technical capacity of developing countries to undertake EIAs has been emphasized by development funding agencies and should continue to improve.[69] The lack of capacity in developing countries extends beyond technical issues and includes more structurally oriented difficulties relating to the ability of states to disseminate the results of EIA studies and to effectively consult with affected populations.[70] Some of these difficulties relate to larger issues, such as literacy rates and inadequate communication and transportation infrastructure, but they also relate to questions

[65] For example, the World Bank provides avenues for affected persons to bring forward complaints regarding failure to comply with the World Bank's EIA requirements, discussed below at ch. 4.4.

[66] Wood, *Comparative Review* at 303.

[67] Ronald Bisset, "Devising an Effective Environmental Assessment System for a Developing Country: The Case of the Turks and Caicos Islands" in Biswas and Agarwala, eds., *Environmental Impact Assessment for Developing Countries* (Boston: Butterworth-Heinemann, 1992) 214.

[68] Wood, *Comparative Review* at 303.

[69] The United Nations Environment Programme has been instrumental in this regard, preparing training manuals and sponsoring training programs and workshops, as well as assisting in the preparation of EIA legislation in developing countries, discussed in Donald Kaniaru *et al.*, "UNEP's Program of Assistance on National Legislation and Institutions" in Lin and Kurukulasuriya, *UNEP's New Way Forward: Environmental Law and Sustainable Development* (Nairobi: UNEP, 1995) 153 at 162. See also UNEP, *Environmental Impact Assessment Training Resource Manual* (2nd edn, Nairobi: UNEP, 2002).

[70] See, for example, H. Fowler and A. de Aguiar, "Environmental Impact Assessment in Brazil" (1993) 13 Environmental Impact Assessment Review 169.

respecting the openness of the government decision-making process in highly centralized political cultures.[71]

The top-down orientation of EIA in many developing countries suggests that the structure and role of EIA may differ depending on the social and economic context. For example, it has been noted that EIA approaches in Russia and states formerly part of the Soviet Union are more oriented toward an expert-centered approach to environmental assessment, with a consequential lesser emphasis on public consultation.[72] Of particular concern is whether there is a sufficiently strong and broad-based commitment to environmental outcomes underlying the EIA system to ensure that environmental values are considered with genuine concern. The presence of well-organized actors who are able to promote environmental principles and challenge agency and proponent positions is another key element that has been identified as crucial to the interest-coordination role of EIA that will differ significantly from country to country. To some degree this role will be played by development agencies, but there remains a need to develop broad-based environmental values and the institutions, such as judicial review, to support meaningful public exchanges and accountability.

It would be inaccurate to consider the development of EIA systems in developing countries as "falling short" of a defined set of ideal EIA processes. Instead, it should be recognized that EIA processes must be adapted to different political, economic and social contexts. Such an examination is well beyond the scope of this study, but the implications for the development of international EIA commitments should be borne in mind. To the extent that international EIA requirements seek to impose procedural commitments on states and those requirements fail to appreciate the diverse cultural contexts and differing levels of capacity in which they are intended to be implemented, they may be less likely to succeed.[73] Moreover, insofar as the international community itself has its own political and institutional context or multiple contexts, similar questions arise about the suitability and adaptation of EIA to those distinct contexts.

[71] Hironaka and Schofer, "Decoupling" at 224, noting cases where EIAs have been classified as secret or completely disregarded.

[72] See Kobus, "Comparison and Evaluation" at 164.

[73] Asit K. Biswas, "Summary and Recommendations" in Biswas and Agarwala, eds., *Environmental Impact Assessment for Developing Countries* (Boston: Butterworth-Heinemann, 1992) 235.

2.6 Application of domestic EIA beyond the state

Domestic EIA requirements have had a more direct influence on the regulation of environmental impacts beyond the state by requiring the assessment of extraterritorial impacts independently of international obligations to perform EIAs. In the event that domestic EIA processes on their own are sufficient to provide decision-makers with adequate information respecting extraterritorial impacts and to ensure that the interests of affected persons outside the state of origin are accounted for, then there may be less need for the development of distinct international EIA obligations. An approach that minimizes formal international legal processes is viewed with favor by Peter Sand who notes in relation to transboundary environmental issues: "Instead of internationalizing a local issue (via an enormous detour to the respective national capitals), a more economic solution in most cases would be to adapt local decision-making processes so that they can handle transfrontier problems like ordinary local ones of comparable size."[74] In other words, where environmental issues can be successfully addressed unilaterally, there is less justification for the development of international rules. Conversely, legal and political limitations to the extension of domestic EIA requirements beyond the state inform our understanding of the need for, and the form of, international rules governing EIA.

The need for the examination of transboundary impacts was recognized in a number of domestic EIA systems both in practice and more explicitly through implementing instruments. A number of early US court decisions concerning NEPA treated the application of EIA processes to transboundary effects as uncontroversial. For example, in *Wilderness Society* v. *Morton*,[75] it was assumed that the EIS requirements for a proposed oil pipeline located in Alaska included an assessment of the impacts on the natural environment in Canada. A similar assumption was made in *Swinomish Tribal Community* v. *Federal Energy Regulation Commission*,[76] where the court considered the impacts of a Washington state dam project on Canadian environmental interests. In both of these cases, Canadian intervenors were granted standing before the courts to challenge the adequacy of EISs affecting Canadian environmental resources. The presumption in favor of the transboundary application of NEPA was reinforced by an Executive Order issued in 1979 which was intended to

[74] Peter Sand, "The Role of Domestic Procedures in Transnational Environmental Disputes" in OECD, *Legal Aspects of Transfrontier Pollution* (Paris: OECD, 1977) 146 at 159.
[75] 463 F 2d 1261 (DC Cir. 1972). [76] 627 F 2d 499 (DC Cir. 1980).

require federal agencies to consider the extraterritorial effects of their actions under certain conditions, including where major federal actions significantly affected the environment of another state or the global commons.[77] Unfortunately, the 1979 Executive Order was complicated by the fact that it also addressed the issue of the application of NEPA to projects undertaken outside the US, which raises concerns regarding the limits of a state's prescriptive jurisdiction.[78] However, in relation to activities undertaken within US territory, but having potential impacts outside the US, there is little doubt of the jurisdictional ability of source states to impose EIA requirements that include assessing transboundary impacts.[79]

In 1997, the Council on Environmental Quality (CEQ) issued a "Guidance" document addressing what it refers to as "practical considerations" regarding the assessment of transboundary impacts.[80] The CEQ Guidance indicates that a determination of whether transboundary impacts are present should be made during the scoping process. In the event that the potential for transboundary impacts is identified, it is suggested that the agencies in the affected country with relevant expertise be notified, although the guidance does not give any indication of how those agencies may be identified. In most cases, the scoping and screening of projects is undertaken by agency personnel and consultants who may have difficulty in identifying the relevant foreign agency on an *ad hoc* basis. The Guidance is also silent on the question of notification in the event that a likelihood of significant transboundary impact is found to exist. The CEQ's approach suggests that notice should take place not by reference to jurisdictional boundaries, but rather on the basis of who is affected. But, again, this requires that the agencies have the capacity to identify the relevant foreign agencies and public institutions to ensure

[77] Executive Order No. 12,114, 3 CFR 356 (1980), reprinted in 18 ILM 154 (1979), para. 2–3(a) and (b).

[78] See Karen Klick, "The Extraterritorial Reach of NEPA's EIS Requirement after Environmental Defense Fund v. Massey" (1994) 44 Am. U. L. Rev. 291 at 301–303.

[79] The current line being drawn by the US courts is to focus on whether the application of the EIA requirements could impinge on another country's sovereignty. See *Natural Resources Defense Council* v. *Department of the Navy*, 2002 WL 32095131 (CD Cal. 2002) (NEPA applicable to sonar tests in high seas and EEZ). See also *Center for Biological Diversity* v. *National Science Foundation*, 2002 WL 31548073 (ND Cal. 2002), and *Born Free USA* v. *Norton*, 2003 US Dist. LEXIS 13770 (DDC 2003).

[80] CEQ guidance documents are not binding on agencies, but the US Supreme Court has on previous occasions upheld the right of the CEQ to interpret NEPA and has held that the CEQ's interpretation should be given "substantial deference." See *Andrus* v. *Sierra Club*, 442 US 347 (1979).

notice is effective. It also leaves unaddressed the question whether notice should extend to affected individuals or just to state agencies. Finally, because the adequacy of an EIS will depend upon knowledge of both the project and the receiving environment, transboundary assessment is further complicated by difficulties in source state agencies accessing baseline environmental information in another jurisdiction and assessing the adequacy of that information. The Guidance document suggests that agencies are under the same obligation to use a "rule of reason" in determining the adequacy of information and to identify gaps in information where they exist.

A similar approach to the assessment of transboundary impacts is evident in other jurisdictions. So, for example, in Canada and in Europe, the need for transboundary EIA was recognized early on,[81] and there have been numerous examples of states within these regions conducting transboundary EIAs, including notice to, and consultation with, other states that predates their treaty obligations.[82] In Canada, section 47 of CEAA allows the Minister of the Environment in his or her discretion to refer a matter to mediation or a review panel under CEAA, where the proposal may cause significant adverse environmental effects outside Canada's territorial jurisdiction and the project is not otherwise subject to the federal EIA process.[83] Thus, the presence or likelihood of a transboundary impact allows the federal government to assert jurisdiction over the matter for EIA purposes where the federal government would not otherwise have jurisdiction. This could include projects subject to provincial EIA or not subject to any EIA process, such as certain private sector projects. This approach overcomes the difficulty of federal agencies being unable to assess transboundary impacts because of a lack of jurisdiction over the activity itself. The difficulty with CEAA is that, like NEPA, it provides no detail respecting notification of transboundary impacts or of participation by non-residents. A determination of whether a transboundary impact exists will be the responsibility of individual agencies or the project proponent and will involve similar challenges in identifying appropriate foreign agencies and notifying affected persons in outside jurisdictions to those identified in connection

[81] Environmental Assessment and Review Process (EARP) Guidelines Order, SOR/84–467, s. 4(1)(a); EC Directive, Art. 7.

[82] UNECE, "Current Strategies in Transboundary EIA" (Geneva: UNECE, 1996) at 19–20 (listing instances of the transboundary application of domestic EIA processes prior to the Espoo Convention).

[83] CEAA, s. 47.

with NEPA. Moreover, the ability to petition the Minister to initiate a transboundary proceeding under section 47 of CEAA is limited to provincial governments, and foreign governments or "subdivisions thereof," which would exclude matters being petitioned by nongovernmental organizations and affected individuals. The result of this limitation is that members of the public located outside Canada must in effect have their concerns taken up by their government. Whether a project warrants an assessment under section 47 is a matter wholly within the Minister's discretion. To date, no project has been referred by the Minister to mediation or a review panel under section 47 of CEAA.[84] The experience in Europe prior to the enactment of the Espoo Convention was similar in that the EC EIA Directive recognized the importance of assessing transboundary impacts, and required affected member states to be notified, but provided no details on implementation. The result was that these requirements were unevenly implemented.[85]

The discretionary nature of applying the transboundary provisions underscores the lack of reciprocity that may exist between states in the transboundary application of their domestic EIA processes. A state has wide-ranging authority to impose EIA requirements over activities within its own territory or in connection with its own agencies,[86] but what a state very clearly cannot do is require that a project that is undertaken in another state with impacts in its own territory be subject to its own or the source state's EIA processes. Consequently, states affected by activities outside their jurisdiction can only rely on the domestic EIA regime of the source state to provide notice, assess impacts and provide for avenues of participation. One immediate concern that arises is that a state will apply its domestic EIA laws in such a way as to protect its own environment and to involve its own citizenry, but will be reluctant to extend these protections to areas and persons outside the state

[84] David Boyd, *Unnatural Law: Rethinking Canadian Environmental Law and Policy* (Vancouver: UBC Press, 2003) at 154.

[85] For example, the obligation did not extend to impacts to non-Member States or the global commons. In the UK, the 1985 Directive's transboundary provisions were not implemented until the Town and Country Planning (EIA) (England and Wales) Regulations 1999, SI 1999 No. 293, discussed in Stuart Bell and Donald McGillivray, *Environmental Law* (5th edn, London: Blackstone Press, 2000) at 369.

[86] It is common for states, for example, to require EIAs for international development projects undertaken by their national development agencies. In the US, see USAid Environmental Procedures Regulation, 22 CFR 216. In Canada, see Canadian International Development Agency, "Environmental Assessment at CIDA," www.acdi-cida. gc.gov. ca.

and outside its own polity. While the foregoing discussion suggests that domestic EIA requirements are not purposely structured so as to privilege the domestic environment, the different levels of coverage of EIA processes between countries and the broad discretion granted to agencies and officials over whether and how to apply EIA processes point to the need for coordination of EIA processes between states.

These concerns are borne out in two recent transboundary disputes between Canada and the United States. In one dispute, the state of North Dakota proposed to divert water from the Missouri/Mississippi water basin into waters that flowed northwards into Canada and which ultimately drained into the Hudson Bay water basin. The province of Manitoba and Canada objected to the proposal out of concern that the diversion would lead to the introduction of foreign biota into Canadian waters. Of particular concern was that the environmental review process conducted by the state of North Dakota was inadequate, leading to several court challenges,[87] and calls by the Canadian government to refer the matter to a bilateral commission, the International Joint Commission, for an independent review. In another case involving a proposed power-generating station in Washington state on the border with British Columbia, there was extensive cross-border consultation with Canadian agencies and sub-state governments in respect of potential air quality issues.[88] The project was approved by Washington state, but was subject to a second environmental review process in Canada owing to the fact that the transmission lines connecting the plant to the distribution network were located in Canada and subject to regulatory approval. The Canadian review process included a review of the generating station itself and its impacts on Canadian residents, notwithstanding that this project had been fully canvassed in the Washington proceedings. The transmission line proposal was not approved in Canada on the basis of unacceptable air quality impacts from the generating station. In upholding the agency decision, the (Canadian) Federal Court of Appeal commented on the positions of the respective approval authorities:

[87] *Government of the Province of Manitoba* v. *Norton*, 398 F Supp 2d 41 (DDC 2005). Manitoba also joined US environmental groups in challenging the North Dakota state government's decision to move ahead with diversion of Devil's Lake without an adequate EIA: *People to Save the Sheyenne River* v. *North Dakota*, 2005 ND 104 (NDSC 2005).

[88] See *In Re Sumas 2 Generating Facility PSD Permit No. EFSEC/2001-2*, PSD Appeal Nos. 02-10 and 02-11, Environmental Appeal Board, US Environmental Protection Agency, decision issued March 25, 2003, www.epa.gov/eab/orders/sumas.pdf.

> Suffice it to say that the EFSEC [the Washington state approval authority] was concerned with the impact of the project from a US perspective, while the Board had to consider the Canadian perspective. Both were seeking to advance their respective public interests, which in this case did not coincide. In that context, the Board was not obliged to defer to the EFSEC or to alter in any way its assessment of the factors which it considered relevant.[89]

The fact that the project was subject to multiple and contradictory approval processes suggests the potential for improved coordination of decision-making concerning projects with transboundary impacts. But of greater concern is the acceptance by the Court of a somewhat parochial approach, without consideration of whether there existed a more transcendent understanding of the public interest. In other words, because the project was assessed without reference to shared normative criteria, there was little consideration of the reciprocal rights of each state.

A further set of complications arises in respect of projects that may impact environmental resources that are part of the global commons or that raise issues of global common concern, such as biological diversity. While there are mixed indications that states are willing to extend their domestic EIA legislation to account for impacts to the global commons,[90] there is no indication that states have considered notifying other states in relation to projects affecting the Antarctic environment or the open oceans, in the absence of international obligations to do so.[91] In the absence of naming a particular international body to whom notice might be given, it is not clear which states or bodies might be notified given the interest that all states have in global commons resources. A similar problem presents itself with issues of common concern, such as biological diversity or climate change. States may have an interest in ensuring that activities undertaken outside their territorial boundaries do not adversely impact resources that may be of benefit to all humankind. However, states cannot require that activities under the

[89] *Sumas Energy 2 Inc.* v. *Canada (National Energy Board)* [2005] FCJ No. 1895 at para. 27.

[90] For example, both Canada and the United States include areas outside the jurisdiction of any state within the definition of environment. However, the original EC EIA Directive did not extend to the global commons, but was limited to situations where projects had effects on the environment of another Member State: EC, Council Directive 85/337, OJ 1985 L175/40, Art. 7.

[91] A number of US cases have considered and accepted the applicability of NEPA to the global commons: see *Environmental Defense Fund Inc.* v. *Massey*, 986 F 2d 1345 (DC Cir. 1981) (Antarctic); *Natural Resources Defense Council* v. *Department of the Navy*, 2002 WL 32095131 (CD Cal. 2002); and *Center for Biological Diversity* v. *National Science Foundation*, 2002 WL 31548073 (ND Cal. 2002) (high seas and EEZ).

control of another state be subject to EIAs since to do so would likely be contrary to the limitations on a state's ability to exercise prescriptive jurisdiction extraterritorially.[92] Moreover, even where a state may have a jurisdictional connection to the activity, the rules of international comity suggest that it still must respect the sovereignty of the state in which the activity is occurring. This preference for avoiding conflict with another state's environmental requirements found expression in *Born Free USA* v. *Norton*,[93] where a US district court refused to apply NEPA to an import permit for the importation of elephants from Swaziland on the basis that Swaziland was obligated under the Convention on International Trade in Endangered Species to issue an export permit that requires an assessment of whether the importation will be detrimental to the survival of the species.[94] To require a further assessment under NEPA would have the effect of "second-guessing the validity of Swaziland's determination."[95] In this case, international law dictated the nature of the analysis to be undertaken prior to the export/import of the species in question, effectively determining the roles of the exporting and importing states, which points to the need for a level of coordination between states to determine who should carry out an EIA when a project is subject to the jurisdiction of two or more states. In the absence of international cooperation of this nature, even widely held environmental goals can be undermined by a lack of reciprocity between states over the kinds of impacts that should be accounted for in EIA processes.

2.7 Conclusion

As an example of a globalized norm of environmental law, EIA appears to be highly successful. Over a period of less than forty years, EIA has gone from a requirement to provide a detailed statement of environmental effects consequent on governmental activities to a highly elaborate scientific, legal and political tool used in virtually every corner of the globe. EIAs have been adopted in a variety of regime types and across

[92] For a discussion of the international rules respecting jurisdiction, see Peter Malanczuk, *Akehurst's Modern Introduction to International Law* (7th edn, New York: Routledge, 1997) at 109–113.

[93] 2003 US Dist. LEXIS 13770 (DDC 2003).

[94] Convention on International Trade in Endangered Species of Wild Flora and Fauna, Washington DC, March 3, 1973, in force July 1, 1975, 993 UNTS 243; 12 ILM 1055.

[95] Malanczuk, *Modern Introduction to International Law* at paras. 38–39.

all levels of development, suggesting a high degree of universality. However, despite the wide-ranging adoption of EIA requirements in domestic settings, there remain questions about the role that EIA plays within domestic environmental governance structures and its effectiveness in influencing environmental outcomes. The adoption of EIA in international settings appears to be intuitively attractive, particularly where EIA is conceived of as an admonition for decision-makers to account for the environmental consequences of their proposed activities in a systematic and transparent way. But it is also clear that the ability of EIA processes to impact environmental outcomes depends on the presence of institutional and political factors that will vary across different settings.

As a purely instrumental and information-driven tool, EIA is an expert-driven and technical exercise, which may lend itself to highly bureaucratized environments, but should also raise concerns about capacity that are ubiquitous in international environmental governance. A central criticism of EIA processes in domestic settings has been the unrealistic reliance on prediction in a highly uncertain informational environment. In international settings, these concerns may be exacerbated by difficulties in obtaining environmental (baseline) information in foreign jurisdictions and the global commons. In addition, because the principal policy response to prediction difficulties has been the incorporation of follow-up measures, there are further complications relating to the implementation of monitoring and feedback mechanisms by source states in areas outside their territory. Going beyond the purely informational role of EIA, similar questions arise regarding the implementation of notification and consultation requirements outside the state. Thus while domestic EIA has provided international law with a template for bringing environmental values to bear on policy decisions respecting activities that are likely to impact the environment, the application of EIA norms in international settings requires interstate cooperation.

The proceduralized structure of EIA is justified in domestic settings in part because there is a recognition that activities subject to EIA require a contextual decision-making framework and involve the balancing of competing social objectives. It follows that, where EIA processes are understood to operate as political vehicles, either as a site for bargaining between interest groups or for social learning and transformation, the effectiveness of EIA would seem to turn on the presence of shared political institutions and shared normative understandings that cannot be assumed to exist outside the state.[96] To this end, the next chapter considers the role of general principles of international law in generating commonly held environmental norms that transcend particular state interests and might themselves structure state interactions in relation to extraterritorial environmental impacts.

[96] See Joseph Weiler, "The Geology of International Law – Governance, Democracy and Legitimacy" (2004) 64 ZaöRV 547.

3 EIAs and general principles of international environmental law

3.1 Introduction

One tentative conclusion that can be drawn from the previous chapter is that the extension of domestic EIA obligations to include impacts beyond the state without further international cooperation will not be adequate on its own to address the challenges posed by extraterritorial environmental impacts. The form that this international cooperation takes will be affected by the presence of environmental norms shared between states – which is to say that the development of international EIA commitments will not occur in a vacuum, but will reflect general principles of international environmental law. In this regard, this chapter outlines the relationship between international EIA processes and three sets of background norms: nondiscrimination, the harm principle and sustainable development.

The relationship between the harm principle and international obligations to perform EIAs has long been acknowledged. As early as 1980, Günther Handl argued that a state's obligation to prevent environmental harm to areas beyond its own territory requires it to investigate the potential impacts of its activities, while the duty to cooperate requires a source state to give notice of any impacts to an affected state. In short, Handl suggested that a generalized duty to undertake EIAs arose by necessary implication from the existence of the harm principle and the duty to cooperate.[1] This view is not, however, without controversy. For example, John Knox has argued that the procedural structure of EIA commitments in international law is at odds with the substantive

[1] Günther Handl, "The Environment: International Rights and Responsibilities" (1980) 74 Proc. Am. Soc. Int'l L. 223 at 224–228. See also Günther Handl, "Environmental Security and Global Change: The Challenge to International Law" (1990) 1 YBIEL 3 at 21.

orientation of the harm principle.[2] If it were the case that EIA obligations in international law were derived from the harm principle, then one would expect EIA obligations to require the prevention or mitigation of assessed harms. An evaluation of EIA obligations in international instruments shows this is not the case, resulting in Knox's argument that EIA obligations are in fact better explained as reflecting the principle of nondiscrimination. Knox's argument is a good point of departure for the present discussion because it underscores the relationship between EIA obligations and substantive norms in international law. In the previous chapter, I described the essential structure of domestic EIA as being a combination of specific procedural requirements directed toward broad substantive ends. The perspective advanced suggests a similar relationship between process and substance in international EIA commitments. Beyond structuring the relationship between EIAs and substantive values, these background norms also influence the form of EIA commitments by recognizing, *inter alia*, the role of individuals, the continuing obligation of states to prevent harm and the international significance of certain environmental resources. In addition, they help explain the types of international environmental problems that give rise to a demand for EIA processes and the roles that EIA processes are called upon to fulfill in relation to the broader structure of the regulation of international environment problems.

3.2 Nondiscrimination

Nondiscrimination, as an environmental principle,[3] requires that states apply their own environmental laws without discriminating between internal environmental harm and environmental harm to areas external to the state. An associated principle, the principle of equal access, requires that states provide all persons affected by environmental decisions access on an equal basis to participatory decision-making processes regardless of whether they reside within or outside the state in question. The principle of nondiscrimination in environmental matters was first formally applied in the 1974 Nordic Environmental Protection

[2] John Knox, "The Myth and Reality of Transboundary Environmental Impact Assessment" (2002) 96 AJIL 291.

[3] The principle of nondiscrimination also exists as a fundamental principle of international economic law: see Michael Trebilcock and Robert Howse, *The Regulation of International Trade* (3rd edn, New York: Routledge, 2005) at 28–30.

Convention.[4] This treaty between the four Nordic states provides that, where a state determines that an environmentally harmful activity to be carried out within its territory may entail a "nuisance of significance" to another state party, the originating state must provide notice of the activity and allow the nationals of the affected state to make representations regarding the effects of the activities.[5] Moreover, the parties agreed that, in regulating activities, the effects of a nuisance occurring in another state shall be treated as though those effects occurred in the state of origin.[6] The Convention is formulated on the basis of nondiscrimination in the sense that the contracting parties are required only to extend procedural rights to nationals of the other contracting parties to the same extent that those rights are available to its own nationals and are required to treat transboundary impacts as they would treat domestic impacts. As a result, parties are not required to enact new environmental rules, to strengthen their existing environmental laws or to set up new institutions. Nor does the Convention require that parties maintain minimum procedural or substantive standards. Parties must rely instead on the existing laws of the source state.

The principle of nondiscrimination was further developed by the OECD in the mid-1970s through a series of OECD recommendations respecting transboundary pollution, recommending that national laws should not impose lower standards or quality objectives in relation to polluting activities that are more likely to have a transboundary impact, than those likely to have a wholly internal impact,[7] and equal rights of access to information and to existing administrative and judicial procedures should be extended to foreign nationals within an affected state.[8] In a subsequent OECD document, these procedures expressly included access to environmental impact studies and procedures.[9]

In both the Nordic Convention and the OECD Recommendations, the stated objective is clearly to improve environmental protection, but the underlying mechanism is based on a broad principle of equity, as

[4] Stockholm, February 19, 1974, 13 ILM 591.

[5] Nordic Environmental Protection Convention, ibid., Arts. 2–5.

[6] Ibid., Art. 2.

[7] OECD, "Recommendation of the Council on Principles Concerning Transfrontier Pollution," November 14, 1974, C(74)224; "Recommendation of the Council on Equal Right of Access in Relation to Transfrontier Pollution," May 11, 1976, C(76)55 Final; and "Recommendations on the Implementation of a Regime of Equal Access and Non-discrimination in Relation to Transfrontier Pollution," May 17, 1977, C(77)28 Final.

[8] C(77)28 Final, ibid., Art. 4.

[9] OECD, C(78)77 Final, Art. 3.

opposed to any substantive environmental value. While both approaches speak in vague terms about policy harmonization, this is not required. Nondiscrimination does not require reciprocity. As a result, where a country's environmental laws are weak, the same weak rules apply to transboundary impacts. Nondiscrimination is only as effective as the domestic laws of each participating state.

As applied to EIA, the principle of nondiscrimination requires that states assess transboundary impacts in the same manner as impacts on the state's own environment. For example, an impact may not be considered more or less significant merely because it affects the environment of another state. Nondiscrimination, or, more precisely, the principle of equal access, would also require that impacted persons outside the state of origin be entitled to the same procedural rights within the EIA process, such as notice and rights of participation, as those persons within the originating state. Nondiscrimination supplements existing domestic rules respecting transboundary EIA by specifying, in a broad sense, who should receive notice and be afforded rights of participation. What nondiscrimination does not do, however, is impose any minimum EIA requirements on the state of origin. Thus, where domestic projects are not subject to EIA requirements or those requirements are weaker than those of the impacted state, the principle of nondiscrimination does not give the impacted state any right to impose a more onerous set of requirements on the originating state. Even where the source state extends equal rights of notice and participation to non-citizens, the affected state or its inhabitants are reliant on the sufficiency of source state laws. For example, all of those actions that are statutorily exempt from NEPA or exempt under the CEQ regulations would not be subject to EIA requirements regardless of their impact on the natural environment of another state.

Nondiscrimination as a basis for transboundary EIA imposes its own structure on EIA commitments that may have implications for the role that EIAs play in addressing transboundary environmental issues. First, the non-reciprocal nature of nondiscrimination results in there being no minimum requirements for transboundary EIA. The determination as to whether an EIA is undertaken for an activity with potential transboundary impacts remains within the sole discretion of the originating state. The assumption that underlies nondiscrimination is that transboundary environmental issues do not differ from domestic environmental issues. Consequently, nondiscrimination does not afford any privileged status to the concerns of an affected state. Instead, the affected state or groups and individuals within the state are treated like any other commenting agency; their comments are duly considered but they are not privileged in any way. However, in one sense, non-resident interested parties differ from those interested parties within the state of origin in that they do not partake (or are less likely to partake) in the benefits of the project. The economic development associated with the project will likely produce jobs and tax revenue within the state of origin, but those are not likely to be shared. The responsible authority in the state of origin may account for any distributional consequences of the project, but it is not required to do so.

Accepting that the requirements for transparency and participation have an accountability function through the political pressures brought to bear on decision-makers through the notification, access to information and public involvement requirements, it is doubtful whether groups located outside the state are able to generate the same level of political pressure in having their interests accounted for. The difficulty here is that nondiscrimination relies on the efficacy of the domestic EIA system to ensure competing interests are fairly represented, but such a model, based on pluralistic politics inherently disadvantages groups that exist outside the domestic polity. It follows that impacted persons from outside the state of origin cannot appeal to instrumental reasoning; rather they must by necessity appeal to the principles that underlie the EIA system. However, the principle of nondiscrimination on its own is not underlain by a set of shared values that exist outside the domestic EIA regimes. Instead, nondiscrimination accepts a purely procedural understanding of the role of EIA and ignores the possibility that transboundary EIA requirements may be premised on objectives and values that are determined by the international community. From the perspective of the impacted person (or state), their perspective is only given equal consideration when it coincides with the values and priorities of the domestic regime.

A related limitation to the principle of nondiscrimination as the basis for international cooperation on EIA is that nondiscrimination does not recognize the unique normative dimensions of international environmental issues. Consider the case of the Antarctic. While NEPA may apply to projects undertaken by US agencies in the Antarctic, the threshold standard under NEPA, likelihood of significant environmental impacts, may not reflect the uniquely sensitive nature of the Antarctic natural environment. However, under international law, the Antarctic's unique sensitivity is integral to the approach to assessment and is reflected in the use of a much lower threshold standard, namely, more than a minor or transitory impact.[10] The point being that a purely domestic approach treats domestic and international environmental issues as undifferentiated, when in fact that is not the case. As the Antarctic example illustrates, the very nature of the natural environment may require special considerations. From a practical perspective, questions regarding who receives notice and a determination of whether notice was given in a timely fashion will be impacted by whether the impact is domestic, transboundary or in the global commons. NEPA requires that notice be given to "persons or organizations who may be interested or affected."[11] However, such a determination in connection with a potential impact to a migratory species, greenhouse gas levels or with respect to the marine environment is not immediately clear in the absence of further international agreement.

At the very least, international cooperation is required to impose minimum procedural requirements among states which would result in an acceptable level of predictability respecting the circumstances under which an assessment is triggered and how an assessment is to be conducted. Going beyond the need for harmonization of EIA procedures, an argument can be made for a deeper level of cooperation rooted in shared principles respecting the environment. EIA commitments are situated within a broader set of values shared among the participants in the system. The extension of EIA commitments to transboundary harms logically requires a similar extension of the normative environment, if EIAs are to play a similar, i.e. interest-coordinating and transformational, role within international environmental governance structures.

3.3 The harm principle

The harm principle in international environmental law is well-trodden ground, and, as such, I do not intend to describe its coming into being at great length.[12] The harm principle has a long-established pedigree in international law starting with the *Trail Smelter* arbitration between Canada and the United States where, in connection with a dispute over Canadian responsibility for damage occurring in the United States

[10] The EIA regime under the Antarctic Protocol is discussed in detail below at ch. 5.

[11] 40 CFR § 1503.1(a)(4).

[12] See Phoebe Okowa, *State Responsibility for Transboundary Air Pollution in International Law* (New York: Oxford University Press, 2000) ch. 3; and Xue Hanqin, *Transboundary Damage in International Law* (Cambridge: Cambridge University Press, 2003) ch. 5.

arising from air pollution from a smelter located in Canada, the panel formulated its much-quoted *dicta* regarding state responsibility for transboundary harm:

> No state has the right to use or permit the use of its territory in such a manner as to cause injury in or to the territory of another or the properties of persons therein, when the case is of serious consequence and the injury is established by clear and convincing evidence.[13]

More recently, the harm principle has been codified first as Principle 21 to the Stockholm Declaration[14] and then again in Principle 2 of the Rio Declaration,[15] and was confirmed by the ICJ as forming "part of the corpus of international law relating to the environment."[16] Inherent within the harm principle, as set out in both the Stockholm and Rio Declarations, is that the obligation to prevent harm must be balanced against each state's sovereign right to development and to exploit their own natural resources. The dyadic structure of the harm principle means that states can neither insist on an untrammeled right to engage in activities within their jurisdiction regardless of impacts outside their jurisdiction nor insist that other states refrain from all activities that are likely to have transboundary environmental impacts. The recognition that the harm principle is underlain by these competing objectives has resulted in two central qualifications to the obligation to prevent harm.

The first qualification respecting the harm principle is that it only applies to situations where there is a likelihood of "significant" harm to the environment. Both the Stockholm and Rio Declarations speak simply to the prevention of damage, unqualified, to the environment, suggesting that any adverse impact regardless of its scale could trigger the obligation. However, in the *Trail Smelter* arbitration, the panel limited its considerations to activities which cause injury of "serious

[13] *Trail Smelter Arbitral Decision (United States v. Canada)*, 3 RIAA 1905, reprinted in (1939) 33 AJIL 182 (decision dated April 16, 1938) and in (1941) 35 AJIL 684 (final decision dated March 11, 1941) (citations hereinafter refer to the RIAA report).

[14] United Nations Conference on the Human Environment, Stockholm Declaration, June 16, 1972, UN Doc. A/Conf.48/14, reprinted in 11 ILM 1416 (1972).

[15] United Nations Conference on Environment and Development, Rio Declaration on Environment and Development, June 14, 1992, UN Doc. A/Conf.151/5/Rev.1, reprinted in 31 ILM 874 (1992).

[16] *Legality of the Threat or Use of Nuclear Weapons*, Advisory Opinion, (1996) ICJ Rep 15 at para. 29.

consequence" to be established by "clear and convincing evidence."[17] Likewise, in the *Lac Lanoux* arbitration (between France and Spain in respect of a shared watercourse), the tribunal required that the harm resulting from the proposed French diversion of waters be "serious and real."[18] International agreements have similarly used the terms "substantial" or "significant" in the context of defining an appropriate threshold of environmental harm to trigger international obligations.[19] The International Law Commission (ILC), in their commentaries to the Draft Articles on Prevention of Transboundary Harm from Hazardous Activities,[20] describes the term "significant" as "something more than 'detectable' but need not be at the level of 'serious' or 'substantial'."[21] This indication that "significance" as a threshold is lower than "serious" or "substantial" is consistent with the greater appreciation the international community has of the implications of environmental harm, even at low thresholds, since the *Trail Smelter* arbitration.[22]

The term "significant," which appears to be the preferred term in these circumstances, is not without ambiguity and will be determined, for the most part, in relation to a specific factual context. However, as the ILC points out, the "significance" threshold is meant to be measured by objective standards,[23] and as such it is not intended to provide states with the discretion to determine for themselves when there are international consequences flowing from their activities. International agreements that contain environmental standards have a legal relevance

[17] *Trail Smelter* arbitration, at 1965. This standard appears to have been derived from similar standards used in US domestic law cases involving interstate pollution, such as *Missouri* v. *Illinois*, 200 US 496 (1906) and *New York* v. *New Jersey*, 256 US 296 (1921), both of which were cited by the arbitral panel in the *Trail Smelter* case.

[18] *Lac Lanoux Arbitration (France* v. *Spain)*, (1957) 24 ILR 101 at 125.

[19] See, for example, Convention on Long-Range Transboundary Air Pollution, Geneva, November 13, 1979, 18 ILM 1442, in force March 16, 1983, Art. 5; and Vienna Convention for the Protection of the Ozone Layer, Vienna, March 22, 1985, (1990) UKTS 1; 26 ILM 1529 (1987), in force September 22, 1988, Art. 1. The notable exception is the Protocol on Environmental Protection to the Antarctic Treaty, Madrid, October 4, 1991, 30 ILM 1461, in force January 14, 1998, where a lower threshold is used.

[20] International Law Commission, "Commentaries to the Draft Articles on Prevention of Transboundary Harm from Hazardous Activities," in *Report of the International Law Commission, Fifty-Third Session*, UN GAOR, 56th Sess., Supp. No. 10, UN Doc. A/56/10 (2001) 377.

[21] Ibid., Art. 2, Commentary 4.

[22] See K. Sachariew, "The Definition of Thresholds of Tolerance for Transboundary Environmental Injury Under International Law: Development and Present Status" (1990) 37 Neth. Int'l L. Rev. 193.

[23] ILC, "Commentaries to Draft Articles on Prevention of Transboundary Harm," Art. 2, Commentary 4.

that is similar to the way in which regulatory standards are used as a measure of "significance" under domestic EIA legislation. That is, that satisfaction of an international standard will not be determinative of an absence of "significance," or *vice versa*, but such standards may be evidence of the international community's understanding of tolerable levels of environment harm.[24] "Significance" will also depend to a high degree on scientific understandings of the nature of pollutants and natural systems. To this extent, the meaning of "significance" is necessarily dynamic and will change as scientific knowledge respecting the environment changes.[25] The intent of qualifying the harm principle in this manner is to ensure that states can carry on with activities which have impacts falling below the threshold. To maintain otherwise would result in too great an interference with a state's sovereign right to engage in economic activity within its territory. The requirement that environmental harm exceed a threshold of significance also correlates more closely with domestic environmental regulation, which allows for the release of many pollutants within identified levels.

Secondly, notwithstanding the strict liability approach found in the *Trail Smelter* arbitration, the obligation to prevent harm is understood to impose an obligation of conduct, not result. Thus, the obligation is not triggered solely by the existence of transboundary environmental harm exceeding the significance threshold; rather, it is contingent upon the failure of a state to take reasonable steps to prevent that harm. This approach is supported by the International Court of Justice's decision in the *Corfu Channel Case*.[26] While this case dealt with Albanian liability for damage to British warships caused by mines in its territorial waters, the Court's reasoning is widely cited as supporting the duty to prevent environmental harm.[27] Here, the Court's decision to hold Albania liable was partly based on the finding that every state is under an obligation "not

[24] See Okowa, *State Responsibility* at 89–90.

[25] This is acknowledged by the ILC in the "Commentaries to Draft Articles on Prevention of Transboundary Harm," Art. 2, Commentary 7 (where it is noted that "a particular deprivation at a particular time might not be considered 'significant' because at that specific time scientific knowledge or human appreciation for a particular resource had not reached a point at which much value was ascribed to that particular resource. But some time later that view might change and the same harm might then be considered 'significant'.").

[26] (1949) ICJ Rep 4.

[27] See, for example, Patricia Birnie and Alan Boyle, *International Law and the Environment* (2nd edn, New York: Oxford University Press, 2002) at 109; and Philippe Sands, *Principles of International Environmental Law* (2nd edn, Cambridge: Cambridge University Press, 2003) at 192.

to allow knowingly its territory to be used for acts contrary to the rights of other states."[28] The use of the word "knowingly" in this case imposes a subjective element into the determination of liability. However, the Court acknowledges the evidentiary difficulties that such a subjective test causes and bases its own decision on inferences of knowledge.[29] What is clear from this case is that a state cannot be required to prevent harm of which it has no knowledge or which is not reasonably foreseeable.

The ILC, in a commentary to its rule regarding the duty to prevent harm contained in its Draft Articles on Prevention of Transboundary Harm describes the obligation in the following terms:

> due diligence is manifested in reasonable efforts by a State to inform itself of factual and legal components that relates foreseeably to a contemplated procedure and to take appropriate measures in timely fashion to address them.[30]

But this in itself does not significantly clarify the nature of the obligation, as it does not specify what steps a state must take to discharge the obligation. By basing the duty on a standard of reasonableness, satisfaction of the duty will be determined with reference to objective criteria.[31] But this leaves unanswered what those standards might be. The difficulty here is not unlike the employment of the reasonableness standard in domestic law, where what is reasonable will depend upon the particular circumstances of each case, including the nature of the potential harm, the risk it poses, and the location of the harm in relation to natural features and other human activity. Moreover, in international environmental law, it is arguable that reasonableness will also depend upon the particular capabilities of the state in question.[32]

What is important is that there is an obligation on states to take steps to understand the environmental consequences of their activities. International law does not dictate the modalities of discharging this

[28] *Corfu Channel Case*, at 22. [29] Ibid. at 18–19.

[30] ILC, "Commentaries to Draft Articles on Prevention of Transboundary Harm," Art. 3, Commentary 10.

[31] *Alabama Claims Arbitration* (1872) 1 Moore's International Arbitration Awards 485.

[32] See, for example, United Nations Convention on the Law of the Sea, Montego Bay, December 10, 1982, 21 ILM 1261 (1982), in force November 16, 1984, Art. 194 (qualifying the obligation with the words "in accordance with their capabilities"); and American Law Institute, *Restatement (Third) of Foreign Relations Law of the United States* (St. Paul, MN: American Law Institute, 1987) at § 601. See also Pierre Dupuy, "Due Diligence in the International Law of Liability" in OECD, *Legal Aspects of Transfrontier Pollution* (Paris: OECD, 1977) 369 at 375–376.

obligation. Instead, the legislative or administrative steps required to be undertaken are left for states to determine.[33] In this regard, there are numerous sources of minimum international standards of due care, including more specific standards set out in treaties or those adopted by international organizations, as well as evidence of consistent practice by individual states within their domestic legal systems. Treaty practice and state practice as used here do not have to amount to an independent customary duty to be legally relevant because they are resorted to as evidence of what is reasonable state practice. By analogy to domestic law, it is common for courts to look to whether there are common industry practices in determining whether a defendant has acted reasonably.[34] While the practice or standard is not binding, it is strong evidence of measures that a state acting reasonably may employ to prevent harm.

EIAs are clearly one of the central mechanisms used by states to acquire knowledge respecting the environmental consequences of their actions. EIAs address foreseeability by requiring project proponents to comprehensively analyze the likely impacts of proposed activities, including transboundary impacts. In addition, EIA addresses the reasonableness of the activity undertaken through the requirement to look at the feasibility of alternatives to the proposal. The existence of an obligation of due diligence does not suggest that undertaking an EIA is necessary to satisfy the more general duty of prevention, nor does it suggest that EIAs are sufficient to satisfy the duty. For example, a system of carefully controlled emission standards or mandatory pollution control technology, which is adequately implemented could satisfy the requirement in many instances. Indeed, the existence of adequate regulatory schemes will be considered a key factor in determining due diligence.[35] However, insofar as the international community views EIAs

[33] This is the approach adopted by the ILC in the "Commentaries to Draft Articles on Prevention of Transboundary Harm," Art. 3, Commentaries (5) and (6), and Art. 5.

[34] See Henry Hart Jr. and Albert Sacks, *The Legal Process: Basic Problems in the Making and Application of Law*, prepared for publication from the 1958 tentative edition by Eskridge and Frickey (Westbury, NY: Foundation Press, 1994) at 423.

[35] For example, the ILC notes that, in connection with the Sandoz chemical spill into the Rhine river, the Swiss government acknowledged responsibility arising out of its failure to exercise due diligence in the adequate regulation of industrial activities: "Commentaries to Draft Articles on Prevention of Transboundary Harm," Art. 3, Commentary 8. See also Hans Ulrich and Jessurun d'Oliveira, "The Sandoz Blaze: The Damage and the Public and Private Liabilities" in Francesco Scovazzi and Tullio Francioni, eds., *International Responsibility for Environmental Harm* (London: Graham & Trotman, 1991) 429.

as a reasonable mechanism by which a state may determine the foreseeable consequences of its activities, EIA implements a state's due diligence obligation to inform itself of the environmental effects of proposed activities.

One of the central difficulties with respect to the relationship between EIA and the harm principle arises from the ambiguous status of the requirements of due diligence in relation to the law respecting state responsibility for environmental harm. The confusion arises in large part because of the existing uncertainty as to the rules respecting state responsibility for transboundary environmental damage, more generally. This uncertainty is recognized in both Principle 22 of the Stockholm Declaration and Principle 13 of the Rio Declaration, which call upon the international community "to develop further international law regarding liability and compensation for adverse effects of environmental damage caused by activities within their jurisdiction or control to areas beyond their jurisdiction."[36]

The legal relationship between environmental harm and state liability has also been at the center of the ILC's work on state responsibility and state liability, out of which the Draft Articles on Prevention of Transboundary Harm arose.[37] The ILC has long drawn a distinction between state responsibility, on the one hand, and liability, on the other. The former arises only upon breach of an international obligation, while the latter could arise in relation to lawful activities. The concern which the ILC sought to address here was liability for unforeseeable environmental harm or harm that could not be prevented by reasonable means. Under international law, in the absence of breach of due diligence, the affected state would have no remedy: it must bear the costs of the environmental damage itself, notwithstanding its own innocence in causing the damage.[38] This distinction led to the separate consideration by the ILC of "Liability for Injurious Consequences of Acts Not Prohibited by International Law," a topic that focused almost entirely on environmental

[36] Quoting Principle 13 of the Rio Declaration.

[37] Discussed in Alan Boyle, "Codification of International Environmental Law and the International Law Commission: Injurious Consequences Revisited" in Alan Boyle and David Freestone, eds., *International Law and Sustainable Development: Past Achievements and Future Challenges* (New York: Oxford University Press, 1999) 61. See also Jutta Brunnée, "Of Sense and Sensibility: Reflections on International Liability Regimes as Tools for Environmental Protection" (2004) 53 ICLQ 351.

[38] See Boyle, "Codification" at 76–77, noting that Art. 21 of the 1996 ILC Draft Articles on State Responsibility sought to address this issue by placing a duty on the state of origin to negotiate compensation for victims of unavoidable environmental harm.

liability. Perhaps recognizing that there was little support in international law for liability without fault, except in limited circumstances, such as ultra-hazardous activities, and no appetite in the international community for the imposition of such a regime, the ILC has since refocused this project. The result of this reorientation was a further distinction being drawn between liability regimes and prevention regimes, with the Draft Articles on Prevention of Transboundary Harm being the culmination of the ILC's work on prevention.[39]

While it is clear that international law will hold a state liable for damages that arise out of activities undertaken without due diligence, it is less clear what the consequences are for failing to exercise due diligence in the absence of environmental damage. If due diligence is only conceived of as a defense to a claim for compensation for environmental damages, it would follow that failure to exercise due diligence has no legal consequences in the absence of actual harm.[40] This in turn implies that a potentially affected state cannot require the state of origin to take steps to ensure that its activities will not have significant environmental impacts in advance of the activity actually causing harm. Another way to conceptualize this approach is that, because due diligence is not a discrete obligation, but rather is an element of a broader obligation not to cause transboundary environmental harm, its breach does not give rise to state responsibility and access to the remedy of cessation. Such an approach is very clearly at odds with the preventative objective of the harm principle. The better view is that due diligence gives rise to a separate duty on states to take measures to prevent harm. Failure to take such measures does not render the proposed activity unlawful *per se*, but the affected state has the right to insist that the state of origin comply with its due diligence obligations.

The latter approach is consistent with the approach of the ILC, in that the Draft Articles on Prevention of Transboundary Harm clearly contemplate state responsibility for the breach of due diligence

[39] The liability aspect of this topic resulted in the adoption by the ILC of the Draft Principles on the Allocation of Loss in the Case of Transboundary Harm Arising Out of Hazardous Activities, UN Doc. A/CN.4/L662 (2006). These draft principles move away from the concept of liability toward characterizing the obligation as one of "allocation of loss."

[40] This appears to be the position taken by Okowa, *State Responsibility* at 169, noting: "A state that has failed to undertake environmental impact assessment, or enter into consultations with affected states, may be precluded from asserting that the harm did not occur for want of diligence."

obligations.[41] This approach is also consistent with state practice and judicial understandings of the nature of due diligence obligations. For example, in the *Nuclear Tests Cases*, it was argued by New Zealand that France's proposal to conduct underground nuclear tests without first undertaking an environmental impact assessment was illegal, notwithstanding the absence of actual harm.[42] Similar arguments were put forward by Hungary in the *Gabcikovo-Nagymaros Case*, in connection with potential (but not actual) environmental harm from a dam project on the Danube River,[43] and most recently by Ireland in relation to the operation by the United Kingdom of a nuclear reprocessing plant located on the Irish Sea.[44] In all of these cases, the potentially affected state sought to prevent the originating state from carrying out the proposal until they had complied with their due diligence obligations.

The more controversial question in relation to the harm principle is its substantive content. The obligation as set out in the Rio Declaration is quite plainly an obligation of substance, requiring states to refrain from those activities that cause environmental harm to other states and to the global commons. It would seem to follow from this that, where a country complies with its procedural obligation to assess harm and that assessment discloses that significant transboundary harm is likely, then a state is under a positive obligation to mitigate that harm or refrain from the activity. It is based on this understanding of the harm principle that John Knox argues that an international EIA obligation that originates in the harm principle would require states, as part of the EIA obligation, to mitigate transboundary environmental harm. But, since international EIA obligations do not require harm prevention, the argument continues, EIA obligations do not arise out of the requirement to prevent harm.[45] Knox's argument tends to view the harm principle in isolation, whereas in fact it must be read and understood in conjunction

[41] ILC, "Commentaries to Draft Articles on Prevention of Transboundary Harm," Art. 1, Commentary 6. See also Alan Boyle, "State Responsibility and International Liability for Injurious Consequences of Acts Not Prohibited by International Law: A Necessary Distinction?" (1990) 39 ICLQ 1.

[42] Request for an Examination of the Situation in Accordance with the Court's Judgment of December, 1974 in the Nuclear Tests (New Zealand v. France) Case, (1995) ICJ Rep 288.

[43] *Case Concerning the Gabcikovo-Nagymaros Project (Hungary/Slovakia)*, September 25, 1997, (1997) ICJ Rep 7.

[44] *MOX Plant Case (Ireland* v. *United Kingdom)*, Memorial of Ireland, July 26, 2002, Permanent Court of Arbitration, www.pca-cpa.org.

[45] Knox, "Myth and Reality."

with the related duty of state cooperation in preventing or minimizing transboundary harm.

3.4 The duty to cooperate

The duty to cooperate, which includes both a duty of notification and a duty of consultation, has its origins in the law respecting shared natural resources, and is most notably expressed in the *Lac Lanoux* arbitration.[46] In this case, France had proposed to divert a watercourse that flowed from France into Spain. In planning for the project, France had notified the Spanish government of its proposal and entered into consultations with the Spanish respecting the proposal, which did not result in Spain's agreement to the project, but did result in some modifications to the project. Spain took the position in the arbitration that the project could only proceed with its prior agreement. The arbitral panel, in rejecting the Spanish position, held that, in the case of a shared watercourse, a state which proposed to alter the watercourse had an obligation to notify an affected state and to enter into consultations with that state in good faith in an attempt to resolve any outstanding differences. However, the proponent state was not required to obtain the consent of any affected state prior to commencing a project.[47]

This structure, whereby states are required to notify one another and exchange information and consult one another about the potential impact of proposed activities, but do not have the right to exercise a veto over another state's project, has formed the basis of the procedural obligations placed on states that share common resources. The approach, which recognizes the fact that each state must respect the sovereign rights of other states to utilize shared resources in an equitable manner, is reflected in the *Lac Lanoux* arbitration where the panel notes:

> France is entitled to exercise her rights; she cannot ignore Spanish interests. Spain is entitled to demand that her rights be respected and that her interests be taken into consideration. As a matter of form, the upstream State has, procedurally, a right of initiative; it is not obliged to associate the downstream State in the elaboration of its schemes. If, in the course of discussions, the downstream State submits schemes to it, the upstream State must examine them, but it has the right to give preference to the solution contained in its own scheme provided that it takes into consideration in a reasonable manner the interests of the downstream State.[48]

[46] *France* v. *Spain* (1957) 24 ILR 101. [47] Ibid. at 130. [48] Ibid. at 140.

The right that a state possesses to proceed with a project without the prior consent of another affected state is a result of the sovereign right of a state to pursue activities in its own self-interest. When faced with the possibility of an affected state raising objections to a planned activity involving a shared resource, the state of origin is under a clear obligation to take those objections into account and, significantly, it must do so in a good faith effort to resolve those objections.

This approach was reflected in the ILC Draft Articles on the Non-Navigational Uses of International Watercourses and subsequently in the UN Convention on the Non-Navigational Uses of International Watercourses.[49] It is noteworthy in the context of this discussion that the UN Watercourses Convention includes an obligation on states to prevent harm to a shared watercourse, in addition to the requirement to utilize shared watercourses in an equitable manner.[50] Article 7(2) indicates that, in the event of harm that cannot reasonably be avoided, states are still required to consult with one another, having regard for their equitable obligations, to eliminate or mitigate the harm, or, if appropriate, provide compensation. Within this structure, the duty to cooperate provides the framework for achieving equitable utilization and harm prevention, through requirements for notification, exchange of information and consultation.[51]

The duty to cooperate has been applied outside the context of shared natural resources to transboundary environmental effects more generally.[52] For example, the duty to cooperate is included as Principle 24 of the Stockholm Declaration and reiterated in Principle 7 of the Rio Declaration. A general duty of cooperation is also found, *inter alia*, in the UNCLOS,[53] the US–Canada Air Quality Agreement,[54] and the UNECE Convention on Long Range Transboundary Air Pollution.[55] The more specific obligations relating to notification and consultation are also found in international instruments respecting the environment, including the Stockholm and Rio Declarations. Like their counterparts in

[49] 36 ILM 719 (1997), not in force. [50] Ibid., Arts. 7 and 6, respectively.

[51] Ibid., Art. 8(1). Arts. 11–19 set out more detailed procedural requirements in relation to planned measures.

[52] See Alan Boyle, "The Principle of Co-operation: The Environment" in Vaughan Lowe and Colin Warbrick, eds., *The United Nations and the Principles of International Law* (London: Routledge, 1994) 120.

[53] UNCLOS, Art. 194.

[54] Agreement between United States and Canada on Air Quality, Ottawa, March 13, 1991, Can TS 1991 No. 3; 30 ILM 676, Arts. V–VII.

[55] November 13, 1979, 18 ILM 1442, entered into force March 16, 1983, Arts. 2–5.

shared resource regimes, the obligations to notify and consult in the event of potential transboundary environmental harm stops short of requiring prior consent and the threshold for triggering these obligations is the potential of significant transboundary environmental harm.

Good faith stands at the center of the duty to cooperate because in its absence the rights of affected states are subject to abuse, particularly in light of the lack of a requirement of prior consent. Good faith as a principle of international law has, of course, significance well beyond the duty to cooperate. The principle is found in both the UN Charter,[56] in relation to the fulfillment of legal obligations, and in the Vienna Convention on the Law of Treaties,[57] in connection with the interpretation of treaties. In the *Fisheries Jurisdiction Case*, the ICJ refers to the principle of good faith in the context of the duty to negotiate in respect of a shared resource: "The task before . . . [the Parties] will be to conduct their negotiations on the basis that each must in good faith pay reasonable regard to the legal rights of the other, [to] . . . the facts of the particular situation, and having regard to the interests of other states with established . . . rights."[58]

While consultation differs from negotiation, both processes are clearly oriented toward the same ends, namely, to bring about a workable consensus between parties with potentially divergent interests. In the *Gulf of Maine* case, the panel described the duty to negotiate in good faith as entailing "a genuine intention to achieve a positive result."[59] Similarly, the ICJ, in the *North Sea Continental Shelf Case*, held that negotiation must be something more than "a formal process"; instead it must be "meaningful," which in turn requires a willingness to genuinely consider the position of others.[60] In the context of consultation, the panel in the *Lac Lanoux* arbitration also links good faith with an obligation not to treat consultations as "mere formalities."[61]

At a minimum, the requirement that notification and consultation be meaningful implies that the state of origin supply sufficient information about the project and its effects so as to enable the potentially impacted state to make a reasoned assessment of the potential impacts on its interests and so as to enable the impacted state to engage in a consultation process to safeguard those interests. In addition, good faith

[56] Charter of the United Nations, June 26, 1945, Can TS 1945 No. 7, Art. 2(2).

[57] Vienna Convention on the Law of Treaties, Vienna, May 23, 1969, 1155 UNTS 331, Arts. 26 and 31(1).

[58] *United Kingdom* v. *Iceland*, (1974) ICJ Rep 3 at 33.

[59] (1984) ICJ Rep 292 at 299.

[60] (1969) ICJ Rep 3 at 47.

[61] *Lac Lanoux* arbitration at 119.

requires that both states conduct consultations in a genuine, as opposed to a formal or perfunctory, manner. In the *Lac Lanoux* arbitration, the panel spoke to both good faith and the "rules of reason."[62] While not elaborating on what was meant by the latter phrase, the requirement of genuineness suggests that a state that proposes a planned activity must consider objections with an open mind and on a principled (reasoned) basis. Put another way, a state that proposes a planned activity that may cause significant transboundary harm has an obligation not to act in an arbitrary or high-handed manner. It is difficult to conceive how the obligation of good faith could be discharged in the absence of a response from the state of origin to the objections raised by the impacted state, as good faith would seem to require an assessment of the reasons given by the state of origin justifying its actions in the face of objections. The good faith requirement, in other words, requires that consultation be an iterative, ongoing process.

International duties of notification and consultation are for the most part framed in broad language, leaving unanswered crucial questions such as when the duty arises, who is to be notified, when they are to be notified, what information is to be provided and what constitutes reasonable consultation. EIA may again be best seen as implementing these broader duties by providing a standardized set of procedures defining what information gets provided in what form and to whom. EIA commitments also require that affected parties, including members of the public, are afforded opportunities to comment and that these comments must be taken into account and responded to. Good faith consultation as required by the principle of cooperation is operationalized by EIA requirements, providing an international analogue to NEPA's hard look doctrine.[63] By providing more specific rules with respect to notification, disclosure of information and requiring parties to respond to objections raised, EIA commitments ensure that the duty of cooperation is viewed by states as more than a lofty ideal, but is an enforceable obligation, the breach of which would engage state responsibility.[64]

As with the relationship between EIA and the harm principle, the relationship between the duties of notification and consultation and EIA requirements is not that the existence of the former logically necessitates the latter. Notification and consultation can be carried out in the

[62] Ibid. [63] Discussed above at ch. 2.

[64] Stephen McCaffrey, *The Law of International Watercourses: Non-Navigational Uses* (New York: Oxford University Press, 2001) at 403.

absence of an EIA. However, notification and consultation are only meaningful if they are accompanied by sufficient information respecting the potential effect of a proposed project. EIAs, as a source for that information, enable a state to fulfill these obligations in good faith. Thus, whereas the harm principle requires that a state, as a matter of due diligence, inform *itself* of the possible environmental consequences of its activities, the principle of cooperation requires that a state inform *others* of the details of its activities that may affect them.

3.5 The proceduralization of the harm principle

Viewing the harm principle and the duty to cooperate as integrated obligations points to the largely procedural nature of the duty to prevent harm. The proceduralization of the harm principle is evident when one considers a scenario where a state proposes an activity that poses a likelihood of significant transboundary impact. Under international law, that state is required to undertake an assessment, to notify and exchange information with affected states and to enter into good faith consultations with affected states. If, however, the parties to the consultation cannot arrive at a mutually satisfactory arrangement, the state of origin can proceed with the project. In the event of subsequent damage to the environment, the question of liability will turn on the reasonableness of proceeding with a project in the face of knowledge of that project's harm. In assessing the reasonableness of the state decision, international law requires more than formal adherence to the procedural requirements, but a judgment as to whether in all the circumstances the actual decision taken meets the standard of reasonableness. Thus, as a *liability* principle, the harm principle has substantive bite. It is beyond the scope of this chapter to address the precise contours of that standard, but the degree to which the harm that occurred was foreseeable, the feasibility of mitigation, the importance of the project itself and whether the foreseeable damages contravened commonly accepted standards, are relevant considerations.[65]

The more germane question for the purposes of this discussion is the legal position of both the state of origin and the potentially affected state prior to any damages being suffered by the affected state. Here, the

[65] These factors are similar in many respects to the factors set out in International Law Commission, "Draft Articles on Prevention of Transboundary Harm from Hazardous Activities," in *Report of the International Law Commission, Fifty-Third Session*, UN GAOR, 56th Sess., Supp. No. 10, UN Doc. A/56/10 (2001) 370, Art. 10.

consideration of the harm principle is not in relation to state liability for damages, but rather relates to the legal right of a state to undertake activities that pose a threat to other states. As independent and necessarily preventive obligations one might expect that an affected state would be able to enjoin a state which proposes a harmful activity from carrying out that activity unless the impacts are mitigated. However, the duty of cooperation does not necessarily provide an affected state with a right to veto projects with significant transboundary impacts. This question was left unanswered by the panel in the *Lac Lanoux* arbitration because the panel found no evidence that the proposed dam would in fact cause significant harm to Spain's interests.[66] It is, in fact, far from clear that an affected state is entitled to enjoin a state from carrying out activities that are likely to cause significant transboundary impacts.

For example, the approach of the ILC is to deny that such a right exists. What the harm principle entitles an affected state to do is to have its concerns taken into account, as is made clear in Article 9(3) of the ILC Draft Articles on Prevention of Transboundary Harm:

> If the consultations referred to in paragraph 1 fail to produce an agreed solution, the State of origin shall nevertheless take into account the interests of the State likely to be affected in case it decides to authorize the activity to be pursued, without prejudice to the rights of any State likely to be affected.

The latter phrase, which preserves the rights of affected states in the event of damages, is in keeping with the ILC's decision to treat prevention separately from questions of state liability for damages. The duty to take the affected state's interests into account is described by the ILC in the following terms: "The State of origin, while permitted to go ahead with the activity, is still *obligated*, as a measure of *self-regulation*, to take into account the interests of the States likely to be affected."[67] On the one hand, there is a duty to take account of an affected state's interests, but on the other hand, as a matter of self-regulation, the duty appears to be of a voluntary nature. If this requirement is to avoid self-contradiction, it has to be considered in light of the overarching obligation of good faith, and in particular an obligation to justify the decision taken in light of the available evidence of the potential for environmental harm.

[66] *Lac Lanoux* arbitration at 129.

[67] ILC, "Commentaries to Draft Articles on Prevention of Transboundary Harm," Art. 9, Commentary 10 (emphasis added).

The objective of the duty to consult is to effect a balancing of competing interests, which must be done in an "equitable" manner.[68] In order to assess whether a state has discharged its obligation to take another state's interests into account, there must exist a set of objectively determinable relevant considerations. As a consequence, the discretion that the state of origin has in determining whether to proceed with a planned activity is qualified by the equitable factors listed in Article 10 of the Draft Articles on Prevention of Transboundary Harm. This is principally a procedural qualification because none of the factors listed are determinative of whether an activity with transboundary impacts can be legally undertaken. Indeed, the very terms of Article 10 suggest that social and economic factors can under circumstances outweigh environmental factors. It would, however, be a mistake to view the state of origin as having untrammeled discretion to do as it pleases so long as it goes through the procedural motions. A state that acts in an arbitrary or clearly unreasonable manner by either ignoring or giving insufficient weight to relevant considerations or taking into account irrelevant considerations cannot be said to have acted in good faith. It is questionable that recourse to equitable considerations is a requirement of customary law, and, as such, may be seen as being posed by the ILC as progressive development of the law, instead of being a codification of existing customary law.

Despite its uncertain normative status, the ILC's approach remains instructive, as it points to the difficulty in formulating a substantive preventive obligation of general application. Koskenniemi identifies the difficulty as arising out of the structure of transboundary environmental disputes whereby both the state of origin and the affected state can couch their respective positions in terms of their own inviolable sovereignty.[69] The recourse to equitable considerations is, under this view, inevitable, as is the proceduralization of the harm principle.[70] Koskenniemi views the move to process as a move toward *ad hocry* and away from principled decision-making.[71] He does not see this move away from principles as a negative development, as he views any principles as being necessarily disputed and the contextualized format of dispute settlement that results more reflective of the actual political nature of the decisions taken. An alternative understanding, and one that is

[68] "Draft Articles on Prevention of Transboundary Harm," Art. 9(1).

[69] Martti Koskenniemi, "Peaceful Settlement of Environmental Disputes" (1991) 60 Nordic JIL 73 at 74–76.

[70] Ibid. at 84. [71] Ibid. at 86.

more sympathetic to the relative autonomy of law, maintains that equitable considerations do not confer absolute discretion, but rather constrain decisions by limiting the range of choices available to the state of origin.[72]

There is a danger here in conflating the harm principle and the duty to cooperate such that it appears to rob the duty to prevent harm of any substantive content. The characterization of the harm principle as substantive or procedural is not an either/or determination. To portray the harm principle as "mythic," as Knox does,[73] on the basis that it fails to provide states with a consistent and quantifiable prescription, may be the result of the creation of a straw man, as it criticizes the harm principle for failing to achieve substantive results that are not intended. The harm principle identifies both ends and means. The objective, the prevention or reduction of transboundary harm, cannot be reduced to a single standard because transboundary environmental harm is necessarily contextual. This is not the equivalent of saying that the determination of harm is unprincipled. Whether it is by reference to the factors identified by the ILC or like criteria drawn by analogous circumstances in domestic or other areas of international law, the harm principle requires decisions respecting potentially harmful activities to be made on an objective and reasoned basis. Having said that, there is undeniably a penumbra of uncertainty that threatens the ability of the harm principle to constrain state actions. Consequently, the harm principle turns to procedure, which tends to transcend context, in order to ensure that decision-making processes have recourse to a consistent set of considerations and take into account all relevant viewpoints. The requirement that these procedures be exercised in good faith, again a condition that is both substantive and procedural in nature, further narrows the range of acceptable outcomes.

Knox, in tracing the development of transboundary EIA obligations in international law, extends his criticism to international lawyers who have characterized transboundary EIA obligations as flowing out of this mythical understanding of the harm principle. But, again, the criticism rings hollow, if one accepts a procedural understanding of the harm principle. In fact, when one considers the kind of procedural mechanism that is required to implement the harm principle, it would be difficult to conceive of something that did not look a lot like modern EIA obligations.

[72] See, for example, *Malta–Libya Continental Shelf Case*, (1985) ICJ Rep 39 at para. 45.
[73] Knox, "Myth and Reality."

In particular, what is required is a process that allows for highly contextualized decision-making. The process, triggered by the likelihood of significant environmental harm, must include provisions for providing notice of potential environmental impacts to affected states and must allow for the affected state to participate meaningfully in the decision-making process. In this regard, in implementing the harm principle, the mechanism should not confer substantive rights, but instead it should structure dialogue between parties with often competing interests. The mechanism should account not only for environmental effects, but also economic and perhaps even strategic interests. It is unlikely that, in implementing the harm principle, states should adopt procedures that would require in an absolute fashion the prevention or mitigation of environmental damage, even where such damage is likely to occur. Instead, the implementing procedure must seek to ensure that interactions between the parties are carried out in good faith and that decisions taken have genuinely accounted for the interests of affected states. This, in turn, suggests that the decisions themselves must be accompanied by reasons so as to allow interested parties to satisfy themselves that their interests were accounted for and the decision itself was determined on the basis of relevant factors. In this regard, it is noteworthy that the ILC indicates that preexisting environmental standards contained in domestic, regional and international instruments are a relevant factor, as is the availability of alternative methods to carry out the proposed undertaking.[74] The extent to which actual EIA obligations in international law respond to the requirements of the harm principle is taken up in the next chapter.

Describing the harm principle as encompassing a set of procedural obligations, but without including a substantive obligation to mitigate significant environmental harm, leaves this formulation open to the criticism that, in the absence of definable substantive rights, the principle is too easily abused. Of particular concern in this context is whether weaker states will be subjected to greater amounts of transboundary pollution from stronger states. The concern here is that a procedural understanding of the harm principle takes the law out of the harm principle, reducing the decision-making process itself to the expediency of politics. However, such a view may depend too much on a sharp dichotomy between law and politics. Determining whether the extent to which economic factors should be allowed to compromise environmental

[74] "Draft Articles on Prevention of Transboundary Harm," Art. 10(e) and (f).

objectives is a political question, but the discretion that inheres in that question is not absolute. Here again, there are strong parallels with domestic EIA structures, where discretion does not amount to whim and the process itself is inclined toward the objective of harm prevention. Decisions that are perceived as being contrary to the goal of harm prevention will carry a greater burden of justification. This points to one further aspect of the role of the harm principle. A principle, and not a rule or standard, it is aimed less at determining the formal validity of a particular decision, than it is with the legitimacy of the decision.

3.6 Sustainable development

The relationship between international EIA commitments and sustainable development norms is on one level obvious and fundamental since at the center of each is the idea that environmental considerations must animate and inform public policy. The policy statement in NEPA anticipated a number of the goals of sustainable development, including integration of environmental, economic and social considerations, inter-generational equity, and the maintenance of natural diversity, demonstrating a long-standing link between EIA and sustainability.[75] The connection between EIA and sustainable development is ubiquitous in international policy instruments developed since the publication of the report of the World Commission on Environment and Development (WCED).[76] For example, sustainable development is explicitly referenced as the objective of the UNEP Goals and Principles of Environmental Impact Assessment,[77] and the Espoo Convention. Prior assessment of planned activities was identified by the WCED Experts Group on Environmental Law as an emerging principle of international law.[78] The Rio Declaration, included, as Principle 17, a commitment on states to conduct EIAs, and there are numerous references to EIA in Agenda 21.[79]

[75] Section 101.

[76] World Commission on Environment and Development, *Our Common Future* (New York: Oxford University Press, 1987).

[77] UNEP Res. GC14/25, 14th Sess. (1987), endorsed by GA Res. 42/184, UN GAOR, 42nd Sess., UN Doc. A/Res/42/184 (1987).

[78] Experts Group on Environmental Law of the WCED, *Environmental Protection and Sustainable Development: Legal Principles and Recommendations* (London: Graham & Trotman/Martinus Nijhoff Publishers, 1987) at 62.

[79] Report of the United Nations Conference on Environment and Development, Annex II ("Agenda 21"), UN Doc. A/Conf.151/26 (vol. 1), paras. 9.12(b), 11.23(b), 13.7(a), 15.5(k), 17.6(d) and 22.4(c).

Despite the early and continuing identification of the importance of EIA for promoting sustainable development, the precise nature of this linkage has suffered from the conceptual ambiguity of the concept of sustainable development itself. The result has been a huge volume of academic literature and policy analysis examining the contributions of EIA to sustainable development and the reform of EIA processes to better account for sustainability criteria.[80] A review of this literature is beyond the scope of this study, but several common trends salient to the development of international EIA commitments are emerging from it.

First, the emphasis on the integration of environmental considerations with economic and social considerations, commonly referred to as the three pillars of sustainable development, indicates an increased need to assess activities beyond the project level through strategic environmental assessment (SEA). This link between sustainability and integration is elevated to the status of principle in the Rio Declaration, where Principle 4 notes: "In order to achieve sustainable development, environmental protection shall constitute an integral part of the development process and cannot be considered in isolation from it."[81] SEA, which requires the assessment of decisions respecting policies, plans and programs, implements the goal of integrated decision-making by requiring consideration of environmental impacts at an earlier stage in the development process and across broader spatial and temporal horizons, capturing inter-sector and cumulative impacts.[82] Integrated decision-making can be accomplished through a variety of measures, and so, like the relationship between the harm principle and EIA, the increased demand for integrated decision-making does not necessitate a move to SEA.[83] However, in light of the preexistence of EIA norms in both domestic and international settings, the extension of assessment tools toward strategic level decision-making provides an avenue to

[80] Notable examples include Barry Sadler, *Environmental Assessment in a Changing World: Final Report of the International Study of the Effectiveness of Environmental Assessment* (Ottawa: Canadian Environmental Assessment Agency, 1996), ch. 7; Hussein Abaza, Ron Bisset, and Barry Sadler, *Environmental Impact Assessment and Strategic Environmental Assessment: Towards an Integrated Approach* (Nairobi: UNEP, 2004); Barry Dalal-Clayton and Barry Sadler, *Strategic Environmental Assessment: A Sourcebook and Reference Guide to International Experience* (London: Earthscan Publications, 2005); and Clive George, "Testing for Sustainable Development Through Environmental Assessment" (1999) 19 Environmental Impact Assessment Review 175.

[81] Rio Declaration, Principle 4.

[82] Abaza, Bisset and Sadler, *Towards an Integrated Approach*, ch. 5.

[83] See John Dernbach, "Achieving Sustaining Development: The Centrality and Multiple Facets of Integrated Decision-Making" (2003) 10 Indiana J. Global Legal Stud. 247.

implement integration without the development of new tools. That said, there remains a need for careful consideration of the suitability of SEA for decision-making in international settings. For example, flowing from the discussion on the harm principle, international obligations to prevent harm are only triggered by the likelihood of direct physical harm, which is unlikely to be triggered by proposed strategic-level decisions.

Integration also suggests the need for a greater appreciation of complex ecological interrelations, which in turn points to the presence of scientific uncertainty as a characteristic of environmental decision-making. The recognition of the limits of scientific knowledge militates in favor of instituting precautionary measures into decision-making processes. The precautionary principle provides a normative justification for tempering the synoptic approach of EIA processes with corrective mechanisms such as post-project monitoring and feedback mechanisms.[84] The move away from traditional sectoral approaches to environmental management finds further recognition in the extension of EIA processes to areas such as biological diversity and climate change.[85]

The WCED report also stresses the fundamental importance of access to information and participation to realizing the goals of sustainable development, noting:

> Recognition by states of their responsibility to ensure an adequate environment for present as well as future generations is an important step towards sustainable development. However, progress will also be facilitated by recognition of, for example, the right of individuals to know and have access to current information on the state of the environment and natural resources, the right to be consulted and to participate in decision-making on activities likely to have a significant effect on the environment, the right to legal remedies and redress for those whose health or environment has been or may be seriously affected.[86]

The connection made by the WCED between sustainable development and increased transparency of environmental decision-making processes and increased participation in those processes by individuals potentially affected by those decisions has clear implications for EIA – implications of which the WCED appears to have been aware in its recasting of EIA as a tool to bring about sustainable development. Seen in this light, the political dimension of the role of EIA is enlarged because it is partially aimed at ensuring that decisions regarding the environment reflect the values of those they affect. By this understanding, access to information

[84] Discussed above at Ch. 2. [85] CBD, Art. 14; UNFCCC, Art. 4(f).
[86] WCED, *Our Common Future* at 330.

and participation are not optional or peripheral aspects of international EIA obligations, as suggested in earlier formulations, but are at the center of EIA. The importance of public participation and access to information is affirmed in Principle 10 of the Rio Declaration. There is no explicit link between Principles 10 and 17 (requiring EIAs), but in light of the transparent and participatory nature of many domestic EIA processes, EIAs should be viewed as one of the main mechanisms by which Principle 10 can be achieved.[87] Also of significance is the inclusion of an obligation to notify and consult in the event of activities that may have significant transboundary effects.[88] Here, the obligation extends beyond the context of shared natural resources to include transboundary environmental impacts more generally. Again this provision must be read together with Principle 17, whereby the assessment is the mechanism upon which notification, information exchange and consultation will occur. The express requirement that consultation take place on the basis of good faith demonstrates the integral nature of good faith within the broader requirements respecting transboundary harm.[89]

The focus on participation points to the strongly procedural character of sustainable development. Sustainable development rarely, if ever, points to particular outcomes but rather mediates between the competing goals of economic development and environmental well-being by requiring states and other transnational actors to consult one another in good faith and to justify their actions in light of shared goals. Vaughan Lowe describes sustainable development as operating "interstitially," by which he means to suggest that sustainable development does not operate directly on states or other actors as a primary norm or rule, but rather operates indirectly by directing how primary norms should interact with each other.[90] The International Court of Justice's decision in the *Gabcikovo-Nagymaros Case* nicely illustrates the procedural character of sustainable development.[91] Here, the Court invoked the principle of

[87] This link is expressly noted by Jeffrey Kovar, a member of US delegation to the Rio Conference, who notes that "the inclusion of strong public participation principles, including the use of environmental impact assessments as set out in Principle 17, was one of the primary objectives of the United States, the European Community, Canada and the Nordic countries": see Jeffrey Kovar, "A Short Guide to the Rio Declaration" (1993) 4 Colorado J. Int'l Envt'l L. & Pol'y 119 at 131.

[88] Rio Declaration, Principle 19. [89] Ibid.

[90] Vaughan Lowe, "Sustainable Development and Unsustainable Arguments" in Alan Boyle and David Freestone, eds., *International Law and Sustainable Development: Past Achievements and Future Challenges* (New York: Oxford University Press, 2001) 19 at 31.

[91] *Case Concerning the Gabcikovo-Nagymaros Project (Hungary/Slovakia)* (1997) ICJ Rep 6.

sustainable development in support of its decision to require the parties to negotiate a resolution to a dispute over the use of a shared watercourse in light of their respective rights and the prevailing principles of international environmental law.[92] The Court's approach was to maintain the discretion of the states to determine the actual outcome, but to require the parties to exercise that discretion on a principled basis. Alan Boyle describes the court's approach in the following terms:

> [I]t seems that the Court viewed sustainable development . . . as a value or objective that the parties were legally obliged to take into account in their decisions on development projects. If this is correct, then the Court's use of sustainable development has implications primarily for the process of decision-making by the parties and not for the decision itself. It is in this sense that requiring states to evaluate and assess environmental impacts and apply new environmental norms and standards becomes part of the process for giving effect to the objectives of sustainable development. From this perspective, sustainable development may also entail commitments to public participation in decision-making, environmental impact assessment, and the application of the precautionary principle, but it dictates no particular outcome or result and leaves the parties free to give effect to this fundamental value in almost any way they choose.[93]

A further overarching aspect of sustainable development is the move away from compartmentalizing environmental problems as either domestic concerns or as international concerns, in favor of recognition that even activities that occur solely within a state and whose direct effects are felt within the state have implications for other states and individuals within other states.[94] The transnationalism of sustainable development is exemplified by the approach to principles in the Rio Declaration that are not directed to the international context, but rather are formulated as principles of sound environmental governance regardless of their context. For mechanisms such as EIAs, transnationalism means that there is no clear line differentiating domestic EIA from international EIA. This requires states to appreciate the global dimensions of domestic environmental activities and to ensure that in assessing the effects of activities that these global dimensions are accounted for. The application of EIA to biological diversity illustrates this trend,

[92] Ibid. at para. 140.

[93] Alan Boyle, "The Gabcikovo-Nagymaros Case: New Law in Old Bottles" (1997) 8 YBIEL 13 at 18.

[94] WCED, *Our Common Future* at 4, noting, "[u]ntil recently, the planet was a large world in which human activities and their effects were neatly compartmentalized within nations, within sectors . . . and within broad areas of concern . . . These compartments have begun to dissolve."

since the physical impacts from a loss of biodiversity will be state-based, but very clearly the international community has a broader interest in the preservation of biological resources. The move toward transnationalism represents a move away from the state as the sole actor of consequence in international environmental governance. There is a recognition here that individual citizens and other non-state entities, whose views may not coincide with the state in which they reside, are often best able to contribute to international environmental governance directly, as opposed to through the state.

3.7 Conclusion

There is nothing to suggest that each of these influences must operate in a mutually exclusive fashion. Each has its advantages and disadvantages. The principles of nondiscrimination and equal access have the advantage of focusing on existing domestic processes and on the impacted individuals themselves, as opposed to the affected state. What the harm principle offers that nondiscrimination does not is a foundation for reciprocal obligations between states. Whereas nondiscrimination provides for no minimum standards of conduct, the harm principle supplies a clear baseline of procedural requirements. The harm principle also recognizes that affected states are in a different position from domestic affected persons. They are less likely to participate in the benefits of a project located outside the state and they may subject their own industries and project proponents to a more rigorous set of environmental standards. The harm principle views transboundary pollution from the perspective of both the source state and the affected state and considers as relevant the regulatory framework in both states. The harm principle also provides a basis for the imposition of EIA requirements outside the context of strictly transboundary harm between states. For example, the formulation of the harm principle under Principle 21 extends the obligation to all "areas beyond the limits of national jurisdiction," which would include the global commons and issues of common concern. Sustainable development provides the institutional context in which international EIA norms are formulated and implemented. Like the harm principle, sustainable development points to the substantive ends to which EIA processes are directed, but on a much broader scale.

Without wanting to overdraw the point, each of these sets of background norms points to the different roles that EIA may play in international environmental governance structures. Nondiscrimination is principally focused on EIA as an information-driven process, requiring states to seek out environmental information beyond their borders, but does not acknowledge the political dimensions of EIA. The harm principle and sustainable development, on the other hand, structure transnational interactions that are underlain by shared environmental values. The procedural orientation of both sets of background norms suggests that international EIA processes will involve bargaining between states and between transnational actors, but EIA commitments rooted in either framework will also require decision-makers to justify outcomes in light of substantive norms, with possible transformative consequences.

Part III EIA commitments in international law

4 Sources of international EIA commitments

4.1 Introduction

In light of the background norms examined in Chapters 2 and 3, this chapter and the next provide a detailed examination of the international commitments to conduct EIAs themselves. While a principal purpose in these chapters is to describe the commitments themselves as a matter of positive law, this task is undertaken with several additional objectives in mind. First, I want to explore the relative impact of the different background norms on the development of international EIA commitments. The purpose in tracing the relationship of the EIA commitments to the normative influences previously discussed goes beyond merely describing the evolution or development of these commitments, but is also informed by the idea that these different influences will impact the structure and meaning of the commitments themselves. For example, the extent to which international EIA commitments are underlain by substantive considerations, in addition to procedural ones, has implications for the role of EIA. Secondly, by looking across different international contexts where EIA commitments form part of the overall approach to protecting the natural environment, we can draw some tentative conclusions as to why EIA commitments have become prevalent within international environmental governance structures, the type of problems EIAs are being called upon to address and the factors which are contributing to the formation of EIA commitments. Finally, by focusing in on the structural features of EIA commitments, this chapter and the next provide the basis for the broader discussion that follows in Chapters 6 and 7 on the role of EIA commitments in international environmental governance structures.

Describing the existing obligations to perform EIAs in international law presents an initial difficulty in how to differentiate between the kinds of EIA obligations that exist in international law. EIA commitments take a variety of forms and can be differentiated along a number of different lines. In this regard, international EIA commitments are reflective of a more general trend toward the use of a multiplicity of legal instruments that structure obligations between states, as well as involving sub-state and non-state actors. The diversity of instrument choice speaks to the adaptability of EIA processes to a variety of contexts, across both domestic and international, and public and private divides. It is common to distinguish between formally binding and non-binding commitments, commonly referred to as the hard law versus soft law distinction.[1] Yet, this distinction captures only one aspect, albeit an important one, of the structure of EIA obligations and is itself difficult to determine with exactitude. For example, EIA commitments are contained in political declarations, such as the Rio Declaration, that are clearly not formally binding, but which because of their prominence and the consensus surrounding their adoption have a strong persuasive value. On the other hand, EIA commitments are also contained in formally binding instruments, for example, the Convention on Biological Diversity (CBD), but the specific obligation is qualified in such a way as to suggest a degree of discretion inconsistent with a formal notion of bindingness.[2] Similarly, there are EIA obligations contained within treaties which are drafted in binding but ambiguous terms, such that their indeterminate nature appears to leave states with broad discretion.[3] From the perspective of determining the role of EIA in international governance structures, it is equally important to understand why the states involved adopted the approach that they did and the extent to which the commitments nevertheless raise behavioral expectations among parties. Clearly, those instruments which contain detailed commitments will tell us the most about the structure of EIA obligations. However, the mere presence (and, for that matter, the absence) of EIA obligations in certain regimes is also informative of the kinds of environmental issues for which EIAs are seen to be relevant.

[1] For a comprehensive exploration of legal issues related to the soft law/hard law divide, see Dinah Shelton, ed., *Commitment and Compliance: The Role of Non-Binding Norms in the International Legal System* (Oxford: Oxford University Press, 2000). See also Alan Boyle, "Some Reflections on the Relationship of Treaties and Soft Law" (1999) 48 ICLQ 901.

[2] United Nations Convention of Biological Diversity, Rio de Janeiro, June 5, 1992, 31 ILM 818, in force December 29, 1993, Art. 14, where the EIA obligation is qualified by the phrase "as far as possible and as appropriate."

[3] See, for example, United Nations Convention on the Law of the Sea, Montego Bay, December 10, 1982, 21 ILM 1261 (1982), in force November 16, 1994, Art. 206.

The distinction between treaty norms and customary law is not centrally important in the case of EIAs because customary law is not a principal source of EIA obligations in and of itself. In this regard, I am sympathetic to the argument advanced by Daniel Bodansky, who questions the relevance of customary law in the context of international environmental governance structures that are largely treaty-based and whether, in any event, there are many true instances of customary obligations in the field of international environmental law.[4] Central to Bodansky's argument is a tendency for those positing the existence of a customary rule to do so on the basis of declarations of intention, rather than true instances of state practice.[5] Moreover, the bulk of interactions between states do not occur in a judicial forum where the normative status of a rule or principle is of paramount importance, but rather on a less formal level where the objective is to persuade other states to act in accordance with accepted norms.[6]

I do not take Bodansky to be saying that the status of a rule in international law does not influence state behavior, but rather that the degree of its influence, or "compliance pull," to use Franck's term,[7] is dependent on other factors, such as the norm's specificity. However, it is important to note that a lack of specificity is not an exclusive condition of customary obligations. As noted, many of the EIA obligations contained within environmental treaties do not include detailed rules setting out the specific steps and requirements these obligations entail. In a number of instances, the ambiguity surrounding EIA obligations has led to international disputes. For example, the second *Nuclear Tests Case*, the *MOX Plant Case* and the *Singapore Land Reclamation Case* all involve the application of unelaborated EIA obligations.[8] Even in the *Gabcikovo-Nagymaros Case*, where there was no formal EIA requirement, the parties were split over the adequacy of the assessments conducted and the need to conduct further assessments.[9]

[4] Daniel Bodansky, "Customary (and Not So Customary) International Environmental Law" (1995) 3 Indiana J. Global Legal Stud. 105. See also David Wirth, "Teaching and Research in International Environmental Law" (1999) 23 Harvard Envt'l L. Rev. 423 at 435–436.

[5] Bodansky, "Customary (and Not So Customary)," at 112–116.

[6] Ibid. at 116–118.

[7] Thomas Franck, *The Power of Legitimacy Among Nations* (New York: Oxford University Press, 1990) at 24–26.

[8] *MOX Plant Case (Ireland* v. *United Kingdom)*, Provisional Measures, 41 ILM 405 (2002); *Singapore Land Reclamation Case (Singapore* v. *Malaysia)*, Provisional Measures, unreported (the order and pleadings may be found at www.itlos.org); and *Request for an Examination of the Situation in Accordance with the Court's Judgment of December 1974 in the Nuclear Tests (New Zealand v. France) Case*, (1995) ICJ Rep 288.

[9] *Case Concerning the Gabcikovo-Nagymaros Project (Hungary/Slovakia)* (1997) ICJ Rep 6.

The presence of both elaborated and unelaborated EIA obligations in international law presents a bit of a puzzle both from a standpoint of customary law and in relation to the interpretation of treaty provisions. On the one hand, there exists, as a customary rule or as an unelaborated treaty obligation, a general obligation on states to perform some kind of environmental assessment. However, that obligation lacks the specificity necessary to result in predictable and uniform outcomes. On the other hand, there does exist a significant body of treaty obligations, rules and procedures from international organizations and domestic EIA practice that contains a high degree of detail. A natural question that arises is the extent to which states, international courts and international organizations can turn to elaborated obligations as a basis to fill in the gaps and ambiguities present in the unelaborated obligations. This is a distinct question from determining the contours of a customary obligation because the base obligation to perform EIAs is likely to be rooted in an unelaborated treaty commitment. It does, however, point to the need to consider the influence of these various sources of EIA norms upon one another. To this end, the first part of this chapter outlines the various sources of explicit international EIA commitments, with a view to examining the institutional context of the commitments, such as which actors are creating the commitments, upon whom are they intended to operate, the degree of specificity and the binding nature of the commitments themselves. The second part of this chapter considers the extent to which a customary EIA obligation can be usefully determined, but it also focuses on the possibility for, and limitations of, the normative elaboration of treaty-based EIA obligations. This examination is made with reference to recent interstate disputes concerning the nature and content of EIA commitments. Since the intent in this chapter is to examine the broad structural contours of international EIA commitments, the precise details of how these obligations address the different elements of the EIA process is taken up in Chapter 5.

4.2 Explicit EIA commitments

4.2.1 Formally non-binding instruments

EIA as a useful tool for environmental decision-making was acknowledged by the international community soon after the enactment of NEPA, and well in advance of the establishment of EIA in many domestic settings. EIA was raised at the United Nations Conference on the Human

Environment (UNCHE) and was partially reflected in an early draft of the Stockholm Declaration.[10] While the draft article was left out of the final version of the Stockholm Declaration due to concerns raised by several developing countries over the possible constraints that the draft article would have on the right to develop,[11] environmental assessment was included in several recommendations contained in the "Action Plan for the Human Environment" that was produced at the UNCHE.[12]

After the Stockholm Conference, EIA references continued to be incorporated into instruments produced by the United Nations (UN), largely in relation to transboundary harm and the development of shared resources. For example, the failed draft article from the Stockholm Declaration was revived as part of UNGA Resolution 2995, which recognized the importance of the exchange of "technical data" respecting proposed activities in preventing transboundary harm.[13] In 1978, the UN Environment Programme (UNEP) prepared the Principles on Conservation and Harmonious Utilization of Natural Resources Shared by Two or More States (UNEP Draft Principles of Conduct), which included a specific reference to EIA in Principle 4.[14] The structure of the UNEP Draft Principles of Conduct also reflected the close relationship between the harm principle and the duty to cooperate, on the one hand, and EIA, on the other, with the UNEP Draft Principles of Conduct including explicit references to the duty to prevent harm, as well as the obligation to exchange information and consult.[15] Nevertheless, the approach here remained fairly

[10] Declaration of the United Nations Conference on the Human Environment, June 16, 1972, UN Doc. A/Conf/48/14/Rev.1, reprinted in 11 ILM 1416 (1972) (Stockholm Declaration). The draft itself can be found in UN Doc. A/Conf/48/4, Annex. Principle 20 of the Draft read: "Relevant information must be supplied by states on activities or developments within their jurisdiction or under their control whenever they believe, or have reason to believe, that such information is needed to avoid the risk of significant adverse effects on the environment in areas beyond their national jurisdiction." Quoted in Wade Rowland, *The Plot to Save the World* (Toronto: Clarke, Irwin and Co., 1973) at 54.

[11] Philippe Sands, *Principles of International Environmental Law* (2nd edn, Cambridge: Cambridge University Press, 2003) at 580. See also Louis Sohn, "The Stockholm Declaration on the Human Environment" (1973) 14 Harvard ILJ 423 at 431; and Steven Bernstein, *The Compromise of Liberal Environmentalism* (New York: Columbia University Press, 2001) at 43 (noting that the draft article was blocked by Brazil over concerns over the article's implications for an ongoing dispute with Argentina).

[12] Report of the United Nations Conference on the Human Environment, Stockholm, June 16, 1972, UN Doc. A/Conf.48/14/Rev.1 (1972) at 7, Recommendations 51 and 61.

[13] "Co-operation between States in the Field of the Environment," UNGA Resolution 2995 (XXVII), UN GAOR, 27th Sess., Supp. No. 30 (1972) at 42.

[14] 17 ILM 1094 (1978).

[15] Ibid., Principles 3 and 5, respectively.

narrow in that the UNEP Draft Principles of Conduct viewed participation as extending only to state actors and international institutions.[16] In addition, impacts were not anticipated to extend beyond the shared resource itself.[17] A more inclusive approach that was developed in the same timeframe is found in the World Charter for Nature prepared by the International Union for the Conservation of Nature and adopted by the UN General Assembly.[18] Here, too, the document expressly recognizes EIAs as a central mechanism to control the adverse consequences of planned activities, but the formulation is much stronger in that it requires EIAs to be carried out for activities that "disturb" nature, and specifically requires that activities be planned and carried out so as to minimize potential adverse impacts.[19] The threshold requirement of "disturbing" the environment is lower than the usual threshold of "significant effect," and suggests almost any level of impact would trigger an EIA. In addition, the formulation of the requirement under the World Charter for Nature imposes a substantive obligation to mitigate environmental harm in an unqualified way. Unlike previous formulations of the harm principle that have recognized the competing right to develop, the World Charter for Nature is less equivocal in its posture toward harm prevention.

These early formulations of EIA commitments provided a commitment to undertake EIAs, but they did not provide detailed requirements for carrying out EIAs. In this regard, the development of EIA commitments at the international level was akin to the broad, unelaborated requirement under NEPA prior to its being fleshed out by the courts and through subordinate legislation. As a result, more specific requirements of how EIA would work in the context of international law were required, if states were to make use of EIAs in connection with transboundary and other impacts of an international nature. UNEP, in fulfillment of its mandate to develop principles and guidelines of international environmental law, began, in 1983, a process to develop the details of a set of elaborated EIA requirements. The scope of this project went beyond looking at applying EIA to activities that may have a transboundary impact. Instead,

[16] Ibid., Principle 10.

[17] This is best reflected in ibid., Principle 3, para. 3, which particularizes the kinds of adverse effects to be avoided as those having repercussions for another state's usage of the resource, threatening the conservation of the resource or, more broadly, endangering the health of the population of another state.

[18] GA Res. 37/7, UN GAOR, 37th Sess., UN Doc. A/Res/37/7(1982), reprinted in 22 ILM 455 (1983).

[19] Ibid., Art. 11(c).

the resultant UNEP Goals and Principles of Environmental Impact Assessment,[20] were aimed at creating a set of foundational principles that could be used as a guide for the formulation of domestic and international EIA requirements. The dual domestic and international agenda of the UNEP EIA Goals and Principles is established within the stated goals which identify as key objectives both the promotion of domestic EIA procedures[21] and "the development of reciprocal procedures for information exchange, notification and consultation between States when proposed activities are likely to have significant transboundary effects on the environment of those States."[22]

The first meeting of the Working Group established to develop the UNEP EIA Goals and Principles was convened in Washington at the invitation of the United States. Prior to the UNEP initiative, the US had shown considerable interest in the development of international rules respecting EIA; for example US State Department officials had been active in the development of the UNEP Draft Principles of Conduct. In addition, in 1978, the US Senate had passed a resolution calling for the creation of a treaty on "International Environmental Assessments."[23] The draft treaty that was proposed by the Senate required EIAs to be conducted when an activity could reasonably be expected to have a significant adverse effect on another state or on the global commons. The EIA would be submitted to both affected parties and UNEP and would form the basis of consultations. Consultations were to be carried out with a "view towards preventing or minimizing adverse impacts," but the process did not require mitigation.[24] Nothing came of the draft treaty itself, but the senator who introduced the resolution calling for the creation of the EIA treaty in 1978 addressed the UNEP Working Group at the Washington meeting, suggesting strong US interest and influence in the preparation of the UNEP EIA Goals and Principles.[25] The other important development that was occurring at the time of the Working Group meeting was the development of the European Community EIA Directive,[26] which was in final

[20] UNEP Res. GC14/25, 14th Sess. (1987), endorsed by GA Res. 42/184, UN GAOR, 42nd Sess., UN Doc. A/Res/42/184 (1987) ("UNEP EIA Goals and Principles").
[21] Ibid., Goal 2. [22] Ibid., Goal 3.
[23] US, Senate Resolution 49, 95th Congress, 2nd Sess. (Congressional Record, v.124, No. 111 (July 21, 1978)), pp. S 11523–11524, reprinted in 17 ILM 1082 (1978) (the resolution contains the draft treaty).
[24] Ibid. at 1082 (cited to ILM).
[25] Will Irwin, "Impact Assessment – First Session of the Working Group of Experts" (1984) 13 ELP 51 at 52.
[26] EC, Council Directive 85/337, OJ 1985 L175/40.

draft form. The Working Group members heard presentations regarding the US experience under NEPA, and the pending EC Directive.[27]

The influence of both NEPA and the draft EC Directive is evident in the UNEP EIA Goals and Principles. For example, the UNEP EIA Goals and Principles include a "menu" of possible mechanisms that could be used to determine whether an activity will have a "significant" environmental effect. The suggested approaches to the determination of significance include an "initial environmental evaluation" (the NEPA approach), the use of lists of activities or geographic areas where significant effects are presumed and the use of further criteria to define significance (both of which appear in the EC Directive).[28] The description of what an EIA should include is very similar to NEPA's description of an EIS, including a requirement to describe practical alternatives, as well an indication of where the environment of another state or "areas beyond national jurisdiction is likely to be affected."[29] The latter requirement, which is clearly aimed at transboundary impacts, also captures impacts to the global commons (echoing the similar reference in the US Senate proposal). The minimum EIA requirements also provide that a "brief, non-technical summary" of the assessment be provided.[30] This should be seen as a decisive move away from the view (as seen in UNGA Resolution 2995) of EIA as a purely technical exercise carried by and for the benefit of experts. Instead, by requiring a level of accessibility, the UNEP EIA Goals and Principles indicate an understanding of EIA as being, at least partially, a political process. Principle 5, which requires the degree of detail of an assessment to be commensurate with the activity's likely environmental significance, is, in essence, a codification of the judicially (under NEPA litigation) derived "rule of reason."[31] The iterative structure of NEPA is also present in the UNEP EIA Goals and Principles through the inclusion of a requirement to provide for review and comments by the public and other agencies, and by requiring the ultimate decision made to be in writing and accompanied by reasons.[32] There is no absolute requirement here for harm prevention or mitigation, as indicated by the inclusion of the words "if any" to qualify the requirement to include provisions respecting prevention and mitigation in the written

[27] Irwin, "Impact Assessment." [28] UNEP EIA Goals and Principles, Principle 2.
[29] Ibid., Principle 4. [30] Ibid., Principle 4(h).
[31] See, for example, *Marsh* v. *Oregon Natural Resources Council*, 490 US 360 (1988), and *Natural Resources Defense Council Inc.* v. *Hodel*, 865 F 2d 288 at 294 (DC Cir. 1988).
[32] UNEP EIA Goals and Principles, Principles 7–9.

decision.[33] Principle 10, concerning "follow-up" procedures, led to considerable debate during the drafting sessions, with some experts being of the view that post-project monitoring was essential to the integrity of the EIA process, while others saw monitoring requirements as going beyond EIA's planning role and thereby impinging on the state's regulatory function.[34] The result is a highly qualified requirement for decisions subject to EIAs to be subject to "appropriate supervision" where it is "justified."[35]

The transboundary requirements are contained in Principles 11 and 12. The principles do not set out a separate assessment procedure for transboundary impacts. Instead, the unstated assumption is that transboundary impacts will be identified through the domestic EIA process. But, where transboundary impacts are found to be likely, an additional set of obligations arise, namely, the obligations to notify, exchange information and consult. Where the UNEP EIA Goals and Principles advance the development of international EIA obligations is that they make explicit what was until that time largely presumed – that notification, exchange of information and consultation shall be undertaken on the basis of the information contained within the EIA document. What is surprising is that the UNEP EIA Goals and Principles only require consultation in connection with a specific proposal where consultation is agreed upon by both states, which would appear to be an unnecessary deviation from early acceptances of the duty to consult.[36] This reluctance to accept mandatory consultation may be explained as arising from residual concerns from developing countries regarding the potential for EIA processes to impede or delay initiatives to develop natural resources that arose in connection with EIA in the Stockholm process and as evidenced in UNGA Resolution 2995. Notwithstanding the weak duty to consult, what remains clear is that in a transboundary context EIAs are viewed as a mechanism by which to implement the duty to cooperate. The more general EIA requirements, such as allowing for a sufficient amount of time for comments/consultations and to provide written reasons for its decision, would apply in the transboundary context.

[33] Ibid., Principle 9.

[34] See John Bonine, "Environmental Impact Assessment – Principles Developed" (1987) 17 ELP 5.

[35] UNEP EIA Goals and Principles, Principle 10.

[36] For example, the duty to consult was already accepted by UNEP in its Principles on Shared Natural Resources.

One area of procedural innovation that was present in the 1978 US Senate draft treaty on international EIA that does not appear in the UNEP EIA Principles is the more active role assigned to UNEP in the case of potential impacts to the global commons. Under the Senate draft treaty, UNEP would have acted as a sort of guardian of the global commons, being the institution that would be consulted in the event of likely impacts to the global commons and even being able to initiate consultations. It is not surprising that this rather extraordinary role for UNEP has not been pursued, as it goes well beyond UNEP's established mandate.[37] It does, however, point to a difficulty with the extension of transboundary EIA to the global commons. In such cases, the rights of all states are potentially implicated, giving rise to complex questions respecting who, in the absence of a responsible international institution, should be notified of the potential impact and with whom does a state consult.

The next major development at the UN that bears on EIA obligations was the publication of the WCED report,[38] which led to the convening of the 1992 UNCED in Rio de Janeiro. As discussed in Chapter 3, the UNCED did not so much further develop the concept of international EIA, as it placed EIAs firmly within the sustainable development paradigm by underlining the transnational and participatory aspects of EIA obligations.[39] However, by 1992, EIA was firmly established as a central aspect of international environmental governance, as evidenced by the growing number of multilateral environmental agreements containing EIA commitments.

4.2.2 MEAs as a source of international EIA

The first treaty to contain a commitment to perform EIAs was the 1978 Kuwait Convention for Cooperation on the Protection of the Marine Environment from Pollution.[40] Here, the parties are obliged to "endeavor to include an assessment of the potential environmental effects in any planning activity entailing projects within its territory, particularly in the coastal areas, which may cause significant risks of pollution in

[37] UNEP's role is discussed in Sands, *Principles of International Environmental Law* at 83–85.

[38] World Commission on Environment and Development, *Our Common Future* (New York: Oxford University Press, 1987).

[39] See above at ch. 3.6.

[40] Kuwait Regional Convention for Co-operation on the Protection of the Marine Environment from Pollution, Kuwait, April 24, 1978, 1140 UNTS 133, 17 ILM 511 (1978), in force July 1, 1979.

the Sea Area."[41] There is consistency between the Kuwait Convention requirements and the approach developed within domestic and global EIA frameworks insofar as the threshold for undertaking EIAs is "significance," EIA is understood as involving both the assessment itself and the communication of its contents to affected parties,[42] and is explicitly linked to the minimization of harmful impacts on the marine environment.[43] The Kuwait Convention was developed under the UNEP Regional Seas program and the EIA provisions contained in it were subsequently adopted in other regional seas conventions developed under this program.[44] The obligation under the Kuwait Convention is normatively weak, as are most of the formulations under regional seas conventions concluded in the 1980s, but the trend in more recent regional seas conventions has been toward the use of mandatory, unqualified language in EIA obligations,[45] with the level of commitment tending to reflect the presence of EIA systems in the parties to the agreement.

In 1982, the United Nations Convention on the Law of the Sea (UNCLOS) was adopted after almost ten years of negotiation.[46] The provisions respecting marine pollution (Part XII of the UNCLOS), which at the time

41 Ibid., Art. XI; the "Sea Area" is defined in Art. II(a). 42 Ibid., Art. XI(b) and (c).

43 The Kuwait Convention is structured as a framework convention and was also accompanied by an Action Plan, which also contained provisions referring to EIA, ibid., Art. III(b), providing for the formulation and adoption of further protocols. See also Action Plan for the Protection and Development of the Marine Environment and the Coastal Areas of Bahrain, Iran, Iraq, Kuwait, Oman, Qatar, Saudi Arabia and the United Arab Emirates, 17 ILM 501, paras. 10–17.

44 Convention for Co-operation in the Protection and Development of the Marine and Coastal Environment of the West and Central African Region, Abidjan, March 23, 1981, 20 ILM 746, entered into force August 5, 1984, Art. 13; Convention for the Protection of the Marine Environment and Coastal Area of the South-East Pacific, Lima, November 12, 1981, International Environmental Legal Materials and Treaties 981, entered into force May 19, 1986, Art. 8; Regional Convention for the Conservation of the Red Sea and Gulf of Aden Environment, Jeddah, Saudi Arabia, February 14, 1982, 9 EPL 56, entered into force August 20, 1985, Art. XI; Convention for the Protection and Development of the Marine Environment of the Wider Caribbean Region, Cartagena de Indias, March 24, 1983, 22 ILM 221, entered into force October 11, 1986, Art. 12; Convention for the Protection of the Natural Resources and Environment of the South Pacific Region, Noumea, New Caledonia, November 25, 1986, 26 ILM 25, entered into force August 22, 1990, Art. 16.

45 See Convention on the Protection of the Black Sea Against Pollution, Bucharest, April 21, 1992, 32 ILM 1110 (1993), in force January 15, 1994, Art. XV(5); Convention on the Protection of the Marine Environment of the Baltic Sea Area, Helsinki, April 9, 1992, in force January 17, 2000, Art. 7 (Helsinki Convention). But see Framework Convention for the Protection of the Marine Environment of the Caspian Sea, Tehran, November 4, 2003, in force August 12, 2006, Art. 17.

46 December 10, 1982, 21 ILM 1261 (1982) , in force November 16, 1994.

were both a codification of existing international law and an exercise in progressive development,[47] are underlain by the general obligation "to protect and preserve the marine environment."[48] The article addressing EIAs, Article 206, which is included in this Part, states:

> When States have reasonable grounds for believing that planned activities under their jurisdiction or control may cause substantial pollution of or significant and harmful changes to the marine environment, they shall, as far as practicable, assess the potential effects of such activities on the marine environment and shall communicate reports of the results of such assessments in the manner provided in article 205.

The inclusion of a provision on EIA arose fairly early in the negotiating process and it does not appear to have been seriously opposed by any state.[49] An early proposed draft of the EIA provision required a state that undertakes an activity that may lead to "significant alteration of the marine environment" to file an "environmental impact statement" with the "international organization concerned."[50] The draft provision linked the preparation of an EIA with the duty to consult affected states "with a view to avoid damage to other interests and to preserve the environment against pollution."[51] The use of the term "environmental impact statement" strongly suggests the early influence of NEPA, which uses the same term in reference to its full EIA requirement.[52]

In its final wording, Article 206 reflects the originally proposed structure with a number of important qualifications, which provide the state of origin with a measure of discretion: first, by requiring "reasonable" grounds for believing activities may cause significant harm to the marine environment and, secondly, by tempering the obligation with the phrase "as far as practicable."[53] It would, however, be a mistake to consider the obligation to conduct EIAs under UNCLOS as being non-binding. The reasonableness requirement maintains an objective standard for the determination of the threshold. As a matter of practice, the state of origin will likely be given some leeway in determining whether reasonable grounds exist, but this is no different from the deference

[47] Ibid., preamble.

[48] Ibid., Art. 192 (this general obligation is expanded upon in Art. 194).

[49] Myron Nordquist, *United Nations Convention on the Law of the Sea: A Commentary* (Boston: Martinus Nijhoff, 1985) at para. 206.2 (noting that the first reference to EIA appeared in 1973 in a working paper submitted by Norway (A/AC.138/SC.III/L.43 (1973, mimeo), Art. XV)).

[50] Ibid. [51] Ibid.

[52] National Environmental Policy Act, 42 USC §§ 4321–4370(f) (2000), s. 102(c).

[53] Nordquist, "UNCLOS Commentary" at para. 206.6(b).

normally granted to a domestic agency in its determination of whether significant impacts are "likely" to occur.

The second qualification that EIAs shall be undertaken "as far as practicable" arises only after the threshold has been met and, as such, does not relieve a state from its obligation to carry out an EIA, but instead impacts the level of detail and depth to which an EIA must be carried out. While the preparatory materials do not disclose the purpose behind including this phrase, the most likely reason is to account for differing capacities among states to carry out assessments. Sensitivity to capabilities is an integral part of the structure of the marine protection provisions of UNCLOS, and is reflected in the convention's general duty to prevent harm, which is qualified by the phrase "in accordance with their capabilities."[54] It may be taken as significant that Article 206 does not use the term "environmental impact assessment," nor does it refer to an "environmental impact statement," as was the case in the original draft provision. Instead, by referring to the more ambiguous term "assess," Article 206 does not fix the requirements for an EIA, but rather allows states to make such a determination in accordance with their capabilities and their domestic legislation – a matter of considerable importance to developing states and states in transition whose capacity to carry out EIAs would in many instances be lower than developed states, particularly in 1982, when UNCLOS was adopted.

By the time of the Rio Conference, the inclusion of unelaborated EIA commitments was a common practice in environmental treaties at both the regional level[55] and the global level, including the Convention on Biological Diversity (CBD)[56] and the United Nations Framework Convention on Climate Change (UNFCCC).[57] Again, in these treaties the obligations to conduct EIAs were framed in qualified terms. The UNFCCC simply acknowledges a role for EIA without imposing an obligation to perform EIAs under specified conditions, while the CBD goes somewhat further by requiring that EIAs be conducted, "as far as possible and as appropriate," where proposed projects are likely to have a significant adverse effect on biological diversity. Given the qualifying language of

[54] UNCLOS, Art. 194(1).

[55] Prominent among these treaties were the ASEAN Agreement on the Conservation of Nature and Natural Resources, Kuala Lumpur, July 9, 1985, 15 EPL 64, Art. 14(1); and the Agreement between the United States and Canada on Air Quality, March 13, 1991, Can TS No. 3, in force March 13, 1991, reprinted 30 ILM 676 (1991).

[56] 31 ILM 818 (1992), June 5, 1992, in force December 29, 1993, Art. 14(1)(a).

[57] New York, May 9, 1992, 31 ILM 851 (1992), in force March 21, 1994, Art. 4(1)(f).

the obligation in the CBD, it is clear that states have a degree of discretion in terms of whether and how to implement the requirement to conduct EIAs in connection with biological diversity. The language provides a greater degree of flexibility than does the wording of the EIA commitment under the UNCLOS, as the determination of 'appropriateness' is oriented more toward a subjective determination by the state of origin. Given the impact of the CBD on domestic decision-making and the high participation rate among developing countries with less domestic EIA experience, this is to be expected. Nevertheless, where a country has an existing EIA system and a demonstrated capacity to conduct EIAs, the obligation to ensure that the system incorporates biological diversity considerations is strengthened.

The objective of including EIA commitments in the CBD and the UNFCCC differs from the EIA commitment in UNCLOS in that the focus is on expanding the coverage of domestic EIA systems by requiring that they account for impacts on biological diversity or climate change in the carrying out of assessments, as opposed to structuring transboundary interactions. Consequently, the demand that these regimes give rise to is not for detailed procedures on the conduct and content of EIAs, but on the more technical issues of how to actually account for the diffuse and cumulative impacts associated with climate change and biological diversity.[58] The underlying assumption here is that the actual modalities of conducting the EIA will be addressed in domestic legislation and through other bilateral, regional and multilateral instruments. For example, the CBD contains a normatively weak obligation to notify and consult in the event of transboundary harm to biological resources, but it specifically contemplates that these rules will be formulated elsewhere.[59]

More surprising is the weak formulation of the EIA commitments contained within watercourse treaties such as the 1992 UNECE Convention on the Protection and Use of Transboundary Watercourses and Lakes, which simply lists EIA as one of the measures parties shall apply in order "to prevent, control and reduce transboundary impact,"[60] and the UN Convention on the Law of the Non-Navigational Uses of International Watercourses (UN Watercourses Convention),[61] where the

[58] See Barry Sadler, *Environmental Assessment in a Changing World: Final Report of the International Study of the Effectiveness of Environmental Assessment* (Ottawa: Canadian Environmental Assessment Agency, 1996) at § 7.3.
[59] CBD, Art. 14(1)(c).
[60] 31 ILM 1312 (1992), Helsinki, March 17, 1992, in force October 6, 1996, Art. 3(1)(h).
[61] New York, May 21, 1997, 36 ILM 719, not in force.

potential application of EIA to "planned measures" is not itself mandated, but rather EIA is assumed to be a source of "technical data and information."[62] The mention of EIA in the UN Watercourses Convention goes further than the ILC in their Draft Articles on the Non-Navigational Uses of International Watercourses (upon which the UN Watercourses Convention is based), which make no mention of EIA at all.[63] The eventual inclusion of the reference to EIA arose as a compromise between states that wanted to include a separate EIA requirement in the UN Watercourses Convention and those which opposed its inclusion.[64] The result is that states that are otherwise obligated to perform an EIA, whether by virtue of another international obligation or in accordance with domestic requirements, shall be required to disclose the "results" of the EIA as part of its general obligation to notify and exchange information, but states are not subject to an independent obligation to conduct EIAs.

The only formally binding treaties that set out detailed requirements for the conduct of EIAs are contained in two agreements, the Convention on Environmental Impact Assessment in a Transboundary Context (Espoo Convention)[65] developed by the UNECE and the Protocol to the Antarctic Treaty on Environmental Protection (the Antarctic Protocol),[66] developed within the framework of the 1959 Antarctic Treaty.[67] The impetus for the UNECE's development of rules respecting EIA arose from meetings in the mid-1970s between Eastern and Western European countries held for the purposes of exploring areas of mutual cooperation, which led to the identification of EIA as one such area.[68] Originally, the Espoo Convention was conceived as a framework agreement, similar to the UNEP EIA Goals and Principles and requiring further bilateral agreements for implementation, but during the negotiation process this approach was abandoned in favor of the preparation of a treaty imposing

[62] Ibid., Art. 12.

[63] International Law Commission, "Draft Articles on the Non-Navigational Uses of International Watercourses" in *Report of the International Law Commission, Forty-Sixth Session*, UN GAOR, 49th Sess., Supp. No. 10, UN Doc. A/49/10 (1994).

[64] Stephen McCaffrey, *The Law of International Watercourses: Non-Navigational Uses* (New York: Oxford University Press, 2001) at 408.

[65] 30 ILM 802 (1991), Espoo, Finland, February 25, 1991, in force January 14, 1998.

[66] Madrid, October 4, 1991, 30 ILM 1461, in force January 14, 1998, Art. 8 and Annex 1.

[67] Washington DC, December 1, 1959, 402 UNTS 71, reprinted in 19 ILM 860 (1980).

[68] Final Act of the Conference on Security and Co-operation in Europe, 14 ILM 1307 (1975). See also Robert Connolly, "The UN Convention on EIA in a Transboundary Context: A Historical Perspective" (1999) 19 Environmental Impact Assessment Review 37 at 38.

direct obligations on parties.[69] As such, the Espoo Convention differs from the UNEP EIA Goals and Principles in the level of detail included in the treaty. It also differs from the UNEP EIA Goals and Principles in that it is focused on the environmental assessment of transboundary impacts only, defined to exclude both exclusively domestic impacts and those impacts that are "exclusively of a global nature."[70] As a UNECE treaty, the Espoo Convention was originally formulated as a regional convention open to UNECE members only. In February 2001, the parties to the Convention agreed to amend the Convention to allow non-UNECE members to become parties to the Convention with the approval of the membership.[71] As a result of this change, there is at least the possibility that the Espoo Convention may become the basis for a global transboundary EIA treaty.[72]

The Espoo Convention differs in another significant way from other treaty-based EIA obligations, in that the Espoo Convention is not part of a discrete international environmental regime. Rather, the Espoo Convention cuts across environmental problems, as demonstrated by the inclusive definition of "impact" contained in the Espoo Convention.[73] Most treaty-based EIA obligations are oriented toward a particular environmental problem, be it biological diversity or marine pollution. The Espoo Convention has application across a wide variety of environmental problems so long as the effects of those problems are felt in a state outside the source state. The result is the potential for overlap between the Espoo Convention and other EIA obligations. For example, an activity that has potential transboundary impacts on another countries marine environment may be subject to EIA obligations under UNCLOS, a regional seas convention and the Espoo Convention. In this regard, the Espoo Convention would be the vehicle by which the transboundary aspects of the required EIA are implemented where there is common membership. This role is explicitly recognized in the Helsinki Convention which imposes an obligation on source states to notify and consult with other affected states "whenever consultations are required

[69] Connolly, "The UN Convention on Transboundary EIA" at 42.

[70] Espoo Convention, Art. 1.

[71] See Amendment to Espoo Convention, Meeting of the Parties to the Convention on Environmental Impact Assessment in a Transboundary Context, Report of the Second Meeting, UN Doc. ECE/MP.EIA/6, September 13, 2004, Decision II/14 (the proposed amendment is not yet in force).

[72] This possibility is discussed in John Knox, "Assessing the Candidates for a Global Treaty on Transboundary Environmental Impact Assessment" (2003) 12 NYU Envt'l LJ 153.

[73] Espoo Convention, Art. 1.

by international law or supra-national regulations applicable to the Contracting Party of origin."[74] This is a reference to the Espoo Convention and the EC Directive.[75] The CBD similarly anticipates that transboundary notification and consultation obligations will be concluded through other agreements, such as the Espoo Convention, which clearly applies to impacts to biological resources.

The link between EIA commitments and the harm principle is made explicitly in the Espoo Convention through the inclusion of a general provision requiring states to "take all appropriate and effective measures to prevent, reduce and control significant adverse transboundary impact from proposed activities."[76] John Knox has commented that this provision contains no substantive obligation due to its ambiguous wording and the lack of a binding mechanism to resolve disputes regarding its application.[77] It is true that this provision is unlikely to be relied upon as a basis for imposing *ex post facto* liability for damages suffered given that the focus of the Convention is on the prevention of harm. However, it is not the intent of this provision to serve as a basis for the imposition of liability in the event of harm, nor is it, for that matter, the nature of the duty to prevent harm, which has been quite deliberately separated from the question of *ex post facto* liability. As discussed in Chapter 3, divorcing the duty to prevent transboundary harm from liability does not rob the provision of its prescriptive force.[78]

The Antarctic Protocol offers a further distinct model for the basis of international EIA obligations. Here, the regime is rooted in the status of the Antarctic as part of the global commons and not, therefore, subject to the exclusive sovereignty of any one country. The Antarctic Protocol, concluded within the framework of the Antarctic Treaty,[79] governs the "comprehensive protection" of the Antarctic environment and

[74] Helsinki Convention, Art. 7(2).

[75] A similar overlap exists between the members of the Espoo Convention and the Convention for the Protection of the Marine Environment of the North-East Atlantic, Paris, September 22, 1992, 32 ILM 1072, in force March 25, 1998 (OSPAR Convention), but under the OSPAR Convention there is no direct incorporation of international EIA standards; the relationship of the Espoo Convention to the OSPAR and Helsinki Conventions is discussed in David Dzidzornu, "Environmental Impact Assessment Procedure Through the Conventions" (2001) 10 Eur. Envt'l L. Rev. 15.

[76] Espoo Convention, Art. 2(1).

[77] John Knox, "The Myth and Reality of Transboundary Environmental Impact Assessment" (2002) 96 AJIL 291 at 305. See the discussion above at ch. 3.

[78] Above at ch. 3.5.

[79] Washington DC, December 1, 1959, 402 UNTS 71, reprinted in 19 ILM 860 (1980), in force June 23, 1961.

designates Antarctica "as a natural reserve, devoted to peace and science."[80] In light of the absence of existing economic activity, the focus of the environmental governance of the Antarctic is on avoiding or minimizing adverse environmental effects of planned activities. In this regard, EIA lies at the center of the Antarctic environmental protection regime and is highly developed within the Antarctic Protocol. The underlying legal basis for the imposition of EIA obligations is the duty on states to prevent harm to a commons resource. The approach to environmental management here is ecosystem-based, with EIAs being required for virtually all activities regardless of the source or type of impact. The Antarctic EIA system, in keeping with the regime's strong conservationist ethos, and in recognition of the unique fragility of polar ecosystems, employs a different threshold to trigger EIA, requiring an assessment where an activity has at least a "minor or transitory impact," as opposed to the usually-resorted-to trigger of "significance."[81]

Both the Espoo Convention and the Antarctic Protocol prescribe quite specific rules for the conduct of EIA in their respective contexts. The elements of the EIA process prescribed generally map onto the basic elements of domestic EIA discussed in Chapter 2. The details of each step are described in Chapter 5. What is important to note here is that detailed rules are required here because the intention of both the Espoo Convention and the Antarctic Protocol is to provide for minimum requirements to ensure reciprocity between the parties concerning the content of EIAs and with respect to the requirements of notification and consultation. As a result, unlike the unilateral extension of domestic EIA, the approach taken in both treaties is to go beyond the reliance on extending domestic EIA rules by requiring states to adhere to a common set of procedural requirements – an approach that is reflective of the harm principle, as opposed to nondiscrimination. In this connection, it is noteworthy that the three members of the North American Agreement on Environmental Cooperation[82] prepared a draft agreement on transboundary EIA[83] that relied more heavily on the principle of nondiscrimination. Here, the approach was not to set out minimum standards, but simply to rely on the extension of existing domestic rules to transboundary impacts. The strong emphasis on nondiscrimination, as opposed to the development of common EIA procedures, appears to be at the root of the

[80] Protocol on Environmental Protection to the Antarctic Treaty, Art. 2.

[81] Ibid., Art. 8(1). [82] 32 ILM 1480 (1993), in force September 14, 1993.

[83] "Draft North American Agreement on Transboundary Environmental Impact Assessment," http://cec.org/pub_info_resources/law_treat_agree/.

unresolved issues between the parties. Part of the difficulty is reported to relate to the lack of reciprocity between parties on the application of the agreement. Canada and the United States have federal EIA legislation that applies only to federal projects or approvals, while Mexico's national EIA legislation would apply to a broader range of activities. An approach based largely on nondiscrimination would appear not to satisfy Mexico, as many projects in Mexico with potential impacts in the US would trigger the transboundary procedures, but similar projects in the US would not since these are under state jurisdiction.[84] The deadlock over this issue suggests that a minimum level of reciprocity may be required to successfully conclude a transboundary EIA agreement.

4.2.3 EIA guideline documents

A related source of EIA commitments are sets of non-binding guidelines adopted by treaty bodies to provide further guidance to member states in conducting EIAs in light of the particular environmental objectives and challenges associated with that regime. For example, under the Antarctic Protocol, the Antarctic Treaty Consultative Meeting adopted guidelines to assist proponents in the preparation of Antarctic EIAs and to promote consistency in fulfilling EIA obligations by member states.[85] Similarly, the parties to the Espoo Convention have further elaborated on the content of the EIA duties under that regime through the work of the governing body of the treaty, the Meeting of the Parties. To this end, the parties have adopted guidelines on matters such as public participation[86] and implementation and sub-regional cooperation.[87]

The CBD regime has also taken steps to provide further guidance to its members with respect to the implementation of the EIA requirement. The guidance takes the form of a decision of the Conference of the Parties under the CBD endorsing a set of draft guidelines for incorporating biodiversity-related issues into environmental impact assessment

[84] Discussed in Knox, "Myth and Reality" at 307.

[85] "Guidelines for Environmental Impact Assessment in Antarctica," adopted by Resolution 4 (2005), attached to the Final Report of XXVIIIth ATCM, 2005.

[86] Guidance on Public Participation in Environmental Impact Assessment in a Transboundary Context, Meeting of the Parties to the Convention on Environmental Impact Assessment in a Transboundary Context, Report of the Third Meeting, UN Doc. ECE/MP.EIA/6, September 13, 2004, Decision III/8.

[87] Guidance on Good Practice and on Bilateral and Multilateral Agreements, Meeting of the Parties to the Convention on Environmental Impact Assessment in a Transboundary Context, Report of the Third Meeting, UN Doc. ECE/MP.EIA/6, September 13, 2004, Decision III/4.

legislation and/or processes and in strategic environmental assessment (the CBD EIA/SEA Draft Guidelines),[88] and provides a framework by which biodiversity concerns can be integrated into domestic EIA and SEA processes. The CBD EIA/SEA Draft Guidelines define EIAs, in a manner consistent with most elaborated EIA systems, as "necessarily" involving screening, scoping, the identification and assessment of impacts and mitigation measures, decision-making and post-project analysis. The purpose of the guidelines is to ensure that within each of these stages parties will incorporate specific criteria related to the assessment of biological diversity. To this end, the guidelines provide suggestion for a general framework and criteria that may be used to measure impacts to biodiversity at each of the various stages of the EIA process.

In the above examples, the guideline document seeks to elaborate on an existing treaty obligation, but in relation to Arctic environmental cooperation the Arctic states have adopted a stand-alone set of guidelines in the absence of a treaty commitment to conduct EIAs. Unlike the commons status of the Antarctic, the Arctic is subject to the exclusive jurisdiction of eight states,[89] it is inhabited by both indigenous peoples and subsequent settlers, and its resources, both living and non-living, are subject to exploitation. As a result, the approach to international environmental cooperation in the Arctic is less comprehensive and centralized than that found in the Antarctic Protocol.[90] In 1991, in an effort to address some of the deficiencies in the international management of the Arctic environment, the Arctic states concluded the Arctic Environmental Protection Strategy (AEPS), a formally non-binding instrument that sets out environmental objectives and identifies key environmental problems. Subsequently, in 1996, the Arctic states created the Arctic Council, as a sort of umbrella organization whose purpose is to coordinate Arctic cooperation, but without authority to bind member states. The AEPS is now administered through the Arctic Council.

[88] "Guidelines for Incorporating Biodiversity-Related Issues into Environmental Impact Assessment Legislation and/or Processes and in Strategic Environmental Assessment," Report of the Sixth Meeting of the Conference of the Parties to the Convention on Biological Diversity, UN Doc. UNEP/CBD/COP/6/7, Annex, www.biodiv.org/decisions/default.aspx?m = cop-06. Revised draft guidelines were issued by the CBD Secretariat in July 2005, www.biodiv.org/programmes/cross-cutting/impact/guidelines.shtml.

[89] The Arctic states are Canada, Denmark, Finland, Iceland, Norway, Russia, Sweden and the United States.

[90] Donald Rothwell notes that, as of 1991, some twenty-six global conventions apply to the Arctic environment: see Donald Rothwell, "The Arctic Environmental Protection Strategy and International Environmental Co-operation in the Far North" (1995) 6 YBIEL 65 at 73.

It is under the auspices of the AEPS, that the 1997 Guidelines for Environmental Impact Assessment in the Arctic (Arctic EIA Guidelines) were developed.[91] Like other international EIA guideline documents, the Arctic EIA Guidelines are not intended to supplant existing domestic and international rules (six of the eight Arctic states are members of the Espoo Convention), but rather they are used as a resource by those setting domestic and international EIA policy and by those who are conducting EIAs themselves. Timo Koivurova has aptly described the role of the Arctic EIA Guidelines as providing "adaptation rules,"[92] which is to say that the Guidelines help implement EIA requirements by situating the elements of EIA in the context of the unique environmental and social context of the Arctic, including the fragile nature of Arctic ecosystems and the environmental vulnerability of indigenous groups.

Guideline documents are, by their very nature, non-binding. But they remain normatively significant in a number of ways. First, they underline the international community's acceptance of a basic uniform structure of EIA processes. Each guideline document accepts and amplifies the basic structural features of EIA, and they also provide support for those aspects of domestic and international EIA, such as strategic environmental assessment and post-project assessment, that are not firmly established in binding documents. In addition to elaborating on the procedural aspects of EIA in the context of a particular international environmental issue area, the guideline documents point to the relationship between the procedural obligations and substantive environmental requirements. This is most clearly demonstrated in the CBD EIA/SEA Draft Guidelines which reference substantive criteria in other international environmental treaties, such as the Convention on the Conservation of Migratory Species of Wild Animals and the Convention on Wetlands of International Importance,[93] as being relevant to identifying important biological features and species.[94] The various guideline documents also incorporate in varying degrees the background norms

[91] 1997 Guidelines for Environmental Impact Assessment in the Arctic, adopted by the Arctic Council in the 1997 Alta Declaration on the Protection of the Arctic Environmental Protection Strategy, http://finnbarents.urova.fi/aria ("Arctic EIA Guidelines").

[92] Timo Koivurova, *Environmental Impact Assessment in the Arctic: A Study of International Legal Norms* (Aldershot: Ashgate Publishing, 2002) at 172.

[93] 19 ILM 15 (1980), in force November 1, 1983, and 11 ILM 963 (1972), in force December 21, 1975, respectively.

[94] CBD Draft Guidelines, para. 6 and Appendix 2. See also "The Ramsar Convention and Impact Assessment: Strategic, Environmental and Social," Resolution VII.16 of the Conference of the Parties to the Ramsar Convention, www.ramsar.org/key_res_vii.16e.htm.

associated with international EIA commitments. For example, the Arctic EIA Guidelines provide further details on the obligation of states to notify and consult in the event of transboundary harm, as required by the duty to cooperate, as well as noting that transboundary participation should be extended to include broad rights of public participation by affected individual in accordance with the principle of nondiscrimination.[95] The CBD EIA/SEA Draft Guidelines incorporate principles associated with the sustainability paradigm such as ecosystem approaches to environmental management, sustainable use of resources and participation by vulnerable minorities. There may be a temptation to view the references to these open-ended principles as being of little normative value, but the experience with domestic EIA shows that the value of EIA is the projection of open-textured environmental norms into concrete decision-making processes. Moreover, because interactions around EIA are underlain by a duty of good faith, guideline requirements, which point to best practices, provide a measure by which states can assess good faith.

4.3 International organizations

The practice of international organizations, whose membership is made up of individual states, provides a further indication of state understandings of what good EIA practice should consist of. Attributing the practice of international organizations to states is not straightforward since international organizations may develop interests that are independent of the interests of member states.[96] Nevertheless, World Bank practice has been cited as evidence of state practice by at least one judge of the ICJ in connection with EIAs.[97] The practice of international organizations is also relevant to international EIA insofar as international organizations incorporate international EIA norms, such as assessing transboundary and global impacts into their own requirements.

The most prominent set of EIA requirements adopted by an international organization are those of the World Bank. The World Bank's current requirements are found in Operational Policy (OP) 4.01 and Bank

[95] Arctic EIA Guidelines at 39–40.

[96] See Michael Barnett and Martha Finnemore, *Rules for the World: International Organizations in Global Politics* (Ithaca: Cornell University Press, 2004) at 20–29, discussing sources of autonomy of international organizations.

[97] See *Gabcikovo-Nagymaros Case* at 111, *per* Judge Weeramantry.

Procedure (BP) 4.01,[98] which were adopted in 1999 and replaced a previous set of policies regarding environmental assessment first adopted in 1989.[99] The stated purpose of OP 4.01 is to ensure that bank-financed projects are "environmentally sound and sustainable."[100] In seeking to achieve this objective, the World Bank relies on a range of instruments falling under what it terms "environmental assessment" (EA),[101] which includes EIA, regional or sectoral EA, environmental audit, hazard or risk assessment, and environmental management plans.[102] It is the borrower's responsibility to carry out the EA, with the bank reviewing the EA work to ensure consistency with the bank's policies and conducting a substantive review of the identified impacts themselves.[103] The scope of the EA requirements is broad, taking into account impacts on the natural environment, human health, as well as social impacts.[104] The environmental impacts include both transboundary impacts and "global environmental" impacts, the latter defined as including climate change, ozone-depleting substances, pollution of international waters, and adverse effects on biodiversity.[105] The World Bank provides further guidance and direction regarding the implementation of transboundary and global commitments in its *Pollution Prevention and Abatement Handbook*. The express linkage of EA processes to substantive environmental standards and objectives points to a significant role for the World Bank's EA process in the implementation of environmental treaties.

The specific requirements for EA resemble more sophisticated EIA processes in domestic and international instruments, and include detailed screening requirements, identification of adverse impacts, as well as gaps in knowledge, an analysis of alternatives and public consultation at both

[98] World Bank, *Operational Policies – Environmental Assessment*, January 1999, OP 4.01; World Bank, *Banking Procedures – Environmental Assessment*, January 1999, BP 4.01, www4.worldbank.org/legal/legen/legen_assessment.html. OP 4.01 sets out the Bank's principal policies respecting environmental assessment, while BP 4.01 sets out the Bank's internal processes for conducting and reviewing environmental assessments.

[99] OP 4.01 and BP 4.01 replaced a number of directives and operational memoranda (listed in OP 4.01), the most prevalent being World Bank, Operational Directive 4.01, "Environmental Assessment."

[100] OP 4.01, para. 1.

[101] The use of the term "environmental assessment" in the context of OP 4.01 should not be confused with the narrower use of the same term under NEPA, the latter referring to an initial environmental assessment undertaken as a screening mechanism.

[102] OP 4.01, para. 7. [103] Ibid., para. 5.

[104] Ibid., para. 3. [105] Ibid., para. 3 and n. 4.

the scoping stage and once a draft EA document has been prepared.[106] The World Bank also requires monitoring and is developing SEA guidelines.[107] Perhaps the most innovative development respecting environmental assessment at the World Bank is the use of inspection panel reviews as a mechanism to ensure compliance with the bank's policies and procedures, including the EA procedures.[108] The Inspection Panel is an independent body that considers complaints from individuals or groups who believe that they have been harmed by a failure of the World Bank to follow its internal requirements. Upon review of a complaint, the Inspection Panel may recommend to the Bank's management that a further investigation be undertaken, and the Inspection Panel is responsible for carrying out such investigations where authorized. Sands notes that the largest number of complaints received under this process have related to compliance with the Bank's EA policies.[109] Complaints may be initiated by persons who are directly affected or by their local representatives. In essence, the Inspection Panel procedure is a form of administrative review akin to judicial review proceedings available to correct procedural deficiencies in domestic legal systems. Like judicial review, the Inspection Panel review process is procedurally oriented, but the substantive bite of the process is demonstrated by panel decisions that have led to the withdrawal of Bank financing or to the implementation of further remedial actions.[110] Outside the World Bank framework, EIAs have been adopted by a host of other regional development banks,[111] by the International Seabed Authority,[112] and by treaty bodies in their internal

[106] The *Pollution Prevention and Abatement Handbook*, World Bank Group, http://lnweb18.worldbank.org/ESSD/envext.nsf/51ByDocName/PollutionPreventionandAbatementHandbook/ at 22–26, contains a good description of the Bank's EA process.

[107] World Bank, *Strategic Environmental Assessment in World Bank Operations: Experience to Date – Future Potential* (Washington DC: World Bank Group, 2002).

[108] See Resolution No. IRBD 93–10; and Resolution No. IDA 93–6, creating the Inspection Panel in 1993.

[109] Sands, *Principles of International Environmental Law* at 211.

[110] See ibid. at 822.

[111] Regional development banks that require EIAs to be conducted for projects involving bank-assisted financing include the Asian Development Bank, the African Development Bank, the European Bank for Reconstruction and Development and the Inter-American Development Bank: see M. Sornarajah, "Foreign Investment and International Environmental Law" in Sun Lin and Lal Kurukulasuriya, eds., *UNEP's New Way Forward: Environmental Law and Sustainable Development* (Nairobi: UNEP, 1995) 283 at 288.

[112] Agreement relating to the Implementation of Part XI of the United Nations Convention on the Law of the Sea, UN Doc. A/RES/48/263, July 28, 1994, Annex, section 7, www.un.org/Depts/los/convention_agreements/texts/unclos/closindx.htm.

decision-making procedures, such as the approval of projects under the Clean Development Mechanism in the climate change regime.[113]

4.4 EIA and interstate disputes

EIA commitments have been the subject of a number of interstate environmental disputes. The significance of these disputes as an independent source of EIA obligations is limited for several reasons. Foremost, none of the disputes in question, except for the *Gabcikovo-Nagymaros Case*, has been determined on the merits. Consequently, the judicial considerations of EIA commitments are confined to separate opinions or provisional measures proceedings. Secondly, the EIA commitments subject to interstate disputes have been principally treaty-based. As a result, the arguments and decisions, such as do exist, are oriented toward ambiguities in treaty-based EIA obligations, and not toward an independent customary rule or general principle of international law. The treaty-based nature of EIA obligations supports Bodansky's contention that customary law is likely to be of secondary importance in international environmental law. What these disputes do indicate, though, are conflicting understandings of the nature and scope of EIA requirements, and the context in which these disputes are likely to arise. These disputes also point to the complex relationship between overlapping EIA treaty commitments and between treaty-based EIA commitments and customary rules of international environmental law.

Nuclear Tests Cases. These proceedings were initiated by Australia and New Zealand in 1973 before the ICJ, which sought to enjoin France from conducting atmospheric nuclear tests in the atolls of the South Pacific. The Court at that time declined to take jurisdiction over the dispute because France had issued a number of unilateral statements committing to conduct no further atmospheric tests, but the Court left open the possibility of resumption of the proceedings in the event that the facts giving rise to the Court's declining jurisdiction (i.e. France's unilateral commitment) changed.[114] Subsequently, France did proceed with a program of underground nuclear tests, and, in the face of a 1995 decision by France to continue these activities, New Zealand sought to

[113] Modalities and Procedures for a Clean Development Mechanism defined by Article 12 of the Kyoto Protocol, UN Doc. FCCC/CP/2001/13/Add.2, Draft Decision -/CMP.1, Annex, s. 37, UNFCCC, http://unfccc.int/resource/docs/cop7/13a02.pdf#page = 20.

[114] *Nuclear Tests Cases (New Zealand v. France)* (1974) ICJ Rep 457.

resume the proceedings against France.[115] As part of these proceedings, New Zealand argued that France breached its international obligation to conduct a prior EIA of its proposed underground testing program.

New Zealand's submissions with respect to France's obligation to conduct an EIA were based on both an explicit obligation under the Noumea Convention[116] and on customary international law. The Noumea Convention EIA provision requires parties, "within [their] capabilities," to assess the potential effects of major projects that might affect the marine environment, and includes, "where appropriate," public consultation and consultation with affected states, as well as dissemination of the assessment through the South Pacific Regional Seas Commission. New Zealand argued that these provisions required France to conduct a prior, "systematic, comprehensive and public scrutiny by independent scientists and others . . . if international standards are to be met." New Zealand explicitly linked the conduct of an EIA to the duty on states to protect the environment, going so far as to argue:

> Thus, there is no need to look for a specific, legal obligation to conduct an EIA. That duty flows from the legal duty to protect the environment: it is logically inseparable. You cannot have a legal duty to protect the environment without there being a legal duty to ensure, *in advance*, that an activity in contemplation does not contain a risk to the environment.[117]

The submissions on the existence of a customary rule to perform EIAs are closely related to this argument, in that the position put forward was framed less in terms of actual state practice, and more to demonstrate, with reference to the large number of explicit EIA obligations in existence at the time, that EIAs have been accepted worldwide as the method by which the duty to protect has been implemented. Significantly, France did not deny the existence of a treaty-based or customary duty to conduct EIAs, but rather argued that these obligations must be interpreted as allowing states a "margin of appreciation" in determining how they will prevent harm.[118]

The majority of the Court declined to address the substantive question on the extent of EIA obligations as it found that it did not have

[115] *Request for an Examination of the Situation in Accordance with Paragraph 63 of the Court's 1974 Judgment in the Case Concerning Nuclear Tests (New Zealand* v. *France) Case* (1995) ICJ Rep 288.

[116] Convention for the Protection of the Natural Resources and Environment of the South Pacific Region, 26 ILM 38 (1987), Art. 16.

[117] Oral Pleadings, New Zealand, September 12, 1995, CR/95/20 at 22.

[118] Oral Pleadings, France, September 12, 1995, CR/95/20 at 57.

jurisdiction over the dispute. The judges in the minority, addressing the substantive merits of New Zealand's claim, cautiously embraced New Zealand's approach to interpreting the obligation to conduct an EIA. Judge Weeramantry cryptically notes that the principle of environmental assessment has "reached the level of general recognition at which this Court should take notice of it."[119] Weeramantry's wording suggests an emerging rule of international law that exists independently of specific treaty obligations, although he cites little more than the UNEP EIA Principles in support of this conclusion. The reference to the UNEP EIA Principles is significant as it demonstrates a rejection of the French position that the form of implementing EIA obligations is a matter of state discretion, in favor of a recognition that the term "EIA" refers to a defined process of study and consultation. Ad Hoc Judge Palmer comes to a similarly equivocal conclusion about the presence of a customary rule to conduct EIAs.[120]

Gabcikovo-Nagymaros Case. The *Gabcikovo-Nagymaros Case* presented the International Court of Justice with a slightly different set of circumstances in relation to international EIA obligations. This dispute arose out of a plan proposed jointly by Hungary and Czechoslovakia to develop a dam and electrical power generation project on the Danube River. The project fell apart when Hungary effectively abandoned the project due to environmental concerns, but Czechoslovakia (and subsequently Slovakia) sought to proceed unilaterally with a revised version of the project.[121] Much of the argument between the parties centered on whether an adequate EIA had been undertaken for the main project and for the revised version. It is noteworthy in itself that neither party denied the legal obligation to conduct an EIA in these circumstances, notwithstanding that the 1977 treaty governing the development and operation of the dam contained no express requirement to carry out an EIA.[122] The Court, instead of determining the adequacy of prior assessments undertaken,

[119] (1995) ICJ Rep 288 at 344.

[120] Ibid. at 412, noting that a customary rule to conduct EIAs where an activity may have a significant environmental affect "may have developed."

[121] The facts of the case are summarized in the Judgment, ibid. at paras. 15–45.

[122] See Treaty Concerning the Construction and Operation of the Gabcikovo-Nagymaros System of Locks, September 16, 1977, Czechoslovakia/Hungary, 1109 UNTS 211. While this treaty did not contain specific EIA provisions, it did contain several provisions respecting the environment; in particular Art. 15 required that the parties ensure that the water quality of the Danube is not impaired as a result of the construction and operation of the dam, and Art. 19 provided that the parties ensure "compliance with the obligations for the protection of nature" arising from the construction and operation of the dam.

upheld the 1977 treaty, but indicated to the parties that they were under a joint obligation to consider the environmental impacts of the project as currently proposed and in doing so were required to assess those impacts in light of current environmental standards. What the Court was not prepared to do was to set out what those standards should be, but instead it required the parties to "look afresh at the effects on the environment of the operation of the Gabcikovo power plant."[123]

The majority does not refer specifically to an obligation on states to conduct EIAs, but the majority's approach is instructive in that it demonstrates the tension between the duty to prevent harm and a state's sovereign right to develop its own natural resources. In this case, the tension between these rights is expressed as the principle of sustainable development, and the resolution of this tension requires the parties, not the Court, to negotiate a final result, "taking account" of their respective rights and the principles of international environmental law and the law of international watercourses.[124] The result of the Court's approach is to impose upon the parties a duty to engage in principled negotiations. In this regard, the principles of environmental law do not dictate the outcome, but instead they structure the discourse between the parties. The role of EIA is thus to ensure that environmental impacts and international environmental principles are taken into account in a "meaningful" way in the course of negotiations.[125] The court does not go so far as to suggest that EIA is the sole process by which this may be accomplished, but it does suggest that assessment, notification and principled consultation are required elements of a state's duty to prevent harm.

Judge Weeramantry, in a separate opinion, picks up on his previous comments from the 1995 *Nuclear Tests Case* specifically linking EIAs to the duty to prevent harm and provides greater detail as to what this obligation may entail.[126] Here, Judge Weeramantry notes that EIA obligations should be "read into" treaties where there is a likelihood of significant impact.[127] The particular point that Weeramantry stresses is that EIA should not be confined to prior assessment, but is an obligation of continuing effect, such that a project, due to its magnitude and the possibility for unexpected consequences, should be subject to continuous monitoring.[128] Weeramantry expresses this expanded obligation as

[123] *Gabcikovo-Nagymaros Case* at para. 140. [124] Ibid. at para. 141.
[125] Ibid. at para. 141, quoting the *North Sea Continental Shelf Case*, (1969) ICJ Rep 47, para. 85.
[126] *Gabcikovo-Nagymaros Case* at 111–113. [127] Ibid. at 112. [128] Ibid. at 111.

arising out of the environmental provision of the 1977 treaty and, more generally, from the harm principle. The logic being that, since the obligation to prevent harm continues beyond the planning stage, so too should the obligation to monitor impacts to ensure no adverse impact. Weeramantry draws an explicit link between the duty to continually monitor and EIA, stating that the concept of EIA as a customary legal obligation is not restricted to prior assessment only, but includes an obligation to monitor impacts as long as the project is in operation.[129] EIA is viewed by Weeramantry as being a "specific application of the general principle of caution."[130] It is, in other words, a mechanism by which the more general obligations to prevent harm can be implemented in the context of shared watercourse regimes.

Perhaps the most interesting aspect of Weeramantry's treatment of EIA is how the concept of sustainable development plays out in the development of EIA commitments more generally. What Weeramantry recognizes is that an *ex ante* synoptic approach to environmental management will be inadequate, an observation that Weeramantry links to environmental complexity.[131] In light of the fact that impacts cannot be adequately determined in the planning stages of a project, sound environmental management requires that projects be subject to "continuous monitoring." While Weeramantry does not elaborate on the connection of this approach to sustainable development more generally, it is clear that the recognition of complexity as a constraint to effective environmental planning and the need to use adaptive practices are central aspects of sustainable development. Weeramantry, without making specific reference to requirements to engage in post-project monitoring, does note a "growing international recognition of the concept of continuing monitoring as part of EIA."[132] While the status of post-project monitoring as an integral part of EIA commitments in both domestic and international legal settings is very much a matter of continuing development, Weeramantry's interpretation of EIA obligations through the lens of sustainable development, indicates the normative direction of international EIA commitments is toward a more integrative and adaptive role.

MOX Plant Case. This ongoing dispute between the United Kingdom and Ireland involves the siting of a nuclear fuel reprocessing plant on the United Kingdom coast of the Irish Sea. The *MOX Plant Case* is complicated

[129] Ibid. at 111. [130] Ibid. at 113. [131] Ibid. at 111. [132] Ibid. at 112.

by a multiplicity of proceedings and overlapping jurisdictions;[133] however, the EIA issue has been framed primarily in terms of the obligation to conduct EIAs found in Article 206 of the UNCLOS, requiring assessment of activities that may cause substantial pollution or significant and harmful changes to the marine environment.[134] In this case, the concerns relate to the potential for discharges of radioactive isotopes into the Irish Sea from the operation of the proposed nuclear fuel reprocessing plants at Sellafield. The merits of the dispute have not been addressed by the Annex VII arbitration panel,[135] but the issues in dispute point to the difficulties associated with unelaborated EIA commitments.

Ireland's position was that the United Kingdom had failed to meet its obligation under Article 206 because the only EIA conducted, which was prepared in 1993, had inadequately assessed the potential harm to the Irish Sea by failing to assess, *inter alia*, all of the sources of discharges into the Irish Sea, the cumulative impacts from discharges, the effects from accidental releases of transportation of nuclear material associated with the project. In addition, there was inadequate consideration of alternatives to the project, as well as a failure to update the assessment. Accepting for the moment that Article 206 applies to this project (a point contested by the United Kingdom), it is evident that there is a disjuncture between the unelaborated nature of the EIA obligation under Article 206 and the specific EIA requirements that Ireland has sought to impose on the United Kingdom. In order to provide the necessary detail, Ireland has asked the arbitration panel to draw on other international instruments.[136] In essence, the argument is that the content of the duty to assess should be determined with reference to common standards of EIA accepted by states in other international instruments. In this regard, Ireland relies on the requirements as set out in the UNEP EIA Principles, the Espoo Convention and the EC EIA Directive. Ireland argues that the provisions contained in these instruments (the United Kingdom is subject to obligations under both the Espoo Convention and the EC EIA Directive) provide international benchmarks which are binding on the

[133] See Robin Churchill and Joanne Scott, "The MOX Plant Litigation: The First Half-Life" (2004) 53 ICLQ 643.

[134] *MOX Plant Case (Ireland* v. *United Kingdom)* (Annex VII Tribunal), pleadings and orders, www.pca-cpa.org.

[135] Ibid., Order No. 4, November 14, 2003, suspending proceedings in light of the jurisdiction dispute before the European Court of Justice. See Case C-459/03, *Commission* v. *Ireland*, Judgment May 30, 2006, finding that the European Court of Justice has exclusive jurisdiction.

[136] *MOX Plant Case* (Annex VII Tribunal), Memorial of Ireland, para. 7.16.

United Kingdom in carrying out its obligations under UNCLOS. Ireland goes on to argue that the United Kingdom is also bound to update its EIA given the lengthy passage of time between the original assessment and the actual approval. Here, international instruments are silent on the duty to update, but Ireland relies on the ICJ's decision in the *Gabcikovo-Nagymaros Case*, noting that the Court found that international law (the specific source is not indicated) imposes a "principle of contemporaneity in the application of environmental norms."[137]

The United Kingdom, for its part, rejects the Irish position on three principal bases. First, Article 206 is without application because UNCLOS became binding on the parties subsequent to the approval for the construction of the plant being granted. As a result, there was no "planned activity."[138] Secondly, even if Article 206 was *prima facie* applicable, the threshold requirement to trigger an assessment, "substantial pollution" or a "significant and harmful change to the marine environment," had not been met. Here, the United Kingdom argues that the requirement for there to be "reasonable grounds" introduces an element of state discretion in determining whether the threshold had been met and, in any event, Ireland had not demonstrated that such effects would likely result.[139] Finally, the United Kingdom rejects that the meaning of Article 206 can be elaborated upon with reference to general principles of international law or other international EIA instruments on the basis that Article 206 was intended to leave the details of how to carry out assessments to the source state.[140]

These arguments have not been addressed by the Tribunal on the merits, but for current purposes what is significant is that, like the *Nuclear Tests Cases*, the controversy revolved around the specific details of international EIA obligations, and not the existence of an obligation to assess itself. The approach by both France and the United Kingdom was to argue that the obligation in question afforded the source state broad

137 Ibid., paras. 7.31–7.32.

138 *MOX Plant Case* (Annex VII Tribunal), Counter-Memorial of the United Kingdom, paras. 5.7–5.10.

139 Ibid., paras. 5.11–5.12. On this latter point, it would seem that the United Kingdom's position was borne out to some degree by a finding by the Annex VII Tribunal that Ireland had not demonstrated that small quantities of radionuclides released into the marine environment would meet the "serious" harm threshold required by Art. 290 of UNCLOS to impose provisional measures. See *MOX Plant Case* (Annex VII Tribunal), Order No. 3, June 24, 2003, para. 55.

140 *MOX Plant Case* (Annex VII Tribunal), Counter-Memorial of the United Kingdom, paras. 5.14–5.32.

discretion in implementing their EIA obligations. There is clear potential for this kind of argument, if taken too far, to render EIA obligations in international law meaningless since the essence of any EIA obligation is to fix the common requirements for assessment.

Singapore Land Reclamation Case.[141] This case, between Malaysia and Singapore, concerned a land reclamation project by Singapore in and around the Straits of Johor. It was contended by Malaysia that these works constituted a threat of serious harm to the marine environment and, as a result, Singapore was obliged, *inter alia*, to conduct an environmental assessment and to notify and consult with Malaysia. Malaysia instituted proceedings against Singapore pursuant to Article 287 of UNCLOS before an Annex VII tribunal, and, pending the constitution of the arbitral tribunal, sought provisional measures from the International Tribunal for the Law of the Sea (ITLOS). Here, too, the core of the dispute was over the application of the duty to assess, with Singapore maintaining that the threshold for triggering Article 206 obligations had not been met.[142] Notwithstanding this contention, Singapore agreed to exchange information on the project and to consult with Malaysia. These assurances formed the basis of a provisional measures order that required the parties to establish a group of experts to study the environmental effects of the land reclamation and to recommend mitigation measures.[143] The group of experts was duly constituted and the contemplated study was undertaken. The study itself was not formally referred to as an EIA, but in many respects it conformed to the requirements of an EIA.[144] The screening of the study was effectively carried out by the provisional measures order where the tribunal notes that the possibility of harm to the marine environment from the proposal could not be excluded.[145] The terms of reference of the study were scoped in consultation with the parties, and the report itself sets out mitigation measures. The expert's report formed the basis of a settlement of the dispute entered into in April 2005.[146]

[141] *Case Concerning Land Reclamation by Singapore in and Around the Straits of Johor (Malaysia v. Singapore)* (September 4, 2003) ITLOS Case No. 12, pleadings and orders at www.itlos.org.

[142] Ibid., Response of Singapore, para. 144.

[143] Ibid., Provisional Measures Order, ITLOS, October 8, 2003.

[144] *Report of the Group of Independent Experts in the Matter of ITLOS Order of October 8, 2003*, November 5, 2003, www.mfa.gov.sg/Internet/press/land/GOE-Final_Report.pdf.

[145] *Case Concerning Land Reclamation by Singapore*, Provisional Measures Order, para. 96.

[146] Ibid., Settlement Agreement, April 26, 2005, www.mfa.gov.sg/Internet/press/land/Settlement_Agreement.pdf.

Pulp Mills of the River Uruguay Case.[147] The adequacy of an EIA is also central to proceedings initiated by Argentina against Uruguay alleging that Uruguay has violated the terms of the Statute of the River Uruguay, a bilateral treaty governing issues relating to a shared watercourse. The basis of concern is the construction of two pulp and paper mills on the river by Uruguay without notification and consultation with Argentina through a bilateral river commission set up under the treaty. The matter proceeded to a hearing on provisional measures, which were denied.[148] The Statute of the River Uruguay does not expressly require that an EIA be conducted (which is not surprising given that the treaty was concluded in 1975), but an EIA for each project was undertaken.[149] Uruguay has argued that it has discharged all of its legal obligations, of both a procedural and a substantive nature, in relation to the proposed mills, including consultation with Argentine officials and members of the public. Despite assurances from Uruguay of further consultation and information exchange and that effluent discharges will be monitored to ensure compliance, Argentina has maintained that it is not satisfied with the environmental studies to date and that it is entitled to a higher level of procedural protection, including a qualified right of consent to the project.[150]

A number of summary observations can be drawn from these examples of interstate disputes. First, the existence of an obligation to assess the environmental impacts of activities that have the potential to have impacts outside the source state is not disputed. In large part this is due to the presence of treaty-based obligations, but the *Gabcikovo-Nagymaros Case* and the *Pulp Mills of the River Uruguay Case* indicate that even in the absence of specific EIA obligations both states and international courts have an expectation that prior assessment will be undertaken. What are in dispute are the specific requirements that assessment obligations entail, and, given the prevalence of unelaborated EIA obligations in international instruments, one can expect further disputes concerning the amount of discretion states may exercise in carrying out assessments. The presence of both unelaborated and elaborated EIA requirements gives rise to questions respecting the relationship between customary

[147] *Pulp Mills on the River Uruguay (Argentina v. Uruguay)* (ICJ) (2006), pleading and orders at www.icj-cij.org.

[148] Ibid., Request for Provisional Measures, Order, July 13, 2006.

[149] See International Financial Corporation, www.ifc.org/ifcext/lac.nsf/Content/Uruguay_Pulp_Mills for EIA documentation.

[150] Request for Provisional Measures, Order, July 13, 2006, para. 50.

law and treaty law and between overlapping treaty obligations. What remains unexplored, but is clearly raised by the form of argumentation in both the *Nuclear Tests Case* and the *MOX Plant Case*, is the extent to which complementary obligations can be used to interpret ambiguous international obligations.[151] Also evident in these cases is the complex relationship between process and substance in international environmental law. Even in cases where EIAs have been undertaken, states tend to resort to process-oriented arguments in environmental disputes. EIA requirements become substitutes for absent substantive environmental requirements.

4.5 Customary obligations to perform EIAs

As discussed in Chapter 3, there is a close relationship between the development of EIA obligations in international law and the prior customary obligations of harm prevention and cooperation in transboundary matters, and this relationship is relied upon in support of the claim for a distinct customary obligation requiring EIAs to be conducted. The basis of this argument is that due diligence will require that a state inform itself of the environmental consequences of any potential environmentally harmful activities it proposes, and the duties of notification and consultation further require that this information be shared with potentially affected states, at least to the extent that it enables affected states to come to their own conclusions about the effects of the project on their interests and to engage in meaningful consultation in respect of the project. The argument continues that, if we accept the prior existence of these duties, then an obligation to perform EIAs can be deduced.[152]

On one level, this argument is sound. These prior duties clearly require an assessment of sorts, as well as an exchange of information. Moreover, from a theoretical standpoint, there is some attractiveness to the idea that certain obligations arise deductively by virtue of imperatives of state co-existence.[153] But the obligation to conduct an EIA that arises

[151] See Philippe Sands, "Sustainable Development: Treaty, Custom, and the Cross-Fertilization of International Law" in Alan Boyle and David Freestone, eds., *International Law and Sustainable Development: Past Achievements and Future Challenges* (New York: Oxford University Press, 1999) 39.

[152] See, for example, Günther Handl "The Environment: International Rights and Responsibilities" (1980) 74 Proc. Am. Soc. Int'l L. 223.

[153] See Michael Byers, *Custom, Power and the Power of Rules: International Relations and Customary International Law* (New York: Cambridge University Press, 1999) at 138–139, citing Serge Sur, *La coutume internationale* (Paris: Libraries Techniques, 1990).

by way of implication is almost entirely open-ended, such that it leaves unanswered critical questions regarding the scope, extent and nature of the assessment process. In fact, the deduced obligation can scarcely be viewed as a helpful development because in the absence of further procedural specificity it does little that the prior obligations of harm prevention and cooperation do not do on their own.[154]

Most arguments in support of a customary EIA obligation go beyond the simple assertion of an obligation by necessary implication. The argument is usually presented as consisting of a recognition that the implication of the harm principle and the duty to cooperate requires a consideration of environmental consequences and an exchange of information and then evidence, in the form of examples of treaty and soft law practice, that EIA is the preferred mechanism by which states implement that requirement.[155] The prior obligations are therefore necessary, because they frame the purpose for which EIAs are undertaken, but are not sufficient conditions for the existence of a customary EIA obligation.

This approach exemplifies the central criticism given by those, like Bodansky, who remain skeptical of the whole exercise of describing customary rules in international environmental law. Namely, by relying solely on treaty and soft law practice in support of a customary norm, these commentators tend to confuse what states say with what they do. For example, as early as 1982, the International Law Association concluded that the duty to perform environmental impact assessments was a "rule of international law in the stage of development" on the basis of an implied obligation arising from the duty to prevent harm and the duties to notify and consult, the UNEP Draft Principles of Conduct,[156] OECD Recommendations,[157] and the EIA provisions in the early regional seas conventions and UNCLOS (then a draft).[158] The Experts Group on Environmental Law of the WCED came to a similar conclusion in 1987

154 See Andre Nollkaemper, *The Legal Regime for Transboundary Water Pollution: Between Discretion and Constraint* (Boston: Nijhoff/Graham & Trotman, 1993) at 181.

155 See, for example, Experts Group on Environmental Law of the WCED, *Environmental Protection and Sustainable Development: Legal Principles and Recommendations* (London: Graham & Trotman/Martinus Nijhoff Publishers, 1987); and International Law Association, "Legal Aspects of the Conservation of the Environment" *Report of the Sixtieth Conference* 157 at 171.

156 Co-operation in the Field of Environment Concerning Natural Resources Shared by Two or More States, GA Res. 34/186, UN GAOR, 34th Sess. (1979).

157 OECD Recommendation C(79)116, "The Assessment of Projects with Significant Impact on the Environment," in OECD, *OECD and the Environment* (Paris: OECD, 1986).

158 ILA, "Legal Aspects of Conservation" at 174.

on the strength of a similar mixture of binding and non-binding instruments.[159] In none of these examinations is the conclusion respecting the status of the EIA obligation rooted in an analysis of state practice in relation to EIAs.

In fairness to these commentators, none of them goes as far as to suggest that the conclusion of treaties and other instruments containing EIA commitments (which are often themselves in a weak normative form) amounts to a fully formed customary obligation. Instead, they appear to be engaging in some degree of progressive development of international law, and to that end are noting a trend toward greater acceptance of EIA in an international setting (and, in that regard, they were undeniably correct).[160] But, beyond this criticism, there are two other serious difficulties with this approach to custom. First, the assumption that these commentators seem to accept is that EIA is the only way by which the harm principle can be implemented. And, secondly, when one considers the unelaborated nature of the treaty or soft law provisions in support of these arguments (only the UNEP EIA Principles contain detailed provisions – but these relate as much to domestic EIA as they do to transboundary EIA), it is doubtful that the customary EIA norm would substantially advance the implementation of the harm principle.

The harm principle, if it is to usefully influence state behavior, requires further, more specific rules. EIA, as we have now come to recognize it through domestic law and elaborated international instruments, provides procedural specificity of a defined sort. However, it must be accepted that the harm principle (due diligence) can be implemented in other ways. Most notably, international instruments can provide for substantive specificity through the creation of standards for emissions or required pollution control methods. In domestic law, substantive specificity is the predominant form of environmental regulation with an ever-increasing number of air and water quality standards, point source emission standards and mandated pollution control technologies. In international law, regimes employing substantive standards include the air pollution treaties such as those addressing ozone-depleting substances, and long-range transboundary air pollution or, in a different

[159] WCED Experts Group, *Legal Principles*.

[160] This is certainly true of the ILA and the WCED, who refer to the obligation as "emerging." Judge Weeramantry's cryptic characterization of EIA obligations as having "reached the level of general recognition at which [the ICJ] should take notice of it" suggests a similarly inchoate obligation.

context, those that identify specific endangered species and restrict their trade. Substantive regimes still involve an assessment of environmental consequences, but on a much more generalized and abstracted level, as opposed to requiring states to engage in case-by-case assessments. Substantive specificity tends to be possible where there is a high degree of certainty respecting future effects, as well as agreement on the specific objectives sought to be achieved. Procedural specificity, on the other hand, is more likely to arise in cases where there remains considerable uncertainty, especially outside a known context, and only agreement on a broader set of environmental objectives. Procedural specificity may take the form of an EIA, but there are other methodologies such as risk assessment that are being used in international agreements, as well. When one looks across the larger field of environmental law, the requirement for due diligence is implemented in different ways that are dependent upon the characteristics of the subject matter under regulation.

The ILC Draft Articles on Prevention of Transboundary Harm support a customary obligation to assess environmental effects that is not limited to EIA.[161] Article 7 of the Draft Articles on Prevention of Transboundary Harm requires states, prior to the authorization of an activity that presents a risk of significant transboundary harm, to conduct "an assessment of the possible transboundary harm caused by that activity, including any environmental impact assessment."[162] This provision captures the limitations of a customary obligation to perform EIAs in that it recognizes that EIAs are a predominant form of assessment, but are not the only method of assessment. The commentaries to this provision note that the specifics of the content of the obligation should be left to the domestic laws of the state.[163] In the context of the Draft Articles on Prevention of Transboundary Harm, the absence of specified procedural duties does not reduce the obligation to assess to a subjective requirement as it is clearly linked to the substantive duty to prevent harm and to other procedural obligations to notify and consult. At a minimum, this requires that the assessment undertaken be sufficient to allow an affected state to fully understand the environmental implications

161 International Law Commission, "Draft Articles on Prevention of Transboundary Harm," in *Report of the International Law Commission, Fifty-Third Session*, UN GAOR, 56th Sess., Supp. No. 10, UN Doc. A/56/10 (2001) 370 at Art. 7.

162 Ibid.

163 International Law Commission, "Commentaries on Draft Articles on Prevention of Transboundary Harm," in *Report of the International Law Commission, Fifty-Third Session*, UN GAOR, 56th Sess., Supp. No. 10, UN Doc. A/56/10 (2001) 377, Art. 7, Commentary 7.

of proposed activities. The ILC's approach is supported by the absence of EIA obligations in watercourse treaties. One might reasonably infer that, if EIA was the sole modality by which the harm principle could be implemented, there would not have been debate regarding the inclusion of an EIA obligation in the UN Watercourses Convention. Instead, the approach there was to acknowledge that EIA is one instrument among a variety of choices by which harm can be prevented.

The development of more detailed EIA commitments in international instruments, as well as in domestic legal systems, supports Bodansky's contention that norms that appear to be accepted by states in declaratory instruments are likely to require further implementation.[164] Bodansky's point here is that these types of normative statements tend to be formulated at the level of broad principles and not as detailed sets of rules, whether of a procedural or substantive nature. Whether the norm has achieved customary status is of secondary importance where the norm itself lacks the necessary detail to influence behavior.

The development of detailed EIA rules in international and domestic instruments may lend some credence to the view that these instances of elaboration are sufficiently uniform and consistent among states as to constitute further state practice in support of a more detailed customary norm. Certainly, since the Rio Declaration, EIA obligations have been included in treaties addressing a broad range of environmental subject areas and have been accepted by states from every region and from economies of every level. However, elaborated obligations have been more regionally based, being contained in treaties such as the Espoo Convention and the Antarctic Protocol that have limited memberships consisting of more developed states. Moreover, this type of argument suffers from the difficulty of trying to establish a customary obligation that is distinct from the treaty obligation. In other words, agreement to specific requirements in the context of a treaty cannot be taken in and of itself as proof of a more generalized intention to be bound by those requirements outside the treaty.

The relationship between treaty practice and customary law is unsettled and too complex to be addressed in this context,[165] but for present purposes, it suffices to say that evidence of consistent state practice

[164] Bodansky, "Not So Customary" at 118–119.

[165] The relationship between treaty and custom is explored in the *North Sea Continental Shelf Case (Federal Republic of Germany/Denmark; Federal Republic of Germany/Netherlands)* (1969) ICJ Rep 3. See also A. D'Amato, *The Concept of Custom in International Law* (Ithaca, NY: Cornell University Press, 1971), ch. 5 at 105 *et seq.*

beyond agreeing to treaty and soft law provisions is still a requirement to demonstrate a customary rule to conduct EIAs. But here the presence of extensive treaty provisions further complicates matters because it is very difficult to discern where domestic state practice in relation to EIAs arises as a result of an existing treaty obligation or as a result of a distinct customary duty. The most salient evidence of state practice in support of a customary EIA obligation may be the existence of domestic legislation requiring assessment of transboundary impacts of projects under that state's jurisdiction.[166] As discussed in relation to the US, Canada and the EC, this appears to be a requirement in all three systems, with evidence of transboundary assessment predating treaty obligations.[167]

The point here is not that there is an absence of state practice with regard to transboundary EIA as has been suggested by some.[168] There are numerous examples of states and state agencies notifying one another of possible environmental impacts and involving other states in their EIA processes.[169] The difficulty lies in attributing the practice to the state itself, since EIA is often carried out by a proponent other than the state, or will be carried out at the sub-state level. It will also be difficult to discern the extent to which this activity is motivated by a sense of international legal obligation, or whether notification and participation in EIA processes is simply comity or professional courtesy between agencies.

Finally, the presence of so many elaborated and unelaborated EIA treaty commitments makes the question of custom somewhat beside the point. As noted above, in the interstate disputes in which the precise

[166] Domestic legislation is commonly accepted as a form of state practice in support of a customary rule: see Peter Malanczuk, *Akehurst's Modern Introduction to International Law* (7th edn, New York: Routledge, 1997) at 39.

[167] Discussed above at ch. 2.6.

[168] See, for example, P. Okowa, "Procedural Obligations in International Environmental Agreements" (1996) 67 BYIL 275 at 281.

[169] Sources discussing specific instances of transboundary EIA include UNECE, *Current Policies, Strategies and Aspects of Environmental Impact Assessment in a Transboundary Context*, Environmental Series No. 6, UN Doc. ECE/CEP/9 (discussing the practice in ECE member countries prior to the Espoo Convention coming into force); Koivurova, "EIA in the Arctic" at 273–286 (discussing Vuotos Reservoir, Finland/Sweden); Arctic EIA Guidelines at 39 (discussing Outokumpu Steel Factories, Finland/Sweden); and M. Nazari, "The Transboundary EIA Convention in the Context of Private Sector Operation Co-financed by an International Financial Institution: Two Case Studies from Azerbaijan and Turkmenistan" (2003) 23 Environmental Impact Assessment Review 441. In the North American context, see the discussion of the cases above in ch. 2, and the examples discussed below in ch. 6.

content of EIA requirements has been raised, the controversy centered on the elaboration of treaty obligations and the extent to which treaty-based EIA obligations could be amplified by more detailed EIA requirements in international law.

4.6 Elaboration of existing EIA commitments

The elaboration of EIA commitments, unlike the search for a stand-alone customary obligation, begins with an existing, treaty-based commitment to undertake EIAs or in some cases "assessments." The principal interpretive question is to what extent the use of the term "EIA" or "assessment" imports the more specific requirements found in elaborated obligations. One approach to this question is to argue that the absence of elaboration could be taken as an indication that the parties intended to confer broad discretion on states to determine the content and form of the assessment. This was the type of argument put forward by France in the *Nuclear Tests Cases* and the United Kingdom in the *MOX Plant Case*. Given that assessment processes are going to be undertaken through national instruments, some "margin of appreciation" is necessary to allow assessment obligations to be integrated into domestic processes. However, at least insofar as obligations that specifically require that EIAs be undertaken, as opposed to those, like Article 206 of the UNCLOS, that require assessments, there is a strong argument that the term "EIA" has developed a specialized meaning in international law.

Article 31(4) of the Vienna Convention provides that special meanings of terms used in treaties shall be accepted where it is established that that was the parties' intention.[170] It is in this regard that the consistent elaboration of the term "EIA" in international and domestic instruments is relevant. The specialized meaning at the international level was established in the UNEP EIA Principles and is further evidenced by the consistent requirements contained in elaborated EIA commitments, such as the Espoo Convention and the Antarctic Protocol, as well as in domestic legislation. In light of this consistent and widespread treatment of the term "EIA," it is reasonable to attribute awareness of this specialized meaning to parties negotiating treaties containing unelaborated obligations. Indeed, in many instances, the same parties have negotiated elaborated and unelaborated treaties. This position is strengthened by the presence of other treaties that use the term "assessment," which

[170] Vienna Convention on the Law of Treaties, Vienna, May 23, 1969, 1155 UNTS 331.

indicates intent to include a broader scope of processes to assess impacts. If parties had intended to require processes that were less narrowly focused than EIA processes, they would have used the term "assessment," or at the very least avoided the use of the more technical term "EIA." Following from this, for those treaties negotiated after the mid-1980s, where the term "EIA" is used it should be interpreted to include the minimum core of procedural requirements set out in the UNEP EIA Principles, unless some contrary intention can be shown. This approach still provides considerable scope to allow states to implement these requirements in the context of their own domestic EIA systems.

Using the provisions of one instrument or sets of instruments to amplify the commitments contained in another requires considerable caution and sensitivity to the precise wording of the provision subject to interpretation. For example, the arbitration tribunal in the proceedings brought under the OSPAR Convention,[171] relating to the MOX plant litigation,[172] rejected arguments by Ireland that the access to information provisions contained in the OSPAR Convention should be interpreted in light of the more inclusive practice found in the Aarhus Convention[173] and an EC Directive,[174] which Ireland argued was indicative of the prevailing principles of international law. Instead, the tribunal was careful to restrict its interpretation to the provision before it, and rightly focused on the intent of the parties to the OSPAR Convention. The other treaty provisions, while perhaps illustrative of a general trend toward greater openness, were not probative of the intent of the parties.[175] Unlike the interpretation of EIA discussed above, this case did not involve the interpretation of a term with a specialized meaning. However, this decision does suggest that sensitivity to the precise wording is of paramount importance.

The interpretation of terms with specialized meanings should be distinguished from the interpretation of scientific standards and understandings that are contained in treaties. In giving effect to these types

[171] OSPAR Convention.

[172] *Dispute Concerning Access to Information under Article 9 of the OSPAR Convention (Ireland* v. *United Kingdom)*, Final Award (OSPAR Ar. Trib., July 2, 2003), www.pca-cpa.org.

[173] Convention on Access to Information, Public Participation in Decision-Making and Access to Justice in Environmental Matters, Aarhus, Denmark, June 25, 1998, 38 ILM 517, entered into force October 30, 2001.

[174] EC Directive 90/313, OJ 1990 L158/56.

[175] For a brief summary of and comment on this decision, see T. McDorman, "Access to Information under Article 9 of the Ospar Convention (Ireland v. United Kingdom), Final Award" (2004) 98 AJIL 330.

of treaty requirements – and the scientific considerations in determining the threshold of "significant impact" is an example of such a provision – scientific understandings and standards should be construed contemporaneously in light of current knowledge. For example, in the *Gabcikovo-Nagymaros Case*, the ICJ held, in connection with the requirement that the parties "look afresh" at the environmental impacts of the proposed hydroelectric facility, that this should be done with reference to those standards prevailing at present rather than those prevailing at the time of the 1977 treaty.[176] Determining the content of a duty to assess in the context of a treaty obligation should not be interpreted in a dynamic fashion such that advancements in assessment methodologies are to be read into commitments over time. This is not to say that as a matter of implementation states will not apply prevailing approaches to EIA. However, as a matter of obligation, a specialized term such as "EIA" must be understood in light of the intention of the parties at the time the obligation was concluded. Unlike the determination of "significant impact," the construction of the duty to assess is not a factual determination to be made at the time of the dispute.[177]

The interpretive relevance of elaborated EIA commitments is not limited to fleshing out the requirements associated with the use of the specialized term "EIA." Take, for example, the commitment to assess contained in Article 206 of the UNCLOS. The use of the term "assess" in this provision indicates an intention that a broad range of assessment approaches beyond EIAs may satisfy this requirement. In this regard, the commitment under Article 206 is similar to the customary obligation to assess in that the modality of assessment is left to the state, but the obligation is not robbed of its objective content because the assessment undertaken will still have to be sufficient to discharge the duty to prevent harm that underlies it. In both cases, however, evidence of treaty and domestic EIA practice are relevant in that they provide examples of reasonable state behavior in response to potential impacts to the environment.

To return to the arguments of Ireland and the United Kingdom in the *MOX Plant Case*, the Irish position that the tribunal should look to

[176] At para. 140. See also *Kasikili/Sedudu Island Case (Botswana/Namibia)* (1999) ICJ Rep 1045 at 1060.

[177] On the rule that treaties are to be interpreted by reference to the circumstances and understandings that prevailed at the time the treaty was concluded, see *Land and Maritime Boundary Between Cameroon and Nigeria (Cameroon* v. *Nigeria)* (2002) ICJ Rep at para. 59.

the UNEP EIA Principles, the Espoo Convention and the EC EIA Directive as indications of what the "United Kingdom is bound to cause to be prepared,"[178] goes too far. It cannot be said that Article 206 imports all of the requirements of an EIA. However, insofar as the United Kingdom is under a duty to exercise due diligence, a failure to adhere to commonly accepted standards is surely evidence of a lack of due diligence. The due diligence obligation can be discharged by some other form of assessment, but that assessment would have to include sufficient information to allow the affected state to make a meaningful determination of whether its interests are impacted. The contention by the United Kingdom that states retain "an element of discretion" to determine whether the threshold has been met is contrary to the objective determination of due diligence. Indeed, the use of the term "reasonable grounds" in Article 206 supports the objective nature of the requirement. Ireland's argument that the existence of other EIA obligations provides evidence of what is practicable is surely correct. Here, the presence of other treaty obligations demonstrates the level of assessment that a state is capable of. States should not be allowed to claim that a full EIA is not practicable in the face of international practice to the contrary. Evidence of EIA practice at the domestic level would also be probative of the standard of conduct that is required to satisfy due diligence obligations.[179] In this context, because the evidence of treaty and domestic practice is not oriented toward establishing an independent state obligation, there is no requirement that this conduct meet the requirements of uniformity and consistency demanded of state practice in support of custom. Rather, because the base obligation to assess is established in a treaty, the question that remains is an interpretive one regarding the content of that base obligation.

4.7 Conclusion

One of Bodansky's concerns with legal scholars' over-attention to a rule's normative status is that it emphasizes an area of international interaction, namely, interstate adjudication, which is infrequent and of lesser influence in determining state behavior than more informal

[178] *MOX Plant Case*, Memorial of Ireland at para. 7.24.

[179] In this regard, Ireland, in the *MOX Plant Case*, cites the EIA practice of the US in relation to a similar type of facility as evidence of the standards of assessment required in the context of MOX facility approvals: ibid. at paras. 7.75–7.80.

interactions.[180] The emphasis on litigation may in fact have a distorting effect on our perception of how law operates in these less formal settings, if it leads to the impression that states are only influenced by those norms that are likely to be formally recognized as part of the positive system of international law. Bodansky, drawing on Franck's model of compliance, suggests that formal bindingness may be less important than specificity in determining outcomes in state-to-state interactions.[181] While Bodansky focuses on specificity, it is important to bear in mind that Franck's analysis suggests that compliance pull is affected by a combination of factors including the coherence of norms with other principles and rules within the system and their connection to secondary rules of interpretation and application.[182] All of these factors, of course, contribute to the overall legitimacy of the norm in question, which is, for Franck, the paramount determinant of compliance pull.

When the various normative strands of EIA commitments are considered in the context of these less formal and more common interactions, a more cohesive picture of international EIA commitments begins to emerge. In Europe, the overlapping and reinforcing nature of EIA commitments is clearly anticipated in some treaties, where the assessment requirements in one treaty are elaborated by the rules contained elsewhere.[183] Here, the institutionalization of a unified form of implementation is explicitly anticipated. However, the high density of EIA commitments, their relationship to broader customary rules, soft law instruments and to domestic practices suggests that these different normative elements taken as a whole will exert influence over state behavior regardless of their formal status. The desire for normative coherence results in states adjusting their domestic EIA processes to account for broader environmental norms that arise in international settings. For example, Canada applies the transboundary EIA provisions of CEAA in relation to non-parties to the Espoo Convention, such as the United States, as well as

[180] Bodansky, "Not So Customary" at 117.

[181] Ibid. at 118, citing Thomas Franck, *The Power of Legitimacy Among Nations* (New York: Oxford University Press, 1990).

[182] Discussed in Franck, ibid. at 135–194. See also Thomas Franck, *Fairness in International Law and Institutions* (New York: Oxford University Press, 1995) at 38–46.

[183] This is acknowledged and explored in a series of informal UNECE reports looking at the relationship of the Espoo Convention to other treaties, namely, the Convention on Long Range Transboundary Air Pollution, the Convention on Transboundary Effects of Industrial Accidents, the Convention on the Protection and Use of Transboundary Watercourses and Lakes, and the Convention on Biological Diversity. The reports are available at www.unece.org/env/eia/eiaresources.html.

parties to that Convention without differentiation.[184] The United States in its application of domestic EIA to transboundary issues explicitly justifies this on the existence of customary commitments, such as the duty to prevent harm and the duty to notify.[185]

Conceiving of EIA commitments in less formal terms is somewhat at odds with the regime-based approach to international environmental law in the sense that regime theorists tend to understand different environmental regimes as being independent of each other. However, each of the separate regimes which contain EIA commitments of varying degrees of specificity is implemented in an undifferentiated fashion at the domestic level. There is no distinct transboundary pollution, climate change or biological diversity EIAs. Rather, all of these objectives are implemented through a single domestic process that will also reflect domestic environmental values. There is a dynamic aspect to the development of EIA commitments in that processes and norms are developed at both the international and domestic levels and then filter both vertically and horizontally to different systems.

In the latter regard, EIA commitments have a transnational character that is consistent with the turn to sustainable development as the touchstone of environmental governance. The incorporation within EIA processes of many of the principles inherent in the concept of sustainable development, such as participatory norms, the need for integration of environmental decision-making with other decision-making processes and the incorporation of biological complexity and scientific uncertainty into decision-making processes through monitoring and adaptive management plans, underscores the close link between EIA commitments and sustainable development. This in turn points to the less instrumental nature of EIA processes. For example, the open and participatory nature of EIAs is both a means and, as an integral part of sustainable development, an end in itself. Similarly, the investigation and evaluation of environmental effects and the consideration of those effects in the context of a project's social and economic impacts are directed toward the goal of environmental protection and sustainability, but the process itself defines those ends – it gives meaning to sustainability.

[184] Canadian Environmental Assessment Act, SC 1992, c. 37, as amended, s. 47.

[185] *CEQ Guidance on NEPA Analyses for Transboundary Impacts*, issued July 1, 1997, CEQ NEPANET, http://ceq.eh.doe.gov/nepa/regs/transguide.html.

5 The structure of international EIA commitments

5.1 Introduction

The most visible influence of domestic EIA systems on their international counterparts is the adoption of the same elements in international EIA commitments. Not surprisingly, many of the difficulties found in domestic EIA are evident in international disputes over EIA, such as disputes regarding whether an EIA is required, and the adequacy of any EIA reports prepared. However, translating domestic decision-making processes into an international context raises a unique set of challenges which have necessitated the development of distinctly international responses. The requirement to involve other states and the publics of other states, for example, requires the creation of specialized rules regarding notice and consultation, as well as mechanisms for receiving extraterritorial environmental information. The uncertain availability of judicial review, which has played a critical role in the development of domestic EIA,[1] raises questions about the need for mechanisms that will both resolve disputes and provide for authoritative interpretations and elaboration of EIA obligations. In addition to these more procedurally oriented differences, international law also presents a distinct substantive context for EIA commitments. As in domestic EIA systems, the link between substantive environmental outcomes and international EIA commitments is often made in explicit, but highly abstracted terms. In this connection, this chapter describes how the various elements of the EIA process are implemented in international EIA commitments with an emphasis on how these commitments reflect and implement the wider international context. Because I am principally concerned with

[1] See Serge Taylor, *Making Bureaucracies Think: The Environmental Impact Statement Strategy of Administrative Reform* (Stanford, CA: Stanford University Press, 1984) at 232.

examining the overall structure and role of EIAs in international environmental governance, the approach in this chapter is to look at how each of the elements of EIA are addressed across a variety of different international EIA commitments.

5.2 Screening

The threshold requirement for conducting an EIA in almost all cases is the likelihood of a significant environmental effect. Significance is the required threshold in, *inter alia*, the UNEP EIA Goals and Principles, the Espoo Convention, the CBD, the US–Canada Air Quality Agreement and the regional seas agreements. The UNCLOS confusingly uses the two thresholds of "substantial pollution of or significant and harmful changes to the marine environment." The term "substantial" may suggest a higher threshold, but, given that the two standards are disjunctive, the lower standard of "significant and harmful change" will apply in any event. The choice of significance as the threshold reflects the use of that threshold in domestic EIA, as well as the threshold requirement for triggering obligations under the harm principle. Adopting the same threshold as domestic EIA requirements facilitates the implementation of international EIA obligations as it will not require the consideration of a separate, international standard for triggering EIA. Thus, the threshold also reflects the principle of nondiscrimination in that the resulting structure is the non-differentiation between domestic and international impacts as a trigger for EIA. The one exception to the use of significance as the threshold is the Antarctic Protocol where an EIA is to be conducted if an activity has at least a "minor or transitory impact."[2]

Few attempts have been made to define significance in the abstract,[3] but the preferred attempt has been to determine whether the threshold has been met on a case-by-case basis. The difficulty faced in domestic EIA is that, because determining significance is both a technically complex and context-specific exercise, it is difficult for agencies to develop a consistent approach. The challenge then is that the threshold requires an objective assessment of the potential for harm, but in actuality the

[2] Protocol on Environmental Protection to the Antarctic Treaty, Madrid, October 4, 1991, 30 ILM 1461, in force January 14, 1998, Art. 8(1).

[3] But see UNEP Principles on Conservation and Harmonious Utilization of Natural Resources Shared by Two or More States, UN Doc. UNEP/IG.12/2 (1978), reprinted in 17 ILM 1094 (1978), defining "significantly affect" as "any appreciable effects on a shared natural resource and excludes *de minimis* effects."

determination is highly subjective. The contested nature of this determination is evident from the interstate disputes involving EIA discussed in the previous chapter, which all involved disagreement over the characterization of the potential environmental impacts. In domestic settings, disagreements about whether the threshold has been met are subject to judicial review, but courts have tended to defer to the more specialized expertise of agencies. However, part of the justification for deference in a domestic context is concern over the legitimacy of the judicial branch exercising a strong supervisory role over an area delegated to administrative decision-makers – in essence, a separation-of-powers concern.[4] In the international context, the separation-of-powers argument has less purchase since the controversy is between competing sovereign claims. Consequently, the democratic legitimacy of the original decision cannot be solely rooted in internal political structure of the source state, but must appeal to the shared values of the particular regime.

Under the Espoo Convention, the determination of whether the threshold condition for conducting an EIA is triggered uses both lists of activities and criteria for determining significance. Under the scheme, a state of origin is required to carry out an EIA for a "proposed activity listed in Appendix I [to the Espoo Convention] that is likely to cause a significant adverse transboundary effect."[5] The list of activities contained in Appendix I includes a wide range of both public and private sector projects, which are generally of a large scale.[6] For those activities not listed in Appendix I, Article 2 requires parties to enter into "discussions" on whether the proposed activity is likely to cause a significant adverse transboundary impact and, in the event that the parties agree that a project is likely to have such an effect, it is treated as a listed item and subject to the EIA requirements under the Espoo Convention. Therefore, for non-listed activities, the requirement to conduct a transboundary EIA is permissive even if they appear likely to cause significant adverse transboundary impacts, with the only obligation to "discuss" subjecting the project to a transboundary EIA. The Espoo Convention also contains a list of general criteria by which the significance of non-listed activities may be determined.[7]

Unlike the EC Directive where a listed activity is automatically subject to an EIA, under the Espoo Convention an initial environmental

[4] Richard Stewart, "The Reformation of American Administrative Law" (1975) 88 Harvard L. Rev. 1669.

[5] Espoo, Finland, February 25, 1991, 30 ILM 802, in force January 14, 1998, Art. 2(3).

[6] Ibid., Appendix I. [7] Ibid., Appendix III.

assessment or some other internal screening mechanism is required to determine whether an activity listed in Appendix I is likely to cause significant adverse environmental impact. Ebbeson has argued that the listing of activities should be treated as a "presumption" that the activities do in fact cause significant transboundary effects, requiring notification of all listed projects except where it is "manifest that there is no risk of causing significant adverse transboundary impact in the neighbouring state."[8] The reasoning here is that the use of listed activities appears redundant if states must undertake an independent assessment of the significance of the activity's impact. This interpretation, which appears to suggest that the onus is on the source state to disprove the likelihood of an activity having a significant adverse transboundary impact, does not, however, seem warranted by the wording of Article 2, which clearly imposes a two-part test consisting of inclusion on the list and a finding of significant adverse transboundary impact. The better view is that the significance of listing categories of projects in a separate appendix is related to the application of the inquiry procedure under Article 3.[9]

Under the inquiry procedure, where a party considers that a proposed activity listed under Appendix I is likely to have a significant transboundary impact, but the state of origin has not given notice of the project in accordance with the Convention, then the potentially affected party may require exchange of sufficient information regarding the project and engage the state of origin in discussions respecting the application of the EIA requirements. In the event of continued disagreement, either party may submit the question of whether the threshold has been met to an inquiry commission in accordance with the procedures detailed in a further appendix to the Convention.[10] The inquiry procedure is only available for those projects listed in Appendix I, so, in the event of a disagreement about a non-listed activity, the state of origin retains greater discretion to determine the threshold, subject only to "discussions" with the state of origin, but not the inquiry procedure.

As a means for resolving disputes over whether the threshold has been met, the inquiry procedure is not analogous to domestic judicial review. Rather, it operates more like a hearing *de novo* in the sense that the process calls for the appointment of an independent inquiry commission, at the request of either the source state or the affected state, which

[8] Jonas Ebbeson, "Innovative Elements and Expected Effectiveness of the 1991 EIA Convention" (1999) 19 Environmental Impact Assessment Review 47 at 51.

[9] Espoo Convention, Art. 3(7). [10] Ibid., Appendix IV.

conducts its own inquiry as to whether the threshold has been met. To this end, the inquiry procedure is structured on the premise that a determination of significant transboundary impact is predominantly a technical and scientific matter, as indicated by the requirement that the commission's members shall be experts and that the commission's final opinion "be based on accepted scientific principles."[11] The commission's findings are recommendations, and as such are non-binding. Instead, the inquiry procedure, which allows for other parties to intervene and the results of which are circulated to the parties, relies on appeals to accepted scientific norms and community pressure to bring about compliance.

The screening of activities under the Antarctic Protocol uses a system of Initial Environmental Evaluation (IEE) similar to the use of initial environmental assessments under NEPA. A preliminary assessment of the proposal, done in accordance with "national procedures," is used to determine whether an activity has a minor or transitory impact.[12] If it has less than a minor or transitory impact, the proponent may proceed with the proposed activity. But, where an activity has at least a minor or transitory impact, an IEE must be prepared, which includes a description of the activity, alternatives to the activity, as well as any impacts that the activity may have.[13] If the IEE discloses more than a minor or transitory impact, a more detailed Comprehensive Environmental Evaluation (CEE) must be prepared. The IEE is not subject to the scrutiny of other parties, but operates as a self-assessment tool, although each party is required to provide an annual list of IEEs prepared and any consequent decisions taken.[14] The adoption of the term "minor or transitory" as the threshold was chosen by the parties to the Antarctic Protocol in order to provide greater clarity than the term "significant," which was used under the 1987 Antarctic EIA Guidelines, and does not denote a lower threshold.[15] Despite the change in wording, there remain disputes over the common meaning of the term, and, while the Committee for Environmental Protection (the treaty body that oversees the Protocol)

[11] Ibid., Appendix IV, paras. 2 and 14.

[12] Protocol on Environmental Protection to the Antarctic Treaty, Madrid, October 4, 1991, 30 ILM 1461, in force January 14, 1998, Art. 8 and Annex I, Art. 1.

[13] Ibid., Art. 2. [14] Ibid., Art. 6.

[15] See Kees Bastmeijer and Ricardo Roura, "Environmental Impact Assessment in Antarctica" in Kees Bastmeijer and Timo Koivurova, eds., *Theory and Practice of Transboundary Environmental Impact Assessment* (Leiden: Martinus Nijhoff, 2007) 177.

has been invited to elaborate on the meaning, it has opted to continue to make this determination on a case-by-case basis.[16] The Antarctic EIA Guidelines note that it may be useful to consider how similar impacts have been assessed in similar circumstances,[17] although, in the absence of a mechanism by which information from past EIAs could be fed into future EIA processes, it is difficult to see how this might be accomplished.

Other international EIA instruments acknowledge the difficulties associated with screening, and provide further elaboration on the methodology of screening, but not as a legal test. In keeping with their adaptation role, the CBD Draft EIA Guidelines provide suggestions for biodiversity criteria, noting that reference should be made to existing national and international standards, such as protected species legislation and treaties that protect specific biological resources.[18] The Arctic EIA Guidelines also indicate that, where case-by-case determinations are made, care must be taken to ensure that screening procedures account for the particular sensitivity of the Arctic environment. To this end, the Arctic EIA Guidelines provide lists of potentially sensitive features and note that other instruments addressing the Arctic environment should be referenced in determining significance.[19]

The CBD Draft EIA Guidelines acknowledge that determining threshold values is, in part, a political process. This is not a surprising acknowledgment. The political dimension of determining significance has long been acknowledged in domestic EIA, but it does point to a legitimacy difficulty in international law. As noted, the legitimacy of screening

[16] Discussed in Donald Rothwell, "Polar Environmental Protection and International Law: The 1991 Antarctic Protocol" (2000) 11 EJIL 591 at 600–602, citing reports prepared by New Zealand and Australia.

[17] "Guidelines for Environmental Impact Assessment in Antarctica," adopted by Resolution 4(2005), attached to the Final Report of XXVIIIth ATCM, 2005, para. 3.3.3.

[18] "Guidelines for Incorporating Biodiversity-Related Issues into Environmental Impact Assessment Legislation and/or Processes and in Strategic Environmental Assessment," Report of the Sixth Meeting of the Conference of the Parties to the Convention on Biological Diversity, UN Doc. UNEP/CBD/COP/6/7, Annex, www.biodiv.org/decisions/default.aspx?m=cop-06. Revised draft guidelines were issued by the CBD Secretariat in July 2005, www.biodiv.org/programmes/cross-cutting/impact/guidelines.shtml, s. 13, Appendix 2.

[19] 1997 Guidelines for Environmental Impact Assessment in the Arctic, adopted by the Arctic Council in the 1997 Alta Declaration on the Protection of the Arctic Environmental Protection Strategy, http://finnbarents.urova.fi/aria/, at 12 ("Arctic EIA Guidelines").

decisions in international law cannot necessarily rely on the corrective functions of judicial review or on the connection of the decision-makers to democratically elected institutions. The turn to standards or criteria in other international instruments as a basis to assess significance provides a shared, and more legitimate, basis to determine whether an EIA should be undertaken.

To return to the Espoo Convention model, the inquiry commission process provides an alternative to a solely unilateral approach to threshold considerations by providing for a neutral, science-based opinion on the question of significance. In the only proceedings under the inquiry commission procedures, a dispute between Romania and the Ukraine regarding the effects of a proposed navigation channel in the Danube Delta, the result appears to be mixed. The inquiry commission determined that the project was likely to have significant transboundary impacts, a decision that was supported by a wide range of technical reports. However, the Ukrainian government has reiterated its intention to proceed with the project. Despite the technical focus of the inquiry commission, the report itself acknowledges and seeks to address the political dimension of the dispute. In the conclusion to the report, the commission, in recognition of the fact that the proposed navigation route is likely to remain a source of controversy between the parties, recommends the formation of a "Bilateral Research Programme related to activities with transboundary impacts in the framework of the bilateral cooperation under the Espoo Convention."[20] The recommended approach responds to the scientific shortcomings, which in this case included gaps in baseline knowledge and difficulties in predicting impacts, and the continued political dispute by proposing a continuing program of improving baseline environmental information and monitoring of impacts. It is suggested that these activities may be connected to existing institutions, such as the International Commission for the Protection of the Danube Delta, and EU-based environmental programs. This recommendation appears to go beyond the technical orientation of the inquiry commission's role contemplated under the Espoo Convention, but it evinces an understanding by the commission that cooperation on transboundary issues requires an ongoing process of information exchange and principled dialogue.

[20] Espoo Inquiry Commission, "Report on the Likely Significant Adverse Transboundary Impacts of the Danube–Black Sea Navigation Route at the Border of Romania and the Ukraine," July 2006, at 62, UNECE, www.unece.org/env/eia/inquiry.htm.

5.3 Scoping and the contents of EIA reports

International EIA obligations have provided only skeletal requirements for the determination of the scope and contents of required EIA reports, preferring to leave the detailed requirements to domestic decision-makers. In some respects, this is not surprising, since the scoping and preparation of EIA reports will not raise distinctly international issues requiring specialized rules. The one exception to this approach is the Antarctic Protocol, which is drafted much more like a stand-alone EIA regime. Here, each of the three levels of EIA reflects increasingly more demanding requirements as the likelihood of harm increases. For example, the preliminary (screening level) assessment must simply follow "appropriate national procedures,"[21] while the Initial Environmental Evaluation (IEE) includes minimum requirements, including the consideration of alternatives.[22] The requirements for a Comprehensive Environmental Evaluation (CEE) are very detailed, consistent with the requirements of well-established domestic EIA systems. For example, a CEE shall include consideration of alternatives and the consequences of each alternative, a description of baseline environmental information, a description of analysis methodology, consideration of indirect impacts and cumulative impacts, identification of mitigation measures and a non-technical summary of the CEE.[23] Despite the high level of detail for the CEE, the Antarctic Protocol does not include any obligation on the state responsible for preparing the CEE to consult with other member states as to the appropriate scope of the CEE prior to its being prepared.

The Espoo Convention also contains a list of minimum requirements for inclusion in an EIA report that is similar to the requirements of a CEE.[24] However, in the Espoo Convention, the requirement for the consideration of alternatives, including the "no-action alternative," is framed as being required "where appropriate."[25] The use of the term "appropriate" would seem to signal that the decision to consider alternatives is best left to the source state, which makes sense insofar as states have different requirements for considering alternatives, depending on the screening process. The term "appropriate" here should be interpreted in light of state domestic practice such that, where alternatives are required under domestic legislation, it is appropriate to consider alternatives in the context of transboundary harm. This interpretation is in keeping with the principle of nondiscrimination, by requiring

[21] Protocol on Environmental Protection to the Antarctic Treaty, Annex I, Art. 1.
[22] Ibid., Art. 2. [23] Ibid., Art. 3(2). [24] Espoo Convention, Appendix II. [25] Ibid.

states only to consider alternatives under the same circumstances as would be required for purely domestic harm. This qualification for an essential aspect of conducting an EIA, if viewed as allowing states to depart from domestic practice in their discretion, seems an unnecessary deviation from domestic practice, particularly among UNECE members.[26]

The difficulty with leaving the determination of alternatives solely in the hands of the source state is that the range of alternatives examined can have profound effects on the outcomes of EIA processes.[27] In the international context, the alternatives requirement is particularly important because of the relative absence of substantive environmental standards at the international level. Without a consideration of alternatives, it will be more difficult for affected states to be able to make a principled assessment of whether the potential for transboundary harm is acceptable in the circumstances. The importance of considering alternatives was recognized in the context of preventing transboundary harm by the International Law Commission in their Draft Articles on Prevention of Transboundary Harm.[28] Here, alternatives are recognized as an evaluative measure of the reasonableness of state activity. Where the ends sought by the source state can be achieved through an alternative and less harmful manner, proceeding with a more harmful alternative should be regarded as less reasonable in the absence of other compelling factors.

Apart from setting minimum procedural requirements, international EIA commitments will impact the scoping and content of EIA processes by requiring states to include consideration of substantive international environmental issues that they may not have otherwise considered. For example, international EIA commitments require the geographical extension of EIA beyond the state, as well as the assessment of impacts on issues of common concern, such as biological diversity and climate change. In relation to the latter, the international obligations may operate without the involvement of other states or international organizations, but these obligations require states within their domestic

[26] See, for example, Christopher Wood, *Environmental Impact Assessment: A Comparative Review* (2nd edn, Harlow: Prentice Hall, 2003) at 139, noting consistent practice of considering alternatives among the seven EIA systems examined.

[27] See, for example, *Calvert Cliffs' Co-ordinating Committee Inc.* v. *United States Atomic Energy Commission*, 449 F 2d 1109 at 1128 (DC Cir. 1971).

[28] International Law Commission, "Draft Articles on Prevention of Transboundary Harm from Hazardous Activities" in *Report of the International Law Commission, Fifty-Third Session*, UN GAOR, 56th Sess., Supp. No. 10, UN Doc. A/56/10 (2001) 370, Art. 10.

decision-making processes to consider issues of international concern. The inclusive definition of impact under the Espoo Convention and the Antarctic Protocol, which include consideration of effects on human health, landscape, historical monuments, cultural heritage or socio-economic conditions resulting from physical impacts, may also enlarge the scope of EIAs undertaken.[29]

A further omission from the required scope of transboundary EIA under the Espoo Convention is any mention of the assessment of the cumulative impacts of proposed activities. Cumulative effects assessment requires the project proponent to consider not only the impacts from their project by itself, but also how the effects of the project, when combined with the effects from other projects, will impact the environment.[30] The failure to include cumulative impacts is a deviation from the description of the minimum contents of an EIA contained in the UNEP EIA Goals and Principles, which included a provision requiring an "assessment of the likely or potential environmental impacts of the proposed activity and alternatives, including the direct, indirect, cumulative, short-term and long-term effects."[31] This is also a deviation from established domestic rules respecting EIA, many of which require proponents to assess cumulative impacts.[32] The Antarctic Protocol explicitly requires the assessment of cumulative impacts, pointing again to the more advanced state of Antarctic EIA.

5.4 Notification and consultation

Unlike the contents of an EIA report where the requirements are similar in both domestic and international settings, notification and consultation at the international level have required a more extensive set of rules owing to the introduction of a new set of actors to the EIA process. Under the Espoo Convention, when the obligation to notify is triggered, the state of origin is required to notify "any Party which it considers

[29] Espoo Convention, Art. 1; Protocol on Environmental Protection to the Antarctic Treaty, s. 3(1).

[30] See Alan Gilpin, *Environmental Impact Assessment: Cutting Edge for the Twenty-First Century* (New York: Cambridge University Press, 1995) at 31.

[31] UNEP Goals and Principles of Environmental Impact Assessment, UNEP Res. GC14/25, 14th Sess. (1987), endorsed by GA Res. 42/184, UN GAOR, 42nd Sess., UN Doc. A/Res/42/184 (1987), Principle 4(d).

[32] See, for example, Canadian Environmental Assessment Act, SC 1997, c. 37, s. 16(1); CEQ, *Considering Cumulative Impacts Under the National Environmental Policy Act* (Washington DC: CEQ, 1997).

may be an affected Party as early as possible and no later than when informing its own public about that proposed activity."[33] In order to overcome any difficulties that source states may face in identifying the appropriate agency to notify, the Espoo Convention requires that each party provide designated points of contact.[34] To further regularize the notification process, the Meeting of the Parties adopted a standard format for transmitting notification.[35] The notification itself must contain certain prescribed information relating to the proposed activity and its potential impacts. The Espoo Convention also addresses the difficulty that a source state may have in receiving adequate information about the affected environment beyond its own borders by placing an obligation on the affected state to furnish "reasonably obtainable information" at the request of the party of origin.[36] The notification procedures, while operating principally on a state-to-state level, also require that the public of the affected party be informed of the proposed activities and be provided with an opportunity to comment on or object to the proposal.[37] The structure of the notification requirement is influenced by both the principle of nondiscrimination and the harm principle. For example, the affected state and their public are afforded rights of notification equal to those given to the public of the party of origin.[38] However, since the Espoo Convention provides for a minimum level of public involvement, a state of origin cannot avoid public scrutiny in an affected state by denying rights of participation to members of its own public. In this regard, the Espoo Convention goes beyond the nondiscrimination principle and reflects the requirements of the duty to cooperate. The reciprocal nature of the duty to exchange information is also reflective of the duty to cooperate.

The obligation to notify affected states is coupled with a duty on the source state to consult with the affected state.[39] The duty to consult arises after the completion of EIA documentation, which is required to be distributed to affected states and members of the public of affected states. Since the source state is not required to consult affected states prior to the completion of the EIA, there is no obligation under the Espoo

[33] Espoo Convention, Art. 3.

[34] As required by Decision 1/3 of the Meeting of the Parties to the Espoo Convention, *Report of the First Meeting of the Parties*, November 10, 1998, UN Doc. ECE/MP.EIA/2, UNECE, www.unece.org/env/eia/eia.htm.

[35] Decision 1/4 of the Meeting of the Parties to the Espoo Convention, ibid.

[36] Espoo Convention, Art. 3(6). [37] Ibid., Art. 3(8).

[38] Ibid., Arts. 2(6) and 3. [39] Ibid., Art. 5.

Convention for the source state to provide opportunities for affected state participation during the scoping or report preparation stages of the EIA. The importance of providing for consultation during the scoping process is recognized as being an integral part of that process.[40] Effective consultation with potentially affected parties can focus the EIA process on the issues of principal concern, can assist in identifying an appropriate range of alternatives, and may identify additional sources of environmental information.[41] This latter aspect of scoping is, for example, emphasized in the Arctic EIA Guidelines, where it is noted that early involvement by indigenous and other communities allows those conducting EIAs to draw on the specialized knowledge these groups have of the Arctic environment.[42] Interestingly, the obligation to consult with the actual public of an affected state, which is formulated on the basis of nondiscrimination, may be stronger under the Espoo Convention than the duty to consult affected states themselves under Article 5. Under Article 2(6), source states are required to ensure that the public of an affected state is provided opportunities of participation equivalent to those afforded to the public of the source state. As a result, where the source state is required, or decides on its own volition, to consult its own public during the scoping phase, that right of participation must be extended to the public of the affected state. Nondiscrimination in this context has the effect of raising the minimal requirements.[43]

One innovation associated with the requirements of notification and consultation in a transboundary context is the use of geographic factors to trigger notification. Under the US–Canada Air Quality Agreement, which contains an unelaborated EIA obligation and a separate obligation to notify and consult,[44] each party is required to provide notification of new sources of air pollution located within 100 kilometers of the US–Canada border.[45] Sources are identified by reference to quantified

[40] Barry Sadler, *Environmental Assessment in a Changing World: Final Report of the International Study of the Effectiveness of Environmental Assessment* (Ottawa: Canadian Environmental Assessment Agency, 1996) at para. 5.2.

[41] Ibid. [42] Arctic EIA Guidelines, p. 15.

[43] Discussed in John Knox, "The Myth and Reality of Transboundary Environmental Impact Assessment" (2002) 96 AJIL 291 at 314.

[44] Agreement between the United States and Canada on Air Quality (1991) Can TS No. 3, in force March 13, 1991, reprinted 30 ILM 676 (1991), Art. V(1) and (3), respectively.

[45] The 100 km notification zone matches the proposed notification zone set out in the draft transboundary EIA agreement prepared by the NACEC, showing a degree of

emission limits.[46] This system has led to a large number of notifications between the parties,[47] which in turn have resulted in transboundary consultations. The results of an EIA may be incorporated within the notification and consultation processes, but whether they are depends upon the particular regulatory framework into which the planned activity falls.

Outside the context of transboundary harm, the question of which state to notify in the event of potential harm to areas beyond the territorial jurisdiction of any one state is complicated by the collective nature of environmental rights in commons areas. The response to this difficulty has been the use of international institutions to disseminate information relating to EIAs and to coordinate the involvement of other states. The most advanced system of this nature is found in the Antarctic Protocol where the Committee for Environmental Protection and the Antarctic Treaty Consultative Meeting both play a role in reviewing and disseminating Comprehensive Environmental Evaluations (CEEs). Parties are required to circulate drafts of CEEs to all parties and to the Committee.[48] A final decision in relation to the activity subject to assessment cannot be taken until the Antarctic Treaty Consultative Meeting has had an opportunity to consider the draft.[49] The draft CEE is also required to be made "publicly available." The current practice is for material to be made available on the Antarctic Treaty Secretariat website.[50] There is, of course, no affected public *per se*, and in that regard there are no provisions allowing for formal non-state participation in the EIA review process by the Committee for Environmental Protection or the Antarctic Treaty Consultative Meeting.

The obligation to notify affected states under UNCLOS requires states to communicate a report of the results of an assessment in the manner provided in Article 205. Article 205 requires states to "publish" these reports or provide the reports to "the competent international organizations," that in turn are required to make the reports available to all states.[51] There is no indication as to what is meant by "publish" in this

commensurability between the proposed NACEC EIA process and the transboundary air quality regime between the US and Canada.

[46] Discussed in the *US–Canada Air Quality Agreement 2002 Progress Report* prepared by the bilateral Air Quality Committee, www.ec.gc.ca/pdb/can_us/qual/2002/index_e.html.

[47] The notifications are available at www.ec.gc.ca/pdb/can_us/canus_applic_e.cfm (for Canadian) and at www.epa.gov/ttn/gei/uscadata.html (for the US). The notification tables indicate in excess of seventy-five notifications between the parties.

[48] Protocol on Environmental Protection to the Antarctic Treaty, Annex I, Art. 3(3).

[49] Ibid., Art. 3(4). [50] See www.ats.aq. [51] UNCLOS, Art. 205.

context, although earlier drafts of Article 205 made reference to the term "disseminate," a term often used in this context in the regional seas conventions.[52] The alternative means of communicating the results of an assessment is equally vague, with no further elaboration as to what organizations were being contemplated here. Early references to UNEP were abandoned in favor of less precise wording. The most obvious candidates for "competent international organizations" are the regional seas commissions set up under the regional seas conventions. This role is, for example, expressly given to both the Commission on the Protection of the Black Sea Against Pollution established under the Convention on the Protection of the Black Sea Against Pollution,[53] and to the Baltic Marine Environment Protection Commission under the Convention on the Protection of the Marine Environment of the Baltic Sea Area, 1992.[54] However, in the absence of an organization that is clearly identified as having competence over assessments, states are required to satisfy their obligation under Article 205 by way of publication.

What is most surprising in this context is that there is no express obligation in Articles 205 or 206 to notify those states whose marine environment is likely to be affected by a planned activity. This omission can in part be explained as arising out of an understanding that harm to the marine environment is a matter of global interest and, consequently, requires that all states have equal access to information respecting potential harms.[55] Article 205 should also be read in conjunction with the other provisions contained in Part XII, particularly the obligation to cooperate and Article 198 requiring notification to other states in "cases in which the marine environment is in imminent danger of being damaged or has been damaged by pollution." Here, the principle underlying Article 198 is that a state likely to be affected by harm arising from the pollution of the marine environment is entitled to notification, although in Article 198 the circumstances where this obligation arises are limited to cases where damage has already occurred or is imminent. In respect of planned activities, damage is unlikely to be

[52] Discussion of early drafts in Myron Nordquist, *United Nations Convention on the Law of the Sea: A Commentary* (Boston: Martinus Nijhoff, 1985), paras. 205.1–205.4.

[53] Bucharest, April 21, 1992, 32 ILM 1110 (1993), in force January 15, 1994, Art. XVII (establishing the Commission). See also Art. XV(5) (requiring the parties to communicate the results of assessments to the Commission).

[54] Helsinki, April 9, 1992, in force January 17, 2000, Art. 19 (establishing the Commission), Art. 7 (requiring notification of the Commission where an assessment is required).

[55] Nordquist, *Commentaries* at para. 205.3.

found to be imminent prior to approval. However, it would be contrary to the preventive purpose of UNCLOS (as clearly set out in Articles 192 and 194) to allow a state that undertakes an assessment that discloses that a planned activity is likely to cause substantial pollution or significant and harmful impacts to the marine environment to not notify the affected state until such time as the damage would be imminent. The better interpretation is that an obligation to notify affected states may be implied by the term "publish" in the context of Article 205. In essence, this interpretation suggests, more realistically, that, where an effect is localized and therefore not of interest to the entire community of states, the state of origin is only required to direct its efforts to those states that would reasonably seem to have an interest.[56] Such an approach is consistent with the duty to cooperate found in Article 197 and is in keeping with the regionalized approach to marine management that the UNCLOS promotes.

5.5 Public participation

The public participation requirement under the Espoo Convention should be seen as part of a continuing trend toward transnationalism in environmental law as discussed in relation to the WCED report, the Rio Declaration and the UNEP EIA Goals and Principles. The difference between the Espoo Convention and these other processes, beyond the formally binding nature of the Espoo Convention, is that the Espoo Convention does not address EIA in a purely domestic setting. It is not aimed at the reform of internal institutions *per se*, but at regulating the interactions between states. Whereas, under previous instruments, public participation was seen as an integral part of domestic EIA, thereby requiring an agency to engage its own public in environmental decision-making. Under the Espoo Convention, public participation is viewed as an integral part of transboundary EIA requiring an agency or the state itself to engage the affected public of another state.[57] To this end, the Espoo Convention operates on both a state-to-state level and a state-to-individual level. In its final decision, the state

[56] An argument along these lines was put forward by Ireland in the *MOX Plant Case*, Memorial of Ireland (Annex VII Tribunal), paras. 8.56–8.75, and by Malaysia in the *Singapore Land Reclamation Case*, where it was argued that Singapore's failure to assess the effects of a proposal to reclaim land located in the Straits of Johor and to notify Malaysia was a breach of Arts. 205 and 206.

[57] Espoo Convention, Arts. 2(6), 3(8) and 4(2).

of origin is required to take "due account" of both state-to-state consultations, as well as the comments received by the public of the affected state.[58]

In a "guidance" document adopted by the Meeting of the Parties under the Espoo Convention, the objectives of the public participation requirements are laid out.[59] As was seen with domestic EIA, the participatory nature is justified as a means toward improving the quality of environmental decision-making and more generally as a way to mitigate environmental impacts. The Meeting of the Parties also understands public participation in EIA to lead to "balanced and open" decision-making, to prevent conflicts and to "develop an understanding of final decisions."[60] These latter justifications support the political and democratic function of EIA. For example, the "Guidance on Public Participation" also explicitly notes that EIA will help promote civil society and democracy within member states.[61] The process is equally oriented toward engendering the acceptance and legitimacy of environmental decisions both at the state level and at an individual level.

The trend toward granting environmental rights directly to individuals is continued in the Convention on Access to Information, Public Participation in Decision-Making and Access to Justice in Environmental Matters (the Aarhus Convention),[62] a treaty, also negotiated under the auspices of the UNECE, setting minimum standards for access to information and public participation in environmental matters. The Aarhus Convention supplements the Espoo Convention by providing an additional set of obligations on states to notify the public of proposed activities that may have a significant impact and to provide procedures for the public to provide comments and additional information relevant to a proposed activity. The Aarhus Convention scheme is similar to that of the Espoo Convention in that it contains an annex listing activities to

[58] Ibid., Art. 6(1). The definition of "public" is the subject of an amendment that inserts the words "and, in accordance with national legislation or practice, their associations, organizations or groups," the effect of which is to make clear that non-governmental organizations and other groups can participate. Amendment to Espoo Convention, Meeting of the Parties to the Convention on Environmental Impact Assessment in a Transboundary Context, *Report of the Second Meeting*, UN Doc. ECE/MP.EIA/6, September 13, 2004, Decision II/14 (the proposed amendment is not yet in force).

[59] Guidance on Public Participation in Environmental Impact Assessment in a Transboundary Context, Meeting of the Parties to the Convention on Environmental Impact Assessment in a Transboundary Context, *Report of the Third Meeting*, UN Doc. ECE/MP.EIA/6, September 13, 2004, Decision III/8.

[60] Ibid. [61] Ibid. at para. 8.

[62] Aarhus, Denmark, June 25, 1998, 38 ILM 517, into force October 30, 2001.

which the public participation requirements apply, although the listing under Aarhus is much more extensive.[63]

The Aarhus Convention is not aimed principally at transboundary environmental issues (or EIAs for that matter), but on environmental decision-making more generally. Consequently, where activities listed under Annex I to the Aarhus Convention are proposed, the state of origin will be required to notify and extend participation rights to the public regardless of whether the proposed activity is likely to have a significant adverse transboundary impact. The Aarhus Convention does not differentiate between the public of the decision-making state and the public of the affected state. Instead, the right to participate in environmental decision-making is extended to the "public concerned," which is in turn defined in terms of those persons "affected or likely to be affected by, or having an interest in, the environmental decision-making."[64] The approach is not dissimilar to the identification of affected persons under domestic EIA systems, such as NEPA, which is made without reference to national boundaries. The Aarhus Convention includes a detailed obligation of nondiscrimination that ensures that the public will have rights of access to information, participation in environmental decision-making and access to justice in environmental matters without discrimination on the basis of citizenship, nationality or domicile.[65] But, like the Espoo Convention, the Aarhus Convention goes further than nondiscrimination by providing for minimum standards for notification and public participation. The Aarhus Convention also contains mandatory requirements for public participation during the preparation of plans and programs relating to the environment,[66] as well a requirement to "strive to promote" public participation in the preparation of regulatory instruments respecting the environment.[67]

The relationship between the Espoo Convention and the Aarhus Convention is not explicitly set out in the Aarhus Convention (the later of the two).[68] However, one of the categories of activities to which the public participation provisions in the Aarhus Convention apply is activities

[63] Ibid., Art. 6(1)(a). [64] Ibid., Art. 2(5).

[65] Ibid., Art. 3(9). [66] Ibid., Art. 7. [67] Ibid., Art. 8.

[68] Ebbeson notes that, during the negotiation of the Aarhus Convention, there was a proposed article addressing the participatory aspects of EIA, but this was eliminated: Jonas Ebbeson, "The Notion of Public Participation in International Environmental Law" (1998) 8 YBIEL 51 at 88.

subject to an EIA procedure under national legislation.[69] As a result, parties are required to fulfill all of the Aarhus requirements for any activity subject to a national EIA process regardless of whether it is otherwise enumerated in Appendix I to the Espoo Convention. The greater detail respecting notification and access to information under Aarhus fleshes out the more general requirements respecting public participation that exist under the Espoo Convention. Where both conventions apply, the effect of the Aarhus Convention is actually to lower the threshold for notification of transboundary impacts, since a member of the public is entitled to notice by virtue of the proposed activity having a likely effect[70] (as opposed to a "significant adverse transboundary impact"). The one difference being that under the Aarhus Convention the duty to notify would not extend to affected states *per se*, but only to their respective "publics." There is considerable overlap between the parties to the Aarhus Convention and Espoo Convention, but there are fewer parties to the Aarhus Convention.

The Aarhus Convention, unlike the Espoo Convention's reference to the harm principle, contains no substantive rules of international law. Its objective, set out in Article 1, is to "contribute to the protection of the right of every person of present and future generations to live in an environment adequate to his or her health and well-being." But this is clearly set out as a policy objective, not as a prescriptive principle. There is, under the Aarhus Convention, a more explicit linkage between human rights and the environment.[71] The same justifications for public participation noted in the "Guidance on Public Participation" under the Espoo Convention appear in the preamble to the Aarhus Convention, reinforcing the legitimization and democracy-enhancing role of public participation.

Public participation requirements in international EIA commitments also recognize the unique position of indigenous people and other environmentally vulnerable groups in accordance with Principle 22 of the Rio Declaration, which states:

[69] Aarhus Convention, Annex I, para. 20.

[70] The threshold is derived from the definition of "public concerned" which means "the public affected or likely to be affected by, or having an interest in, the environmental decision-making": see Aarhus Convention, Art. 2(5).

[71] In the preamble to the Aarhus Convention, the parties recognize that adequate protection of the environment is essential to basic human rights, and further asserts that "every person has the right to live in an environment adequate to his or her health and well-being."

> Indigenous people and their communities, and other local communities, have a vital role in environmental management and development because of their knowledge and traditional practices. States should recognize and duly support their identity, culture and interests and enable their effective participation in the achievement of sustainable development.[72]

The Arctic EIA Guidelines recognize the importance of traditional knowledge to the EIA process, which is viewed as a complement to established scientific methods.[73] Part of the acknowledged difficulty in incorporating traditional knowledge into EIA processes is ensuring that modern scientists recognize its methods, which may differ in many respects from established scientific methodologies. The Arctic EIA Guidelines address this by establishing a normative commitment to respect traditional knowledge and values. Neither Principle 22 nor the Arctic EIA Guidelines seeks, in a substantive way, to privilege the rights of indigenous peoples over other affected persons. However, by providing special recognition of traditional practices and knowledge, the Arctic EIA Guidelines raise a presumption that this information should be accounted in the decision-making process. The Arctic EIA Guidelines also acknowledge that the presence of remote indigenous communities presents a further challenge in conducting transboundary EIA, such as coordinating consultation with geographically remote groups. In this regard, the Guidelines note the potential role of transnational groups such as the Inuit Circumpolar Conference, the Saami Council and the Indigenous Peoples Secretariat could play in coordinating participation on a transboundary level.[74] The CBD EIA/SEA Draft Guidelines similarly recognize the unique position of indigenous communities and recommend specific policies for including vulnerable groups in EIA processes.

5.6 Final decisions

As with domestic EIA processes, there is no obligation on states to follow the recommendations contained within a completed EIA report. However, it is equally clear that international EIAs are conducted with specific environmental objectives in mind. The Espoo Convention, for

[72] United Nations Conference on Environment and Development, Rio Declaration on Environment and Development, June 14, 1992, UN Doc. A/Conf.151/5/Rev.1, reprinted in 31 ILM 874 (1992), Principle 22.

[73] Arctic EIA Guidelines at 37. [74] Ibid. at 41.

example, is clearly structured as a measure to enable states to meet their due diligence obligations pursuant to the harm principle. The form of the due diligence obligation that is implemented through the Espoo Convention, as discussed in Chapter 3, is proceduralized in the sense that Article 2 of the Espoo Convention is not intended in a formal and absolute sense to prohibit a state from engaging in activities that have significant transboundary impact. The underlying premise of the harm principle is that a determination of acceptable levels of transboundary harm is context dependent and therefore requires a state to fully investigate the environmental consequences of its proposal, as well as to carefully consider the interests of those affected.[75] in the domestic context, the non-determinative nature of EIA reports is a recognition that given the complex and unique nature of individual project decisions, the competing interests implicated by the decision are best resolved through self-regulatory processes. In the transboundary context, the same dynamic recognizes that competing sovereign interests are best resolved through good faith consultation. The harm principle does not, however, devolve into pure proceduralism, as parties are still obligated to justify their respective positions, and their good faith will be assessed, in light of the substantive principle to prevent environmental harm.

Instead of dictating a particular outcome, the Espoo Convention requires that the source state take "due account" of the EIA report, as well as the comments received both from affected states and from members of the affected states' public.[76] This obligation is operationalized by a further requirement for the source state to provide the reasons and considerations upon which the final decision was based.[77] The requirement is one of justification whereby a state that proposes a potentially harmful activity must justify their actions in light of the substantive environmental values animating the Espoo Convention.

The same structure is evident in other international EIA commitments. In the Antarctic Protocol, the state that proposes a particular activity retains control over the final decision, with the Committee for Environmental Protection or the Antarctic Treaty Consultative Meeting providing only recommendations as to whether the activity should proceed. To some degree, this is surprising because the Antarctic Protocol contains fairly explicit language requiring that activities be planned

[75] See discussion above at ch. 3.5. [76] Espoo Convention, Art. 6(1).
[77] Ibid., Art. 6(2). See also Aarhus Convention, Art. 6(9).

so as to limit adverse impacts and to avoid other specified impacts.[78] In addition, the only non-environmental objective recognized in the Antarctic Protocol is the value of the Antarctic as an area for scientific research. By and large, however, the Antarctic EIA system relies on the use of community pressure through a consultative and transparent decision-making process to ensure that decisions adhere to the substantive requirements of the Antarctic Protocol.

The Espoo Convention includes a provision for a continuing obligation of disclosure respecting additional relevant information not available at the time a decision was taken.[79] This requirement reinforces the iterative nature of the process by adding a dynamic element to the duty to exchange information. This requirement is accompanied by a further obligation to conduct consultations, if requested, on whether the final decision must be revised in light of the new information. The requirement of supplementation raises a difficult issue with respect to the finality of the EIA process. As a planning mechanism, there must be some end to the duty to gather and assess new information. The approach taken under the Espoo Convention is to impose a duty of supplementation on both the state of origin and the affected state until "work on that activity commences."[80] This obligation is further qualified by the requirement that only new information that could have "materially affected" the original decision is subject to the supplementation requirement. Both of these qualifications leave room for considerable debate as to their precise application. For example, do changes to the proposed activity itself constitute new information and when precisely does "work" on an activity commence? There is no requirement that the new information itself be subject to a supplemental EIA, as is the case under NEPA,[81] which raises the question of exactly how it is determined whether

[78] Ibid., Art. 3(2). The specified impacts include: adverse effects on climate or weather patterns; significant adverse effects on air or water quality; significant changes in the atmospheric, terrestrial, aquatic, glacial or marine environments; detrimental changes in the distribution, abundance or productivity of species or populations of species of fauna and flora; further jeopardy to endangered or threatened species; and degradation of, or substantial risk to, areas of biological, scientific, historic, aesthetic or wilderness significance.

[79] Ibid., Art. 6(3). [80] Ibid.

[81] 40 CFR § 1502.9(c). The general rule respecting supplementation in the US requires a supplemental EIA to be prepared where the information is "relevant" to the environmental concerns of the proposed activity. See *Marsh* v. *Oregon Natural Resources Council*, 490 US 360 at 374 (1988), applying a "rule of reason" to the determination of relevance.

the new information will "materially affect" the decision.[82] The Antarctic Protocol does not contain a supplementation requirement. The efforts to confine the EIA process to pre-decision activities reinforce the understanding of EIA procedures as having a planning, as opposed to a regulatory, role. However, as evidenced by the *Gabcikovo-Nagymaros Case*, there is a discernible trend toward imposing ongoing obligations on states to ensure that their activities, once constructed and operating, do not cause significant adverse transboundary impacts.

5.7 Post-project monitoring

Post-project analysis is described in the Espoo Convention as including the surveillance of the activity and the determination of any adverse transboundary impact and may be undertaken for the following objectives:

(a) Monitoring compliance with the conditions as set out in the authorization or approval of the activity and the effectiveness of mitigation measures,
(b) Review of an impact for proper management and in order to cope with uncertainties,
(c) Verification of past predictions in order to transfer experience to future activities of the same type.[83]

The regulatory nature of post-project analysis is evident in the references to monitoring compliance with conditions and proper management, both of which suggest an ongoing attempt to maintain agreed upon environmental standards. The acknowledgment that uncertainties may need to be addressed is also important as it addresses the criticism that EIA processes rely too heavily on limited predictive capabilities. Post-project analysis compensates for this limitation by allowing for new information regarding actual impacts to feed into ongoing environmental management of the project. Finally, the stated objectives indicate that monitoring can also provide a valuable feedback mechanism whereby predictive methods and proposed mitigation measures can be continually refined in light of information respecting past activities. Perhaps

[82] The requirement to disclose new information contained in Art. 6 should be distinguished from the obligation to prepare an EIA that may arise in situations where a state proposes "major changes" to an activity subject to a decision of a competent authority: see Espoo Convention, Art. 1(v).
[83] Ibid., Appendix V.

what is most remarkable about the post-project analysis requirement is the further stipulation that:

> When, as a result of post-project analysis, the Party of origin or the affected Party has reasonable grounds for concluding that there is a significant adverse transboundary impact or factors have been discovered which may result in such an impact, it shall immediately inform the other Party. The concerned Parties shall then consult on necessary measures to reduce or eliminate the impact.[84]

This provision confirms the centrality of the harm principle to the Espoo Convention and, in fact, extends the application of the harm principle beyond the planning stages of an activity by placing an obligation on states that agree to post-project analysis to notify and consult each other in respect of actual and possible significant impacts stemming from approved projects. This requirement is consistent with the position Judge Weeramantry outlined in his separate opinion to the *Gabcikovo-Nagymaros Case* respecting the obligation of continual monitoring flowing from the harm principle.[85]

The value of ongoing monitoring as part of EIA is recognized in the Antarctic Protocol, which contains mandatory requirements for monitoring impacts for activities subject to a CEE,[86] and permissive monitoring requirements for activities subject to IEE.[87] The stated rationale for monitoring is to provide a source of information to assess whether actual impacts of planned activities are consistent with the Antarctic Protocol, including information for determining whether activities need to be modified or suspended. The monitoring provision does not, however, recognize the contribution that monitoring can make toward verifying past predictions and transferring experience to future activities.[88] This is unfortunate because the need for such a process has been noted in connection with determining thresholds.[89] Monitoring under the Antarctic Protocol is not subject to the oversight of either

[84] Ibid., Art. 7(2). [85] (1997) ICJ Rep 7 at 111.
[86] Protocol on Environmental Protection to the Antarctic Treaty, Art. 5.
[87] Ibid., Art. 2(2).
[88] As suggested by the Espoo Convention, Appendix V.
[89] A report from a meeting of the parties to the Antarctic Treaty noted: "The terms 'minor' and 'transitory' are interpreted by the Treaty Parties in the implementation of Annex I and a great deal of experience in producing IEEs and CEEs has accumulated. Many IEEs and CEEs have been presented as Information Papers at ATCM meetings. However, there is at present no systematic approach to utilizing and learning from this experience." *Final Report of the Twenty-First Antarctic Treaty Consultative Meeting* (Christchurch, May 19–26, 1997), para. 138, quoted in Rothwell, "Polar Environmental Protection" at 600.

the Committee for Environmental Protection or the Antarctic Treaty Consultative Meeting, although the Antarctic Protocol does provide for "inspections" to ensure compliance, which have included consideration of monitoring programs.[90] Post-project monitoring is also recognized in the CBD EIA/SEA Draft Guidelines[91] and in the Arctic EIA Guidelines,[92] both of which expressly recognize the limitations of a purely predictive approach to EIA. Ongoing monitoring was included as part of the settlement of the *Singapore Land Reclamation Case* and was recommended by the Bystroe Navigation Channel Inquiry Commission. The move to enhanced monitoring of environmental impacts as part of EIA is consistent with the same trend in domestic EIA processes and implements the broader requirements for continuous monitoring in international law. Where projects are approved on the basis that the project will achieve quantified environmental standards, the linking of monitoring to EIA has the benefit of providing benchmarks against which environmental performance can be measured.

5.8 Strategic environmental assessment

Article 2(7) of the Espoo Convention directs that EIAs be undertaken as a minimum at the project level, but also encourages parties to apply EIA to "policies, plans and programmes." The non-obligatory nature of the requirement to undertake assessments beyond the project level reflects the uncertain status of strategic-level assessments in domestic EIA legislation at the time that the Espoo Convention was negotiated. Since that time, strategic environmental assessment (SEA) has emerged as an important element in domestic environmental decision-making processes, particularly in Europe where a European Directive on SEA was promulgated in 2001.[93] The increasing acceptance of SEA is also reflected in the Aarhus Convention, which extends the public participation requirements to plans and programs,[94] World Bank environmental

[90] Protocol on Environmental Protection to the Antarctic Treaty, Art. 14.

[91] Paras. 32 and 33. [92] Arctic EIA Guidelines at 27–29.

[93] "Assessment of the Effects of Certain Plans and Programmes on the Environment," EC, Council Directive 01/42, OJ 2001 L197/30.

[94] For a discussion on the relationship between the SEA Protocol, the EC SEA Directive and the Aarhus Convention, see Simon Marsden, "SEA and International Law: An Analysis of the Effectiveness of the SEA Protocol to the Espoo Convention, and of the Influence of the SEA Directive and Aarhus Convention on Its Development" (2002) 1 ELNI Rev. 1.

policies[95] and the CBD EIA/SEA Draft Guidelines.[96] More broadly, the embrace of SEA has been influenced by the emphasis on integration in environmental decision-making coming out of the WCED report and the UNCED[97] – a linkage that is made explicit in Principle 4 of the Rio Declaration.[98]

SEA responds to the criticism that project-based EIA tends to occur after broader social and economic policy decisions have been made. The potential consequence of the separation of environmental assessment from the broader policy setting is that the environmental consequences of plans and programs are less likely to be subject to rigorous analysis. In the event that these broader issues are raised at the project level, the existence of prior policy decisions may constrain the ability to examine a full range of alternatives. The response to these criticisms has been to emphasize the need for greater integration of EIA processes with top-level decision-making.[99] Here, the idea is to move away from viewing EIA as a technical exercise, where the environmental inputs are one consideration among many, but do not pervade the decision-making process, toward a decision-making culture where environmental considerations are accounted for throughout the process.[100] By requiring an environmental assessment of these more abstracted policy documents, SEA seeks to integrate environmental considerations with economic and social policy. To the extent that SEA succeeds in having environmental values reflected in planning and programmatic decisions, subsequent project-level EIAs are less likely to encounter marginalization because they are at odds with a previously determined policy direction. In this regard, SEA and EIA are most effective when the processes are themselves vertically integrated through tiered assessment requirements.[101] This is most successfully done where approvals processes create explicit linkages

[95] OP 4.01, para. 7, recognizing regional and sectoral plans. See also K. Ahmed, J. Mercier and R. Verheem, "Strategic Environmental Assessment – Concept and Practice" (2005) Environment Strategy Note No. 14.

[96] Para. 1(b).

[97] For a discussion on the role of integration in international environmental law, see John Dernbach, "Achieving Sustainable Development: The Centrality and Multiple Facets of Integrated Decisionmaking" (2003) 10 Indiana J. Global Legal Stud. 247.

[98] Rio Declaration, Principle 4, stating: "In order to achieve sustainable development, environmental protection shall constitute an integral part of the development process and cannot be considered in isolation from it."

[99] US, CEQ, *The National Environmental Policy Act: A Study of Its Effectiveness after Twenty-Five Years*, January 1997, at 12–13, http://ceq.eh.doe.gov/nepa/nepa25fn.pdf.

[100] Ibid. at 11. See also Sadler, "International EA Study" at § 5.1.1.

[101] Sadler, ibid. at § 6.4.3.

between programmatic and project-level assessments.[102] SEA may also assist in addressing cumulative impacts by providing a framework for conducting project EIAs that contribute to a common environmental problem.

In 2003, the parties to the Espoo Convention adopted a protocol on SEA.[103] However, unlike the Espoo Convention, the SEA Protocol is not confined to transboundary impacts. Instead, the SEA Protocol requires that parties carry out SEAs for identified plans and programs that are likely to have significant environmental, including health, effects, regardless of where those impacts are located.[104] More particularly, the SEA Protocol requires an SEA to be carried out for plans and programs that are prepared in identified sectors and which "set the framework for future development consent" for projects listed in the SEA Protocol.[105] Determining whether a plan or program sets the framework for future development is liable to be controversial given the ambiguity of that phrase. Presumably, the intent of including this further qualification was to capture those plans and programs that have the effect of narrowing the discretion of decision-makers to determine the scope of project EIAs. There is also provision for a case-by-case assessment of the need for SEA based on likelihood of environmental effects for unlisted projects,[106] and a set of criteria for determining significance.[107]

The SEA Protocol provides for the preparation of an environmental report that includes identifying "reasonable alternatives" and includes a more detailed listing of requirements that should be included in such a report, where reasonable.[108] Like the Espoo Convention, public participation is an integral part of the SEA process – a requirement that links the SEA Protocol to the requirements of the Aarhus Convention. Significantly, nongovernmental organizations are expressly identified as part of the "public."[109] The SEA Protocol does not define the nature of public participation, except to provide that the public shall have an opportunity to express its opinion on the plan and the environmental report in a reasonable timeframe. There is also a provision for transboundary consultation. Notification is given at the determination of the state of

[102] Examples of such explicit linkages are found in NEPA, the New Zealand Resource Management Act, and in Dutch energy and waste management plans. Discussed in ibid.

[103] Protocol on Strategic Environmental Assessment to the Convention on Environmental Impact Assessment in a Transboundary Context, adopted May 21, 2003, not in force, UNECE, www.unece.org/env/eia/sea_protocol.htm ("SEA Protocol").

[104] Ibid., Art. 4(1). [105] Ibid., Art. 4(2). [106] Ibid., Art. 5(1). [107] Ibid., Annex III.

[108] Ibid., Art. 7(2) and Annex IV. [109] Ibid., Art. 8(3).

origin where it considers that the implementation of a plan or program is likely to have a significant transboundary impact.[110] Alternatively, a state that is likely to be significantly affected may request notification, although they would need to demonstrate the plan or program's significant effect. Unlike the Espoo Convention, there is no inquiry procedure to which states can turn when they are unable to agree upon whether notification is required. Where notification does occur, there is a corollary obligation for parties to enter into consultation at the affected party's request and to agree to measures allowing for participation by the public of the affected state.[111]

The state of origin is expressly required to take "due account" of the environmental report,[112] and explain how it has accounted for the comments received and to provide reasons for its decisions "in the light of the reasonable alternatives considered."[113] The wording of this requirement is similar to Article 6 of the Espoo Convention which also addresses the factors that must be accounted for in the final decision. In several respects, the SEA Protocol goes beyond the Espoo Convention. The requirement to look at alternatives and to specifically justify the decision in light of those alternatives exceeds the qualified obligation to look at alternatives under the Espoo Convention.[114] The more explicit reference to account for the prevention, reduction or mitigation of adverse effects found in the SEA Protocol, while certainly an implicit part of the final decision under the Espoo Convention, emphasizes the centrality of these considerations and places the objective of harm prevention at the forefront of the SEA Protocol. Lastly, the requirement for monitoring under the SEA Protocol is mandatory, with the provision recognizing that the purpose of monitoring is both to identify unforeseen adverse effects and to be able to take remedial action.[115] The inclusion of mandatory monitoring continues the trend in domestic EIA toward utilizing environmental assessment processes as adaptive management tools, and not simply as *ex ante* planning measures.

Because the SEA Protocol is directed at environmental decision-making generally, as opposed to transboundary environmental harm alone, the SEA Protocol impinges to a much greater degree on traditional areas of state sovereignty. Here, the focus of the SEA Protocol is to

[110] Ibid., Art. 10(1). [111] Ibid., Arts. 10(3) and (4).
[112] Ibid., Art. 11(1). [113] Ibid., Art. 11(2).
[114] Recall that, in Appendix II to the Espoo Convention, which lists the required information for inclusion in the EIA document, reasonable alternatives are only required where appropriate: ibid., Appendix II.
[115] SEA Protocol, Art. 12.

create minimum standards for internal decision-making processes. Interestingly, the SEA Protocol is premised on the basis that each state shall have an internal environmental assessment system, which is a requirement under EC legislation, but not a requirement in international law. The justification for imposing internal standards on domestic decision-making processes is rooted firmly in the transnationalism of sustainable development, that is, a recognition that environmental degradation and consequent human health impacts are of international concern regardless of where they occur. In this regard, the preamble references Principles 4 (integration) and 10 (public participation), not the harm principle (Principle 2). The principle of nondiscrimination is also reflected in the SEA Protocol as it relates to the exercise of rights by the public.[116] As with the Espoo Convention, the SEA Protocol is open to all UN members to sign (not just UNECE members). At present, all of the signatories are European countries.

5.9 Implementation

International EIA commitments are most likely to be implemented through the incorporation of international requirements directly into national EIA procedures.[117] In relation to transboundary impacts, the approach has been to extend national EIA procedures to include transboundary impacts, as opposed to the creation of a separate transboundary process. The result is that transboundary EIA requirements can be implemented without significant changes to domestic policy, so long as the domestic system meets the minimum content requirements under international commitments, which are specified for the Espoo Convention only. A review of implementation of the Espoo Convention undertaken by the parties in 2002 showed that most parties have legislation in place implementing their requirements under the Convention and that application of the Convention is increasing.[118] While the review pointed to a number of shortcomings, these weaknesses tended to be

[116] Ibid., Art. 3(7).

[117] For example, the Espoo Convention defines "environmental impact assessment" as a "national procedure": Espoo Convention, Art. 1(vi).

[118] The review was authorized by the Meeting of the Parties at its second meeting and was undertaken by a task force set up by the parties: see Review of Convention, Meeting of the Parties to the Convention on Environmental Impact Assessment in a Transboundary Context, *Report of the Second Meeting*, UN Doc. ECE/MP.EIA/6, September 13, 2004, Decision II/10. The review itself is contained in UNECE, *Convention of Environmental Impact Assessment in a Transboundary Context: Review of Implementation*, www.unece.org/env/eia/documents/Review%of%Implementation%2003.pdf.

of a technical nature, relating to matters such as the adequacy of the contents of notification, inaccuracy in the points of contact and difficulties in translation of EIA documents.[119] An earlier implementation review of the Espoo Convention in the Nordic countries raised particular concerns regarding the adequacy of public participation in transboundary EIA processes and with the exact nature of the consultation that is contemplated under the Espoo Convention.[120]

The Espoo Convention does not create any multilateral institutional structure for the purpose of carrying out EIAs or reviewing EIA documents, although there are provisions for parties to conclude further bilateral or multilateral agreements in order to give further detail to EIA arrangements between states, which could include provisions on joint EIA or joint monitoring.[121] The dispute settlement provisions are non-binding and have not been resorted to.[122] The parties have, however, adopted a compliance monitoring mechanism.[123] Described as a "non-adversarial and assistance-oriented" procedure, the compliance mechanism allows parties to bring issues of non-compliance before an Implementation Committee, which can make recommendations respecting general compliance measures and assistance to the non-complying party. The mechanism should add to the treaty's normative strength by providing a public process for the evaluation and resolution of claims of non-compliance. There has been some limited discussion on the possibility of non-state actor involvement in the non-compliance process, but at present the development of procedures has focused on the parties themselves.[124]

Implementation of EIA commitments under the Antarctic Protocol is also conducted pursuant to national procedures, but these are likely to require greater adjustment since the screening process, which uses different threshold terminology and divides the EIA process into three different levels, is less likely to be reflected in existing domestic EIA

[119] Review of Implementation, ibid. at 24.

[120] Arne Tesli and Stig Roar Husby, "EIA in a Transboundary Context: Principles and Challenges for a Co-ordinated Nordic Application of the Espoo Convention" (1999) 19 Environmental Impact Assessment Review 57 at 80–83.

[121] Espoo Convention, Art. 8 and Appendix VI.

[122] Ibid., Art. 15.

[123] Review of Compliance, Meeting of the Parties to the Convention on Environmental Impact Assessment in a Transboundary Context, *Report of the Third Meeting*, UN Doc. ECE/MP.EIA/6, September 13, 2004, Decision III/2.

[124] See *Report of the Fifth Meeting of the Implementation Committee*, Meeting of the Parties to the Convention on Environmental Impact Assessment in a Transboundary Context, Working Group on Environmental Impact Assessment, UN Doc. ECE/MP.EIA/WG.1/2004/4.

requirements. In addition, the application and scope of the EIA requirements may require many states to assess activities not normally subject to domestic EIA. For example, the application of the EIA processes to private tour operators will require states to ensure that Antarctic tour operators conducting business from those jurisdictions are subject to either the domestic EIA process or a similar process in order to ensure compliance with the Antarctic Protocol requirements. The result has been that some countries have created separate Antarctic EIA processes outside the framework of their domestic system.[125] There is no formal compliance mechanism under the Antarctic Protocol, but the oversight by the Committee for Environmental Protection and the Antarctic Treaty Consultative Meeting through the review of CEEs and lists of IEEs, as well as through official inspections, ensure that EIA activities are subject to scrutiny by the contracting parties.

The implementation of EIA commitments relating to issues of common concern requires a slightly different approach. Here, the international requirements do not seek to extend domestic EIA geographically, but rather seek to ensure that domestic EIA accounts for issues of common concern. This may require amendment to ensure the full range of environmental impacts, such as those affecting climate or biological diversity, are included in the scope of assessments. However, these requirements are more likely to be implemented in the actual conduct of assessments themselves. Sets of adaptation rules, like the CBD EIA/SEA Draft Guidelines and the Arctic EIA Guidelines, can be particularly helpful in this regard because they are oriented more toward reforming EIA practice, as opposed to creating legislative rules regarding minimum requirements.

5.10 Conclusion

5.10.1 *Determinants of international EIA commitments*

Looking at the development of EIA commitments in international environmental governance structures as a whole, some general conclusions

[125] In Canada, the requirements are implemented in An Act Respecting the Protection of the Antarctic Environment, SC 2003, c. 20. Here, activities subject to the Antarctic Protocol that are under Canadian jurisdiction must receive a federal permit, which in turn is tied to the undertaking of an EIA. The US requirements are contained in the Antarctic Conservation Act of 1978, 16 USC §§ 2401 *et seq*. Governmental activities are subject to National Science Foundation regulations for assessing impacts of activities in the Antarctic: 45 CFR 641.10–641.22. Non-governmental activities are subject to EPA oversight and special regulations: "Environmental Impact Assessment of Nongovernmental Activities in the Antarctic," 40 CFR Part 8.

can be drawn with respect to the conditions that contribute to the formation of international EIA commitments. In particular, the existence and characteristics of a domestic EIA system, the nature of the norms within specific regimes and the nature of the impact itself may each influence the kinds of EIA commitments that states are willing to accept.

With the inclusion of EIA commitments in the UNCLOS, regional seas agreements and the CBD, there appears to be broad-based support for the use of EIAs in an international context. The globalization of EIA commitments at the international level is consistent with the same trend at the domestic level, as evidenced by the growing numbers of domestic EIA systems, although the degree to which states are willing to accept EIA commitments still has a strong regional bias. For example, the multilateral environmental agreements with near global membership that contain EIA commitments couch those commitments in broad and often qualified language. While those treaties that provide more detailed EIA requirements, such as the Espoo Convention, the Arctic EIA Guidelines and the Antarctic Protocol have more limited memberships, which tend to include states with more demanding EIA requirements domestically. States which have preexisting EIA systems into which the international commitments can be integrated will be more inclined to accept EIA commitments at the international level, so long as the international commitments do not require significant changes in the domestic regime.

Many of the qualifications regarding EIA commitments in regime-specific treaties condition the commitment on the practicability of undertaking assessments within the national system. Consequently, those states that do not have well-developed EIA systems by which to implement the requirement are still willing to agree to EIA commitments on the basis that the obligation will be interpreted in light of that state's capabilities. One way of reading the EIA commitments in treaties such as the UNCLOS, the CBD and the UNFCCC is that the commitment requires only those states which have the capacity to carry out EIAs, as demonstrated by a functioning domestic system, to assess the particular impacts addressed under the treaty. This approach would be consistent with the principle of common but differentiated responsibilities that is integral to the post-Rio normative landscape.[126] It also suggests that the prospects for strengthened international EIA commitments are

[126] For a general discussion of common but differentiated responsibilities, see Philippe Cullet, "Differential Treatment in International Law: Towards a New Paradigm of Interstate Relations" (1999) 10 EJIL 549; and Christopher Stone, "Common But Differentiated Responsibilities in International Law" (2004) 98 AJIL 276.

improving given that domestic EIA capabilities are themselves increasing, both regionally and globally. While EIA capacity is a factor that contributes to the formation and nature of international EIA commitments, it cannot be separated from international commitments (as an independent variable), since the presence of international EIA commitments includes obligations to share research and, in some cases, to provide financial assistance to improve developing state capabilities.[127]

The second factor that bears on the formation of international EIA commitments relates to the normative structure of the regime itself. Where the regime consists of open-textured principles, as opposed to more determinative standards, EIA commitments are more likely to be present. As discussed in connection with domestic EIA, EIA, as a form of, or approach to, regulation is very different from command-and-control-type regulation. The latter identifies a particular outcome, usually in the form of a quantified standard, and then requires adherence to the standard. EIA identifies only broad objectives, but leaves the determination of specific outcomes to the EIA process itself. This same distinction is valid in international governance structures. As discussed above, many atmospheric pollution regimes identify particular emission limits, such as the greenhouse gas emission reductions under the Kyoto Protocol, and require that states comply with those specific limitations.[128] Often, however, international agreements cannot achieve the kind of consensus required to identify specific standards and must instead turn to more abstract principles. The harm principle itself is an example of this tendency. In order to give effect to these principles, they must be applied in a particular context. There is, therefore, a demand for mechanisms, such as EIA, which can contextualize these principles. Looking at the types of agreements and other instruments that contain EIA commitments, the approach to regulation tends to be more abstracted and reliant upon states applying principles to specific known contexts. The dynamic in

[127] E.g. Espoo Convention, Art. 9; CBD, Art. 17; United Nations Framework Convention on Climate Change, New York, May 9, 1992, 31 ILM 851 (1992), in force March 21, 1994, Art. 6. Sources of financial assistance include development banks, and possibly the Global Environmental Facility, which has contributed to EIA training programs through the United Nations Development Programme, discussed in Hussein Abaza, Ron Bisset and Barry Sadler, *Environmental Impact Assessment and Strategic Environmental Assessment: Towards an Integrated Approach* (Nairobi: UNEP, 2004), ch. 2 at 15 *et seq.*

[128] Other examples of regimes that include specific standards and do not include EIA requirements are found principally in the atmospheric pollution area, such as the Convention on Long Range Transboundary Air Pollution and the Convention on the Protection of the Ozone Layer.

specific international regimes is similar to that of NEPA, in that policies are articulated and are intended to have normative force. However, in order to operationalize the principles, there is a need for an "action forcing" mechanism.

There exist other mechanisms by which abstract principles can be applied to specific contexts. Adjudication processes often require decision-makers to apply abstract principles, such as equity or reasonableness, to specific circumstances. Again, the harm principle provides an example, as it has certainly formed the basis of interstate claims that can be litigated. But, as states are generally reluctant to concede decision-making authority under conditions of uncertainty,[129] EIA has a comparative advantage over adjudication because the source state retains ultimate control over the decision-making process. The Antarctic Protocol presents the best example of the use of EIA to operationalize environmental goals. The Antarctic Protocol contains no quantified standards, but it has clear environmental objectives. The majority of the environmental concerns arise from the potential impacts from activities undertaken in the Antarctic or its environs, and are addressed principally through the imposition of detailed EIA requirements, without formally conceding authority to other states or to the treaty institutions. Informally, of course, the Antarctic environmental regime depends upon community pressure through the circulation and review of CEEs to other parties in order to bring about decisions that respect the regime's environmental objectives.

Thirdly, the acceptability of international EIA commitments may also be a function of the nature of the impacts sought to be addressed. Transboundary impacts are not on a global scale but are more localized in their effects. As such, there is little motivation for countries that are physically remote from one another to conclude an agreement with one another regarding the rules for an interaction (over transboundary environmental harm) that is unlikely to occur.[130] The demand for international agreements respecting EIA arises where there is a possibility that the activities of one country impact on the rights of another. In the case of the Espoo Convention, the member countries are proximate to one another and are often faced with transboundary impacts arising from proposed activities. In this regard, EIA is a natural fit to address the

[129] See Richard Bilder, "The Settlement of Disputes in the Field of the International Law of the Environment" (1982) 144 Rec. des Cours 139 at 225.

[130] See John Knox, "Assessing the Candidates for a Global Treaty on Transboundary Environmental Impact Assessment" (2003) 12 NYU Envt'l LJ 153 at 157.

environmental issues that arise in the Antarctic, even though the impacts themselves are not of a transboundary nature, because each state's activities will have potential impact on the rights of the other member states. The dynamic is one of a potential clash between sovereign rights.

To some degree this also explains why EIA obligations in treaties that address global issues such as UNCLOS, the CBD and the UNFCCC do not contain elaborated EIA obligations. In these regimes, the impacts contemplated tend not to interfere directly with the sovereign rights of any one state, but rather impact on the global commons or on issues of common concern. In these cases, the obligations of notification and consultation are not triggered, obviating the need for detailed provisions respecting notification and consultation. Under the UNCLOS, the impacts on the marine environment could also have direct impacts on other states, but it is anticipated that the details of interactions arising from more localized impacts would be addressed under regional seas arrangements, and may also be addressed by regional EIA agreements such as the Espoo Convention or the EC Directive.[131]

These factors suggest that there will likely be little future demand for a global transboundary EIA treaty, notwithstanding the overtures of the UNECE to open up the Espoo Convention to global membership. The desirability of a global EIA treaty has been commented on by a number of scholars, who have evaluated the possible basis upon which such a treaty could be formed.[132] The current diversity of domestic EIA systems provides an initial obstacle to a global approach to EIA. This is not to foreclose the possibility that a greater consensus of approach may arise regarding EIA processes. Indeed, there are many examples of international institutions actively promoting EIA models and enhancing EIA capacity in developing countries.[133] However, it must be understood that, because the same EIA procedures are intended to operate on both a domestic and a transnational level, a global approach to EIA necessarily

131 There remains an issue with respect to how these sets of rules interact with one another, with a possibility for competing jurisdictions over EIA. These jurisdictional issues have been integral to the ongoing MOX plant litigation: see Robin Churchill and Joanne Scott, "The MOX Plant Litigation: The First Half-Life" (2004) 53 ICLQ 643.

132 See Knox, "Assessing the Candidates"; and Kevin Gray, "International Environmental Impact Assessment: Potential for a Multilateral Environmental Agreement" (2000) 11 Colo. J. Int'l Envt'l L. & Pol'y 83.

133 The two most prominent international institutions in this regard are UNEP and the World Bank, both discussed above at ch. 4.3.

involves domestic institutional reform. Moreover, implementation of EIA within domestic systems requires sensitivity to political and social conditions that militate in favor of EIA reform from within.

The transnationalism of EIA processes, which is to say that a single domestic procedure regulates domestic, transboundary and global impacts, also explains why states are unwilling to agree to international EIA commitments that exceed the requirements of their existing domestic EIA systems. The difficulty is that, because changes initiated at the international level are integrated into the domestic system, their impact extends to a range of domestic actors as well. For example, agreeing to assess policies, plans and programs (strategic environmental assessment) for transboundary impacts would likely require the introduction of SEA across the domestic regime, which carries its own costs.[134] The one regime that does impose EIA requirements that in many instances exceed domestic requirements, the Antarctic Protocol, is the one set of EIA requirements that can be implemented outside the state's domestic EIA system. The separability of Antarctic EIA system from domestic EIA provides greater freedom for the member states to agree to more stringent EIA requirements, such as a different threshold condition and mandatory post-project analysis.

The need for international EIA commitments to be sensitive to diverse domestic EIA requirements points to the importance of "adaptation rules" of EIA.[135] Adaptation rules include the Arctic EIA Guidelines, the Antarctic EIA Guidelines and the CBD EIA/SEA Draft Guidelines. Unlike EIA commitments that are intended to provide states with defined requirements for EIA procedures, adaptation rules are oriented toward the actual conduct of EIAs in relation to a specific context. As discussed in relation to the Arctic EIA Guidelines, adaptation rules elaborate on how the various EIA steps, for example screening, scoping and participation, may be carried out to achieve the particular objectives of the broader regime. So, in the Arctic context, there is an emphasis on issues that are unique to that regime, such as how to involve remote indigenous populations in the EIA process, the integration of traditional knowledge into EIA and the implications of the particular fragilities of the Arctic environment. Likewise, the CBD EIA/SEA Draft Guidelines set out strategies for adapting EIA processes to account for issues that are unique to

[134] The smaller number of UNECE members that have ratified the SEA Protocol may be explained in part by the onerous domestic requirements imposed by the SEA Protocol, many of which were included in the EC SEA Directive.

[135] This term is taken from Koivurova, *EIA in the Arctic* at 172.

the biodiversity regime. For example, the guidelines address the measurement of "significance" in the context of biodiversity and seek to ensure that assessments consider impacts at the different levels of biodiversity (for example, genetic, species, ecosystem).

5.10.2 *Structure of EIA commitments*

Looking at international EIA commitments, it is possible to discern how the different strands of normative influence identified in Part II, namely, domestic EIA, the principle of nondiscrimination, the harm principle coupled with the duty to cooperate, and sustainable development norms have impacted the structure of EIA commitments in international law. The view presented here is that these principles have each clearly influenced the development of EIA commitments and, as a basis for structuring international EIA commitments, these influences co-exist comfortably. The broad acceptance of EIA commitments generally and the more limited acceptance of elaborated EIA commitments suggests a distinction between different levels upon which international EIA operates, each of which give rise to their own structural characteristics. The levels correspond to the nature of the broader duties owed to other states in respect of environmental harm and can be described as transboundary impacts, impacts to the global commons and impacts of common concern.

On the transboundary level, and here I refer to impacts which arise from activities under the jurisdiction of one state but which are felt in another, the structure of EIA processes is inextricably tied up with the harm principle and notification and consultation. Here, the procedural specificity of EIA compensates for the lack of, or substitutes for, substantive specificity. Because EIAs are oriented toward generating outcomes in circumstances where the substantive guidance is in the form of principles not rules, the requirements for notification and consultation are integral to EIA obligations. EIA obligations both reflect and implement these requirements by providing more precise guidance as to who gets notified, when they are to be notified, what information must accompany notification and the basis upon which consultations must be held, i.e. on the basis of good faith and in light of the assessment and the views of affected parties.

The development of the duties of notification and consultation out of the law on shared natural resources carries with it the same concern for balancing the sovereign rights of the state of origin and the affected state. To privilege the rights of the state of origin or the right of the affected state (by way of a "veto") would result in the negation of the sovereign rights of the other. The result is to require states, as a matter of self-regulation, to reach their own determination on how to balance their respective rights. The domestic analogy that can be drawn here is to the rationale for turning to widespread public involvement in administrative decision-making, including domestic EIAs. In the absence of substantive rules that constrain the discretion of decision-makers, allowing those who are affected by the decision to participate in the decision-making process legitimizes the outcome. Legitimization is required in the domestic context because non-elected officials are given wide discretion to make determinations that impact others. In the context of transboundary harm, legitimization is required because the state of origin is given wide discretion (unconstrained by previously agreed substantive standards) to make decisions that impact the sovereign rights of another state. In both instances, the critical requirement is that the decision-maker take due account of the interests of the affected party. What this suggests is that EIAs, which are turned to in order to implement these requirements, should require states to do those things that will enhance their ability to negotiate a solution.

There is, however, something else at play here because the harm principle still requires outcomes to adhere to a substantive direction. As noted in connection with NEPA, the harm principle, while providing parties with discretion, is not entirely indifferent to outcomes. The purposive nature of EIA is reinforced by EIA treaty provisions that often include a phrase to the effect that EIAs should be conducted with a view to preventing or minimizing or mitigating harm. This view requires that we take seriously the obligation inherent in the harm principle for a state of origin to justify its decision. EIAs promote reasoned decision-making by requiring decisions to be made openly, in writing and accompanied by reasons that account for both the result of the assessment and the comments/objections made by the affected state. The process does not require harm avoidance or mitigation as an operation of a legal right, but, where significant harm can be shown, it does require, as a matter of good faith, that the state of origin justify its decision. In essence, it seeks to lay bare the choices and trade-offs between competing objectives.

On this view, EIA goes beyond pure proceduralism by acknowledging that the entire process is underlain by a substantive environmental purpose. The substantive aspect of EIA is rarely recognized as such because it is not presented as an enforceable, rule-based right. Instead, the substantive principles are self-regulatory obligations. In essence, states are required to take environmental principles seriously, which requires their good faith consideration. What EIA requires then is that states engage one another not from the standpoint of self-interest, but rather from the standpoint of community interest as defined by the underlying and shared principles of the treaty. The substantive nature of EIA comes from the expectation that these interactions are to be based on rational persuasion, that is, with recourse to shared principles not self-interest. In this sense, EIA obligations in a transboundary context reflect the proceduralization of the harm principle, which does not negate the substantive content of the principle but acknowledges that its application will be contingent on its context.

International commitments to perform EIAs go beyond what would be required by simply extending the scope of domestic EIA in accordance with the principle of nondiscrimination. First, nondiscrimination does not provide minimum standards for the conduct of transboundary EIAs, but instead relies upon the adequacy of domestic rules respecting the application of EIA. Therefore, the harm principle provides a basis for policy harmonization that nondiscrimination lacks. International EIA commitments go beyond requiring that transboundary impacts be treated without differentiation to imposing an affirmative duty to assess transboundary impacts. Equally important, nondiscrimination says nothing about the quality of the decision-making process. Nondiscrimination is a form of pure proceduralism at the transboundary level. The environmental values of the domestic system may enter into transboundary EIA, but nondiscrimination does not recognize substance at the international level.

It would, however, be a mistake to discount the influence of the principle of nondiscrimination in the development and ultimate structure of international EIA commitments. The decision to use domestic EIA procedures to address transboundary issues is clearly attributable to nondiscrimination. The participatory aspects of transboundary EIA also arise from the principle of nondiscrimination and equal access requirements. Nondiscrimination treats the possibility of transboundary harm as simply an extension of existing domestic obligations. Those obligations are owed, in a broad sense, to any person who is affected by the potential impacts, resulting in the obligation to provide notice and extend rights of participation to affected persons regardless of their citizenship or residence. This differs from the harm principle which sees the problem of transboundary impacts as an interstate matter. The result under the

Espoo Convention is to recognize both the interstate and the transnational dimension of transboundary harm by imposing obligations to give notice and to consult with both the affected state and affected persons within the state. While the affected state is treated much like any other affected person in respect of notice under the Espoo Convention, the state is accorded a privileged position to initiate the inquiry procedure and to be directly consulted; again demonstrating the influence of the harm principle, which in turn recognizes the primacy of the state in transboundary harm disputes.

Moving beyond the transboundary context, the harm principle, which extends to the global commons, provides a basis for the imposition of EIA commitments to areas such as the high seas and the Antarctic. Under the Antarctic Protocol, for example, the EIA process is quite separate from domestic processes, but is premised on the duty of states to preserve the Antarctic ecosystem. The challenge with assessing impacts to the global commons is that the notification and consultation requirements are not directed toward any particular state, as there is no identifiable impacted state. Instead, the interests of other states in proposed activities with potential impacts to global resources rest on the universal character of these resources. The high seas and the Antarctic EIA provisions reflect this status in that both turn to international institutions as a mechanism for effecting notification and consultation. This approach is highly developed under the Antarctic Protocol, and it is suggested by Article 205 of the UNCLOS, although there is no evidence of institutional involvement on a global scale pursuant to this provision. Instead, regional organizations will be called upon to play this facilitative role. Given that there are only a limited number of states with a declared and active interest in the Antarctic, and the presence of a preexisting institutional structure, the incorporation of institutional intervention was less complicated than under the UNCLOS.

The final level upon which EIA operates is through those regimes, notably the UNFCCC and the CBD, which impose international obligations on a state in relation to the management of its domestic environment. Here, the basis of this intrusion upon state sovereignty is the recognition that the implications of mismanagement will have impacts on other states, i.e. their universal character, characterized as "common concern." The dynamic here is different because in the absence of a more direct interest, other states do not have a right to notification and consultation. Consequently, EIA obligations in this context do not require the elaboration of these latter rights. Instead, they require that states within their domestic EIA systems assess and consider within their decision-making processes the impacts on the particular environmental resource. The more helpful approach here may be through the use of "adaptation rules" that provide guidance to states on how to incorporate issues of common concern into their domestic EIA processes. This may require states to ensure that the scope of their EIA legislation includes consideration of biodiversity and climate change issues or, at a minimum, that officials administering the EIA system are reviewing EIAs with these objectives in mind.

While activities with transboundary impacts are constrained through the involvement of other affected states in the EIA process, no such constraint attaches to issues of common concern. However, the extension of international regulatory interests into the domestic sphere has been accompanied by a parallel requirement for greater public participation in internal environmental decision-making processes. As a result, decisions remain subject to public scrutiny at the domestic level and provide citizens' groups and nongovernmental organizations with opportunities to inject a consideration of these issues into EIA processes. Because EIA processes do not require the state proposing the activity to give up control over the decision-making process, something a state is particularly unlikely to do in the context of harm to its own domestic environment, the requirement that states account for issues of common concern in EIA processes provides an avenue for the consideration issues of common concern without unduly impinging on a state's sovereignty. Here, again, there is a confluence of procedural and substantive requirements. The structure of the obligation is to require that, within their domestic processes, states consider and account for particular environmental objectives identified at the international level. The requirement cannot be ignored because the public nature of EIA allows for transnational actors to scrutinize, and to some degree direct, the process.

Finally, the influence of principles associated with sustainable development is evident in the formal recognition of non-state actors as part of international environmental decision-making, the turn toward greater integration of environmental considerations through SEA and the move away from a purely predictive methodology in EIA. The implementation of these principles maintains the essential structure of EIA in that the implementation of sustainability norms is achieved through procedural requirements, such as the extension of rights of participation to affected groups regardless of their location and independently from their national governments, and the imposition of continuing obligations to monitor impacts and adapt projects and policies in light of evolving scientific knowledge and changing values. The turn to sustainability norms reinforces the non-instrumental nature of EIA through its inherent acceptance of the contingency of science and values.

Part IV The role of EIA commitments in international law

6 EIAs and compliance

6.1 Introduction

International EIA commitments are included in particular regimes in order to further the substantive goals of that regime. Even those EIA commitments that are not directly related to a specified environmental problem still identify substantive environmental objectives, such as the prevention of transboundary environmental harm, as the substantive basis for the EIA commitments. If the purposive nature of EIA commitments is a matter of common sense, answering the question of how EIAs actually achieve environmental ends is not. In the domestic context, competing theoretical approaches to explaining how EIAs affect the policy process have centered on different aspects of the EIA process, and, as a result, have also understood the role of EIA in different terms.[1]

Models of EIA that adopt a comprehensive rationality approach tend to view EIAs, and the policy process more generally, as a technical exercise with a consequent emphasis on the role of science and experts in determining correct courses of action. In rejecting this technical understanding of the policy process, pluralist models emphasize the political dimension of EIA processes. The role of EIA processes is not simply to gather and apply scientific knowledge to a particular problem, but rather EIA provides an opportunity for competing interest groups to press for outcomes that reflect their particular interests. A third model, which may be described as a transformational model, accepts that policy decisions are never neutral and, therefore, EIA processes are inherently political. However, transformational models reject the pluralist assumption that the interests of participants will be fixed. Under this model, the role of EIA is to generate new interests over time through socialization.

[1] See above at ch. 2.

Transformational models tend to be normatively oriented in that they view institutions and policy processes as having substantive objectives, such as sustainability or ecological integrity, in the case of EIA processes. Consequently, while pluralist models emphasize the role of EIA processes in conferring political legitimacy on policy decisions through adherence to accepted processes, transformational models view EIA processes as mechanisms that are capable of conferring a more substantive form of legitimacy on policy decisions based on the decision's adherence to environmental values.

There are clear parallels between these models of domestic policy processes and models developed to explain state compliance with international norms.[2] In their essence, both sets of explanations seek to provide insights into how the structure of institutional arrangements influences policy outcomes and to assess and explain the extent to which those outcomes are consonant with social goals. At a more abstracted level, compliance models similarly distinguish between interest-based explanations and explanations that view normative considerations as having independent influence on actor behavior.[3] One important difference between these sets of models is that explanations at the international level have to account for the absence of a centralized authority that can create, implement and enforce normative arrangements and the role of states as the dominant actors in international society. Given the very different structure in which public policy decisions are made in domestic and international contexts, and in light of the fact that international EIA commitments have been created by states and are institutional arrangements that relate to the broader structure of international environmental governance, this chapter examines the role of EIA commitments to bring about environmental change with reference to explanations of state compliance with international law.

[2] The literature on compliance is vast, but for an excellent introduction see Kal Raustiala and Anne-Marie Slaughter, "International Law, International Relations and Compliance" in Walter Carlsnaes *et al.*, eds., *Handbook of International Relations* (London: Sage Publications, 2001) at 538.

[3] See James March and Johan Olsen, "The Institutional Dynamics of International Political Orders" (1998) 52 Int. Org. 943. A similar divide, referred to as "collective action" and "social practice" models, is discussed in Oran Young, *The Institutional Dimensions of Environmental Change: Fit, Interplay, and Scale* (Cambridge, MA: MIT Press, 2002) at ch. 2. In relation to domestic EIA, see R. V. Bartlett, "The Rationality and Logic of NEPA Revisited" in Larry Canter and Ray Clark, eds., *Environmental Policy and NEPA: Past, Present and Future* (Boca Raton, FL: St. Lucie Press, 1997) 51.

It might appear at first blush that EIA processes are a mechanism ill-suited for promoting compliance. From a rationalist standpoint, compliance typically requires some ability to alter the material incentives of actors from whom compliance is sought. EIA processes very clearly are not directed toward a coercive form of regulation. In fact, not only do EIAs operate in a self-regulatory fashion, they do not even specify, beyond identifying broad environmental objectives, the outcomes with which compliance is required. However, the ambiguity of the substantive environmental norms that underlie EIA commitments is mitigated by several factors. First, the highly contextualized nature of EIA decision-making, and in particular the assessment of alternatives, concretizes the evaluative process. While it may be difficult to decide in the abstract whether a project causes unjustifiable levels of environmental harm, it may be less difficult to determine whether there are less harmful alternatives and whether choosing a more harmful alternative is justifiable. In addition, the reliance within EIA processes on scientific methods, which often have their own evaluative metrics, can flesh out vague environmental principles. That said, the approach to compliance outlined below views compliance in much broader terms than simply mapping behavior onto a chosen rule. The kind of compliance toward which EIAs are oriented is to pull decisions in a direction more consistent with these broad environmental norms. The strength of this approach is that it recognizes that substantive specificity is often difficult to achieve, and, insofar as international environmental governance structures are characterized by the presence of open-textured norms, EIAs are a mechanism that attaches a degree of normative significance to these principles and seeks to operationalize them.

To this end, the first part of this chapter provides a brief overview of compliance explanations developed by process-oriented international legal scholars. As with process-oriented scholarship more generally,[4] there is no single process-oriented approach to understanding the conditions under which states are more likely to comply with international law. However, there are a number of common characteristics that can be distilled from the different process-oriented approaches. The relationship of these characteristics, namely, transparency, participation, discursiveness, contextuality and normativity, to international EIA commitments is then explored. This discussion commences with an analysis of the procedural aspects of compliance. I then discuss the transnational

[4] See the discussion of process-oriented legal method in ch. 1.

nature of international EIA commitments as a backdrop to the subsequent discussion of the contextuality and normativity of EIA processes. Implicit in this approach is a strong connection between the form of implementation and compliance. The transnationalism of EIAs provides a process that is highly permeable to substantive international environmental norms. As these norms are projected into EIA processes at the domestic level, and in the context of a specific project, there are opportunities for decision-makers and nongovernmental actors to consider the application and interpretation of international norms in light of highly contextual information. It is through this process that the outcomes can come to reflect international environmental values. The discussion of EIAs as contributing to compliance in this chapter is illustrated with reference to a number of different EIA systems, but draws in particular on the interaction of global environmental norms in the Canadian federal EIA process.

6.2 Implementation, compliance and effectiveness

Much of the scholarship examining the relationship between state behavior and legal norms is structured around three analytical concepts: implementation, compliance and effectiveness.[5] While these concepts are often treated as being uncontested and unambiguous, they are in fact contingent upon prior understandings of the nature of international law.[6] Rules-based (positivist) approaches to compliance tend to conceive of legal norms as existing separately from the processes into which they are projected. In this way, legal meaning can be determined independently of the context in which the rule operates. The implementation of a legal rule is wholly distinct from its meaning. Moreover, because a rule's binding nature is determined by the validity of its source, compliance is understood in similarly static terms.

[5] These three concepts are the central organizing features of Edith Brown Weiss and Harold Jacobsen, eds., *Engaging Countries: Strengthening Compliance with International Environmental Accords* (Cambridge, MA: MIT Press, 1998); David G. Victor, Kal Raustiala and Eugene B. Skolnikoff, eds., *The Implementation and Effectiveness of International Environmental Commitments* (Cambridge, MA: MIT Press, 1998); and Oran Young, ed., *The Effectiveness of International Environmental Regimes: Causal Connections and Behavioral Mechanisms* (Cambridge, MA: MIT Press, 1999). See also "Symposium on Implementation, Compliance and Effectiveness" (1998) 19 Michigan JIL 303.

[6] Benedict Kingsbury, "The Concept of Compliance as a Function of Competing Conceptions of International Law" (1998) 19 Michigan JIL 345. See also Jutta Brunnée and Stephen Toope, "Persuasion and Enforcement: Explaining Compliance with International Law" (2002) 13 Finnish YBIL 273.

Looking at compliance issues through a process lens alters our understanding of these analytic concepts in several important ways. First, implementation itself is not wholly distinct from the law-making process. Implementation has been defined as "the process by which intent gets transferred into action."[7] This is certainly the case, but it is also a process by which intentions are elaborated upon and interpreted. Unlike formal positivist approaches where rules are generated in a separate law-making process, process-oriented approaches suggest there is no clear line to draw between law-making and law implementation since legal meaning is partly contingent upon the context of its application. Implementation is itself an exercise of interpretation, requiring states to adopt a particular understanding of an international instrument in the process of drafting domestic legislation to implement treaty obligations. A further level of interpretation occurs when frontline bureaucrats apply the implementing legislation or international norms directly in the field. These domestic understandings themselves can and often do filter back up into the international setting, affecting how other states perceive the meaning of the international instrument.[8] EIA commitments, as one of the identified processes by which states are required or encouraged to implement substantive environmental norms, potentially offer interpretive opportunities of this nature.

Because process-oriented approaches tend to view the line between law and non-law as being less distinct, the identification of compliant state behavior is necessarily viewed as being less determinate. Chayes and Chayes capture the dynamic nature of legal meaning when they speak of a "zone" of compliance and "acceptable levels of compliance."[9] Here, the idea is that compliance, like legal normativity, does not operate in a binary manner, but instead operates along a continuum. This again is a move away from a rules-based understanding of compliance, whereby state behavior is mapped onto a static prescription. This results in viewing compliance not as a snapshot, but rather like a film, unfolding over time. Compliance, on this view, is better measured over longer periods of time, across multiple interactions, as opposed to being measured by single incidents.

[7] Victor, Raustiala and Skolnikoff, eds., *Implementation and Effectiveness* at 1.

[8] See, for example, Harold Koh, "Transnational Legal Process" (1996) 75 Nebraska L. Rev. 181 at 194–199.

[9] Abram Chayes and Antonia Chayes, *The New Sovereignty: Compliance with International Regulatory Agreements* (Cambridge, MA: Harvard University Press, 1995) at 17.

The reliance by process-oriented scholars on principles and the overarching desire for normative coherence results in assessments of compliance from a much broader perspective, taking account of how state behavior reflects broader principles. To speak of compliance with principles in a formal context appears problematic because of the inability to determine with precision the acts or omissions of non-compliance. In such cases, the positivist response is likely to deny the legal character of the prescription and the relevance of compliance to principles. By contrast, process-oriented approaches, by attributing greater legal relevance to principles, are more likely to attach significance from a compliance standpoint to provisions within regimes that require adherence to open-textured prescriptions. From a process-oriented perspective, it is possible to conceptualize compliance with a principle because compliance is measured in a "more or less," not a "yes or no," fashion.

Finally, a number of research projects looking at the relationship between international environmental laws and state behavior draw a sharp distinction between compliance and effectiveness on the basis that compliance by itself does not demonstrate a causal relationship between a particular legal rule and the behavior in question.[10] The aim of much of the research looking at the effectiveness of environmental treaties seeks to isolate certain causal factors that impact state behavior in order to determine the extent of their influence. The tendency is to define effectiveness in terms of treaty objectives (i.e. pollution reduction), and to treat these objectives (or preferences) as independent of and unaffected by the legal rules, principles and procedures of the regime.[11] However, under contemporary process-oriented approaches, preferences are not wholly independent of law, and, as such, the relationship between behavioral outcomes and legal norms is not one of strict linear causality. This is not to say that process scholars deny that causal links between rules and behavior cannot be established, but rather that behavioral outcomes are the result of complex and overlapping sources of influence.

[10] See, for example, Harold Jacobson and Edith Brown Weiss, "A Framework for Analysis" in Edith Brown Weiss and Harold Jacobsen, eds., *Engaging Countries: Strengthening Compliance with International Environmental Accords* (Cambridge, MA: MIT Press, 1998) 1 at 4–5; and David Victor, Kal Raustiala and Eugene Skolnikoff, "Introduction and Overview" in Victor, Raustiala and Skolnikoff, eds., *Implementation and Effectiveness* 1 at 6–8.

[11] See ibid. See also the approaches to effectiveness discussed in Oran Young and Marc Levy, "The Effectiveness of International Environmental Regimes" in Young, ed., *The Effectiveness of International Environmental Regimes* 1 at 3–6.

The difficulty in establishing causal connections between international environmental treaties and associated processes, on the one hand, and state actions and policy decisions, on the other, is exemplified by EIAs where the objectives of EIA and the means to achieve those objectives are not easily separable. Because process can at once be both the means and the ends, compliance (adherence to the means) and effectiveness (achievement of the ends) are less distinct themselves because the goal is defined in part by the process. With EIAs the process itself is both directive on a broad level, incorporating exogenous goals of environmental protection and sustainable development, but also non-directive in the sense that particular outcomes are a function of the interactions occurring within the EIA process itself.

A related difficulty is that the outcome by which the effectiveness of EIAs may be measured – policy decisions respecting activities that are likely to impact the environment – are themselves the product of a vastly complicated collection of social, economic and technological forces. Disentangling these different forces presents an enormous challenge to the task of establishing causality.

In light of these complications, the approach adopted here is not to seek to quantify the impact of EIAs as an independent variable, but rather the approach is to examine how EIA processes structure interactions between actors. A process-oriented approach suggests that looking at interactions themselves, particularly the content and nature of the discourse between parties, can inform our understanding of the types of considerations deemed relevant by the parties. As procedural obligations, the ends sought by EIA processes cannot be measured in terms of substantive outcomes, at least not on a decision-by-decision basis. Instead, international EIA obligations should be assessed largely in terms of how the relevant decision-making processes are affected; for example, who makes the decision, whose views are taken into account, and what types of considerations are found to be relevant. Following from this, one measurement of effectiveness that this study employs is to look to the extent to which environmental norms become institutionalized within EIA processes themselves.[12]

[12] This kind of approach to measuring effectiveness is showing up in nascent forms in the research agendas of domestic environmental policy scholars: see, for example, Robert Bartlett and Priya Kurian, "The Theory of Environmental Impact Assessment: Implicit Models of Policy-Making" (1999) 27 Policy and Politics 415 at 425.

6.3 Process-oriented compliance models

6.3.1 *The managerial model*

In their book, *The New Sovereignty*,[13] Abram Chayes and Antonia Chayes present an explanation of compliance that incorporates the central precepts of process-oriented legal scholarship: that legal rules themselves are insufficient to promote adherence and must be projected into interactions between parties; that within these interactions, rules do not determine outcomes but they exert influence by framing issues, justifying positions and determining relevant actors; and that the influence of norms is not the result of coercive measures, but relates to the perceived legitimacy of the norm, which, in turn, is largely a function of right process. Like the development of International Legal Process accounts of international law more generally, Chayes and Chayes sought to provide an alternative to the dominant political realist paradigm that saw virtually no role for law in shaping state behavior.

In challenging the realist model, Chayes and Chayes begin by echoing Louis Henkin's famous observation that "almost all nations observe almost all principles of international law and almost all of their obligations almost all of the time."[14] From this starting point, Chayes and Chayes argue that the sources of non-compliance relate more to inadequate information, ambiguity surrounding rules and a lack of capacity than to willful breaches of rules. If compliance is to be improved, it is these shortcomings that must be addressed and, to this end, Chayes and Chayes turn to the arguments put forward by institutionalist international relations (IR) scholars, who offer a competing understanding of state cooperation to that offered by realists.

Central to the institutionalist focus on cooperation is what political scientists Robert Keohane and Joseph Nye call "complex interdependence."[15] That is, the growing number of transnational, intergovernmental and transgovernmental relationships among states that has the effect of creating complex patterns of mutual dependence. For Chayes and Chayes, interdependence is so central to the relationships between states that they speak of a "new sovereignty" that is grounded, not in the negative right to be left alone, but in the positive right to participate in

13 Chayes and Chayes, *The New Sovereignty*.

14 Abram Chayes and Antonia Chayes, "On Compliance" (1998) 47 Int. Org. 175 at 177, citing Louis Henkin, *How Nations Behave* at 47.

15 Robert Keohane and Joseph Nye, *Power and Interdependence: Politics in a World in Transition* (Boston: Little, Brown & Co., 1977). See also Robert Keohane and Joseph Nye, "Power and Interdependence Revisited" (1987) 41 Int. Org. 725.

international institutions.[16] Sovereignty, under this view, "is status – the vindication of the state's existence as a member of the international system."[17] Interdependence has the effect of limiting the utility of the use of force through the creation of increased points of contact connecting societies on a variety of levels.[18] Moreover, in a world defined by complex interdependence, cooperation and stability can be explained in terms of the ability of international institutions to minimize the impediments to cooperation that arise in an anarchic system, as opposed to the exercise of hegemonic power (the explanation favored by realists).[19]

Institutions (or regimes) can promote cooperation by reducing the high transaction costs normally associated with interstate cooperation. This can occur by using institutions to identify negotiating partners with a common interest in addressing an issue cooperatively,[20] and by reducing bargaining costs through the provision of negotiating forums and shared resources, such as a coordinating secretariat. A related function of regimes is to enhance the exchange of information between states through reporting, verification and monitoring mechanisms, thereby reducing the uncertainty regarding a partner's likelihood of keeping to a bargain. Keohane explains:

> Agreements that are impossible to make under conditions of high uncertainty may become feasible when uncertainty has been reduced. Human beings, and governments, behave differently in information-rich environments than in information-poor ones. Information, as well as power, is a significant systemic variable in world politics.[21]

Related to the information enhancement role of regimes is the ability of regimes to stabilize expectations by providing regularized standards of behavior.[22] This aspect of regimes speaks to the realist insistence that states must focus on each other's capabilities because they can never be sure of intentions.[23] Institutions, by reducing the uncertainty around intentions, lessen the need to examine capabilities. By providing

[16] Chayes and Chayes, *The New Sovereignty*. [17] Ibid. at 27.

[18] Keohane and Nye, *Power and Interdependence Revisited* at 731.

[19] For an influential examination of institutions that puts forward this argument, see Robert Keohane, *After Hegemony: Co-operation and Discord in the World Political Economy* (Princeton, NJ: Princeton University Press, 1984).

[20] Kenneth Abbott, "Modern International Relations Theory: A Prospectus for International Lawyers" (1989) 14 Yale JIL 335 at 399.

[21] Keohane, *After Hegemony* at 245.

[22] Anthony Arend, "Do Legal Rules Matter? International Law and International Politics" (1998) 38 Virginia JIL 107 at 121.

[23] Joseph Grieco, "Anarchy and the Limits of Co-operation: A Realist Critique of the Newest Liberal Institutionalism" (1988) 42 Int. Org. 485 at 500.

standardized and consistent approaches to similar problems, regimes can obviate the need for states to continually recalculate cost/benefit considerations across interrelated issues, allowing states to take advantage of economies of scale. With reference to game theoretic insights, institutionalists note that reputations do matter.[24] Defection may be a desirable short-term strategy, but in a world of repeated transactions this strategy loses its (rational) appeal.[25] Moreover, regimes, through issue linkages, can extend these effects across broad areas, increasing the impact of cooperation.

Like institutionalism, *The New Sovereignty* approaches compliance largely in terms of using legal rules and procedures as an instrument to increase interactional capacity between states.[26] The prominent tools in aid of this objective are process-oriented and managerial. The emphasis is on self-regulation, meaning that compliance is largely achieved through the creation of conditions that allow states to pursue self-interested objectives. The mechanisms proposed, such as broad-based participation, increasing access to information, monitoring and verification procedures, and capacity-building, often facilitated by international institutions, are intended to reduce the costs associated with cooperation and increase the costs of defection. The approach is facilitative and forward-looking, as opposed to being punitive and reactive.

The view so far of legal norms is highly instrumental in that legal rules are used as a means to facilitate more efficient interactions. Within an institutionalist framework, laws (or regimes, more generally) act as a "switching system, facilitating the independent interactions of independent states."[27] Legal norms are not, however, seen as an independent source of influence. To use the terminology of IR theory, law is at best an "intervening variable."[28] However, Chayes and Chayes appear to

[24] Game theoretical approaches in IR and their relevance to international law are discussed in Abbott, "Modern International Relations Theory" at 354–375. The reputational implications of game theory are further explored in Andrew Guzman, "A Compliance-Based Theory of International Law" (2002) 90 California L. Rev. 1823.

[25] Abbott, "Modern International Relations Theory" at 363–365.

[26] "Interactional capacity" refers to how much goods and information can be exchanged, at what speed and over what distances. Increased capacity means there are a greater number of types of interactions with increased intensities. Discussed in Barry Buzan, "The Level of Analysis Problem in International Relations Reconsidered" in Ken Booth and Steve Smith, eds., *International Political Theory Today* (London: Polity Press, 1995) 198 at 204–205.

[27] Chayes and Chayes, *The New Sovereignty* at 229.

[28] Stephen Krasner, "Structural Causes and Regime Consequences: Regimes as Intervening Variables" (1982) 36 Int. Org. 185.

go beyond structural explanations offered by institutionalists by looking, not only at the quantity, velocity and diversity of interactions,[29] but also at the quality of interactions between parties themselves. Here, compliance is explained in terms of a state's response to another state's attributes and behavior. Chayes and Chayes characterize this process as being one of justification and persuasion. From this perspective, the role of law looks quite different.

The managerial approach, as Chayes and Chayes describe it, views institutions as doing more than simply aggregating individual state preferences, but having an independent role, "modifying preferences, generating new options, persuading the parties to move towards increasing compliance with regime norms, and guiding the evolution of the normative structure in the direction of the overall objectives of the regime."[30] Chayes and Chayes describe this process in the following terms:

> The discursive elaboration and application of treaty norms is the heart of the compliance process. The dynamic of justification is the search for a common understanding of the significance of the norm in the specific situation presented. The participants seek, almost in Socratic fashion, to persuade each other of the validity of the successive steps in the dialectic. In the course of this debate, the performance required of a party in a particular case is progressively defined and specified. Since the party has participated in each stage of the argument, the pressures to conform to the final judgment are great. "The process by which egoists learn to cooperate is at the same time a process of reconstructing their interests in terms of shared commitments to social norms."[31]

This transformation appears possible for several reasons. First, there exists a common framework upon which discourse can occur. International legal norms provide broadly accepted background principles, including the "rules of the game." Treaties and customary rules identify the relevant standards of behavior, but, because these are to some degree indeterminate, they also provide the means of authoritative interpretation and elaboration.[32] The range of interpretative possibilities is

[29] This is also referred to as "dynamic density" by John Ruggie, "Political Structure and Dynamic Density" in John Ruggie, *Constructing* at 151.

[30] Chayes and Chayes, *The New Sovereignty* at 229.

[31] Ibid. at 123, quoting Alexander Wendt, "Anarchy Is What States Make of It: The Social Construction of Power Politics" (1992) 46 Int. Org. 391 at 417.

[32] Chayes and Chayes, *The New Sovereignty* at 120, noting: "Alternatively, justification of questioned conduct often relies on broadly accepted background principles rooted in practical experience and common sense: rough fairness, the status quo, precedent, custom."

constrained because treaties and custom provide authoritative starting points.[33] The role of legal norms is not to dictate outcomes, but legal norms will operate to foreclose or limit policy options, and they will generate burdens of justification.

Here, again, process itself is critical. Rules on their own will not promote compliance, rather it is the projection of rules into these discursive processes that will produce compliance. Chayes and Chayes argue that legitimacy plays a key role in the justificatory process because as legitimacy enhances so do the behavioral expectations to follow the prescriptions.[34] The emphasis here, consistent with traditional Legal Process approaches, is on right process, as opposed to the existence of a shared commitment to substantive values. Chayes and Chayes do not seek to go behind the notion of obligation in an attempt to explain its existence, preferring to take the obligatory nature of norms as given.[35]

To a significant degree, Chayes and Chayes fall back on institutionalist logic in explaining compliance, noting that noncompliance with accepted normative principles will have reputational consequences, particularly in a system characterized by complex interdependence.[36] Norms result in a presumption of compliance, and a failure to comply always has some negative consequences because it is contrary to the behavioral expectations of the community. Legal norms will impact state behavior indirectly by narrowing the area in which states can freely act without attracting negative consequences. Procedural or constitutive norms that have a broad legitimizing function, because they operate across multiple regime frameworks, serve to deepen or extend the impact of norms. Ultimately, however, interests are not so much altered by interactions, as they are recalculated in light of the normative environment. What Chayes and Chayes succeed in doing is demonstrating that the extent of the normative environment is significant and, consequently, its impact on state behavior is far-reaching.

[33] Ibid. at 119.

[34] Chayes and Chayes appear to rely on Thomas Franck's work in support of this proposition: see Thomas Franck, *The Power of Legitimacy Among Nations* (New York: Oxford University Press, 1990). For an empirical study linking compliance with legitimacy, see Tom Tyler, *Why People Obey the Law* (New Haven, CT: Yale University Press, 1990).

[35] Ibid. at 116.

[36] Ibid. at 230, noting: "[I]n an interdependent and interconnected world, a reputation for reliability matters. And, in the last analysis, the ability of a state to remain a participant in the international policy-making process depends in some degree on its demonstrated willingness to accept and engage the regime's compliance procedures."

6.3.2 *Transnational legal process*

A further set of assumptions that is shared by both institutionalist and realist IR scholars, and is clearly evident in *The New Sovereignty*, is that states are the principal actors within the international system and that states themselves are unitary and undifferentiated.[37] Consequently, Chayes and Chayes focus on the horizontal interactions between states and the attributes of the international system that shape these interactions. In contrast, Harold Koh argues that, by focusing solely on interactions between states, institutionalist scholars fail to appreciate the significance of "vertical" interactions in promoting compliance with international law. By vertical interactions, Koh means to refer to a broad range of legal and political processes that involve both private and public actors, that occur within both domestic and transnational settings and that draw upon international legal norms as a basis for the claims advanced. Like the managerial approach, Koh views compliance as being generated through discursive interactions that generate authoritative interpretations of international norms, but for Koh compliance is more likely to arise where those interpretations become embedded in domestic institutions that operate more directly on key decision-makers.[38]

For Koh, compliance is seen more as a function of the acceptability of international legal arrangements to domestic audiences, who in turn define state preferences.[39] In this regard, many of the compliance tools suggested by Chayes and Chayes remain important, but their orientation is toward individuals, not states. For example, access to information and participation remain central to compliance, but they are aimed at ensuring that individual views are adequately informed and represented at the domestic level. Similarly, capacity-building for Koh is more likely to be aimed at improving domestic institutions, such as a functioning judiciary or strengthening administrative agencies, with the view to ensuring that individuals can effectively exercise their political

37 Institutionalists and realists do not deny that there are important differences between states and that these differences may impact state behavior, but they view these influences as being less pronounced than structural conditions at the international level. See Barry Buzan, "The Levels of Analysis Problem" at 207–208.

38 Koh's theory of transnational legal process is set out in a series of articles that may be profitably read together. These articles include Harold Koh, "Transnational Legal Process" (1996) 75 Nebraska L. Rev. 181; Harold Koh, "Why Do Nations Obey International Law" (1997) 106 Yale LJ 2599; and Harold Koh, "Bringing International Law Home" (1998) 35 Houston L. Rev. 623.

39 Here, Koh draws heavily on liberal IR theory. See Andrew Moravcsik, "Taking Preferences Seriously: A Liberal Theory of International Politics" (1997) 51 Int. Org. 513.

rights within the domestic system, so as to better ensure that foreign policy decisions are representative of domestic political opinion. Koh seeks to explain compliance as arising from a three-part process of interaction, interpretation and internalization. These interactions occur for the most part within domestic or transnational settings, and involve both state and non-state actors and are sought for the purpose of generating an interpretation in favor of a particular international norm. Through a combination of, *inter alia*, lobbying, transnational public litigation, and norm sponsorship by prominent government and private sector figures – what Koh refers to as "vertical" processes – international legal norms are invoked, argued over and interpreted. These interactions are vertical in that they seek to project global norms into domestic institutions and take advantage of hierarchical legal relationships within the state, such as the ability of domestic courts to impose interpretations on other government agencies or the ability of the executive to incorporate international norms into agency rules and guidelines.

Interpretations may expose contradictions between state behavior and accepted international norms or simply signal to other domestic actors a preferred interpretation. Through the frictions and pressures that are created by repeated interactions and interpretations in support of the norm, politicians, bureaucrats and the judiciary begin to accept these interpretations as authoritative, whereupon they will begin to become internalized within the legal and institutional fabric of the state. Internalization itself can take numerous forms, ranging from treaty ratification, adoption of executive orders, the passing of implementing legislation or bureaucratic procedures.[40] Once a norm becomes internalized, compliance arises because the norm has become enmeshed with domestic decision-making processes.[41] The objective of transnational legal process for Koh is not simply to alter incentives to promote compliance, but to instill a sense of felt obligation, referred to by Koh as "obedience," that is, an allegiance to the norm that arises out of an understanding of what is right. As with the managerial approach, there is an emphasis on self-regulation.

Like *The New Sovereignty*, the focus is on persuasion and justification. Robert Keohane (citing Karl Deutsch) has noted that persuasion relies on the subject being inwardly divided in their thought and that these

[40] Koh identifies three kinds of internalization – social internationalization, political internalization and legal internalization – which are described in Koh, "Bringing International Law Home" at 642–643.

[41] Koh, "Why Do Nations Obey International Law" at 2654–2655.

contradictions "lead to reflection and even attitude change."[42] Transnational legal process operates in such a way as to expose or raise contradictions between a state's behavior and international legal norms. Koh also relies on the general expectation that states will adhere to their commitments and a failure to do so is central to the "frictions" that bureaucracies and politicians seek to avoid.[43] This is most successfully accomplished where state decision-making processes are open and transparent, there exists opportunities for repeated public interactions, and where transnational actors have the ability to access and disseminate information respecting state behavior, which allows for these contradictions to be brought to public attention.

By viewing internalization as the key to compliance, Koh accepts constructivist (IR theory) understandings of the power of interactions to transform interests and, ultimately, the identities of transnational actors.[44] If transnational legal process is constitutive, then norm internalization arises because certain interpretations are more persuasive than others. The normativity of Koh's theory may then be explained as accepting that there are norms whose content are more likely to result in persuasion. However, the difficulty Koh faces is precisely the same difficulty that faces Chayes and Chayes in *The New Sovereignty*. Neither has an adequate explanation of why some norms are privileged over others. As noted, Chayes and Chayes explain a norm's ability to persuade in terms of its legitimacy, but then fail to provide a detailed account of legitimacy. Koh, while criticizing *The New Sovereignty* for its inadequate discussion of legitimacy,[45] is not much clearer himself in explaining the role of legitimacy. However, Koh is clear that the legitimacy of a norm is a significant determinant of whether that norm will be internalized.[46]

6.3.3 *Legitimacy and compliance*

The central role of legitimacy in promoting compliance is an idea that is most readily associated with the work of Thomas Franck, most particularly his book, *The Power of Legitimacy Among Nations*.[47] Franck argues that state compliance with international law is determined in part by

[42] Robert Keohane, "Governance in a Partially Globalized World" (2001) 95 Am. Pol. Sci. Rev. 1 at 10 (quoting Karl Deutsch, *Nationalism and Social Communication* (Cambridge, MA: MIT Press 1953) at 52).
[43] Koh, "Why Do Nations Obey International Law" at 2655.
[44] Koh, "Transnational" at 202.
[45] Koh, "Why Do Nations Obey International Law" at 2641.
[46] Ibid. at 2656. [47] Franck, *Legitimacy Among Nations*.

the perception by states of the legitimacy of the rule in question. Legitimacy exerts what Franck refers to as "compliance pull" – a tendency to promote, but not necessarily determine, compliance.[48] The legitimacy of a rule is a function of the presence of four characteristics: precision or textual determinacy; the ability of the rule to communicate authority (symbolic validation); coherence with other rules and principles in international law; and adherence to secondary rules regarding norm creation. Together these characteristics make up what Franck refers to as "right process." In subsequent writings, right process as a determinant of legitimacy is supplemented with minimum requirements for distributive justice.[49]

For all that Franck unpacks the concept of legitimacy, it is still unclear exactly where legitimacy lies. Legitimacy is presented as characteristic of international rules themselves, but legitimacy also arises from the processes of norm creation and the relationship of the rule to a broader web of rules and principles. Part of the difficulty here is that Franck projects what are essentially dynamic characteristics onto a static rule.[50] By locating the normativity of international law in the rules themselves and not in the processes by which rules are created, interpreted and applied, Franck does not engage in how it is that states and other subjects of international law come to be persuaded. In Koh's view, the missing causal element is transnational legal process.[51] As noted, Koh does not address the sources of legitimacy directly, but, if the constructivist turn taken by Koh is extended to its logical conclusion, a more substance-oriented understanding of legitimacy may be put forward.

Since law is part of the social environment that constitutes the identity and interests of actors, it is artificial to draw a hard distinction between the ends that law serves and the processes that are intended to bring about those ends. Legal reasoning, which is at the heart of compliance for legal process scholarship, must, on this view, appeal to both the procedural legitimacy of a norm and its coherence with shared substantive principles. To place this in the compliance context, a norm, or a particular interpretation, will be more persuasive, and therefore more likely to be internalized, where it is seen to be the product of accepted

[48] Thomas Franck, "Legitimacy in the International System" (1988) 82 AJIL 705 at 712.

[49] Thomas Franck, *Fairness in International Law and Institutions* (Oxford: Clarendon Press, 1995).

[50] This point is suggested by Karen Knop, "Reflections on Thomas Franck, Race and Nationalism (1960): General Principles of Law and Situated Generality" (2003) 35 NYU J. Int'l L. & Pol'y 437at 448.

[51] Koh, "Why Do Nations Obey International Law" at 2645.

procedures and where it is congruent with broadly accepted substantive understandings of right conduct existing within the relevant interpretive community. The existence of shared substantive understandings is not dependent on a commitment to a static and universal set of values, nor does it require the existence of a thickly constituted community that maintains a commitment to shared values. Instead, legitimacy rests on the fact that actors will often share, intersubjectively, common understandings regarding both right process and right substance. Additionally, process-oriented scholars view the relevant interpretive community in broader terms, recognizing that no one institution, public or private, has an interpretive monopoly and that interpretations by private parties, lawyers and bureaucrats will all shape legal meaning.[52] This opening up of norm creation and interpretation is clearly evident in *The New Sovereignty* and even more so in Koh's scholarship, where legal meaning is understood to be shaped by interactions between all manner of actors.[53]

Jutta Brunnée and Stephen Toope, in developing their "interactional" theory of international law, stress the importance of the emergence of "stable patterns of expectation,"[54] upon which discursive interactions rest. In the absence of a shared basis of rhetorical knowledge, persuasion, as distinct from bargaining or signaling, is not possible. It follows that the move to a formally binding, sanction-based framework, in the absence of shared understandings, is less likely to be perceived as a legitimate exercise of authority by those parties whose values are not reflected in the framework,[55] since the justifications offered are unlikely to persuade actors who do not share the principles underlying the framework. Adherence to the rules in such cases necessarily involves coercion, and will be dependent upon the resolve of more powerful players to engage in costly enforcement activities. On other hand, where principles and rules are congruent with shared understandings, law deepens cooperation because actors are open to persuasion. The mechanism that promotes identity and interest-transformation is the reasoned interaction between states. On this view, even where norms are not formally binding and lack precision, they can generate principled discourse between actors. States still act in a self-interested manner, but their understanding of self-interest becomes increasingly identified with broader community interests.

52 See, for example, Robert Cover, "Nomos and Narrative" (1983) 97 Harvard L. Rev. 4.

53 See Koh, "Bringing International Law Home" at 650.

54 Brunnée and Toope, "Persuasion" at 278.

55 Jutta Brunnée and Stephen Toope, "Environmental Security and Freshwater Resources: Ecosystem Regime Building" (1997) 91 AJIL 26.

There is a strong complementarity between Brunnée and Toope's interactional theory and the more overtly process-oriented compliance theory of Koh. The evolutionary approach of Brunnée and Toope posits a link between norm formation and compliance, which recognizes that adherence to regime norms is partly a function of the process by which the norms were agreed upon. Regimes do not arise in response to changed conditions fully formed and without regard to past institutional arrangements.[56] Explaining change in the international relations requires an understanding of both current conditions and the historical path of institutional development.[57] Whereas Koh's theory of transnational legal process takes the existence of norms as a given and provides concrete examples of how legal processes themselves contribute to norm interpretation and elaboration, Brunnée and Toope provide an explanation of how legal norms themselves, particularly their internal characteristics, inculcate a sense of obligation.[58]

Taken together these theories of how international law operates to exert influence over state behavior point to a strong connection between process and substance in international law. The substantive content of international legal arrangements will reflect the interests of those actors represented in the norm creation process. Determining whose interests are at stake, and how those interests will be represented, are procedural matters. Moreover, recognizing the dynamic nature of normative structures means that process must also account for continuing involvement in the interpretation, implementation and application of norms over time. Equally important, continued inclusivity with these practices ensures that those actors whose views were not fully reflected at the initial stages of norm formation continue to participate and voice their views, which will, in turn, increase the chances of broad regime allegiance. Koh extends the importance of process values to the transnational realm because many interests that are implicated by international norms are not adequately represented in formal norm creation processes, but will nevertheless exert influence as norms permeate domestic legal processes.

[56] See Steven Bernstein, *The Compromise of Liberal Environmentalism* (New York: Columbia University Press, 2001), ch. 1.

[57] March and Olsen, "Institutional Dynamics" at 959.

[58] Brunnée and Toope acknowledge this complementarity between their own account of compliance and Koh's transnational legal process: see Brunnée and Toope, "Persuasion" at 292.

Despite the emphasis on norms, it would be a mistake to understand process-oriented approaches as a rejection of rationalist influences on state behavior.[59] Koh convincingly demonstrates that compliance is a function of a variety of causal mechanisms that work together to strengthen and internalize norms. Enforcement proceedings in domestic legal settings that adopt international norms provide both material incentives to comply, but also provide an important signaling effect by demonstrating disapprobation. The enmeshment of norms into domestic institutions also suggests an interplay between rationalist and constructivist explanations that plays out in transnational institutions, whereby transnational actors draw upon the efficacy and legitimacy of domestic institutions to promote normative positions.[60] For example, the effectiveness of norm sponsorship or transnational public litigation depends in part on the preexisting legitimacy of public figures or institutions within domestic settings. Epistemic communities and transnational networks rely on professional standing and the legitimacy accorded to certain kinds of expertise. Similarly, Chayes and Chayes rely on both rationalist arguments regarding the primacy of interests (such as reputational concerns) in determining state behavior, and on more constructivist inspired insights regarding the importance of persuasion and normative influences in altering those interests.

While there are clear differences between the framework adopted by Chayes and Chayes and Koh – the scholars most readily identified with process-oriented thinking in international law – both their approaches reflect the larger process-oriented commitment to rational persuasion. In turn, process-oriented approaches turn to constructivist explanations to provide a richer understanding of the role of norms in qualifying state behavior. Common to process-oriented approaches to compliance is a reliance on process values, such as transparency, participation and a commitment to dialogical interactions, as well as substantive values, as signified by their commitment to discourse based on reason not interests and interactions that are sensitive to context. There is unquestionably a tension between the desire for decision-making to be both principled

[59] See March and Olsen, "Institutional Dynamics" at 952–954, discussing the relationship between the logic of consequences and the logic of appropriateness.

[60] In this regard, there is a parallel between Koh and domestic legal scholars such as Cass Sunstein and Lawrence Lessig, who have incorporated social norms into rationalist explanations of domestic actor behavior. See Lawrence Lessig, "The New Chicago School" (1998) 27 J. Legal Stud. 661; and Cass Sunstein, "Social Norms and Social Roles" (1996) 96 Columbia L. Rev. 903.

and contextual, but as discussed below this form of practical reasoning lies at the heart of international EIA commitments.

6.4 Process values: transparency, participation and discursiveness

6.4.1 *Transparency*

A principal role of transparency in process-oriented compliance explanations is to lower the transaction costs involved in arriving at cooperative solutions to problems that require collective action and to decrease levels of uncertainty, particularly in connection with intentions. In the compliance context, knowledge of intentions often relates to information respecting future compliance.[61] In relation to EIAs, the information that a project proponent must disclose is aimed at ensuring that interested parties understand the nature of the project itself, its potential impacts on the environment, as well as the feasibility and environmental impacts of alternatives to the project. The purpose of disclosure is to ensure that for those projects that are likely to have a significant impact on the environment or an identified part of the environment, such as the environment of another state, the project proponent or state of origin has given full consideration to the environmental consequences of the project.

The interest-coordination aspect of EIA-mandated disclosure is evident in the rules regarding who must receive notification. For example, in the transboundary context, notification is limited to only those states that are likely to suffer a significant impact to their environment. The threshold test both identifies the parties that need to be consulted and provides a standard under which a state of origin need not engage other states. The fact that notification is required to be given as early as possible, and in any event prior to a decision being made, indicates that the purpose of notification and disclosure is to arrive at decisions that will account for the interests of other parties. Like institutions in environmental governance more generally, EIA commitments help reduce transaction costs by identifying negotiating partners and the issues that require cooperative solutions.

[61] Chayes and Chayes, *The New Sovereignty* at 147–149, discussing, *inter alia*, Elinor Ostrom, *Governing the Commons: The Evolution of Institutions for Collective Action* (Cambridge: Cambridge University Press, 1990).

Disclosure of information under EIA commitments provides a measure of procedural protection to both the state of origin and the affected state. For example, an affected party is required upon notification to provide the project proponent or state of origin with an indication of what issues are not satisfactorily addressed and what measures will satisfy their concerns. This requirement is implemented through the duty to consult based on the EIA documentation, which has the effect of limiting the scope of consultations to the issues identified in the screening and scoping processes.[62] By directing the parties to focus their consultations on the matters of interest to them, the EIA process seeks to avoid the inefficient use of resources that would result from studying and reporting on issues that are extraneous to the parties' respective interests. From the project proponent's perspective, the scoping process provides reassurance that objections to a project do not become a "moving target" in the sense that, once an affected state has raised its concerns, it becomes difficult for that state to change those concerns or raise new concerns without adequate justification.

An emerging area related to transparency that bears on compliance is the requirement for proponents to engage in post-project analysis for the purposes of monitoring compliance and verifying predictions.[63] Chayes and Chayes place considerable emphasis on the value of monitoring and verification as a means by which to expose state behavior that fails to adhere to treaty requirements.[64] However, they caution that verification and monitoring processes can become unwieldy and will not always resolve disagreements about the current state of compliance.[65] The recognition here is that the costs of third party monitoring and verification processes may exceed their instrumental value. Consequently, Chayes and Chayes look to less intrusive means of monitoring, such as self-reporting mechanisms.[66]

The post-project analysis requirements, which are becoming more prevalent in domestic and international EIA systems, provide a mechanism by which parties can provide reassurance that the predicted levels of impact are not being exceeded in actual fact. This is, of course, particularly important in situations that involve high levels of uncertainty.

[62] Convention on Environmental Impact Assessment in a Transboundary Context, Espoo, Finland, February 25, 1991, 30 ILM 802, in force January 14, 1998, Art. 5.

[63] Ibid., Art. 7; Protocol to the Antarctic Treaty on Environmental Protection, Madrid, October 4, 1991, 30 ILM 1461, in force January 14, 1998, Art. 5.

[64] Chayes and Chayes, *The New Sovereignty* at 144–148.

[65] Ibid., ch. 8 at 174 *et seq.*

[66] Ibid. at 194–196.

A corollary to post-project monitoring is an adaptive management approach whereby adjustments may be made to projects to mitigate unforeseen impacts.[67] The Espoo Convention leaves the extent, if any, of post-project analysis to be determined by the state of origin, in consultation with other parties.[68] The approach is one of self-monitoring, but critically the Espoo Convention provides that, where post-project analysis discloses significant transboundary impacts, the state of origin must notify the affected state and consult on mitigation measures.[69] There is potential for post-project monitoring to be used to strengthen the future predictive capabilities of EIAs by providing valuable feedback on the accuracy of EIA methodology and on the appropriateness of the specific standards adopted. This learning-oriented purpose is expressly acknowledged in the Espoo Convention.[70] In a review of the implementation of the Espoo Convention, a number of parties indicated that post-project analysis was being undertaken in certain cases, although it was rarely mandatory.[71] The use of post-project analysis under the Espoo Convention has been directed at monitoring for predicted outcomes, but no attempts have been made to integrate that information into future EIA processes as a feedback and learning mechanism.[72]

The use of post-project analysis, which is also emphasized in the Antarctic and biological diversity regimes, is the clearest illustration of EIA processes moving toward a more ongoing, regulatory role, as opposed to its traditional synoptic and predictive approach. This is the role of EIA that is contemplated in the *Gabcikovo-Nagymaros Case* by Judge Weeramantry in his discussion of EIA as part of an obligation in international law for states to continually monitor the environmental impacts of projects and to adapt projects in light of this information.[73]

6.4.2 *Participation*

Requirements providing for participation by affected states in transboundary EIA processes allow for greater access to expertise and

[67] Discussed, in the domestic context, above at ch. 4. [68] Espoo Convention, Art. 7(1).
[69] Ibid., Art. 7(2). [70] Ibid., Annex V.
[71] UNECE, "Convention on Environmental Impact Assessment in a Transboundary Context: Review of Implementation, 2003," released August 30, 2004, at 20, www.unece.org/env/eia/welcome.html. For example, in Canada, whether post-project follow-up is required depends on the type of assessment undertaken, discussed above at ch. 2.
[72] UNECE, ibid. at 20.
[73] *Case Concerning the Gabcikovo-Nagymaros Project (Hungary/Slovakia)* (1997) ICJ Rep 6 at 111–112.

information in an affected state. For example, participation addresses the practical difficulty that a state of origin faces in accessing accurate information regarding baseline environmental conditions and specific expertise regarding local conditions in foreign jurisdictions. In the transboundary context, local environmental agencies will often have the best information regarding the environmental characteristics and capacities of locally affected resources. Under the Espoo Convention, a state of origin may request that an affected party provide "reasonably obtainable information relating to the potentially affected environment under the jurisdiction of the affected party."[74] The objective of this provision is to improve the quality of the environmental information of the assessment and thereby to reduce uncertainty with respect to the outcomes of the projects. Where a state of origin relies on information provided by an affected state, a further level of reassurance is created for the affected state since the assessment is based on information that originates with the affected state itself. The provisions in the Arctic EIA Guidelines regarding the participation of indigenous communities and the use of traditional knowledge demonstrate a similar goal through recognition that groups within a state may possess specialized environmental knowledge and may also harbor concerns about the reliability of the assessments based solely on the proponent's information and methods.[75]

Exposing the scientific analysis that underlies an EIA to public scrutiny provides reassurance that the underlying scientific methods and analysis undertaken in support of EIA are sound and may be reasonably relied upon. By opening the process up to a broad range of actors, particularly during the screening and scoping phases of the EIA processes, participation is likely to enhance the salience of the information contained in the EIA by ensuring that the assessment addresses those issues that are relevant to the parties whose interests are affected.[76] The effectiveness of the scoping process to ensure that issues beyond those determined to be relevant by the proponent are considered will depend on how early

[74] Espoo Convention, Art. 3(6).

[75] 1997 Guidelines for Environmental Impact Assessment in the Arctic, adopted by the Arctic Council in the 1997 Alta Declaration on the Protection of the Arctic Environmental Protection Strategy, http://finnbarents.urova.fi/aria/ ("Arctic EIA Guidelines") at 37.

[76] See David Cash *et al.*, "Salience, Credibility, Legitimacy and Boundaries: Linking Research, Assessment and Decision Making" (Cambridge, MA: Kennedy School of Government/Harvard University Faculty Research Working Papers Series, November 2002).

in the process participation is required. In this regard, both the Espoo Convention and the Antarctic Protocol requirements fall short of requiring public consultation prior to the drafting of the EIA, although both provide for input by affected parties in advance of completion of the EIA document.[77] Within domestic EIA systems, the practice of requiring some consultation during the scoping phase of an EIA is becoming more common and improves the ability of EIA processes to coordinate issues at an early stage.

The transnational nature of EIA is further evidence of the broad participatory nature of EIA commitments. While Chayes and Chayes view participation largely through greater state involvement, Koh recognizes that the state may not always adequately represent or necessarily share the views of its affected citizens.[78] EIA commitments, by providing for notification and disclosure of information to non-state actors and by providing those groups with direct avenues of participation, allows for the political preferences of minority groups or less organized interests to be accounted for.[79] Again, the Arctic EIA Guidelines, with their emphasis on the participation of indigenous communities, can be seen in this light.[80] The importance of public involvement, including that of minority groups, is also emphasized in the CBD EIA/SEA Draft Guidelines.[81]

6.4.3 *Discursiveness*

While improving efficiency and reducing uncertainty enhance the conditions for cooperative behavior, persuasion is at the heart of process-oriented compliance explanations.[82] Processes that require a state to justify its position publicly are more likely to lead states to frame those justifications in terms of shared principles. Chayes and Chayes describe the process of persuasion in this context as being iterative and creative, in the sense that, where states engage one another in a dialogical fashion, the outcome is the product of each participant's input, and, as such,

[77] Espoo Convention, Arts. 3(1) and 4(1); Antarctic Protocol, Annex I, Arts. 3(3)–(6).

[78] See the discussion above at ch. 3.

[79] Espoo Convention, Art. 2(6).

[80] Arctic EIA Guidelines at 37.

[81] Decision VI/7 of the Conference of the Parties to the Convention on Biological Diversity, "Guidelines for Incorporating Biodiversity-Related Issues into Environmental Impact Assessment Legislation and/or Processes and in Strategic Environmental Assessment" in *Report of the Sixth Meeting of the Conference of the Parties to the Convention on Biological Diversity*, UN Doc. UNEP/CBD/COP/6/7, Annex,www.biodiv.org/decisions/default.aspx?m=cop-06 at para. 28 ("CBD EIA/SEA Draft Guidelines").

[82] Chayes and Chayes, *The New Sovereignty* at 25.

each participant is more committed to that outcome given their authorial role.[83]

International EIA processes, when operating on an interstate level, provide a set of processes that facilitate this same type of justificatory discourse. The iterative nature of EIA varies, but, if the screening and scoping requirements include consultation, the result is that the affected state is involved in identifying the environmental issues and the alternatives to the proposal, which can be viewed as a form of agenda-setting.[84] Even in cases where public consultation is limited to reviewing a draft EIA report and providing comments, the structure retains a discursive element because the affected state still has an ability to provide comments on the EIA to which the state of origin is required to respond.[85] Under the Espoo Convention, it is expressly contemplated that the parties shall enter into consultations, in effect mandating that the legitimate concerns of an affected state cannot be ignored.[86]

As presented by Chayes and Chayes, persuasion is possible because through these discursive processes states come to recalculate their interests in terms of their broader concerns for community standing, which is the hallmark of sovereignty.[87] A state's concern for its reputation is amplified where it has mutual points of contact with other states, which in turn depend upon that state being able to reassure its negotiating partners that it will act in accordance with its commitments. Where discussions regarding the outcomes of EIAs are conducted at a state-to-state level through a centralized agency that is cognizant of the broader reputational consequences of its behavior, EIA processes are a part of the greater web of state interrelationships and are subject to the same pressures to conform to shared principles. The structure of the Espoo Convention can be explained as seeking to capitalize on these pressures.[88] Similarly, the Antarctic Protocol's comprehensive environmental evaluation requirements provide a structure that encourages dialogue between state parties through the Committee for Environmental Protection that

[83] Ibid. at 123. See also Keohane, "Governance."

[84] On agenda setting as a source of power, see Chayes and Chayes, *The New Sovereignty* at 275–276.

[85] Espoo Convention, Art. 6(1); Antarctic Protocol, Annex I, Art. 3(6).

[86] Espoo Convention, Art. 5.

[87] Chayes and Chayes, *The New Sovereignty* at 27.

[88] For example, the Inquiry Procedure that may be initiated where parties disagree on the application of the Espoo Convention to a particular project relies on community pressure to adhere to a third-party dispute resolution process: see Espoo Convention, Appendix IV.

has the effect of generating community pressure on individual member states to conform to treaty values.[89]

Even outside formal treaty-based structures, the duty to consult can be drawn upon by states to engage other states in an ongoing dialogue over the potential impacts of planned activities. Certainly in the *MOX Plant Case*, the United Kingdom and Ireland engaged in extensive consultations over the MOX plant facility.[90] Likewise, in the *Gabcikovo-Nagymaros Case*, the parties were required by the ICJ to enter into further negotiation with a view to resolving their differences over, *inter alia*, the environmental consequences of the dam project.[91] While the ICJ did not specify EIA as the modality by which the environmental issues would be resolved, it clearly anticipated that the parties were to consider the environmental implications of the project in light of prevailing environmental standards. Because the ICJ refrained from defining the extent and content of the environmental rights, the result is a negotiation structure that looks much like the one anticipated under EIA commitments in that the parties are required to negotiate a solution in good faith within the framework of broad principles, such as a common commitment to sustainable development.[92]

6.5 EIAs as transnational legal processes

Despite the presence of the above examples, the more common interactions arising out of international EIA commitments are not going to occur at a formal state-to-state level, but rather will involve interactions between agencies and within domestic EIA processes. This will certainly be the case for those EIA commitments, such as those contained in the CBD and UNCLOS, which are to be incorporated directly into domestic EIA regimes. Even under the Espoo Convention, the points of contact for notification purposes for many of the parties are listed as the party's environment ministry or related agency, as opposed to the ministry of

[89] The Committee for Environmental Protection is established under the Antarctic Protocol, Art. 11. The Committee's oversight role is established under Annex 1, Art. 3(4). There have been twenty-one CEEs reviewed by the Committee since 1987 according to a list prepared by the Committee, www.cep.aq.

[90] *MOX Plant Case (Ireland* v. *United Kingdom)* (Annex VII Arbitration), Memorial of United Kingdom, paras. 6.85–6.95, available at www.pca-cpa.org.

[91] *Case Concerning the Gabcikovo-Nagymaros Project (Hungary/Slovakia)* (1997) ICJ Rep 6 at para. 141.

[92] Recall that the ICJ raises sustainable development as a goal in the context of future negotiations between Hungary and Slovakia, ibid.

foreign affairs,[93] signifying that discussions regarding transboundary EIAs will often be conducted directly between environmental officials.[94] The notification process under the US–Canada Air Quality Agreement is also carried out through environmental agencies on both sides.[95] On an even more localized level, there are examples of cooperative agreements between state and provincial environmental agencies, whereby the agencies agree to notify and consult one another regarding major project proposals that are in the vicinity of the other's jurisdiction. For example, in a memorandum of understanding between the Washington State Department of Ecology and the British Columbia Environmental Assessment Office, the two agencies agree to notify, exchange information and provide an opportunity for comment with respect to projects subject to EIA processes that are located close to the border.[96] The implication of the agency-to-agency interactions contemplated under these arrangements is that many transboundary EIA consultations will occur outside the web of interstate relations, raising questions as to whether agencies will be constrained by reputational concerns in a manner similar to national governments.

The direct interaction of government agencies on transboundary issues is an example of a broader phenomenon described by Anne-Marie Slaughter as international governance through transnational government networks, by which she means to describe the increasing tendency of governmental regulators to create informal linkages with their counterparts in other jurisdictions for the purposes of exchanging information, coordinating policies and resolving common problems.[97] One promising aspect of transnational government networks described by

93 A list of the points of contact can be found at www.unece.org/env/eia/points_of_contact.htm.

94 Agency-to-agency discussions of this sort are described by Koivurova in connection with Vuotos Reservoir project: see Timo Koivurova, *Environmental Impact Assessment in the Arctic: A Study of International Legal Norms* (Aldershot: Ashgate Publishing Ltd, 2002) at 273–286.

95 Discussed above at ch. 4.2.2. In a Washington state power generation project with transboundary air pollution impacts, it was Environment Canada, the federal environment department, that became involved in the project, not the foreign affairs department.

96 Memorandum of Understanding between the Washington State Department of Ecology and the British Columbia Environmental Assessment Office, June 20, 2001, www.eao.gov.bc.ca/publicat/MOU-Wash_st-EAO_2004/mou-2003.pdf. The Québec government has entered into similar agreements with some of its border states.

97 Anne-Marie Slaughter, *A New World Order* (Princeton, NJ: Princeton University Press, 2004).

Slaughter is their role in facilitating compliance with community norms and in generating reasoned solutions to collective problems.[98] The success of networks in bringing about cooperative results depends on many of the same types of features identified by Chayes and Chayes. In particular, where officials have repeated, frequent interactions and share similar values and where there are opportunities for reciprocal detriments or benefits, there is a greater likelihood that the parties will adhere to community norms.[99]

In the case of interactions between environmental officials on transboundary EIA matters, it is likely that the participants will have repeated interactions over time. To a significant degree, the interactions are institutionalized through standing committees, such as the US–Canada Air Quality Committee,[100] and through mechanisms such as the points-of-contact provisions under the Espoo Convention. In the instances cited above, where the interacting officials are often found in environment ministries, they are likely to share professional or scientific backgrounds and will face a common set of problems. The technical nature of EIA documents will also tend to result in the involvement of scientists in reviewing transboundary issues. While scientists do not necessarily share similar values, they will often be bound together by a shared sense of professionalism and a commitment to common approaches to resolving science-based disputes.[101] Finally, interactions regarding transboundary impacts are clearly reciprocal insofar as both states will have activities with the potential to cause significant transboundary harm.

The presence of reciprocal burdens and benefits underlines the importance of the principle of nondiscrimination in structuring transboundary EIA processes. Because the intention of compliance-generating processes generally and EIA processes in particular is to engender public-regarding outcomes, the culture of the interactions between participants must be oriented away from undiluted self-interest.[102] Slaughter views the move toward public-spiritedness as being more likely to emerge where parties are offered a fair procedure by which they can have their position heard and considered by others. Certainly, EIA processes are structured to this end. Indeed, they go further by making explicit the

98 Ibid. at 195–212. 99 Ibid. at 199.

100 Set up under the Agreement between the United States and Canada on Air Quality, (1991) Can TS No. 3, in force March 13, 1991, reprinted 30 ILM 676 (1991), Art. VIII.

101 Slaughter, *A New World Order* at 205. See also Peter Haas, "Introduction: Epistemic Communities and International Policy Co-ordination" (1992) 46 Int. Org. 1.

102 Ibid. at 204.

underlying requirement of good faith. Here, good faith requires that decision-makers do more than pay lip-service to opposing or alternative viewpoints, but remain open to the possibility of being persuaded. Nondiscrimination advances this goal because it implements fair treatment by requiring states to treat environmental impacts on areas outside its jurisdiction no differently from those impacts that occur within its jurisdiction.

Slaughter goes on to note that it is in settings in which "both discussion and argument are likely to elicit information, proposed solutions, and contending justifications that will help produce a reasoned and legitimate consensus."[103] The structural features of EIA commitments are intended to create exactly these information-rich, solution-oriented and justificatory processes. This is not to suggest that EIA processes will always produce reasoned and acceptable outcomes. We need only look as far as the *MOX Plant Case* or the *Gabcikovo-Nagymaros Case* for examples of activities where the political sensitivities make acceptable solutions difficult to achieve. However, it does suggest that EIA processes create a decision-making environment that will promote outcomes that are based on accepted principles, and not solely on an aggregation of individual interests.

In the case of those regimes principally associated with issues of global common concern, the EIA commitment is intended less to structure interactions between states and more toward requiring that states consider a particular type of impact within their domestic EIA systems. The structure of these processes is somewhat different given the absence of external pressure from other states or from agency counterparts in other jurisdictions. However, the central characteristics of process-oriented compliance explanations are also evident in these domestic EIA processes.

Here, the compliance model with the most relevance is Koh's theory of transnational legal process that presents an explanation of compliance that accounts for a much broader range of influences than those that arise in interactions between states.[104] For Koh, state compliance with international law will be strongly influenced by pressures from within. The lynchpin of compliance remains persuasion, but for Koh the interactions that are likely to be most effective are those that are directed at a state's domestic institutions. Compliance is enhanced under Koh's model of transnational legal process where international norms can be

[103] Slaughter, *A New World Order* at 206.

[104] Discussed in detail above at ch. 6.3.2.

brought into domestic or transnational processes in which authoritative interpretations of the norm are made and ultimately internalized within the domestic institutions. The question here is whether international EIA commitments have the effect of opening up domestic EIA processes to international normative influences, providing in effect an additional site for the interpretation and internalization of international environmental norms.

The success of EIA processes as a forum for the projection of international norms into domestic institutions depends in large part on the presence of the same process values integral to Chayes and Chayes' managerial approach to compliance, except that the process characteristics are aimed at transnational actors operating within the domestic legal framework. For example, domestic EIA processes are highly inclusive, allowing for the participation of both public and private groups, including what have been termed environmental "norm entrepreneurs."[105] The decision-making processes themselves are relatively transparent in that the environmental information used to assess impacts is made publicly available and is often presented in a format that is accessible to both laypersons and scientists. The nature of the participation allows for active involvement by public and private actors who are not part of the formal decision-making structure. The process is clearly discursive, and, while decision-making authorities do not relinquish their discretion to approve an activity in the face of environmental impacts, a number of factors militate against decisions being made that fail to account for these impacts.

The transparency of the decision-making process, particularly the requirement to give reasons for a decision and to account for both the EIA and the comments made, provides an opportunity for those who stand in opposition to the decision to expose any contradictions between the decision taken and prevailing environmental norms, including international environmental norms. Secondly, domestic EIA systems are often backstopped by a system of judicial review that provides objectors with an additional forum in which to pursue desired environmental outcomes. In the NEPA context, Serge Taylor concluded that, even in the absence of substantive review, the breadth and complexity of procedural review provided environmental groups with leverage to influence

[105] See Martha Finnemore and Katherine Sikkink, "International Norm Dynamics and Political Change" (1998) 52 Int. Org. 887, discussing norm entrepreneurs.

the decision-making process,[106] a process Koh refers to as "bargaining in the shadow of law."[107] The availability of judicial review in the context of environmental decision-making to ensure that state agencies comply with their procedural obligations is itself becoming an international norm through the Aarhus Convention.[108]

Compliance with international legal norms, for Koh, is achieved on a more permanent basis by the internalization of norms within domestic institutions. In essence, domestic decision-makers will seek to avoid the frictions associated with decisions that fail to adhere to international legal norms by adopting practices that institutionalize interpretations consistent with international law. By incorporating the norm into the fabric of the decision-making processes, compliance becomes ingrained.[109] The embeddedness of these norms has an institutional aspect, the international rules and principles form part of bureaucratic operating procedures or perhaps are implemented in more formal ways such as through legislation or regulations, and a cognitive aspect, whereby decision-makers come to fully associate the international norms with their own internal values.[110]

If domestic EIA processes are in fact playing this role, then one could expect to see nongovernmental organizations and government agencies with a particular interest in international environmental issues becoming involved in domestic EIA processes and EIA reform as a way to advance their broader environmental agenda. In addition, international environmental issues and the norms associated with those issues should begin to be invoked in EIA processes. For example, those responsible for producing EIAs would include consideration of the impact of the project on issues of global common concern, such as climate change or biological diversity. Finally, as an indication of some degree of internalization, one could also expect to see some attempts by policy-makers to

106 Serge Taylor, *Making Bureaucracies Think: The Environmental Impact Statement Strategy of Administrative Reform* (Stanford, CA: Stanford University Press, 1984) at 247–248.

107 Harold Koh, "Why Do Nations Obey International Law" at 2639, quoting Robert Mnookin and Lewis Kornhauser, "Bargaining in the Shadow of the Law: The Case of Divorce" (1979) 88 Yale LJ 950.

108 Convention on Access to Information, Public Participation in Decision-Making and Access to Justice in Environmental Matters, Aarhus, Denmark, June 25, 1998, 38 ILM 517, entered into force October 30, 2001.

109 The process of internalization draws on the work of Robert Cover, in particular his notion of "jurisgenesis," whereby successive interactions generate solutions that are subsequently informally, and sometimes formally, codified in state practices. Cover, "Nomos and Narrative."

110 Harold Koh, "Bringing International Law Home" at 627–633.

incorporate the requirements of international law into EIA processes in a regularized fashion, instead of relying on agencies and other participants to raise international issues on an *ad hoc* basis. The participatory aspect is addressed immediately below. I will return to the question of the invocation of international norms and their internalization in the section and chapter that follow, respectively.

In terms of NGO involvement, EIAs have since their outset been an avenue for environmental groups to advocate environmental change. In the early days of NEPA, groups such as the Sierra Club, the National Audubon Society, the National Wildlife Federation and the Natural Resources Defense Council were instrumental in legal challenges aimed at making NEPA more responsive to environmental considerations.[111] While environmental advocacy groups have been active in a broad spectrum of domestic environmental issues, they have also been instrumental in seeking the application of NEPA to extraterritorial effects.[112] In Canada, environmental groups involved in a legislative review of the CEAA made submissions that EIA processes must better account for Canada's international obligations, particularly under the CBD and the UNFCCC, when considering the impacts of planned activities.[113] Environmental advocacy groups have supported these calls for formal recognition of the importance of international environmental commitments through appeals to international norms in EIA processes themselves. For example, Canada's international commitment to reduce greenhouse gas levels has been cited by environmental groups in support of their concerns regarding the impacts on climate change from various fossil fuel extraction projects.[114] Incorporating the concerns of indigenous groups

[111] These groups are cited by Serge Taylor as playing an important early role in NEPA: see Taylor, *Making Bureaucracies Think* at 47, 238–239.

[112] *Environmental Defense Fund Inc.* v. *Massey*, 986 F 2d 528 (DC Cir. 1993) (application of NEPA to activities in the Antarctic); *Natural Resources Defense Council* v. *Department of the Navy*, 2002 WL 32095131 (CD Cal. 2002) (application of NEPA to marine environment in EEZ); see also *Center for Biological Diversity* v. *National Science Foundation*, 2002 WL 31548073 (ND Cal. 2002) (application of NEPA to impacts on marine mammals outside US jurisdiction).

[113] See, for example, CEAA Five Year Review Submissions by the David Suzuki Foundation, February 2, 2000, www.ceaa-acee.gc.ca/013/001/0002/0004/0001/suzuki_e.htm; and CEAA Five Year Review Joint Submission by West Coast Environmental Law Association and Sierra Legal Defense Fund, March 31, 2000, www.ceaa-acee.gc.ca/013/001/0002/0004/0001/wcel_e.htm.

[114] See *Report of the EUB-CEAA Joint Review Panel Cheviot Coal Project* September 2000, at section 5.2.2, www.ceaa-acee.gc.ca ("Cheviot Coal EIA"). See also similar concerns

has also been given prominence in the Canadian EIA process, with specific steps being undertaken to incorporate traditional knowledge into the EIA process and to ensure that the rights and land claims of indigenous groups are accounted for in the EIA process.[115] There is also some indication that NGOs are looking to the Espoo Convention as a possible vehicle to pursue environmental concerns by seeking standing to invoke the non-compliance procedures.[116] Finally, in the context of developing countries, NGOs have been integral to the development of the World Bank's EIA procedures and continue to be involved in these processes.[117]

It should be noted that those seeking to promote a particular international norm through transnational political, legal and administrative channels are not restricted to nongovernmental organizations. In the context of EIAs, government agencies, and individuals within agencies, acting as "administrative entrepreneurs," have been credited with shaping the policy direction of the decision-making framework.[118] Unlike state-centered models of compliance, where the state is treated as having a unified set of interests, the transnationalism of EIA processes acknowledges the heterogeneous nature of government interests by providing avenues of influence for agencies engaged in promoting environmental change. In this context, international legal norms can act as powerful justifications for commenting agencies, particularly environmental agencies, to insist upon more rigorous norms of analysis in relation to a particular environmental issue. For example, Environment Canada,

raised by the Sierra Club of Canada in respect of an oil sands extraction project: *Report of the Joint Review Panel Established by the Alberta Energy and Utilities Board and the Government of Canada: Decision 2004–009; Shell Canada Ltd, Applications for an Oil Sands Mine, Bitumen Extraction Plant, Co-generation Plant and Water Pipeline in the Fort McMurray Area* (Calgary: Alberta Energy and Utilities Board, 2004) at 15.3, www.ceaa-acee.gc.ca ("Jackpine Mine Project").

115 See, for example, *Report on the Proposed Voisey's Bay Mine and Mill Project* (Ottawa: Government of Canada, 1999) at 118–124 ("Voisey's Bay EIA") and *Environmental Impact Statement Final Terms of Reference for the Mackenzie Gas Project*, www.ceaa-acee.gc.ca, at 5–6 ("MacKenzie Pipeline EIA Final Terms of Reference").

116 See *Report of the Fifth Meeting of the Implementation Committee*, April 8, 2004, UN Doc. MP/EIA/WG.1/2004/4, www.unece.org/env/documents/2004/eia/wg.1/mp.eia.wg.1.2004.4.e.pdf, discussing the possibility of NGO involvement in compliance processes.

117 Richard Haeuber, "The World Bank and Environmental Assessment: The Role of Nongovernmental Organizations" (1992) 12 Environmental Impact Assessment Review 331.

118 Geoffrey Wandesforde-Smith, "Environmental Impact Assessment, Entrepreneurship, and Policy Change" in R. V. Bartlett, ed., *Policy Through Impact Assessment: Institutionalized Analysis as a Policy Strategy* (New York: Greenwood Press, 1989) 155.

the federal agency responsible for environmental regulation, has been actively involved in raising climate change issues in a variety of federal EIA processes.[119]

6.6 Substantive values: normativity and context

In compliance explanations, persuasion, as opposed to coercion or other forms of incentive manipulation, works because the participants involved can successfully appeal to norms, principles and values that are shared. The difficulty that one can foresee with EIA commitments as compliance mechanisms is that the norms that underlie the international commitments and are invoked within domestic EIA processes are too ambiguous to exert any persuasive force.[120] This argument also goes to the heart of EIA processes, which are most often characterized as planning, as opposed to compliance, mechanisms – a designation that suggests that EIA processes do not direct policy-makers toward certain outcomes. In the domestic context, much of the debate surrounding the ability of EIA processes to bring about environmental change has focused on the enforceability of substantive norms within EIA processes. However, when viewed from the perspective of international or transnational interactions, where enforceability is the exception not the rule, the ability of EIA processes to influence outcomes in support of international environmental norms is more dependent upon the ability of environmentally concerned actors to generate behavioral expectations on decision-makers to conform to environmental norms – a process that would appear at a minimum to require that norms be specific enough to be able to identify non-compliant decisions or actions.

The response to the questions raised by the requirement for substantive specificity is several-fold. First, in some cases international EIA processes can draw on fairly precise norms and as such can promote compliance with these norms directly. In the majority of cases, though, the norms in question remain at the level of principle and, as such, are open to multiple interpretations. However, EIA processes are structured in such a way as to narrow the interpretive scope of these principles by projecting the principles into highly context-specific decision-making processes where "right" courses of action may be more easily agreed

[119] Environment Canada's role is discussed in Rick Lee, *Climate Change and Environmental Assessment* (Ottawa: CEAA Research and Development Monograph Series, 2001).

[120] This is the form of argument put forward by Thomas Franck, where he suggests that norms that lack precision will have less "compliance pull." See Franck, *Legitimacy Among Nations* at 50 *et seq*.

upon. In addition, EIA processes draw on scientific methods, which contain their own evaluative criteria. The lines between science, politics and law are often blurred, but the structure of EIA processes takes advantage of the relationships between these distinct influences, and serves to strengthen the ability of scientific analysis to influence environmental change. Finally, the kind of compliance that EIA promotes is reflective of the open-textured nature of the underlying environmental norms. In this latter regard, EIA offers a form of compliance mechanism that is well suited to the common circumstances in international environmental governance that finds states able to agree on broad objectives and principles but not on precise rules. Compliance in the face of broad standards is not likely to be determined on a case-by-case basis. Instead, compliance has to be tracked over longer periods of time, and will be evidenced by more subtle shifts in attitudes and approaches in environmental decision-making within agencies and other actors involved in EIA processes.[121]

6.6.1 *Standards and norms in EIA processes*

A consistent structural feature of international EIA commitments, whether they are contained in specific environmental regimes or as stand-alone or customary obligations, is that the procedural obligations that form the heart of EIA processes are directed toward the achievement of a broadly defined environmental end. In transboundary EIA commitments, that end is to prevent transboundary environmental harm.[122] In other regimes, the substantive ends are equally open-ended, but are nonetheless clearly present. While these substantive ends may appear to be incapable of meaningful implementation, in practice the participants in EIAs are able to draw on a variety of normative sources that sharpen the application of the substantive principles invoked.

For example, in a determination of whether an activity meets the threshold test of significant environmental impact, international environmental standards are often drawn upon as evidence of significance. An explicit recognition of using international standards in this manner is found in the CBD EIA/SEA Draft Guidelines, which cite both the Ramsar Convention on Wetlands of International Importance[123] and

[121] This approach is consistent with the approach to the role and influence of EIAs in domestic policy-making presented by R. V. Bartlett: see Bartlett, "NEPA Revisited" in Larry Canter and Ray Clark, eds., *Environmental Policy and NEPA: Past, Present and Future* (Boca Raton, FL: St. Lucie Press, 1997) 51.

[122] See Espoo Convention, Art. 2(1).

[123] Ramsar, Iran, February 2, 1971, 996 UNTS 245; 11 ILM 963 (1971), in force December 21, 1975.

the Convention on Migratory Species.[124] The direction here is that the criteria or the resources identified in these international conventions should be used to inform screening criteria either through inclusion of internationally recognized features in positive lists requiring assessment or in criteria for initial environmental assessments.[125] The intended result is that the requirements of these conventions are implemented by ensuring that activities undertaken do not have adverse impacts on the resources that are the subject of the convention, such as a listed wetland under the Ramsar Convention. For example, the CEAA clearly anticipates that the listing or description of a feature in an international convention will contribute to a determination of significance under the CEAA.[126] Similar references to internationally derived standards are found in the Arctic and Antarctic EIA guidelines,[127] both of which reference further international instruments that identify specific features or ecosystem characteristics.[128]

A related example of the integration of preexisting standards into international EIA processes is the use of preexisting standards to elaborate on a transboundary impact. For example, in an EIA assessment process relating to an electrical generating facility (the "Sumas 2 Generating Station") in the State of Washington that had air quality impacts on neighboring British Columbia, the environmental impact statement prepared by the proponent considered the impact of the project on air quality on both sides of the Canada–US border. In doing so, the EIS had regard for US federal and state air quality regulations and objectives, as well

[124] Bonn, Germany, June 23, 1979, 19 ILM 15 (1979), in force November 1, 1983.

[125] CBD EIA/SEA Draft Guidelines, paras. 8–17 and Appendices I and II.

[126] See Pauline Lynch-Stewart, *Using Ecological Standards, Guidelines and Objectives for Determining Significance: An Examination of Existing Information to Support Decisions Involving Wetlands* (Ottawa: CEAA Research and Development Monograph Series, 2000), listing the Ramsar Convention, the Migratory Birds Convention and the Canada–US Great Lakes Water Quality Agreement as ecological benchmarks to determine significance.

[127] Arctic EIA Guidelines, section 5.4; Antarctic Protocol, Annex I, Art. 3.3.

[128] For example, the Arctic EIA Guidelines reference the "Conservation of Arctic Flora and Fauna" in the Arctic Environmental Protection Strategy, adopted by Canada, Denmark, Finland, Iceland, Norway, Sweden, the Soviet Union and the United States, June 14, 1991, reprinted in 30 ILM 1624 (1991) at 1663, as a source of information regarding sensitive areas, ibid. at 12, while the Guidelines for Environmental Impact Assessment in Antarctica reference special management areas identified under the Antarctic regime, such as the Commission for the Conservation of Antarctic Living Resources Ecosystem Monitoring Program, Specially Protected Areas, and Sites of Special Scientific Interest, adopted by Resolution 4(2005), attached to the Final Report of XXVIIIth ATCM, 2005, at para. 3.1.1.

as Canadian federal and provincial objectives.[129] The use of Canadian standards to address impacts from an American facility is an interesting derivation of the substantive application of the principle of nondiscrimination. In addition to applying local standards to transboundary impacts (nondiscrimination), the EIS accounts for the standards of the affected state, determining that the project would meet those (higher) standards. While the standards referred to here are domestic in origin, their application elaborates on the international obligation to prevent transboundary harm through the implication that affected state air quality standards are a relevant indicator for determining significant harm. The US Environmental Appeal Board, who heard an appeal by Environment Canada and the Province of British Columbia of the project's approval, also referenced the US–Canada Air Quality Agreement, noting that the transboundary harm provisions of that agreement had not been invoked in this case.[130]

Many of the references in the above-noted documents are to standards or principles contained in instruments that are not themselves formally binding. This, however, points to a potential strength of EIAs tied to the non-determinative nature of EIA processes. Because the use of standards in EIA processes does not result in any formally binding result, the value of these sources is not in their normative status, but rather in their ability to persuade. Take, for example, the use of Canadian-based air quality standards in the Sumas EIS: these standards are not binding, but they are clearly persuasive because they indicate levels of acceptable air quality as determined by the authorities of the affected state. Similarly, criteria established under the Arctic Environmental Protection Strategy do not bind any of the participating states, but, given the AEPS's mandate and the role of national governments and other affected parties in establishing these criteria, they have clear relevance and persuasive authority.

The type of function EIA plays in the decision-making process will depend in part on the nature of the relevant substantive norms. Where those norms are specific and binding (standards), EIA processes will act as a mechanism to alert project proponents of these separate requirements at an early stage in the planning process and to implement

129 Washington State Energy Facility Site Evaluation Council, *Sumas Energy 2 Generating Facility, Final EIS*, February 2001, www.efsec.wa.gov/sumas2.html.

130 *Re Sumas Energy 2 Generating Facility*, March 2003, PSD Appeal Nos. 02-10 and 02-11, www.epa/gov/eab/orders/sumas.pdf at 23.

the standard into project planning.[131] The presence of a standard will diminish the exercise of discretion, although it will not entirely extinguish it. Where the relevant norms are contained in formally non-binding instruments and are in the form of principles, the role of EIAs is to implement those norms, but also to supplement their substantive content by elaborating on the norm's application in a specific context. Where binding norms require application and nothing more, non-binding norms require a more reflective attitude regarding the meaning of the norm and the adequacy of the norm to resolve the specific policy question at hand.

6.6.2 Context and EIAs

Given that many of the international principles that are referred to in EIA commitments are more open-ended, the context-specific nature of EIA processes is vital. In process-oriented compliance explanations, legal prescriptions that become divorced from specific circumstances are less likely to be perceived as legitimate. This is particularly the case where the future circumstances of the rule's application are difficult to predict. So, for example, Brunnée and Toope argue that "contextual regimes," which are non-binding and characterized by more open-ended principles than precise rules, allow states to generate normative consensus over time through the application of norms to specific contexts on a self-regulatory basis.[132] A similar evolutionary explanation of normative development is proffered by Koh, who describes obedience to international law as arising from multiple interactions and interpretation of norms within specific contexts. Change is possible under these explanations because participants, through their engagement in legal processes, including EIA processes, are shaped by the normative environment of those interactions. The process of dialogue and justification requires participants to frame their arguments with reference to common principles. Through repeated interactions addressing a variety of contexts, parties can come to better understand the full implications of their principles, which may lead to future elaboration of commitments or acceptance of normative strengthening of the commitments.

[131] A prevalent example is the use of lists of endangered species and the habitat protection requirements that accompany species protection efforts. Endangered species legislation may require that habitat areas be undisturbed. In such cases, EIA processes may disclose unacceptable habitat impact requiring project redesign or abandonment.

[132] Jutta Brunnée and Stephen Toope, "Environmental Security and Freshwater Resources: Ecosystem Regime Building" (1997) 91 AJIL 26 at 31–33.

The integration of climate change considerations into the Canadian federal EIA process provides an instructive example of how the projection of international norms into processes that require the participants to consider the norm in relation to highly specific contexts may lead to increased acceptance of those norms, particularly at the bureaucratic level. From an EIA perspective, climate change is a doubly vexing problem because where a proposed activity releases greenhouse gases it can contribute in a cumulative fashion to global climate change, but independently the effects of climate change will have to be taken into account in making predictions about future environmental conditions. For example, extrapolating past experiences and data regarding temperature conditions, water levels and the presence of permafrost in the Arctic region may not be an accurate predictor of future conditions in light of the dynamic and ongoing nature of global climate change. In other words, decision-makers must consider both the effects of the project on climate change, for example greenhouse gas emissions or carbon sink reductions, and the effects of climate change on the project.

As early as 1988, Environment Canada raised concerns with respect to the impact of climate change on the forecasting of sea levels in connection with the EIA for the Confederation Bridge (a fixed link traversing the Northumberland Strait between New Brunswick and Nova Scotia). Despite the fact that climate change remained an emerging issue during this time period and the science regarding global warming trends was uncertain, the design standard for predicted changes in sea levels was increased from 0.3 m to 1.0 m over the life of the structure.[133] Through the 1990s, Environment Canada raised climate change issues in a number of major projects where global warming could affect water levels, precipitation, evapotranspiration and permafrost.[134] The early application of climate change considerations in EIAs were all driven by concerns that global warming would result in future conditions that would either affect the integrity of the project design itself, or would result in unforeseen environmental consequences unless accounted for.

In a 1999 Environmental Assessment Panel Report on the Voisey's Bay Nickel Mine and Mill Project, the panel conducting the review recommended that the proponent develop an air pollution prevention plan through the reduction of fossil fuel combustion. This recommendation was partially justified on the basis of Canada's Kyoto Protocol commitments, notwithstanding that the Kyoto Protocol was not ratified at the

[133] Project details discussed in Lee, *Climate Change* at 18–20. [134] Ibid.

time.[135] In this instance, the concerns switched from the more technical concerns regarding how to account for climate change considerations in project design and assessment forecasts to the more normative concern of the impacts of human activities on climate change. Similar concerns regarding the impact of a proposal on climate change were raised in a 2000 panel report on a coal-mining project, the Cheviot Coal Mine, in Alberta. Here, the concerns were raised by a coalition of environmental groups.[136] It appears that the question of climate change was addressed in the assessment, although the project was not found to contribute to the problem. Canada's international commitment to reduce greenhouse gas levels was cited by the environmental groups in support of their concern, but the review panel noted that there was no existing regulatory program to cap greenhouse gas emissions.[137] Similarly, in an EIA panel review on a proposed oil sands project, the Jackpine Mine Project, the Sierra Club of Canada indicated that it would be opposed to the project on the basis of climate change concerns alone (although it had other concerns).[138] Here, the concern was broader in that the Sierra Club indicated its opposition to the approval of fossil fuel extraction projects on the basis that bringing additional fossil fuels to market was fundamentally bad policy in light of the contribution fossil fuels make to global climate change. The panel itself noted that climate change concerns were not raised as an issue in the terms of reference, and did not address the broader issue of the policy implications of fossil fuel extraction, although it did note that any environmental changes that result from climate change could be addressed through adaptive management approaches.[139] Finally, in a proposed EIA for a major pipeline project in the Mackenzie River Valley, the final terms of reference for the environmental impact study indicate that considerations of both the effects of climate change on the proposal and the effects of the proposal on climate change must be addressed.[140]

The increasing inclusion of climate change concerns in the federal EIA process started with Environment Canada's technical and scientific concerns with how climate change considerations could affect modeling and other forecasting tools used in EIA. The acceptance of the legitimacy of these concerns from the perspective of the impact of climate change on projects gave credence to the subsequent concerns regarding the impact of the project on climate change. These concerns were

[135] Voisey's Bay EIA, n. 115 above, at 35. [136] Cheviot Coal EIA, n. 114 above, at s. 5.2.2.
[137] Ibid. at s. 5.2.3. [138] Jackpine Mine Project, n. 114 above, at 15.3.
[139] Ibid. at 15.5. [140] MacKenzie Pipeline EIA Final Terms of Reference, n. 115, at s. 22.

first raised on the scale of the impacts from emissions from the project itself, but were expanded in the Jackpine Mine Project EIA to a more comprehensive, policy-level concern regarding fossil fuel extraction. In at least one case, the UNFCCC and the Kyoto Protocol were expressly noted in support of addressing climate change issues. The science-driven concerns of Environment Canada were sufficient to allow for the introduction of climate change issues in advance of international agreement on the subject. The shift toward assessing the impacts of the project on climate change came after the further entrenchment of climate change norms at the international level. Significantly, though, raising the issue of climate change and addressing greenhouse gas reductions in EIA processes preceded the ratification of the Kyoto Protocol, its coming into force, and any legislative response to the issue.

The direct influence of projecting climate change norms into EIAs on domestic policy is difficult to discern, especially since there were a wide range of policy initiatives relating to climate change ongoing over this time period.[141] However, a number of observations can be drawn from this example. First, climate change norms, which are derived from international sources, have clearly shaped the policy discourse within EIA processes by framing the issues relating to climate change and by providing normative justifications to policy entrepreneurs, such as Environment Canada and environmental advocacy groups. Secondly, by providing a specific context for the examination of climate change considerations, EIA processes are able to concretize an otherwise abstract set of normative prescriptions. For example, EIA processes require policy-makers to confront the practical implications of climate change on project design and on relevant environmental inputs, which in turn serves to legitimize the need to address the causes of global climate change. By framing climate change considerations in terms of the impacts on the project, the material interests of the proponent and the responsible authority must be reassessed in light of this new information.

The reference to international environmental issues in EIA processes is not restricted to global climate change. For example, in the Mackenzie Gas Project Terms of Reference, the Rio Declaration is invoked in justification of the adoption of the precautionary principle as one of the

[141] Some of these policies and their interaction with international climate change norms are discussed in Steven Bernstein, "International Institutions and the Framing of Domestic Policies: The Kyoto Protocol and Canada's Response to Climate Change" (2002) 35 Policy Science 203.

governing principles of the study.[142] This study also identifies establishing the project's contribution to sustainability as a fundamental principle for the assessment. Other EIA processes have also recognized sustainability and precautionary principles as being implemented through EIA processes.[143] In a related fashion, biological diversity and the need to recognize and incorporate aboriginal knowledge have also been given status as overriding principles that must govern the EIA process.[144] While none of these principles are exclusive to international law, they are all reflective of an approach that originates in the WCED report and the Rio Declaration.

In these examples, and in international EIA commitments more generally, the contextual nature of EIA aids implementation of the international norms through the assessment of alternatives. In the absence of quantified standards, the assessment of alternatives provides an evaluative basis for decision-making. Alternatives provide a comparative basis by which participants and observers can determine whether the preferred approach to carrying out an undertaking is the most environmentally benign approach that is reasonably available. In a number of regimes, such as Espoo, the CBD and the Antarctic Protocol, the EIA commitment is specifically linked to a goal of harm minimization, making the use of alternatives particularly relevant. For example, the CBD specifically requires that EIAs be undertaken "with a view to avoiding or minimizing" significant adverse effects on biodiversity. Where it can be shown that an alternative is less likely to cause such effects, it places the burden on the proponent to justify why the less intrusive alternative is not taken.

6.6.3 *Science as a normative influence*

As the majority of decisions contemplated under international EIA commitments is not addressed by precise standards, but is to be determined in accordance with the broader objectives of the regime itself, there remains a demand for further normative strengthening of the decision-making environment. Decisions regarding projects that fall within the broad areas of discretion left open by the absence of more precise legal

[142] MacKenzie Pipeline EIA Final Terms of Reference, n. 115 above, at s. 5.5.

[143] Voisey's Bay EIA, n. 115 above, at 9. See also Red Hill Creek Expressway Review Panel, "Environmental Impact Statement Guidelines," October 15, www.ceaa-acee.gc.ca at Annex 4, s. 1.0 ("Red Hill Creek EIS Guidelines").

[144] These values have been emphasized in the Voisey's Bay Project and the Mackenzie Valley Pipeline Project.

norms are not solely determined by the operation of politics. While not wanting to return to a characterization of EIA as an exercise of comprehensive rationality, science, its attendant methods, and unique cultural characteristics play a crucial role in determining outcomes.

The critique of EIA processes as relying too heavily on a comprehensive rationality model of administrative decision-making is largely misplaced in the sense that EIA processes from their inception clearly allowed for political considerations to enter into the decision-making process by opening up the process to non-experts and maintaining decision-maker discretion.[145] However, it is often the case that the broad environmental goals have already been identified and agreed upon. In circumstances where the central dispute is over how to implement shared goals, science can provide authoritative solutions, in the sense that they too provide a persuasive basis for justifying actions.[146] The authoritativeness of scientific processes lies in the acceptance that some questions admit of right answers or, at least, better answers, that there is a group of experts who can determine these better answers and the community can determine who these experts are.[147] These considerations tend to collapse the distinction between science-based, comprehensive rationality approaches to policy-making and the more overtly political pluralist model, by accepting that science itself has political and social dimensions. Karin Bäckstrand, a political scientist, addresses the blurred boundaries between science and politics in the following terms:

> An underlying premise is that scientific knowledge and practices operate inside rather than outside of politics. A key question is what counts as credible, authoritative and legitimate expert knowledge. Instead of taking shared understanding and scientific consensus at face value, the purpose is to unravel the process by which actors come to share common worldviews. Science and politics are in this vein indistinct realms with fluid boundaries subject to negotiation.[148]

International EIA commitments would appear to accept the confluence of science and politics and are well structured to bring politics into the scientific process and *vice versa*.

[145] The rational comprehensive model of EIA and the criticisms associated with that model are described above at ch. 2.4.

[146] Daniel Bodansky, "The Legitimacy of International Governance: A Coming Challenge for International Environmental Law" (1999) 93 AJIL 596 at 622–623.

[147] Ibid. at 620.

[148] Karin Bäckstrand, "Civic Science for Sustainability: Reframing the Role of Experts, Policy-Makers and Citizens in Environmental Governance" (2003) 3 Global Envt'l Politics 24 at 27.

First, the EIA process does not abdicate the decision-making function to the experts, but rather, through the screening and scoping process, those issues that can be appropriately addressed by scientific methods are delineated and agreed upon. To the extent that the scoping process involves consultation with the public and with outside experts, a degree of consensus can be developed around the issues and the methodologies used to address them. The scoping process and the review of draft assessment reports by outside agencies and other interested parties acts much like a peer review process, allowing for input and comment by both experts and laypeople. By institutionalizing review and consultation processes in the preparation of scientific reports, the EIA commitments enhance both the credibility and legitimacy of the assessment, which in turn should improve the influence of the assessment in the decision-making process.[149]

The role that science plays in EIA processes, like the role of legal norms, is not to determine outcomes, but to narrow the range of discretion decision-makers exercise by identifying factual outcomes and linking these to normative requirements. For example, a determination that a particular impact is irreversible or exceeding the carrying capacity of the environment does not decide the matter, but it requires the decision-maker to justify the acceptability of such an impact. EIA processes, far from being impervious to the natural limitations of both science and ideological consensus to provide complete answers to environmental problems, account for those limitations by allowing for the political resolution of those problems. The criticism of domestic EIA processes that arises in response to this residual political authority is that the structure of EIA requirements, particularly the separation of the decision-making body from those that actually undertake the EIA, allows for the results of assessments to be ignored.[150]

One influential analysis, by Serge Taylor, of this problem in the context of NEPA demonstrated that environmental professionals within agencies were in fact able to influence policy outcomes, but their effectiveness in doing so was conditional on the existence of individuals and groups outside the agency that could exert external pressure on senior

[149] Cash *et al.*, "Salience."

[150] See Bradley Karkanian, "Towards a Smarter NEPA: Monitoring and Managing Government's Environmental Performance" (2002) 102 Columbia L. Rev. 903 at 925. See also Richard Stewart, "The Reformation of American Administrative Law" (1975) 88 Harvard L. Rev. 1669 at 1780–1781; and Joseph Sax, "The (Unhappy) Truth About NEPA" (1973) 26 Oklahoma L. Rev. 239.

decision-makers and on the presence of institutions for elaborating and enforcing procedural requirements, in the case of NEPA, a system of judicial review.[151] These components overlap, creating redundancies that reinforce the critical pressure on decision-makers resulting in a decision-making culture that favors improved knowledge creation and the acceptance of environmentally benign outcomes.[152] In a number of important ways, this study mirrors similar findings made by Chayes and Chayes and Koh in relation to compliance. Most significantly, in all three approaches, the efficacy of the process to achieve desired outcomes rests on an ability to expose frictions or contradictions between accepted normative positions and actor behavior (whether actual or proposed). For example, Taylor notes that internal environmental professionals often allied themselves with external environmental NGOs by leaking information, which enabled the NGO to attack the agency decision. These observations coincide with Koh's description of the role of "agents of internalization" in transnational legal processes, such as norm entrepreneurs and norm sponsors, who often form transnational alliances to pressure governments into accepting a particular normative position. Chayes and Chayes also emphasize the catalytic influence of NGOs in mobilizing reputational pressure on states.[153] Moreover, all three explanations point to the important role that institutions, particularly those able to make authoritative interpretations, play in enhancing the relative strength of those seeking to promote compliance.

The influential role of science and environmental professionals in the EIA process maps onto institutionalist explanations of the role of "epistemic communities" in the development of regimes.[154] Epistemic communities are "network[s] of professionals with recognized expertise and competence in a particular domain and an authoritative claim to policy-relevant knowledge within that domain or issue-area."[155] Epistemic communities are often transnational in nature, being united by a shared knowledge base and a shared set of values that transcend domestic politics. One of Taylor's findings in connection with NEPA was that environmental professionals could exert more influence over policy in agencies where they were organized in groups that could be mutually supportive, allowing professions to draw on one another for expertise and reinforcement of shared values. Environmental professionals have been described

[151] Taylor, *Making Bureaucracies Think*, chs. 12 and 15. [152] Ibid. at 263–266.
[153] Chayes and Chayes, *The New Sovereignty*, ch. 11 at 250 *et seq.*
[154] Peter Haas, "Epistemic Communities and International Policy Co-ordination."
[155] Ibid. at 3.

by another policy scholar as acting as "administrative entrepreneurs," actively promoting their own values from within.[156] Again, this description has resonance with descriptions by IR scholars regarding the role of epistemic communities which operate both within and outside state decision-making structures to generate sets of solutions to policy problems around which government policy may converge contributing to regime formation.[157]

In the case of EIAs, the most relevant epistemic community is the network of environmental professionals who are engaged in producing the actual environmental impact reports and who are often involved in the scoping and screening processes. EIA professionals have their own journals,[158] professional organizations[159] and education and research facilities.[160] Through these avenues, EIA professionals exchange information regarding both technical issues, such as appropriate methodologies and policy issues relevant to the carrying out of EIAs. Through their professional interactions, individuals who conduct EIAs get exposure to a variety of international environmental issues and are engaged in an ongoing dialogue about how EIA processes can best address these issues. For example, the International Association for Impact Assessment (IAIA), an association of impact assessment professionals, prepared and presented submissions to the World Summit on Sustainable Development on the link between impact assessment and sustainable development.[161] The IAIA has also been directly involved in the preparation

[156] Geoffrey Wandesforde-Smith, "Environmental Impact Assessment, Entrepreneurship, and Policy Change."

[157] Peter Haas, describes this process in detail in relation to the development of a marine pollution control regime for the Mediterranean Sea, in Peter Haas, *Saving the Mediterranean: The Politics of International Environmental Protection* (New York: Columbia University Press, 1990); but see Steven Bernstein, *The Compromise of Liberal Environmentalism* (New York: Columbia University Press, 2001), who questions the level of influence that epistemic communities had over the development of the sustainability paradigm in international environmental governance.

[158] See, for example, the *Environmental Impact Assessment Review* and *Impact Assessment and Project Appraisal*.

[159] The most prominent perhaps being the International Association for Impact Assessment, which has a mandate to develop and improve best practices in impact assessment, and to promote global capacity and high professional standards in conducting EIAs: see the IAIA website, www.iaia.org.

[160] There exist numerous university-level programs in environmental assessment and research facilities dedicated to studying environmental assessment.

[161] International Association for Impact Assessment, *The Linkages Between Impact Assessment and the Sustainable Development Agenda, and Recommendations for Change: Statements and Policy Briefing for the World Summit on Sustainable Development*, August 2002, www.iaia.org.

of implementation guidelines for EIAs and biological diversity under the CBD.[162] It is through domestic EIA processes that these collective approaches and understandings regarding international issues are put into practice. So, for example, the broad professional acceptance of the need to develop ecosystem-based approaches to assessing the impacts on biological diversity manifests itself in approaches to EIA in domestic systems.[163] Members of epistemic communities engage in activities in both the transnational and the domestic spheres and thus bring global norms developed in their transnational interactions to bear on their understanding of domestic issues.

Climate change considerations again provide an illustrative example of how EIA processes structure the relationship between science, politics and legal norms. At the international level, much of the scientific consensus regarding climate change has arisen through the work of the Intergovernmental Panel on Climate Change (IPCC), a scientific body with broad international membership. The ability of the IPCC to influence policy at the international level has been attributed in part to the credibility of the scientific work undertaken, owing to the perception that the IPCC is engaged in a politically neutral exercise, but also because the IPCC became sensitized to developing state concerns regarding the primary responsibility of developed states for addressing global climate change.[164] One of the challenges to implementing the scientific concerns coming out of the IPCC process was making that information salient to the problems addressed by domestic decision-makers.[165] The examples of domestic EIA processes under the CEAA indicate that EIA processes can be successful in transforming scientific knowledge into information that has saliency on a scale that is helpful to decision-makers. So, for example, identified concerns regarding rising sea levels can be translated through the domestic EIA process into usable information regarding project design.[166]

The issue of scale also impacts the ability of decision-makers to address the impacts of individual projects on climate change. While greenhouse

[162] See CBD EIA/SEA Draft Guidelines.

[163] See, for example, the Voisey's Bay EIA, n. 115 above, at s. 2.2; see also the Red Hill Creek EIS Guidelines, n. 143 above, at s. 2.0.

[164] William Clark *et al.*, "Information as Influence: How Institutions Mediate the Impact of Scientific Assessments on Global Environmental Affairs" (Cambridge, MA: Kennedy School of Government/Harvard University Faculty Research Working Papers Series, November 2002).

[165] Ibid. at 37–38.

[166] See the discussion of the Northumberland Strait Bridge, in Lee, *Climate Change* at 47.

gas emissions from a project can be measured, the scale of the problem, its cumulative nature, and the scientific information generated to address the problem far exceeds any one project. It is not surprising that few concrete policy decisions addressing greenhouse gas emissions have been made in relation to individual projects given the absence of a regulatory program to cap greenhouse gas emissions.[167] However, raising these broader concerns at a project level will generate a demand for assessments on an appropriate scale, perhaps through SEA processes and through the development of policy tools that can better account for cumulative impacts.[168] Given that EIA processes, through the consideration of climate change impacts on project design, acknowledge and often vividly illustrate the environmental consequences of greenhouse gas emissions, it is difficult for decision-makers to ignore concerns raised by environmental groups and agencies about preventing or mitigating future greenhouse emissions.[169]

A related controversy regarding the role of science in environmental decision-making is the way in which we determine what counts as scientific knowledge. This debate has at least two aspects that find expression through EIA processes. First, positivist scientific methodology favors scientific approaches that are subject to reproducible tests and high degrees of scientific certainty. These methods usually require very specialized expertise and technical skills in terms of data collection to ensure accuracy. It is the mutual recognition of these skills and expertise that produces credibility among members of a particular scientific community. One of the implications of this preference for formalized scientific rigor is that it excludes or downplays other forms of knowledge that do not adhere to these standards. The price for maintaining a high degree of credibility between scientists is to sacrifice the legitimacy of the results with certain groups because the scientific studies neglect the input of certain interests.[170] This concern is particularly acute in connection with the use of traditional knowledge held by indigenous

[167] It was on this basis that the panel in the Cheviot Coal Project declined to address greenhouse gas emissions: see Cheviot Coal EIA, n. 114 above, at s. 5.2.3.

[168] For an example of considering greenhouse gas emissions in the context of cumulative impacts, see New Brunswick, Minister of Environment and Local Government, *Final Guidelines for Environmental Impact Assessment Liquefied Natural Gas Receiving, Storage and Processing Facility*, March 25, 2002, at 17, www.gnb.ca/0009/0377/0002/Final-e.pdf.

[169] See, for example, the Voisey's Bay EIA, n. 115 above, at s. 5.3, noting that the proponent "has a responsibility to minimize carbon dioxide emissions through careful attention to energy conservation."

[170] See Clark *et al.*, "Information as Influence."

people. Because traditional knowledge, which is often anecdotal and transferred orally, often does not conform to positivist scientific methods, government and industry scientists may discount it.

To counter this tendency, traditional knowledge is recognized as an important contributor to conservation efforts and sustainable development in the CBD,[171] and forms part of the requirements under the Arctic EIA Guidelines.[172] EIA commitments and processes that recognize traditional knowledge seek to integrate indigenous sources of information and values into traditional scientific approaches.[173] The point here is that not only does EIA provide a means to implement the international community's commitment to respecting and incorporating traditional knowledge, but, in doing so, EIA processes may enhance the ability of the assessment to influence outcomes by enhancing the legitimacy of the assessment with key political interests. This is a good example of a legal process actually acknowledging and confronting the pathologies of science by providing inclusive rules for what counts as relevant knowledge.

The other area where questions arise regarding scientific method is in connection with the application of the precautionary principle. The precautionary principle recognizes the limits inherent to acquiring scientific knowledge, particularly in complex ecological systems.[174] Positivist scientific methodology may minimize the importance of potential ecological impacts because of the levels of uncertainty associated with their prediction.[175] The precautionary principle seeks to overcome this difficulty by requiring that decision-makers not use scientific uncertainty as a basis for refusing to take measures to prevent environmental harm when the failure to act could result in serious or irreversible damage.[176]

171 United Nations Convention on Biological Diversity, Rio de Janeiro, June 5, 1992, 31 ILM 818, in force December 29, 1993, Arts. 8(j) and 17. The Conference of the Parties has identified "Traditional Knowledge, Innovation and Practices" as a cross-cutting theme and has developed a special program of ongoing work to address associated issues: see CBD Secretariat, "Article 8(j) Traditional Knowledge, Innovation and Practices: Introduction," www.biodiv.org/programmes/socio-eco/traditional/default.asp.

172 Arctic EIA Guidelines, ch. 10.

173 The incorporation of traditional knowledge has been a guiding principle of a number of Canadian EIA processes: see the Voisey's Bay EIA, n. 115 above, at s. 2.5, and the MacKenzie Pipeline EIA Final Terms of Reference, n. 115, at s. 5.2.

174 On the relationship between scientific uncertainty and precaution, see Malcolm MacGarvin, "Science, Precaution, Facts and Values" in T. O'Riordan, J. Cameron and A. Jordan, *Reinterpreting the Precautionary Principle* (London: Cameron May Ltd, 2001) at 35.

175 Ibid.

176 See, for example, Rio Declaration on Environment and Development, June 14, 1992, UN Doc. A/Conf.151/5/Rev.1, reprinted in 31 ILM 874 (1992), Principle 15.

EIA processes are again a means of implementation, and will provide opportunities for the elaboration of the precautionary principle. For example, in the Voisey's Bay EIA panel report, the precautionary principle was interpreted so as to require the proponent to demonstrate that the project would not result in serious or irreversible damage and to that end the panel required that the proponent minimize adverse effects and develop monitoring and adaptive management techniques for detecting and addressing unanticipated adverse impacts.[177]

The incorporation of traditional knowledge and the precautionary principle into EIA process is likely to result in further substantive strengthening of EIAs. This is evident in the Voisey's Bay example where the precautionary principle was interpreted to require the minimization of adverse effects. In a different Canadian EIA panel process, the panel further elaborated on the substantive aspect of the precautionary principle, noting that it generally requires

> that the onus of proof should lie with the Proponent to show that a proposed action will not lead to serious or irreversible environmental damage, especially with respect to overall environmental function and integrity, considering system tolerance and resilience.[178]

The precautionary principle favors environmentally benign approaches by placing a higher burden of justification on those engaged in potentially harmful activities. These interpretations go beyond the plain meaning of the principle articulated in international instruments, but the approach adopted highlights that the way in which scientific analysis is institutionalized in decision-making procedures will affect outcomes.

The substantive effect of incorporating traditional knowledge is less directly related to ecological considerations, but it does capture an important element of sustainable development. Integral to the concept of sustainable development is that decisions must reflect social equity between different groups in society, often referred to as intragenerational equity (as distinguished from intergenerational equity). By ensuring that indigenous perspectives are accounted for in the preparation of assessment reports, requirements to include traditional knowledge promotes the integration of indigenous values into the EIA process. Accepting that scientific knowledge will itself be a reflection of the values

[177] See the Voisey's Bay EIA, n. 115 above, at 9, and the MacKenzie Pipeline EIA Final Terms of Reference, n. 115, at ss. 5.5 and 12.9.

[178] Red Hill Creek EIS Guidelines, n. 143 above.

of the community that produces it,[179] incorporating traditional knowledge has a normative dimension through its reflection of indigenous values. For example, the Voisey's Bay report defines aboriginal knowledge as "the knowledge, understanding, and values held by Aboriginal people that bear on the impacts of the Undertaking and their mitigation."[180] Much of the assessment itself considers how the project would contribute to the social and economic well-being of the Inuit and Innu populations.[181] Insofar as traditional indigenous land and resource uses rely on the maintenance of ecosystem integrity, the incorporation of traditional knowledge will indirectly influence outcomes toward outcomes that support sustainable use of these resources.

6.7 Conclusion

Underlying the structure of EIA commitments is the interrelationship between law, politics and science. The efficacy of domestic EIAs has been described variously as a function of each one of these,[182] but EIAs draw on all three in influencing the outcomes of policy decisions. In the next chapter, I discuss how these sources of influence affect the role that EIAs play within international environmental governance structures and how each draws on its own unique form of legitimacy in bringing about environmental change. But, before turning to these questions, it may be helpful to return to the concept of compliance, particularly as it is portrayed here.

In the discussion of process-oriented compliance theory, I noted that process-oriented approaches tend to blur the positivist distinctions between law creation, implementation, compliance and effectiveness. EIAs provide a vivid illustration of this tendency. The substantive legal normativity of EIA processes is derived exogenously from the principles of the regime or treaty in which the EIA commitment is located. These principles define, albeit loosely, the ends to which EIA processes are oriented. The EIA commitments themselves are the means by which these ends are implemented. For example, the Espoo Convention implements the harm principle by requiring the state of origin to consider the transboundary environmental consequences of a proposed activity and to notify and consult with affected states for the purpose of preventing or reducing any likely transboundary harm.

179 Bäckstrand, "Civic Science." 180 Voisey's Bay EIA, n. 115 above, at 10.
181 Ibid. 182 Described above at ch. 2.3.

Implementation in this manner requires each party to interpret the norm in the context of the specific proposal. Each state makes a determination as to whether the harm is likely to be significant and, if it is, each state has to make a further determination whether the state of origin has taken reasonable steps to prevent that harm from actually occurring. The scope of these interpretations is not infinite, and, as discussed above, EIA processes further constrain the range of interpretation by drawing on existing standards and scientific norms of analysis. While states have been unable to elaborate on many of these principles in the abstract, they are often able to agree on the acceptability of impacts in individual instances.

This is not to suggest that each instance of agreement is solely determined by normative influences. On the contrary, EIA processes accept that agreement on shared values will be limited, as will be scientific consensus. Within the bounds of these constraints, interests will guide decision-making. As Taylor concludes in relation to domestic EIAs:

> [S]cience provides one form of consensus, an unforced consensus based on logic and empirical evidence. An equally workable consensus is provided by a society with homogeneous conventional beliefs. When neither scientific nor conventional consensus is strong enough, politics is called upon to fill the spaces left by incomplete knowledge.[183]

However, even in the political sphere, the procedural requirements are aimed at optimizing the possibility of participants identifying their own interests with community interests, or at least coordinating their interests with other actors. On this view, EIAs promote compliance by identifying at the level of principle what those community interests are.

The substantive normativity of the EIA process is clearly not a function of the enforceability of the principles invoked and, as such, implementation does not require that international legal norms be enacted as primary rules with domestic legal systems. In many ways, the characterization of norms in EIA processes resembles what Vaughan Lowe has referred to as interstitial norms. Like interstitial norms, the principles projected into EIA processes are not intended to directly determine outcomes, but rather they operate to provide normative coherence to those outcomes over time. Lowe describes the role of interstitial norms as providing principles of reconciliation, which require decision-makers faced with having to make a choice between primary rules to consider

[183] Taylor, *Making Bureaucracies Think* at 329.

the rules in light of the interstitial principle and the specific factual circumstances, a process Lowe describes as determining whether the principle of reconciliation "fits" or "feels right."[184] Lowe continues:

> The "fit" or "feeling" about principles of reconciliation is not a matter of compliance with legal norms. It is a matter of harmony with what, for want of a better word, one might term experience and common sense. This experience and common sense is an unsystematized complex of moral, cultural, aesthetic, and other values and experiences. But for all its vagueness (or the vagueness of my description of it), it exercises immense power.[185]

EIA processes can be characterized in similar, although not identical, terms. The process of public justification that is so integral to EIAs seeks to establish coherence between the interests of the participants, be they state actors, agencies or private groups and individuals, and the shared environmental values of the community. Much of the vagueness Lowe speaks of is mitigated in EIA processes through the explicit identification of those values and the integration of scientific understandings and experiences. The understanding of compliance as "fit" or coherence accurately portrays the dynamic nature of the kind of compliance toward which EIA commitments seek to contribute.

In any single decision-making event, the application of principles of reconciliation, when viewed in isolation, have an *ad hoc* character because they are so heavily dependent upon context. However, over time, discernible patterns of decision-making may arise. Understood as a mechanism that influences compliance with broad international environmental norms, EIA commitments transcend individual decisions and emerge as broader patterns of governance. The substantive normativity of EIAs inheres in this ongoing process of justifying environmental policy decisions in light of identified environmental principles.

184 Vaughan Lowe, "The Politics of Law-Making: Are the Method and Character of Norm Creation Changing?" in Michael Byers, ed., *The Role of Law in International Politics: Essays in International Relations and International Law* (New York: Oxford University Press, 2000) 207 at 220.

185 Ibid. at 220.

7 EIAs, interests and legitimacy

7.1 Introduction

Identifying international EIA commitments as contributors to compliance suggests that EIAs can fulfill two primary functions in international environmental governance structures. In the short term, on a case-by-case basis, EIAs provide a process for facilitating the coordination of interests. Over the longer term, EIAs can have a more transformational role, shaping actor, including state, interests through the internalization of international environmental norms. These two functions are elaborated on in this chapter, with particular emphasis on the way in which internalization of international norms may occur within domestic EIA systems. Within IR scholarship, these two explanations, the first of which emphasizes interests, and the second of which emphasizes norms, as influencing state behavior, are often presented, at least as ideal types, as alternatives and in competition with one another.[1] It is argued here with reference to EIAs that legal processes can be purposely structured to account for both material and ideational influences on actor behavior.

Not coincidentally, this distinction between EIAs as interest-coordination mechanisms and EIAs as processes by which interests may be transformed also plays out in the domestic policy context. In the context of domestic EIAs, much of the focus on the interest-transformational aspect of EIAs has tended to look at whether individual EIAs can provide opportunities for social learning.[2] The approach taken here looks

[1] The relationship between these explanations is canvassed extensively in James March and Johan Olsen, "The Institutional Dynamics of International Political Orders" (1998) 52 Int. Org. 943. See also Oona Hathaway, "Between Power and Principle: An Integrated Theory of International Law" (2005) 72 Chicago L. Rev. 469.

[2] See Jonathan Poisner, "A Civic Republican Perspective on the National Environmental Policy Act's Process for Citizen Participation" (1996) 26 Environmental Law 53; John

at the transformational possibilities of EIAs from a more institutional and longer-term perspective. As such, the emphasis in this chapter is not on how participation in a single EIA process may impact interests, but rather on how engagement in EIAs over time can lead to shifts in institutional values.[3] This approach of looking at institutional change over longer periods of time maps onto similar claims in process-oriented compliance scholarship where internalization of norms is understood as resulting from multiple interactions over many years.[4]

Process-oriented scholars have associated the ability of norms to influence state behavior with the legitimacy of the norm in question. However, the concept of legitimacy is often presented inconsistently even among process-oriented scholars.[5] One source of the confusion regarding the concept of legitimacy and its role in promoting compliance is that there are different forms of legitimacy, closely related, but which emanate from different sources. International EIA commitments implicate three forms of legitimacy: procedural legitimacy, referring primarily to processes by which authority is exercised; substantive legitimacy, referring to the justness of the outcome itself; and, finally, scientific or expert legitimacy, which recognizes that scientific norms of analysis are themselves often regarded as a basis for justifying the exercise of authority.[6] These forms of legitimacy and the relationship between them are discussed with a view to examining the function of legitimacy within EIA processes as a means to promote compliance with international norms and as an end in itself.

7.2 EIAs and interest-coordination

A rationalist understanding of EIA commitments in international law is to view them as responses to collective action problems. The assumption

Sinclair and Alan Diduck, "Public Involvement in EA in Canada: A Transformative Learning Perspective" (2001) 21 Environmental Impact Assessment Review 113; Heli Saarikoski, "Environmental Impact Assessment (EIA) as Collaborative Learning Process" (2000) 20 Environmental Impact Assessment Review 681.

3 R.V. Bartlett, "The Rationality and Logic of NEPA Revisited" in Larry Canter and Ray Clark, eds., *Environmental Policy and NEPA: Past, Present and Future* (Boca Raton, FL: St. Lucie Press, 1997) 51 at 57.

4 For example, Harold Koh, "Bringing International Law Home" (1998) 35 Houston L. Rev. 623 at 643 and 663–666.

5 See the discussion above at ch. 6.3.3.

6 Daniel Bodansky, "The Legitimacy of International Governance: A Coming Challenge for International Environmental Law" (1999) 93 AJIL 596 at 612.

here is that states in making policy decisions are often faced with transaction costs and costs associated with uncertainty that make cooperative solutions hard to achieve. EIAs, because they promote information collection and analysis and provide for the sharing of that information among interested parties, will facilitate cooperation by reducing uncertainty with respect to outcomes. Moreover, EIAs can be used to efficiently identify negotiation partners and to identify those issues which require further study and evaluation, thereby lowering the costs of cooperation. As a purely procedural mechanism, EIAs conform to the institutionalist models of regime design. It is argued here that EIAs go beyond this facilitative role by cabining the procedural mechanism within a substantive framework, but even from a purely procedural standpoint EIAs provide some innovative features that address barriers to cooperation.

Eyal Benvenisti, in a study on international cooperation in shared natural resource regimes, argues that a significant obstacle to the creation of successful transboundary resource regimes is the ability of rent-seeking minorities within national political structures to exert a disproportionate and distorting influence on national decision-makers.[7] In this way, where the optimal and most public-regarding result would favor resource-sharing and long-term sustainability, interest group politics at the national level often results in sub-optimal outcomes.[8] In order to protect against these distortions, Benvenisti argues that international institutions that provide greater transparency and opportunities for participation and devolve decision-making power to local populations can promote decisions that are more public-regarding and more efficient.[9] Of particular importance to Benvenisti's analysis is the role of the principle of subsidiarity in promoting democratically responsive and efficient institutions. Subsidiarity, as a general principle of governance, requires that decisions be made at the level closest to those affected where practicable. Despite the prominence Benvenisti gives to the principle of subsidiarity in the abstract, he does not point to any specific measures that may aid in the implementation of this principle.[10]

EIAs are well-suited institutional mechanisms for promoting cooperative outcomes in relation to the kind of collective action problems

[7] Eyal Benvenisti, *Sharing Transboundary Resources: International Law and Optimal Resource Use* (New York: Cambridge University Press, 2002) at 53–58.

[8] Ibid. at 64 *et seq.* [9] Ibid. at 89–95.

[10] For a similar, although broader-based, criticism, see Daniel Bodansky, "Review: Eyal Benvenisti, Sharing Transboundary Resources: International Law and Optimal Resource Use" (2005) 99 AJIL 280.

outlined by Benvenisti. In the transboundary context, EIA commitments reflect the transnational paradigm that Benvenisti argues characterizes transboundary resource conflicts, with the same potential for rent-seeking activity whereby well-organized and well-resourced actors with concentrated interests are able disproportionately to influence decision-makers. The two-level structure of transboundary EIAs under the Espoo Convention provides for transparent and participatory opportunities at both the state level and the individual level, allowing for affected local populations to bring their concerns directly to the attention of decision-makers. Whereas state-centered institutions assume that state interests are unitary, international EIA commitments recognize the heterogeneity of interests that exists in relation to environmental issues. EIA processes do not seek to separate out the international dimensions of environmental decision-making from the domestic aspects, but instead integrate these concerns into a single process, allowing decision-makers to understand the full range of competing interests and intentions of interested parties prior to deciding. The transnationalism of EIAs reflects the ecological fact that project impacts cannot be separated into geopolitical units. Moreover, the use of domestic procedures to address environmental issues that have international dimensions also obviates the need for states to set up and fund new institutions resulting in further efficiency gains.[11]

From a rationalist perspective, in order for institutional arrangements to successfully facilitate cooperation, the costs associated with the decision-making process must not outweigh the gains from cooperation. In this regard, EIAs respond to efficiency concerns in a number of ways. The screening and scoping provisions are aimed at identifying at an early stage the issues in contention and then focusing negotiations on those issues. In addition, provisions that provide for lay summaries of technical reports and traditional forms of knowledge to be considered and treated with due regard overcome some of the exclusionary practices associated with positivist scientific method.[12] The case-by-case approach in EIAs does, of course, carry with it substantial costs that may be avoided through standard creation. There is, of course, a lively debate about the desirability of standard creation versus other forms

[11] In cases where impacts are discrete, there may be efficiency gains from creating separate institutions, as appears to be the case with the Antarctic regime.

[12] For example, the Espoo Convention provides that EIAs should include "a non-technical summary including visual presentation as appropriate": Appendix II. The recognition of traditional knowledge is discussed above at ch. 6.4.2.

of environmental regulation that goes beyond the scope of the current discussion.[13] However, for present purposes, it is apparent that there remain, both domestically and internationally, a large number of decisions that are made on a discretionary basis. This decision-making structure is due in large part to the high levels of predictive uncertainty associated with the approval of complex activities with a variety of environmental outputs, making it difficult to calculate optimal levels of environmental protection in the abstract. In these cases, the efficiency gains from standard creation do not offset the losses from sub-optimal decisions arising from the acontextual application of standards.

Given the self-interested nature of disclosure and consultation, one might expect that the notification and information exchange aspects of EIA commitments to be self-enforcing. However, there are a number of factors that make formalization of EIA commitments in international regimes desirable. First, there are, as noted, reasons for states to attempt to gain a short-term advantage with respect to a particular project by not providing information. While central governments may be constrained by fears of future retaliation in the form of an affected state not providing information about its own projects, in many instances the assessment is not undertaken or regulated by the central government. An agency responsible for an EIA may care more about satisfying its own internal objectives, or may be more directly susceptible to pressure from project proponents, leading it to ignore the broader community's interests in maintaining reciprocal notification and disclosure arrangements with other jurisdictions.[14] EIA commitments in these circumstances help prevent rent-seeking activity by agencies or interest groups from interfering with the public-regarding actions of the state. Formalizing procedural requirements also has the effect of lowering the transaction costs associated with having to recalculate on a project-by-project basis the level of desirable disclosure and consultation.

A further condition that facilitates coordination of interests that is common to international EIA commitments and Benvenisti's analysis of common resource regimes is the presence of broad principles, as opposed to precise rules. The flexibility of principles allows states and transnational actors to arrive at self-generated solutions. Again, from an efficiency standpoint, affected parties, so long as they have adequate

[13] For a broad-based discussion on these debates, see Richard Stewart, "A New Generation of Environmental Regulation?" (2001) 29 Capital University L. Rev. 21.

[14] Benvenisti, *Sharing Transboundary Resources* at 115–116.

information, are in the best position to understand their mutual interests and arrive at optimal solutions.[15] The view of EIAs so far looks non-directive in the sense that outcomes are in essence market-driven, that is to say, that the system as a whole is not directed toward identified goals beyond welfare maximization. However, international EIA commitments are not themselves ambivalent to outcomes, but rather they seek to promote outcomes consistent with identified environmental goals, and to this extent it would be a mistake to see EIAs as simply a means for aggregating preferences. EIA commitments, because they have as their end sound environmental decision-making, seek to privilege environmental outcomes in certain ways.

Like Taylor's analysis of NEPA,[16] international EIA commitments advantage environmental interests, not through privileging substantive rules, but by enhancing the bargaining power of those who seek to promote environmental interests relative to those who hold other interests. Most obviously, EIA commitments make careful consideration of international environmental values mandatory, thus one might expect economically marginal projects to be abandoned once the true environmental costs are known. The presence of EIA commitments in relation to specific international issues serves to strengthen the hand of environmental agencies and analysts within the government to insist upon the assessment of impacts relating to the international environment, as was the case with Environment Canada and various NGOs raising climate change concerns in the Canadian federal EIA processes.[17] In connection with transboundary and global environmental issues, the involvement of an affected foreign government or an agency thereof provides a further source of critical engagement and, depending on the level of involvement, it may be more difficult to ignore or marginalize the concerns of foreign governments. This is particularly so in cases where foreign actors have recourse to alternative procedures to press their claims. In much the same way that domestic groups in the US could leverage the costs, delays and uncertainty associated with judicial review,[18] foreign states may be able to exert pressure through the threat of invoking dispute settlement procedures, such as the Espoo Convention inquiry procedure or dispute settlement processes under regional seas conventions

[15] Ibid. at 159–160.
[16] Serge Taylor, *Making Bureaucracies Think: The Environmental Impact Statement Strategy of Administrative Reform* (Stanford, CA: Stanford University Press, 1984).
[17] Discussed above at ch. 6.4.2. [18] Taylor, *Making Bureaucracies Think.*

and UNCLOS.[19] The involvement of foreign governments and agencies may also trigger further internal sources of pressure, such as foreign affairs departments, which would likely be the case in connection with activities covered by the Espoo Convention where many of the official points of contact are both environmental and foreign affairs agencies.[20] Finally, domestic judicial review procedures are often applied in the context of transboundary harm regardless of whether the interested party is resident in the state of origin or the affected state. For example, the provisions of the Aarhus Convention employ this requirement on the basis of nondiscrimination.[21]

The role of substantive norms is to pull the outcome of EIA processes in the direction of the environmental values that underlie EIA commitments. However, in the face of the open-ended nature of the norms that characterize EIAs, the compliance pull exerted is likely to be diluted in the sense that there exists a broad "zone of acceptability." The breadth of discretion will in some instances be narrower owing to factors such as scientific certainty and greater consensus on environmental values that arise in relation to particular problems.[22] But, under a rationalist model, these factors are not affected by the EIA process itself. Instead, decision-makers learn instrumental lessons regarding the circumstances under which they should compromise their economic goals in favor of environmental ones, since, if they do not compromise, their decisions may be subject to delays and additional costs and ultimately may result in reputational costs leading to an erosion of their ability to successfully complete other projects or to exert influence over the projects of other states. Likewise, environmental entrepreneurs, both inside and outside government agencies, learn how to increase or maintain their standing to pursue their environmental goals. But participation in the EIA process will not alter the interests of the agencies involved.

Cooperation is possible because the participants share common, although by no means complete, understandings about the range of outcomes that are acceptable. The normative dimension present in EIAs

[19] Such proceedings include the *MOX Plant Cases* under OSPAR and UNCLOS, the *Singapore Land Reclamation Case* under UNCLOS, and the Bystroe Canal Inquiry under the Espoo Convention (Romania/Ukraine).

[20] A list of the points of contact under the Espoo Convention is available at www.unece.org/env/eia/points_of_contact.htm.

[21] Convention on Access to Information, Public Participation in Decision-Making and Access to Justice in Environmental Matters, Aarhus, Denmark, June 25, 1998, 38 ILM 517, entered into force October 30, 2001, Art. 9.

[22] Discussed above at ch. 5.6.3.

provides the parties with a stable range of outcomes in which to bargain. The parties are committed to those norms because they reflect existing interests. The presence of EIA commitments in both treaty law and as a customary obligation points to the broad consensus regarding the desirability of environmental values. Benvenisti is of the view that in relation to shared natural resources ecologically sound results will arise from market interactions, so long as long-term interests are adequately accounted for and development costs are internalized.[23] International EIA commitments have less faith in the marketplace of ideas, and seek to ensure broad normative coherence on interactions. Environmentally benign outcomes are not assured, but the value of EIAs as a coordinating mechanism is to ensure that the broad consensus regarding environmental values is not subject to non-public-regarding distortions.

7.3 EIAs and interest-transformation

There is, as suggested above, a more robust understanding of EIAs as compliance-promoting mechanisms that arises when one considers EIAs in light of the process-oriented approaches to compliance. Under this understanding, EIA processes provide, in addition to opportunities for interest-coordination, a mechanism for normative social learning whereby interests can be altered through interactions, resulting in the internalization of the environmental values that inhere in the regime. Where a purely rationalist model suggests a policy environment that responds to external change, but does not promote change itself, a transformational model sees change occurring from both within and without, and is therefore intrinsically more dynamic. This model seeks to explain the ability of EIAs to influence decisions by projecting environmental values into deliberations. Over time, those values which persist will influence the interests of actors and ultimately move decision-makers away from their traditional, development-oriented focus toward more ecologically oriented approaches.

International EIA commitments are purposely structured to promote interactions that are premised on reason in addition to interests. Chayes and Chayes expect that states will seek to pursue their own interests, but maintain that normative considerations will constrain their choices. Thus, while the rationalist understanding of EIAs views the

[23] Here, Benvenisti relies on a mixture of game theoretical models and anecdotal evidence: see Benvenisti, *Sharing Transboundary Resources* at ch. 2 at 22 *et seq.*

interactions in terms of calculating the costs and benefits, a process-oriented approach goes further by attributing to norms an independent influence over behavior. States and other actors are required to justify their positions in respect of a project in light of regime norms and outcomes will reflect to varying degrees the persuasiveness of those justifications. The role of examining alternatives is key to this process because alternatives sharpen the discourse over appropriate outcomes. Alternatives help create contradictions by demonstrating that project objectives can be achieved in ways that better adhere to environmental values, i.e. avoiding or minimizing adverse effects on biological diversity.[24] These contradictions can, in turn, be exploited to generate reflection and change. Ultimately, for Chayes and Chayes, the ability of this kind of justificatory discourse to affect outcomes is rooted in a state's desire for standing in the international community, which reflects an instrumental basis for compliance. Nevertheless, it points to the centrality of persuasion in EIA processes.

Persuasion is also central to Koh's theory of transnational legal process, where it is argued that repeated interactions between transnational actors that have a normative dimension lead to the internalization of international norms within domestic political and social structures.[25] Koh's transnational focus lends itself to the dominant mode of implementation of international EIA commitments, which is to integrate those requirements into domestic EIA processes. For the most part, the participants in EIA processes will not be the state as a unified whole, but an agency of the state represented by bureaucrats. Other participants may include environmental officials in other countries, but are also likely to involve individuals and groups from civil society. Here, the reputational concerns of states emphasized by Chayes and Chayes will have less impact, but other pressures arising in the domestic and transnational political contexts will continue to require agencies to evaluate their priorities and approaches in light of continually changing normative and scientific information. Where Koh departs from rationalist explanations is that he accepts that these frictions can result in more permanent adjustments that embed normative influences into agency practices. Compliance becomes routinized because agency officials adopt internal procedures or turn to past decisions to avoid future frictions

[24] United Nations Convention on Biological Diversity, Rio de Janeiro, June 5, 1992, 31 ILM 818, in force December 29, 1993, Art. 14(1)(a).

[25] Discussed above at ch. 5.3.2.

that arise from contradictions between agency behavior and international norms.[26] Ultimately, internalization of international norms in bureaucratic procedures and legislation can contribute to the internalization of norms in a social context, leading to an acceptance of the norm by agency officials, political elites and the public at large. It is not so much that one form of internalization leads to another, but that interactions and forms of internalization are mutually reinforcing.[27]

Koh's approach adds theoretical weight to the emerging understanding of domestic EIA as leading to the "cognitive reform" of agencies, whereby the central role of EIA processes is to instill a broad environmental ethos within bureaucracies.[28] These models of EIA draw on similar theoretical approaches, which stress the ability of institutions, including norms, to transform actor identities and interests.[29] The empirical work in support of a transformational model of EIA has largely focused on social learning processes within specific project EIAs.[30] While these studies indicate that EIAs can provide opportunities for social learning, they require a high degree of openness from the early stages of the planning process, equal opportunities for participation, and access to expertise.[31] The optimal conditions for promoting social learning through deliberation are demanding and difficult to achieve,[32] although the conditions necessary for truly rational discourse are best seen as an ideal from which all processes will derogate to a greater or lesser degree.[33] Having said that, the structure of EIA commitments is clearly oriented toward the facilitation of principled deliberation and persuasion.

Looking at Koh's model of internalization, what one might expect is that domestic agencies that are confronted with international

[26] Harold Koh, "Bringing International Law Home" at 651–653. [27] Ibid. at 643.

[28] James Boggs, "Procedural v. Substantive in NEPA Law: Cutting the Gordian Knot" (1993) 15 Environmental Professional 25 at 25.

[29] Commonly cited in this regard is James March and Johan Olsen, *Rediscovering Institutions: The Organization Basis of Politics* (New York: Free Press, 1989).

[30] See Sinclair and Diduck, "Public Involvement"; Heli Saarikoski, "Collaborative Learning."

[31] See Poisner, "Civic Republican Perspective"; and Sinclair and Diduck, "Public Involvement" at 115, making the same point from a learning theory perspective.

[32] See, for example, the discussion of Habermas' theory of rational discourse in the context of environmental deliberations in Walter Baber and Robert Bartlett, "Towards Environmental Democracy: Rationality, Reason, and Deliberation" (2001) 11 Kansas J.L. & Pub. Pol'y 35. See also Poisner, "Civic Republican Perspective."

[33] Robert Keohane, "Governance in a Partially Globalized World" (2001) 95 Am. Pol. Sci. Rev. 1. See also Shane Mulligan, "Questioning (the Question of) Legitimacy in IR: A Reply to Jens Steffek" (2004) 10 Eur.J. Int'l Rel. 475 at 476.

environmental norms in their day-to-day activities adopt internal rules or procedures that institutionalize these norms. A brief examination of the internal guidelines developed by the Canadian Environmental Assessment Agency, the body that oversees EIA policy in the federal government, suggests such internalization is possible. Throughout the 1990s, while the importance of considering the climate change implications for projects was increasingly accepted, there remained significant variation in the approaches to integrating climate change considerations into the EIA process.[34] Those cases where climate change was accepted as a relevant factor raised the awareness of climate change issues with the agencies involved, many of which were repeat participants in the federal EIA process, and created support for the idea that climate change considerations could in fact be operationalized within decision-making processes. Each instance where climate change was put forward raised new issues with respect to the appropriate scientific and policy approaches to climate change. For example, a study conducted for the Canadian Environmental Assessment Agency noted that, within EIAs where climate change was considered, there was a divergence of opinion regarding the scientific evidence in support of climate change and the appropriate policy response.[35] These instances also resulted in recognition of the need for improved analytical tools to adapt climate science to an EIA framework.[36]

The culmination of these frictions was the adoption by the Canadian Environmental Assessment Agency of a non-binding document directed toward EIA practitioners providing guidance in incorporating climate change considerations into EIA processes.[37] This document does not provide defined parameters for assessing climate change considerations, but it unequivocally asserts that climate change is occurring and that it is attributable to human activities.[38] Given that this starting point has itself been controversial, the guidance document plays an important role in ensuring that climate change considerations are not ignored. The guidance document also references other provincial and federal policy documents that provide substantive guidance to proponents and

[34] Rick Lee, *Climate Change and Environmental Assessment* (Ottawa: CEAA Research and Development Monograph Series, 2001) at 28.

[35] Ibid. at 28. [36] Ibid. at 29.

[37] Canadian Environmental Assessment Agency, *Incorporating Climate Change Considerations in Environmental Assessment: General Guidance for Practitioners* (Ottawa: CEAA, 2003), available at www.ceaa-acee.gc.ca.

[38] Ibid. at s. 1.0.

agencies in assessing and managing greenhouse gas emissions.[39] Perhaps most tellingly, the guidance document anticipates that the incorporation of climate change considerations into EIA processes will have an impact beyond the projects themselves by providing project proponents with additional information to "assist their broader climate change action."[40] This goal is implemented through the adoption of climate change management plans and through post-project follow-up and adaptive management processes.[41] Moreover, by providing direction to agencies and proponents to consider climate change, the guidance will "increase attention to, and awareness of, [greenhouse gas] emissions, stimulate consideration of less emission-intensive ways to realize projects, help proponents minimize the risk associated with climate change impacts on projects, and assure the public that climate change considerations are being taken into account."[42] The guidance acknowledges that climate science will continue to involve considerable uncertainty, and recommends that a precautionary approach be implemented into assessments and management plans.[43]

A similar process of internalization occurred earlier with respect to biological diversity. The consideration of aspects of biological diversity in EIA processes predated the CBD, as biological impacts have long been acknowledged as an appropriate element of EIA. The CBD, however, pointed to the importance of assessing biological resources on an ecosystem basis, stressing the interrelationship between various components of an ecosystem. Like climate change, biological diversity raised new methodological challenges such as assessing the cumulative impact of projects on biological resources and incorporating consideration of genetic diversity, as well as addressing these features in an uncertain scientific environment. The policy response with biological diversity was again to prepare a non-binding guidance document.[44] This document provides a set of guiding principles for the consideration of biodiversity, which include a number of substantive principles such as minimum

[39] For example, the guidance document references the federal government's *Climate Change Plan for Canada* (Ottawa, 2002), available at www.climatechange.gc.ca/plan_for_canada/index.html and Alberta's greenhouse gas emission-reduction targets: see Canadian Environmental Assessment Agency, *Incorporating Climate Change Considerations* at s. 1.0.

[40] Ibid. at s. 1.0. [41] Ibid. at ss. 2.2.4 and 2.2.5.

[42] Ibid. at s. 3.0. [43] Ibid. at s. 1.0.

[44] Canadian Environmental Assessment Agency, *A Guide on Biodiversity and Environmental Assessment* (Ottawa: CEAA, 1995), available at www.ceaa-acee.gc.ca/017/images/CEAA_19E.pdf.

impact on biodiversity, no net loss of ecosystem, species population or genetic diversity, no effect on sustainable use of biological resources, and maintenance of natural processes.[45] The guide also includes lists of specific conditions that would raise biodiversity concerns, such as areas of high biodiversity, critical habitat, fragile ecosystems, and impacts on endangered species.[46] These principles reflect Canada's commitments under the CBD, but are aimed at directing those conducting EIAs to account for particular considerations. The greater specificity and the clearly stated substantive objectives require a more directed justification of any projects that do not minimize these impacts, without sacrificing the formal proceduralism of the EIA processes.

It is noteworthy that these documents were developed notwithstanding the absence of formally binding obligations related to biological diversity and climate change at the international level.[47] The development of bureaucratic guidelines in advance of elaborated international rules supports the view that EIA processes will be particularly useful in the implementation of regimes at their early stages, prior to the creation of standards, if they develop at all. These prescriptions, while developed in a specific domestic context, may filter back up into the international arena. For example, both of the guideline documents prepared by the Canadian Environmental Assessment Agency are referenced by the Espoo Convention Secretariat as a general source of information for other states and EIA professionals to have regard to in the development of EIA documents.[48]

A further example of internalization can be seen in the transboundary context. Under NEPA, the customary rules of harm prevention and the duty to cooperate were first raised in the context of individual EIA processes,[49] but the practice was regularized through a Council on Environmental Quality Guidance, which clearly indicated the obligation to extend EIA processes to impacts outside the state.[50] This guidance specifically references the customary rule, and is a clear example of using the

[45] Ibid. at 3. [46] Ibid. at 6.

[47] For example, the climate change document was adopted well in advance of the Canadian government's ratification of the Kyoto Protocol.

[48] www.unece.org/env/eia/helptopics.htm.

[49] See above at ch. 2.6, citing *Swinomish Tribal Community* v. *Federal Energy Regulatory Commission*, 627 F 2d 499 (DC Cir. 1980); and *Wilderness Society* v. *Morton*, 463 F 2d 1261 (DC Cir. 1972).

[50] *Council on Environmental Quality Guidance on NEPA Analyses for Transboundary Impacts*, issued July 1, 1997, available at CEQ NEPANET, http://ceq.eh.doe.gov/nepa/regs/transguide.html.

EIA processes to implement an international norm, in this case the harm principle. This requirement is given further specificity under the US–Canada Air Quality Agreement notification requirements, which require each party to notify the other of new sources of air pollution that exceed quantified limits within 100 kilometers of the border.[51] The notification requirement raises a presumption of significant impact where a proposal meets defined geographic and emission parameters. In this instance, one recognized difficulty of the harm principle, namely, the absence of an objective standard for determining significance, is addressed through the creation of bureaucratic operating criteria. The approach retains the procedural structure as it acts simply as a screening mechanism, but it ensures that a broad class of activities will be subject to scrutiny.

Koh identifies different forms of internalization that may arise from transnational interactions. Legal internalization is the incorporation of international norms into the domestic legal system, political internalization arises when political elites accept an international norm as the basis for future policy, and social internalization is the broad public acceptance of an international norm. The dominant mode of internalization discussed above is legal internalization through the development of guidelines further elaborating on the consideration within EIA processes of particular kinds of environmental issues that have transnational implications. However, these forms of internalization do not operate independently nor do they necessarily operate in a fixed manner. Part of the stated aim of the climate change guideline is to generate increased attention to greenhouse gas emissions by proponents and to provide broader public assurances that climate change considerations are being addressed[52] – suggesting a recognition that increased regulatory attention through EIAs and post-project monitoring will have an effect on private actor and public values respecting climate change.

Since persuasion is the dominant mode of interaction, the normative dimension of EIAs takes on added importance when EIAs are viewed from a transformational standpoint. As discussed in the previous chapter, the justificatory nature of EIA practices, with their emphasis on principled discourse and attention to context, seeks to produce outcomes that accord with shared values. The Chayesian approach to institutional design clearly draws on this by creating institutional structures that seek to amplify the ability of states to use persuasion as a means to promote

[51] Discussed above at ch. 4.2.2.

[52] Canadian Environmental Assessment Agency, *Incorporating Climate Change Considerations*.

compliance. EIA is an institutional device that draws upon the same design features to pull policy decisions that have environmental consequences in the direction of regime goals. At this juncture, it is worth recalling that EIA processes are mainly concerned with government actors and, in particular, with ensuring that public policy-makers have sufficient regard for environmental values. Where Chayes and Chayes see compliance arising from the behavioral expectations associated with legal normativity, EIAs similarly look to the expectation that public agencies will act in public-regarding ways – a determination that can only be made with reference to normative criteria. In both cases, part of the design strategy is to accept that there will be incentives for actors to evade those expectations and a consequent need to design processes that minimize the ability of actors to do so. Koh's theory of transnational legal process relies in a similar way on the pressure that arises from contradictions between public expectations as identified in international norms and public actions.

Where EIAs differ from these accounts of compliance is in their substitution of procedural specificity and context for substantive specificity. Because the persuasive value of norms is positively affected by greater levels of precision, EIAs rely on a combination of law, science and politics to bring about desired outcomes. The absence of substantive specificity is compensated for in part by ensuring that broad normative goals are considered in factually specific contexts. Because of the contextual sensitivity of EIA, broadly configured norms can be concretized and developed. Bringing open-ended norms into the EIA processes requires decision-makers to confront those norms and to consider them in a principled fashion. Over time, experience in considering the trade-offs between greenhouse emissions and economic growth can lead to improved understandings of the implications of these norms for social and economic policy decisions, which in turn leads to the development of more precise implementation guidelines.

One way to think about internalization is that, prior to internalization, norms are contested and require justification themselves. Here, justification is made by reference to more fundamental and accepted regime principles, as well as to factual claims. Where through deliberation parties come to accept normative propositions as justified, these norms no longer need to be the subject of future deliberation, but instead are internalized and become the basis for the justification of future decisions. In the climate change example, early considerations of climate change issues involved deliberations over both the physical facts of climate change and the application of norms to the problem of climate change; as the justifications became accepted, both the factual and evaluative aspects of the deliberations were internalized in guideline documents, moving the starting point of future deliberations beyond these previously contested areas.

If the strength of EIA is to promote reasoned consideration of environmental norms, EIA commitments may be viewed as an important aspect of what Brunnée and Toope refer to as "contextual regimes."[53] Contextual regimes refer to sets of informal (non-binding) norms that emerge in an issue area, often as a result of converging state practice.[54] As normative agreement crystallizes over time, contextual regimes can become increasingly formalized and precise. Brunnée and Toope tie the emergence of binding legal rules to the regime's increased sense of legitimacy. As parties come to accept the legitimacy of norms, compliance is more likely to arise in a self-regulatory way. The non-determinative nature of EIAs ensures that outcomes that are inconsistent with state interests are not thrust upon states, but through application and consideration of norms in various contexts the implications of norms become clearer. Such an approach does not discount the role of power and interests in shaping state behavior, but it does posit that legal norms and the process of their development can impact outcomes independently of interests.

From a transformational perspective, processes such as EIAs that promote open and principled dialogue as a means to arrive at policy decisions are effective because they seek to ensure that policy decisions adhere to both process values and the nascent substantive values that inhere in the regime. Put another way, because EIA is a mechanism that seeks to legitimize policy decisions, the inclusion of EIA commitments in international governance structures aids in the promotion of compliance with those substantive values by creating conditions by which actors can come to understand their interests as they relate to specific problems in light of identified community interests. The emphasis on legitimacy is what ties process-oriented compliance approaches together – it is the currency of internalization.

[53] Jutta Brunnée and Stephen Toope, "Environmental Security and Freshwater Resources: Ecosystem Regime Building" (1997) 91 AJIL 26 at 31–32.

[54] Ibid. at 33, describing contextual regimes as "recognized patterns of behavior or practice around which expectations converge," quoting Oran Young, "Regime Dynamics: The Rise and Fall of International Regimes" (1982) 36 Int. Org. 277 at 277.

7.4 EIAs and legitimacy

The concept of legitimacy is notoriously slippery, and unpacking that concept in any detail is beyond the scope of this study. However, for present purposes, it may be helpful to make some initial defining comments. Legitimacy as used here refers to the justification of authority.[55] By "justification," I mean to refer to more than simply the giving of reasons, but to the giving of reasons that are intended to be mutually acceptable. There is both a prescriptive and a descriptive dimension to considerations of the concept of legitimacy. Prescriptive approaches look to the conditions under which authority should be justified, while descriptive approaches look to whether an exercise of authority is in fact accepted.[56] These two approaches are very difficult to unravel from one another, particularly in the context of compliance. It is important to note that acceptance or compliance is not in itself proof of legitimacy, since a person or state could comply with a rule not out of an internal sense of the rule's justifiability, but out of fear of reprisals or some other instrumental reason. Distinguishing between compliance and obedience, as Koh does, is meant to differentiate between motivations for rule conformity, with obedience referring only to behavior motivated by an internal sense of "rightness" or justifiability.[57] Finally, the concept of legitimacy is both a means to an end and an end in itself. Legitimacy is desirable from an instrumental standpoint because it can promote compliance, but it is also desirable in the absence of its impact on behavior.

EIAs share with international law a need to rely more heavily on legitimacy as a basis for promoting compliance since coercive measures are either unavailable or are costly to invoke. In this regard, the self-regulatory nature of EIA processes is well suited to international governance as it imposes low costs on state sovereignty.[58] The basis of legitimation in EIA processes is founded on three distinct forms for justification: procedural legitimacy, substantive legitimacy and scientific legitimacy. Each form of justification is problematic and insufficient on its own, but it is suggested here that the real strength of EIA as an element

[55] Here, I adopt the definition of legitimacy put forward by Bodansky, "Legitimacy" at 601.

[56] Jens Steffek, "The Legitimation of International Governance: A Discourse Approach" (2003) 9 Eur.J. Int'l Rel. 249 at 253.

[57] Koh, "Bringing International Law Home" at 628.

[58] Sovereignty "costs" are discussed in Kenneth Abbot and Duncan Snidal, "Hard and Soft Law in International Governance" (2000) 54 Int. Org. 451 at 436–437.

of international environmental governance is the relationship between these forms of justification.

Procedural legitimacy refers to the manner by which a decision is made, what Franck has referred to as "right process."[59] Relevant considerations in determining procedural legitimacy include, who is involved in the decision-making process and the conditions of their involvement. In international law, consent is usually considered the principal basis of procedural legitimacy between states, as no sovereign state can be bound against its will. But, as outlined in chapter 3 in relation to transboundary harm, in the face of competing claims of sovereignty, international rules have turned to participatory forms of democratic decision-making whereby affected states are given notification of potentially harmful activities and the opportunity to be consulted in good faith. To require the prior consent of an affected party would in effect derogate from the sovereign right of the state of origin. But leaving the decision-making power in the hands of the state of origin may affect the sovereign rights of other states. In order to enhance the acceptability of those outcomes for affected states, their views have to be accounted for in the decision-making process.

Given the importance of determining whether an actor is entitled to participate, the inquiry procedure under the Espoo Convention should also enhance procedural legitimacy by increasing the impartiality of that determination.[60] Determining affected parties for issues of global common concern requires a less direct approach given their diffuse nature. In the UNCLOS regime and in the Antarctic Protocol, notification to treaty bodies or other international institutions may partially address the difficulty in determining affected parties.[61] In the case of the Antarctic Protocol, the review mechanisms through the Committee for Environmental Protection and the Antarctic Treaty Consultative Meeting provide opportunities for state participation. The requirement in the UNCLOS to "publish" the results of assessments is less likely to significantly enhance participation in decision-making given the uncertain wording of that provision. But here regional seas organizations are contemplated to provide a forum for notification and consultation.[62] In the case of biodiversity and climate change, participation is anticipated

[59] Thomas Franck, *Fairness in International Law and Institutions* (Oxford: Clarendon Press, 1995) at 7.

[60] The inquiry procedure under the Espoo Convention is discussed above at ch. 5.2.

[61] UNCLOS, Art. 205 and the Antarctic Protocol, Annex I, Art. 3(3).

[62] Discussed above at ch. 5.4.

to occur entirely within the domestic polity and must therefore rely on domestic groups and agencies to represent those broader interests.

Even for those EIA commitments that do not anticipate significant interactions between states, EIA processes provide an alternative basis of legitimacy to consent. For example, in order for international norms to become legally effective in domestic regimes, the state in question must be seen to consent to their implementation through ratification and, in some cases, through affirmative acts of implementation within the domestic legal system. EIA processes provide a different route to the implementation of international norms that does not require formal state consent. Instead, norms are projected directly into domestic decision-making processes. Due to the self-regulatory nature of EIA, international norms that enter into domestic processes do not have formal binding effect, but rather the legitimacy of their application in policy formation depends upon the open and participatory nature of the process and their coherence with accepted norms.

International EIA commitments, by creating a stable set of rules regarding who is notified, and by structuring their participation in the decision-making process, serve to legitimize the decision taken. By contemplating notification to and participation by both state and non-state actors in decision-making processes, international EIA commitments address legitimacy concerns at both the interstate and the transnational levels, in effect overcoming the agency problems associated with the unified state representing the heterogeneous interests of affected citizens. In the same vein, the transnationalism of transboundary EIA requirements also conforms to the democratic principle of subsidiarity. In essence, EIA directs its legitimating function at those persons whose acceptance of the decision is most important.

Procedural legitimacy is not only a function of involving affected persons, but also of ensuring that their involvement is meaningful. To this end, EIA commitments include minimum informational requirements, provide parties with sufficient time to consider the information and ensure that any comments by affected parties are considered in good faith. The importance of full disclosure to legitimacy was highlighted in the *MOX Plant Case*, where one of Ireland's chief complaints was the United Kingdom's failure to disclose relevant information respecting the operation of the facility in question.[63] The link between access to information and EIAs is also acknowledged in the

[63] *Ireland* v. *United Kingdom* (OSPAR Arbitration), Final Award July 2, 2003, www.pca-cpa.org.

Aarhus Convention. Because the proponent is responsible for preparing the EIA documents and must respond to informational requests and even requests for further study, if reasonable, from affected parties, the process requirements lower the burden of participation on affected parties. A number of studies have shown that effective participation requires access to resources to assess technical documents and undertake independent reviews.[64] Some jurisdictions have addressed this requirement through intervenor funding requirements,[65] but these mechanisms are not widespread. At the international level, funding is left to the discretion of states. Unequal conditions of participation are also a concern at the interstate level given that access to expertise related to the conduct of EIAs may be limited in some countries. EIA capacity-building remains an important goal in this regard.

Determining whether EIAs create sufficiently meaningful participation to positively affect legitimacy also raises some concerns. First, legitimacy appears to depend to a high degree on the good faith of the state of origin. EIAs require that decision-makers consider the comments of affected actors with a genuine regard for their views. The requirement to give reasons addresses this concern by requiring decision-makers to make explicit the basis of their determination, although knowing whether sufficient weight has been given to mandatory considerations remains problematic as lip-service may be paid to environmental concerns. The difficulty with policing the genuineness of a decision-making process is that such a determination can only realistically be made with reference to outcomes. Consequently, legitimacy must be derived in part by reference to substantive criteria. This same point is made by Gutmann and Thompson in relation to deliberative processes more generally:

> What reasons count as such a justification is inescapably a substantive question. Merely formal standards for mutual justification – such as a requirement that the maxims implied by laws be generalizable – are not sufficient. If the maxim happens to be "maximize self or group interest," generalizing it does not ensure that justification is mutual. Something similar could be said about all other conceivable candidates for formal standards. Mutual justification requires reference to substantive values.[66]

64 Sinclair and Diduck, "Public Involvement" at 127.

65 See, for example, Canadian Environmental Assessment Act, SC 1992, c. 37, s. 58(1.1), establishing a participant funding mechanism "to facilitate the participation of the public in mediations and assessments by review panels."

66 Amy Gutmann and Dennis Thompson, "Deliberative Democracy Beyond Process" in James Fishkin and Peter Laslett, eds., *Debating Deliberative Democracy* (Malden, MA: Blackwell Publishing, 2003) 31 at 33–34.

The need for substantive criteria leads to a related concern regarding procedural legitimacy. Can international EIA commitments generate sufficient legitimacy in the absence of a shared political culture? Within domestic systems, EIAs operate within the context of a broader political system. Even those actors whose values are not reflected in the outcomes of EIAs may accept those outcomes because EIAs are embedded within a political system that itself enjoys legitimacy through its base commitment to shared community values. In the absence of a thickly constituted global community, states or transnational actors have a limited basis to expect that decision-makers will genuinely account for their views.[67] Of course, it should be noted that participatory processes like EIAs were created as a response to a "legitimation crisis" in national systems of administrative law.[68] However, domestic systems, while acknowledging the potential for rent-seeking, maintain a normative commitment to public-regarding decision-making as a general proposition. At the international level, no such commitment exists, in the sense that states are generally regarded as being self-interested.

EIA commitments, however, do not restrict themselves to procedural matters and, in this regard, they mitigate some of the shortcomings of a purely procedural approach to legitimacy. Because EIA commitments identify broad substantive principles, there exists a common metric by which all participants can assess outcomes. This does require a common commitment to substantive values at the outset, but does not require the existence of a global demos. By identifying substantive goals, EIA processes provide a substantive basis for assessing good faith, but the substantive commitment does not amount to a formal legal obligation. This is the essential structure seen in all international EIA commitments and it is normative in the sense that it provides a basis for evaluation. In keeping with process-oriented understandings of the nature of international legal normativity, EIAs constrain discretion by making environmentally benign choices more politically attractive. As experience with applying the norm to different contexts increases, the more specific applications enjoy legitimacy providing opportunities for

[67] See Bodansky, "Legitimacy" at 615–616.

[68] See Richard Stewart, "The Reformation of American Administrative Law" (1975) 88 Harvard L. Rev. 1669. See also Jonas Ebbesson, "The Notion of Public Participation in International Environmental Law" (1998) 8 YBIEL 51 at 79; and Barry Barton, "Underlying Concepts and Theoretical Issues in Public Participation in Resource Development" in Donald N. Zillman, Alastair R. Lucas and George Pring, eds., *Human Rights in Natural Resource Development: Public Participation in the Sustainable Development of Mining and Energy Resources* (New York: Oxford University Press, 2002) 77 at 96–97.

normative strengthening and internalization. Brunnée and Toope argue that internalization arises from the creation of shared understandings – a process that they describe as relating to practical reasoning – the process of deliberating about future courses of action in light of accepted principles.[69]

The normativity of EIA processes, which promotes interactions that are principled as well as strategic, seeks to enhance the acceptability of policy decisions among affected actors by requiring decision-makers to demonstrate that decisions are taken in light of accepted principles. Because EIAs do not require consensus, outcomes will not necessarily reflect the interests of all of the parties. If those parties whose interests are not reflected in the decision are to accept the result, they must have some reassurances that the decision took their concerns seriously and adhered to underlying values.[70] As noted above, this requirement is captured in the notion of good faith in that good faith requires an assessment of the substantive rationality of the reasons for a decision. The presence of a common commitment to certain substantive ends, often in the context of a particular regime, is itself contingent upon state interests. However, since state interests are not fixed, and are themselves the product of continual reflection and reassessment, participation in deliberative processes offers an opportunity for interests to evolve. In this way, actors who once resisted the inclusion of climate change considerations in domestic EIA processes come to accept the legitimacy of those considerations independently of the strategic value of taking such a position. Accepting that the substantive basis of legitimacy is subject to continuing negotiation dissolves the concern that a substantive pre-commitment interferes with political sovereignty, since states and other actors are part of the negotiation process.[71]

The reliance on substantive legitimacy in EIA processes points to the importance of certain aspects of the EIA process. The examination of alternatives lays bare the substantive trade-offs a particular decision

[69] Brunnée and Toope, "Environmental Security" at 32. See also Stephen Toope, "Emerging Patterns of Governance and International Law" in Michael Byers, ed., *The Role of Law in International Politics: Essays in International Relations and International Law* (New York: Oxford University Press, 2000) 91 at 102.

[70] Some empirical support for this is found in Saarikoski, "Collaborative Learning" at 695–698, noting that legitimacy in domestic EIA processes was enhanced by acknowledgment of different perspectives in final documents. See also Sinclair and Diduck, "Public Involvement" at 124–126, citing data suggesting that lack of information feedback compromises process legitimacy in EIAs.

[71] Gutmann and Thompson, "Deliberative Democracy" at 32.

involves. This is imperative where there are few or no quantifiable standards, as alternatives allow decision-makers to compare and evaluate environmental costs against economic and social costs. Examining alternatives also forces a proponent to consider the project from different perspectives, which requires a consideration of whether the project ends may be achieved by means that better reflect underlying values. Post-project monitoring, which provides opportunities to assess actual environmental outcomes against the decisions made, allows for further reflection on whether the original trade-offs made were in fact acceptable. To the extent that post-project experience can feed into new decision-making processes, there will be further opportunities for social learning, as participants gain a better understanding of how previous measures have impacted environmental outcomes. To date, these types of mechanisms are underdeveloped in international commitments, with only the Antarctic regime providing for mandatory post-project monitoring.[72] However, within domestic EIA processes, there exist agencies which are repeat participants in EIA processes and which have the capacity to generate an institutional memory regarding past practices. NEPA encourages this through the Council on Environmental Quality and the creation of agency-specific regulations for EIA. Likewise, under the CEAA, the Canadian Environmental Assessment Agency has a mandate to assess the effectiveness of EIA processes.[73] The creation of guidelines by the Canadian Environmental Assessment Agency should be seen as a way of creating coherence among the vast number of EIA decisions taken.

The ability of EIAs to engender substantive legitimacy is unquestionably limited by the open-ended nature of the substantive commitments associated with EIAs. However, as discussed in the previous chapter,[74] scientific norms of analysis provide a further basis for strengthening the substantive basis of decisions. Science as a normative influence draws on a distinct form of legitimacy based on expertise.[75] Scientific legitimacy is distinct from procedural and substantive legitimacy because, instead of focusing on the outcome or on how a decision was arrived at, it is concerned with who makes the decision.[76] Again, on its own, scientific legitimacy falls short because of the recognition that scientific knowledge reflects certain values. Without repeating the discussion from the previous chapter, EIA commitments acknowledge the centrality of science in environmental decision-making, but in many ways institutionalize

[72] Antarctic Protocol, Annex I, Art. 5. Discussed above at ch. 5.7. [73] CEAA, s. 62.
[74] Above at ch. 5.6.3. [75] Bodansky, "Legitimacy" at 619–623. [76] Ibid. at 620.

skepticism by subjecting scientific reports to public review and by explicitly acknowledging other sources of expertise, such as traditional knowledge.

Here, we can clearly see that the forms of legitimacy that EIA draws upon are not mutually exclusive and can be reinforcing. For example, the procedural requirements of EIAs serve to democratize the scientific aspects. The requirement for post-project monitoring accepts that the predictive certainty of science is itself limited and sound decision-making requires reassessment and adjustment. Science also plays an important role in the demonstration of good faith. An essential aspect of scientific method is its commitment to objectivity. Where decision-makers concede authority to experts, they signal a willingness to determine outcomes impartially.[77] These claims to objectivity help justify the exercise of authority precisely because they are seen as not reflecting the interests of any one state or party.

7.5 Conclusion

From a theoretical standpoint, there are important differences between rationalist and normative approaches to compliance with international law, but at the level of practice the approaches are not mutually exclusive.[78] The description of the dual role of international EIA commitments provides an example of a mechanism that appeals to both the logic of consequences and the logic of appropriateness. In this final section, I look at how the two logics may fit together.

First, it has been argued here that there is a temporal aspect to how the coordinating and transformative aspects of EIA interrelate. On a case-by-case basis, actors will engage in EIA processes in an instrumental fashion, in the sense that they will be seeking an outcome that best reflects their interests. This is not to suggest that those interests will necessarily be directed toward entirely material ends.[79] Indeed, looking at the range of actors involved in EIA processes, many would appear to be motivated out of ethical concerns for the environment. Finnemore

77 Benvenisti, *Sharing Transboundary Resources* at 146.

78 Oran Young, *The Institutional Dimensions of Environmental Change: Fit, Interplay, and Scale* (Cambridge, MA: MIT Press, 2002) ch. 2 at 29 *et seq*. See also Robert Keohane, "International Relations and International Law: Two Optics" (1997) 38 Harvard ILJ 487; and March and Olsen, "Institutional Dynamics."

79 Martha Finnemore and Katherine Sikkink, "International Norm Dynamics and Political Change" (1998) 52 Int. Org. 887 at 910.

and Sikkink identify what they call "strategic social interaction," where actors make instrumental calculations to maximize their chosen utilities, but those utilities reflect normative commitments.[80] Within the coordination function of EIAs, environmental groups will make rational calculations on how to best achieve outcomes that reflect their commitment to environmental values, including the recognition that there are involved in a "game" with multiple iterations.

A corollary to this point is that persuasion can be part of a rational strategy. Rational institutionalists have always accepted that norms have an instrumental role in shaping outcomes by lowering costs and reducing uncertainty, but they do not admit of the possibility that underlying interests can be altered through interactions. If, however, one accepts the constructivist premise that such changes are possible, and are enhanced by creating conditions where the parties must examine a problem from a variety of perspectives and with an open mind, then leveraging those conditions becomes a rational strategy. Koh's theory of transnational legal process is premised on the idea that norm entrepreneurs will seek out interactions that maximize the pressure on decision-makers to conform to authoritative interpretations of international norms. EIA processes fit comfortably within Koh's theory, in that they are accessible to a wide variety of actors, they are permeable to international norms and they require decision-makers to openly justify their positions in light of those norms.

The creation of shared understandings about both social facts and physical facts is at the heart of interest-transformation. But, here too, there is a relationship between rationalist and transformationalist approaches since the projection of a particular value may lead the parties to uncover certain physical facts or to reassess their significance. In the climate change example, consideration of the climate change norms led proponents to consider the impacts of climate change on design and construction issues. The incorporation of this information was clearly interest-based in that failure to accept the possibility of changes to future water levels or ice conditions could have detrimental impacts on the viability of the project itself. Once the possibility of the impact of climate change on a project was accepted, it was difficult for agencies and proponents not to accept the broader normative position that the effect of the project on greenhouse gas emissions should be assessed and mitigated. On a more general level, the EIA process itself is premised on

[80] Ibid. at 910.

the belief that decision-makers must consider the environmental consequences of their actions. Because this belief is institutionalized, it requires decision-makers to confront a widening range of social and physical facts, including the fact that the decision-making environment is increasingly uncertain. From a coordination standpoint, the changes to the decision-making environment create new incentives to cooperate, but at the same time increase opportunities for persuasion since norm adherence may be the best rational strategy under conditions of uncertainty.[81]

[81] Keohane, "Governance" at 11.

Part V Conclusion

8 EIAs and the process and substance of international environmental law

8.1 Introduction

An underlying theme of this book is that international EIA commitments capture something of the spirit of international environmental governance in the post-Rio era. Insofar as EIAs are reflective of, or respond to, emerging features of international governance, they can provide insights into strategies for designing institutions intended to address transboundary and global environmental concerns. At the center of EIA commitments, at both the domestic and the international level, is the relationship between process and substance. In this concluding chapter, I want to return to the process–substance relationship as an organizing principle for discussing the main findings of this study. I do this not only because of the importance of this relationship to EIA commitments themselves, but also because this relationship plays out in important ways on a number of different levels within this study and within international governance structures more generally. To this end, I return to the central characteristics of international environmental governance identified at the outset of this study, namely, proceduralism, transnationalism and integration. While these characteristics were identified at the outset as having particular relevance for international EIA commitments, at this final stage it is helpful to consider how international EIA commitments respond to these trends, as this points to the future utility and limitations of EIA commitments in international governance structures.

Because this study was framed in terms of process-oriented approaches to international law and the related explanations of compliance, I also reconsider the main theoretical components of process-oriented method in view of the findings regarding the structure and role of international

EIA commitments. The purpose here is to place EIA commitments within the wider framework of process-oriented approaches to international law and compliance. In this regard, I address some of the normative implications of adopting EIA commitments in international environmental governance structures. I also revisit the concepts of implementation, compliance and effectiveness in connection with the role of EIAs in international governance structures. It is argued here that EIAs present a distinct form of governance arising out of procedural specificity that has not been adequately captured in existing considerations of the role of "legalized" institutions in world politics.[1]

8.2 Proceduralism, transnationalism and integration in international environmental governance

In describing international environmental governance structures as being characterized by proceduralism, transnationalism and integration, I do not mean to suggest that these aspects are the only important features of international environmental governance or that they are found in all environmental governance structures. The presence of these features does, however, have significant regulatory implications. In Chapter 3, the turn to process is discussed in relation to a state's duty to prevent transboundary harm.[2] The proceduralism that results has a substantive aspect in that the procedural obligations are directed toward identified ends, but because those ends are loosely defined there remains considerable scope for the generation of particular outcomes. The reasons for the emergence of proceduralism were not addressed in detail, but the presence of opposing claims of state sovereignty, whereby the right of one state to be free from environmental harm originating from another state must be reconciled with the right of a state to economic development, leads to commitments that promote a reflexive, informal, legal rationality.[3] Commitments structured as formal legal

[1] Here, I refer to the concept of "legalization" as described and examined in Kenneth Abbot *et al.*, "The Concept of Legalization" (2000) 54 Int. Org. 401 and the accompanying articles in a special issue of *International Organization* entitled "Legalization and World Politics" (2000) 54 Int. Org. 385.

[2] Discussed above at ch. 3.5.

[3] In this regard, there is a clear link between the jurisprudence of Gunther Teubner and proceduralism in international environmental law. See Gunther Teubner, "Substantive and Reflexive Elements in Modern Law" (1983) 17 Law and Soc'y Rev. 239 (identifying reflexive law as a process-oriented and self-regulatory form of legal structuring).

entitlements are less likely to arise given the diversity of state interests and the difficulty states will have in predicting how substantive rules will affect their interests. In the case of transboundary environmental harm, because the interests in question directly implicate elements of state sovereignty, there is a greater unwillingness by states to make pre-commitments under conditions of uncertainty. This structure is evident in the wide variety of international environmental commitments discussed in Chapters 4 and 5, but perhaps the apotheosis of this approach is the principle of sustainable development, which is itself the defining principle of international environmental governance after the Rio Conference. The proceduralism of the principle of sustainable development is clearly reflected in the *Gabcikovo-Nagymaros Case*, where the International Court of Justice takes the position that the reconciliation between environmental protection and economic development that forms the core of the principle is not a matter to be dictated by the Court, but rather must be determined by the parties through good faith negotiation. In this context, the principle of sustainable development was viewed as self-regulatory, requiring the parties to a dispute to find their own solutions in light of accepted principles.[4]

When the concept of sustainable development is disaggregated, its constituent parts are a mixture of procedural and substantive obligations. The process obligations have greater definition, are more easily subject to judicial treatment, and are therefore more readily identified as having legal normative status. The substantive components, which involve the balancing of competing values, fall outside the accepted institutional competence of judicial bodies in that questions regarding sustainable development involve the resolution of polycentric disputes with allocational consequences – questions which are better left resolved by the parties themselves. The fact that the principle of sustainable development is poorly suited to third party determinations does not rob the principle of its normative character; rather it requires a less deterministic (and more political) form of implementation and application.

International EIA commitments respond to the demands of proceduralism through the promotion of inclusive, information-rich and principled interactions between decision-makers and those impacted by the decision. The opportunity to participate is not premised on formal criteria and the deliberations themselves treat norms, not as formally

[4] *Case Concerning the Gabcikovo-Nagymaros Project (Hungary/Slovakia)* (1997) ICJ Rep 6, para. 141.

binding prescriptions, but as providing a principled basis for persuasion. EIA commitments operationalize the principled nature of proceduralism in international environmental governance by establishing a common commitment to a normative environmental goal, but leaving the question of how that goal is actually reflected in decisions for the parties to determine endogenously. The substantive commitment to environmental goals is implemented by making consideration of matters that may affect those goals mandatory and exercisable in good faith.

The principle of sustainable development institutionalizes the goal of reconciling harm prevention and economic development, but does not limit the principle to interstate activity like the harm principle. Instead, the principle is intentionally transnational in that it applies equally to the domestic environment as it does to impacts that have an international dimension and it applies to both public and private actors. Transnationalism as an element of international environmental governance itself has roots in both procedural and substantive concerns. Transnationalism recognizes there is a broad range of interests that are impacted by environmental decisions and further recognizes that there exist limitations to the capacity of the state to represent those divergent interests. Because transnationalism is concerned with ensuring the appropriate representation of diverse interests, it tends to manifest itself in procedural rules, such as rules of standing, access to information and rights of participation. Consequently, there is a direct link between transnationalism and proceduralism, with EIA commitments addressing the procedural demands of transnationalism. For example, the Espoo Convention addresses these demands through its requirement that states provide public notice of projects with significant transboundary impacts, allow for interested persons to have access to project information, provide comments directly to the foreign proponent and require that the proponent respond to their comments. Other regimes provide specific recognition of the special interests of groups within a domestic polity, such as indigenous groups. The transnationalism of EIAs is also a recognition that desirable outcomes are not simply a matter of aggregating preferences at the domestic or international level, since the determination of outcomes is a function of normative, as well as interest-driven, interactions.

Transnationalism is also reflected in the substance of environmental norms themselves, which are directed to environmental good governance generally, as opposed to existing at either the domestic or the international level. In addition to sustainable development, the precautionary principle, the polluter pays principle, the principle of prevention, and ecosystem integrity all apply without differentiating between levels of governance. Here, transnationalism is a reflection of the nature of environmental problems themselves that cut across borders and across the public/private divide. There is a monist predisposition to transnationalism that validates looking to comparative sources of law, as well as international sources, in decision-making processes. This approach is reflected in the discussion of the principle of sustainable development by Judge Weeramantry in the *Gabcikovo-Nagymaros Case*, who explicitly draws on the practices of traditional legal systems as a source of law in support of sustainable development.[5] The implication of monism for international environmental governance is that, if legal processes are to reflect the full range of normative influences that inform environmental principles, they must be able to give normative effect to these influences without reference to their formal validity. In this regard, the informal legal rationality of EIA processes enables EIA processes to be highly permeable to transnational normative influences. For example, the ability to raise transboundary or climate change norms in relation to a project subject to EIA is not dependent on the formal validity of those norms within international or domestic law. A striking example of the receptiveness of EIA processes to a wide range of normative influences is the EIA for the Sumas 2 generating station, which considered American, Canadian and international sources of environmental standards and principles in its consideration of transboundary air pollution issues.[6]

Transnationalism is further reflected through the implementation of international EIA commitments in a single, undifferentiated domestic EIA system, allowing access by both state and non-state actors to the same processes. In the examples discussed in Chapter 6 regarding the projection of international norms into the Canadian federal EIA process, there was little sense that the decision-makers thought that they were engaged in an international exercise. The distinction between domestic and international law is less relevant in these processes because the decision-makers are not concerned with formal legal validity, and therefore with sources of law. In this respect, the international significance of EIA processes may be overlooked because the interactions between states often occur at an agency level within domestic EIA processes,[7] and do

[5] Ibid. at 96. [6] Discussed above at ch. 2.6.

[7] This is certainly the contemplated approach under NEPA and the CEAA. Even in interactions governed by the Espoo Convention, interstate contacts are likely to be at an agency level.

not have the profile of a formal interstate process, such as a dispute before an international tribunal.

This takes us to integration as a feature of international governance.[8] The need for integration is inherent to both proceduralism and transnationalism. While a formal, substantive, legal rationality tends to view legal principles in a hierarchical fashion, proceduralism requires decision-makers to integrate or reconcile competing objectives. Again, this feature is most easily seen in the principle of sustainable development where environmental, social and economic considerations are expressly recognized as relating to one another in a non-hierarchical fashion, in what is sometimes referred to as a "triple bottom line."[9] Here, the integration is horizontal and issue-based, with decision-makers being required to consider policy questions with multiple objectives in mind. Horizontal integration also seeks to create a more coherent and ecosystem-based regulatory framework for the environment by integrating fragmented sectoral laws and by integrating decisions at various stages of the planning cycle.[10] Integration can also be vertical in the sense that decisions must also account for the interests of actors at a variety of levels both within and outside the state.

Integration is, of course, a stated goal of domestic EIA processes,[11] and is evident in international EIA commitments. For example, the emphasis on an ecosystem approach in the Antarctic and Arctic EIA systems is clearly intended as a means to move away from sectoral approaches to environmental regulation. Similarly, the inclusive definition of impact contained in the Espoo Convention requires the consideration of a broad range of impacts on all manner of environmental media.[12] While many international EIA commitments are contained in sectoral regimes, the fact that they are implemented in domestic systems helps to ensure that project impacts themselves are considered from a broad ecosystem-based perspective.

[8] The concept of integration in environmental decision-making is canvassed in John Dernbach, "Achieving Sustaining Development: The Centrality and Multiple Facets of Integrated Decisionmaking" (2003) 10 Indiana J. Global Legal Stud. 247.

[9] See, for example, Robert Paehlke, *Democracy's Dilemma: Environment, Social Equity, and the Global Economy* (Cambridge, MA: MIT Press, 2003) ch. 4 at 119 *et seq.*

[10] See Hussein Abaza, Ron Bisset and Barry Sadler, *Environmental Impact Assessment and Strategic Environmental Assessment: Towards an Integrated Approach* (Nairobi: UNEP, 2004) ch. 6 at 113 *et seq.* (discussing different forms of integration).

[11] See, for example, NEPA, 42 USC § 4331 (2000); and CEAA, SC 1992, c. 37, preamble.

[12] February 25, 1991, 30 ILM 802 (1991), in force January 14, 1998, Art. 1.

As for the integration of environmental consideration with economic and social considerations, a matter that goes to the heart of sustainable development, it is evident that EIAs are understood as being a primary mechanism to achieve this kind of integration between states. The express connection between EIA and sustainable development is made in the *Gabcikovo-Nagymaros Case*,[13] and in the International Law Commission's Draft Articles on Prevention of Transboundary Harm from Hazardous Activities.[14] In connection with the latter, the ILC in its enumeration of factors involved in an equitable balancing of interests includes taking account of the "advantages of a social, economic and technical character for the State of Origin in relation to the potential harm for the state likely to be affected."[15] The potential for EIA processes to realize the goals of sustainable development is also explicitly noted in the preambles to the Espoo Convention and the SEA Protocol.

Notwithstanding the recognition of the close connection between EIA and sustainable development in the abstract, the successful implementation of sustainable development in EIA processes in practice has proved to be more elusive. The difficulty in using EIA to implement the principle of sustainable development is that EIAs treat the relationship between environmental goals and economic and social goals quite differently than does the principle of sustainable development. Without unpacking the concept of sustainable development in any detail, I would reiterate that sustainable development itself has both procedural and substantive elements. The procedural elements, transparency and participation, are well captured by EIA processes. The most common formulations of the substantive aspect of sustainable development require the equitable distribution of resources between present and future generations, as well as between groups and individuals on an intragenerational basis. Others have gone beyond the traditional focus on material well-being, and have argued that greater attention must be paid to social and cultural factors that cannot be reduced to a single, usually economic, metric.[16] The fact that sustainable development has enjoyed considerable policy traction can be explained in part by the attractiveness that the shift away

[13] *Gabcikovo-Nagymaros Case* at 78.

[14] International Law Commission, "Commentaries to the Draft Articles on Prevention of Transboundary Harm from Hazardous Activities" in *Report of the International Law Commission, Fifty-Third Session*, UN GAOR, 56th Sess., Supp. No. 10, UN Doc. A/56/10 (2001) 377 at 403.

[15] Ibid., Art. 10(b).

[16] Paehlke, "Democracy's Dilemma" ch. 4 at 119 *et seq*.

from the "limits to growth" argument entails.[17] Instead of conceptualizing economic growth as incompatible with environmental goals and as something to be sacrificed in order to achieve environmental goals, sustainable development views economic growth and environmental protectionism as largely reinforcing.

Part of the difficulty with expanding EIA processes to account for a broad range of socio-economic factors is that it risks minimizing the clear consideration of environmental impacts as environmental matters are conflated with economic and social factors under the rubric of sustainability.[18] To be clear, the concern here is not that environmental factors will be subject to trade-offs against socio-economic factors, but rather that, instead of these trade-offs being made in a transparent way by accountable decision-makers, they are at best submerged in the generation of the impact assessment documentation itself, and, at worst, environmental factors are marginalized. To put the concern in slightly different terms, one of the original motivations for developing EIA processes was that environmental considerations were often ignored in favor of agency economic and development objectives; by bringing other considerations into the assessment process, environmental considerations lose their privileged position, with the consequent potential for a loss of bargaining power for those who favor more environmentally benign outcomes.

The success of EIA processes to bring about outcomes that reflect environmental values is dependent on interactions based on principled justifications. The deliberative process does not depend on the existence of a broadly constituted foundation of shared values, but does require a minimal substantive commitment to the identified ends of deliberation. In the case of EIAs, it is a shared commitment to the prevention and mitigation of environmental harm, and, in the case of specific regimes, to preventing specific forms of environmental harm.[19] In the case of sustainable development, while a theoretical reconciliation of these pillars is possible, and ultimately imperative, there is little indication that

[17] See Daniel Esty, "A Term's Limits" (September/October 2001) Foreign Policy 74. See also Steven Bernstein, *The Compromise of Liberal Environmentalism* (New York: Columbia University Press, 2001) ch. 2 at 28 *et seq*.

[18] Jenny Pope, David Annadale and Angus Morrison-Saunders, "Conceptualising Sustainability Assessment" (2004) 24 Environmental Impact Assessment Review 595 at 606 (providing examples of this tendency). See also Esty, "A Term's Limits."

[19] For example, in the case of UNCLOS, harm to the marine environment; or, with the CBD, harm to biological diversity; or, in the case of the polar regimes, to an identified ecosystem such as the Arctic or Antarctic.

as a substantive goal sustainable development can provide at this time a meaningful basis for persuasion. In the words of one commentator, "Unfortunately, in the real world outside the sustainability literature, there is a common, indeed deeply entrenched opinion that the economic pillar and the ecological pillar are foundations of warring houses."[20] In these circumstances, the deliberative process is undermined by setting the range of possible outcomes too broadly, resulting in parties framing their arguments in incommensurate terms. The shallow integration found in the Espoo Convention and the ILC Draft Articles on Prevention of Transboundary Harm avoid these problems by maintaining that environmental goods will generally require trade-offs against other socially desirable ends.

This is not to say that deep integration is not desirable as a goal, but, until such a time as environmental values are more deeply engrained in our understanding of social and economic goals, the original purpose of EIA processes to require environmental issues to be fully aired and to seek to expose the costs associated with meeting environmental objectives should be maintained. EIAs may, of course, play a part in moving toward a sustainability paradigm,[21] but the findings of this study suggest that a reorientation of this nature is best accomplished incrementally and in a bottom-up fashion.[22]

A more modest and more practical approach is to work toward the development of sustainability criteria that can be applied to specific projects. In the environmental assessments conducted under the CEAA, review panels have attempted to give meaning to the goal of sustainable development by requiring projects under consideration to make a

20 Robert Gibson, *Specification of Sustainability-Based Environmental Assessment Decision Criteria and Implications for Determining "Significance" in Environmental Assessment* (Ottawa: CEAA Research and Development Monograph Series, 2000) ch. 2.

21 See, for example, International Association for Impact Assessment, "The Linkages Between Impact Assessment and the Sustainable Development Agenda and Recommendations for Action," August 2002, www.iaia.org. This document, which was prepared by the International Association for Impact Assessment for the World Summit on Sustainable Development, advocates the strengthening and promotion of the full range of impact assessment tools, including, but going well beyond, EIA, in support of sustainable development. However, it contains few concrete policy improvements. For a more technical consideration of this issues, see Hussein Abaza, Ron Bisset and Barry Sadler, *Environmental Impact Assessment and Strategic Environmental Assessment: Towards an Integrated Approach* (Nairobi: UNEP, 2004).

22 On this point, this study supports the claims made by Brunnée and Toope regarding the organic generation of environmental co-operation through "contextual regimes," discussed above at ch. 6.3.3.

positive contribution to the attainment of ecological and community sustainability.[23] These general goals are then given more specific meaning through the evaluation of identified criteria that support the goals. In this way, the goal of sustainable development is placed at the forefront of the analysis, and is given expression with reference to the very specific circumstances of the project under consideration. These criteria will often be science-based, relating to carrying capacities, reversibility of impacts, and net ecological benefits.[24] The advantage of turning to sustainability as the principle normative measure, as opposed to impact mitigation, can be a more onerous standard of net environmental benefit.[25] The approach here, though, is to use sustainability as a justification to push for a higher threshold for trade-offs that can be elaborated upon on a case-by-case basis, as opposed to conflating multiple criteria into a single process.

One recent study prepared by Robert Gibson elaborates on how sustainability criteria might be developed for EIA processes by creating higher burdens of justifications for trade-offs and compromises that favor short-term economic gains over longer-term ecological integrity, by requiring net ecological gains and by discouraging certain trade-offs between different sustainability requirements, such as trade-offs allowing for ecological degradation to be compensated for through the provision of economic or social goods.[26] Significantly, Gibson's study with respect to sustainability criteria was prepared for the Canadian Environmental Assessment Agency in anticipation of the creation of guidelines elaborating on how sustainability criteria can be better integrated into the EIA process under the CEAA. Thus, the trajectory of introducing sustainability criteria looks similar to the internalization process seen with climate change and biological diversity norms. A broad normative goal is introduced, it is projected into contextualized deliberation where the implications of norm application are foreseeable in concrete terms, and

[23] Robert Gibson, "Favouring the Higher Test: Contribution to Sustainability as the Central Criterion for Review and Decisions under the Canadian Environmental Assessment Act" (2000) 10 J. Envt'l L. Prac. 39.

[24] Gibson, *Specification* at ch. 4. [25] Ibid.

[26] Ibid. at ch. 3. Gibson also notes that a number of Canadian provinces have developed sustainability criteria to elaborate on the meaning of sustainability in the context of provincial EIA processes. See, for example, Quebec Ministry of Environment, "Directives Sectorialle," Quebec Ministry of Environment, www.menv.gouv.qc.ca. See also Government of Manitoba, "Manitoba's Provincial Sustainable Development Code of Practice," Manitoba Government, www.gov.mb.ca/gs/psb/SD˙Code˙Practice.pdf.

there are attempts to further institutionalize these elaborations in the form of non-binding guidelines.

As an illustration of the point that there is nothing inevitable about the process of internalization,[27] it is noteworthy that in the case of sustainability criteria no guidelines were in fact adopted, and subsequent review panels have been less enthusiastic about adopting a requirement of no net loss.[28] However, following the logic of transformationalism, it is reasonable to predict that the continued projection of sustainability criteria into EIA processes will result in further deliberations over the utility of sustainable development as a normative basis for decision-making, which in turn can lead to the further elaboration of sustainability criteria, and possibly the internalization of those criteria in the form of bureaucratic guidelines, review panel decisions or more elaborate forms of regulation.

8.3 Process-oriented approaches and EIAs

The starting point for process-oriented approaches to international law is that process matters. However, process-oriented approaches go beyond a simple recognition that how decisions are made will affect outcomes by maintaining that law itself is best viewed as a process, as opposed to a collection of hierarchically structured rules. This characterization of law as process flows out of two related normative considerations that feature prominently in process-oriented legal scholarship. The first is a rejection of "ultimate objectivist foundations" upon which normative justifications can rest, and the second is a commitment to practical reasoning.[29] While the conceptualization of law as process is at the center of process-oriented approaches, there is a considerable amount of theoretical convergence around these two normative considerations that suggests EIAs are part of a broader pattern of governance in international

[27] Brunnée and Toope make this point in reference to the possibility of contextual regimes crystallizing into formally binding sets of rules, which is contingent upon deepening congruence between regime rules and community values. Discussed in Jutta Brunnée and Stephen Toope, "Environmental Security and Freshwater Resources: Ecosystem Regime Building" (1997) 91 AJIL 26.

[28] For example, a decision by the British Columbia Superior Court which held that the CEAA required the responsible authority to demonstrate that it had addressed its statutory duty to promote sustainability was overturned on appeal: *Taku River Tlingit First Nation v. British Columbia (Project Assessment Director)*, 77 BCLR (3d) 310 (BCSC), aff'd (2002) 211 DLR (4th) 89 (BCCA), rev'd [2004] 3 SCR 550.

[29] Frank Michelman, "Traces of Self-Government" (1986) 100 Harvard L. Rev. 4 at 23.

environmental law. Moreover, these considerations provide a basis for a normative justification of international EIA commitments themselves.

The rejection of foundationalist approaches is non-positivist in that it does not rely on an ultimate rule of recognition from which all other rules can derive their validity and, consequently, process-oriented approaches understand law as being contingent upon other social processes. This contingency points to a link between process-oriented legal scholarship and deliberative approaches to democracy, in that both emphasize the importance of reciprocal justifications to agreement and that the process of justification requires appealing to substantive principles that can themselves be the subject of deliberation and adjustment.[30] The requirement for reciprocal justification also points to the importance of reasoned decision-making since justifications that are reciprocal require the consideration of common interests.[31] The form of reasoning that arises is not formal in the sense that outcomes are derived logically from principles and rules. Rather, because norms are contingent and provisional, they must be continually reassessed in light of new factual information and competing norms.

EIA processes reflect the characterization of law as process in several important ways. EIA processes institutionalize contingency in the sense that outcomes are self-generated and norms are treated as being non-binding. This shifts the focus from the validity of a norm to its legitimacy. Where formal legal processes tend to separate decision-making processes from other social processes, EIAs purposely draw on the legitimacy of political and scientific processes, in addition to the legitimacy of norms themselves. The transnationalism of EIAs also rejects formalism by being open to normative influences from both international and domestic sources.

EIAs also reflect the general commitment to reason and the normativity that characterize process-oriented approaches to law. Thus, while rejecting a formal substantive legal rationality, EIAs maintain a commitment to principled decision-making through the requirement for justification. Because EIAs generate context-specific information for the purpose of normative assessment and require decision-makers to look at problems from a range of alternative perspectives in light of

[30] Amy Gutmann and Dennis Thompson, "Deliberative Democracy Beyond Process" in James Fishkin and Peter Laslett, eds., *Debating Deliberative Democracy* (Malden, MA: Blackwell Publishing, 2003) 31.

[31] Abram Chayes and Antonia Chayes, *The New Sovereignty: Compliance with International Regulatory Agreements* (Cambridge, MA: Harvard University Press, 1995) at 120.

non-hierarchical norms, EIA processes should be seen as applications of practical reasoning. In this regard, the absence of formal substantive obligations in EIA is a virtue, not a vice, because it allows for genuine deliberation over norms, while accepting their provisional nature. Nevertheless, norms retain their independence from political interests because as public justifications they are required to be reciprocal. That is, they must appeal to shared values. International EIA commitments identify common principles with the expectation that those principles will be elaborated upon in light of specific project information and in light of scientific norms of analysis. The separation between scientific and ideological judgments is itself fluid. EIAs embrace that fluidity by opening up scientific processes to democratic and ideological influences, and in doing so increases the ability of scientific considerations to influence outcomes.

The link between science and normativity in EIA processes underlines the tendency in process-oriented legal scholarship to see legal institutions as being embedded in a much broader normative environment. Harold Koh speaks directly to the notion of embeddedness through his observation that obedience to international law is directly influenced by the extent to which international norms become enmeshed in domestic institutions.[32] This study demonstrates how institutions can be designed to take advantage of the linkages between international and domestic institutions, and between political, legal and scientific institutions in order to promote environmental goals. At the root of these connections is that each institution draws on legitimacy as the basis of its ability to influence outcomes. These sources of legitimacy are not distinct strands, but can serve to enhance or detract from one another. Koh points to this by showing that the influence of international norms can be enhanced by projecting those norms into domestic processes and drawing on the existing authoritativeness of institutions and processes. Koh does not restrict his analysis to legal processes, but shows how social, political and bureaucratic processes are often simultaneously at work. In a similar vein, international EIA commitments call for the projection of international environmental norms into (mostly) domestic legal processes where scientific, political and ideological influences converge to produce policy outcomes.

A final point of convergence is the understanding of interests and identities as being affected by participation in social processes. This

[32] Harold Koh, "Why Do Nations Obey International Law" (1997) 106 Yale LJ 2599 at 2654–2655.

ties process-oriented scholarship to constructivist approaches in IR and to new institutionalist approaches in policy studies.[33] Law as process captures the recursive character of social cooperation that flows from the endogenous nature of actor interests and identities. EIAs provide an interesting example of how institutional mechanisms can encourage cooperative behavior by purposely structuring interactions through procedural rules in order to foster persuasion. In particular, this study indicates that transformational processes that are directed toward broad goals can be coupled with more rationalistic processes in reinforcing ways.

The connection between principled interactions and interest formation also suggests that EIAs have an important ethical dimension. Participation in deliberative processes is one way in which individuals can discover their interests and identities. International EIA commitments provide an avenue for deliberative interactions over environmental values that can contribute to developing shared understandings of these values in contexts that are identified by the participants as being meaningful to them. Even in cases where a participant's views are not reflected in the outcome, where there is an opportunity for those views to be expressed and accounted for by decision-makers, there is value to the participants in that their views are taken seriously. For example, the requirement that EIA processes consider traditional knowledge has instrumental value in that it can provide decision-makers with information about environmental impacts that they might not otherwise have, but it also has non-instrumental value insofar as it validates indigenous culture by treating traditional knowledge and indigenous environmental values as being relevant and worthy of serious consideration. The important effect is to bring a perspective that was not previously given expression into the common normative environment. Here, again, there is a link back to process-oriented legal scholarship, which has often emphasized the importance of "outsider" perspectives.[34]

[33] The theoretical considerations linking process-oriented approaches to international law to constructivism are discussed in Jutta Brunnée and Stephen Toope, "International Law and Constructivism: Elements of an Interactional Theory of International Law" (2000) 39 Columbia J. Transnat'l Law 19. See also David Frank, Ann Hironaka and Evan Schofer, "The Nation-State and the Natural Environment over the Twentieth Century" (2000) 65 Amer. Soc. Rev. 96 (arguing that domestic environmental policies are affected by institutionalized definitions of the nation-state as a protector of the natural environment).

[34] William Eskridge Jr. and Gary Peller, "The New Public Law Movement: Moderation as a Postmodern Cultural Form" (1991) 89 Michigan L. Rev. 707 at 786.

8.4 Proceduralization as a form of governance

In suggesting that international EIA commitments are part of a broader pattern of governance, my point is that EIA commitments offer an alternative to substantive forms of legalization that may otherwise be overlooked by scholars due to a failure to sufficiently differentiate between procedural and substantive rules in international regimes. For example, legalization as identified as a specific form of institutionalization in world politics focuses principally on the turn to substantive rule-making in particular regimes.[35] Abbott and Snidal's examination of the conditions under which states cooperate through legalized governance structures points out that higher "sovereignty costs" associated with hard legal commitments and uncertainty associated with future conditions addressed by those commitments can make soft legalization an attractive alternative.[36] Under this model, one might expect that international environmental regimes, which often have both high sovereignty costs and high degrees of uncertainty, would have fairly low levels of legalization in the form of formally binding, precise obligations with binding forms of delegated decision-making.[37] While Abbott and Snidal's thesis provides insight into the low levels of substantive legalization in the environmental field, it does not adequately account for proceduralized commitments. For example, both the Espoo Convention and the Antarctic Protocol are precise, formally binding and contain mechanisms, although highly circumscribed, to have disputes resolved by third parties, yet policy-makers in the areas of transboundary impacts and Antarctic ecosystem management face high levels of uncertainty and these ensuing commitments place restraints on domestic policy-makers. My point here is not that the legalization framework is unhelpful, but insofar as it concentrates on substantive forms of legalization it provides a less nuanced understanding of the way by which different normative forms may impact environmental governance. Proceduralized forms of legalization such as EIAs offer a distinct form of governance by allowing states to retain control over the substantive decision-making process, but at the same time facilitating agreement in accordance with regime goals on a case-by-case basis.

[35] Judith Goldstein *et al.*, "Introduction: Legalization and World Politics" (2000) 54 Int. Org. 385.

[36] Kenneth Abbott and Duncan Snidal, "Hard and Soft Law in International Governance" (2000) 54 Int. Org. 421.

[37] See Kenneth Abbott *et al.*, "The Concept of Legalization" (2000) 54 Int. Org. 401.

The legalization framework seeks to identify governance approaches with greater accuracy by unpacking the concept of legalization. One welcome aspect of the legalization project is that it understands that soft legalization is not simply inchoate or underdeveloped law.[38] This is certainly the case with EIAs. This study indicates that EIAs are a superior institutional mechanism in areas of high uncertainty and only provisional agreement on regime objectives. While EIAs can lead to more precise sets of rules, these rules will most often retain a procedural and informal nature.[39] In these circumstances, states that accept proceduralized commitments are relinquishing some of their decision-making powers. However, unlike formal delegation, where authority to make a decision is transferred to an impartial third party decision-maker, under EIA processes the delegation is effectively made to the community of affected persons. The result is a form of power-sharing in the sense that decision-makers are subject to greater external pressures to conform to community norms. As discussed in detail in Chapter 7, these pressures have functional implications for interest-coordination, as well as serving to facilitate greater internalization of community norms.

Proceduralization shifts the focus of legal processes from dispute settlement toward policy formation – again, an aspect not adequately captured by the legalization framework. The formal concept of legality adopted in the legalization framework tends to view norms as coming to legal processes more or less fully formed. Insofar as legal processes do perform elaboration tasks, it is done in accordance with a formal delegation from a centralized source of authority. EIA processes demonstrate that legal normativity is not the sole creation of a central source of authority, but can be a community exercise. In fact, greater community involvement will have a positive influence on compliance, as community norms are identified with internal values. The link between compliance and policy formation highlights the importance of implementation. It also points to the difficulty in distinguishing between implementation and compliance. For example, the understanding of EIA processes as

[38] Kal Raustiala and Anne-Marie Slaughter, "International Law, International Relations and Compliance" in Walter Carlsnaes *et al.*, eds., *Handbook of International Relations* (London: Sage Publications, 2001) 538 at 552.

[39] For example, the development of more precise EIA rules under the CBD, the Antarctic EIA regime and the Arctic EIA regime all took the form of guidelines. Similarly, the rules developed under the CEAA regarding the incorporation of biological diversity and climate change considerations were developed as guidelines.

being "action forcing" speaks to both implementation and compliance because it is through the process of projecting international environmental norms into deliberative processes that norms are both elaborated upon and internalized.

As Finnemore and Toope point out, many of the shortcomings of the legalization framework come from its adoption of a narrow, formal concept of legality.[40] EIA processes, as an example of proceduralization, demonstrate how legal norms can operate in a broader normative landscape to shape policy outcomes in both political and scientific processes. In this regard, where the legalization framework tends to view the turn to legalized institutions as constraining the exercise of political power, EIAs suggest that procedural obligations have a broader range of functions. In particular, EIAs bring transnational actors into the policy-making process, influence the scope and direction of scientific inquiry, and facilitate cooperation between parties.

In a related fashion, the informal legal rationality of EIA processes requires a less binary approach to compliance, in favor of a more directional and long-term understanding of compliance. Conceiving compliance in these terms is still meaningful because, as international EIA commitments demonstrate, open-textured norms are still capable of exerting influence in specific contexts. The result is not unlike the resort to equity in maritime delimitation cases, which Finnemore and Toope point out maintains its legal character and is capable of producing compliance, despite its imprecise nature.[41]

It is important to stress that international EIA commitments are not presented here as a panacea, and proceduralization as a form of institutionalized decision-making cannot operate in isolation. The only example of EIAs being the principal basis of regulation within a regime is the Antarctic Protocol regime. But that regime is unique in that the sources of impacts to the environment are limited and there exist fewer sources of pressure to engage in economic activities. In other regimes, as in domestic environmental governance structures, EIAs are one part of a larger whole. Even the Espoo Convention, which looks like a stand-alone regime on transboundary EIA, is best seen as part of a broader regime on the prevention of transboundary harm, which itself crosses

[40] Martha Finnemore and Stephen Toope, "Alternatives to 'Legalization': Richer Views of Law and Politics" (2001) 55 Int. Org. 743.

[41] Ibid. at 748.

over into other sectoral regimes.[42] The interrelationship between procedural obligations and substantive rules suggests caution in thinking about regimes as being self-contained. As discussed in Chapter 4, various EIA obligations may influence one another and are themselves related to norms of customary law. Finnemore and Toope point to the failure of the legalization framework to account for customary international law as a significant gap. Part of the difficulty here is that legalization as a framework tends to locate sources of rule-making authority in treaty structures and in doing so that ignores the broader coherence of international law – which is to say that legalization downplays or ignores the facts that regime norms are part of a broader system of laws and that regimes cannot be viewed in isolation from one another nor from the sources of normative influence outside law. EIAs, as procedural norms, are subject to these influences (as described in Chapter 4), but also mediate these influences as a site for deliberation over substantive environmental norms.

8.5 The effectiveness of international EIA commitments

Proceduralization also requires a reconsideration of the concept of effectiveness as a measure of normative arrangements. Assessing effectiveness requires a separation of the means by which an objective is attained from the objective itself. While assessing effectiveness in the context of international environmental governance is undeniably an important measure, some care must be taken in defining what those ends are. For example, with EIAs deliberation is both means and ends. It follows that looking at the extent to which EIA processes are successful in bringing international norms into deliberative processes is one way to measure effectiveness.[43] A related objective of international EIA commitments is the legitimation of environmental decision-making processes. This necessitates looking not only at the normative dimension of EIA processes, but also at the scientific and political. Measuring legitimacy as an empirical matter carries its own difficulties, although these are

[42] This is most clearly the case in the area of marine pollution in Europe, where it is anticipated that transboundary marine pollution shall be addressed under the Espoo Convention.

[43] This is the conclusion of John Knox in his consideration of the effectiveness of transboundary EIA commitments: John Knox, "The Myth and Reality of Transboundary Environmental Impact Assessment" (2002) 96 AJIL 291 at 318.

not insurmountable.[44] Finally, and most commonly, effectiveness can be measured in terms of the achievement of substantive environmental goals. But, here too, there are complications because substantive outcomes are influenced by multiple sources, making the establishment of causal connections difficult. Despite these difficulties, identifying proceduralization as a distinct approach to international governance remains helpful because it differentiates between types of legal norms and may lead to more refined understandings of how different types of norms can impact actor behavior. In light of the empirical dimension of effectiveness, the discussion that follows elaborates on indications of effectiveness of international EIA commitments that this study discloses and on the implications of this study for future interdisciplinary research on international EIA commitments.

In relation to its procedural objectives, the effectiveness of international EIA commitments is straightforward in the sense that there is clear evidence that states do in fact carry out transboundary EIAs in accordance with their international commitments and project international environmental norms into their domestic EIA processes. In those cases where states have disputed the extent of their international obligations to conduct EIAs, the existence of a base obligation is rarely disputed, and, in most cases, an EIA has been carried out.[45] Moreover, and more to the point, there is evidence that, when states do engage one another through EIA processes, they seek to justify their proposed activities on reasoned grounds – that is, they appeal to shared scientific and legal norms of analysis. One measure of the effectiveness of international EIA processes is the extent to which international environmental norms are actually being projected into domestic EIA processes. In this regard, this study has shown that EIA processes are effective in the sense of being sites for deliberative interactions over international environmental norms, such as the principles relating to transboundary harm, climate change, biological diversity and sustainability.

The more difficult question arises in response to the central critique of EIA processes that says in essence that "talk is cheap." In other words, actors may pay lip-service to international environmental norms, but decision-makers will pursue their rational interests. The dual role of EIAs as interest-coordination mechanisms and as processes for

[44] See Ian Hurd, "Legitimacy and Authority in International Politics" (1999) 53 Int. Org. 379 at 390–392.

[45] See above at ch. 4.4.

interest-transformation was canvassed in Chapter 7. From an effectiveness standpoint, an important finding of that discussion is that normative influences over actor behavior are most fruitfully measured over multiple interactions across large timeframes. Consequently, one useful measure of effectiveness is to track shifts in how norms are used and by whom within decision-making processes over time, with a view to assessing whether repeated interactions within EIA processes are resulting in greater entrenchment of international environmental norms within those decision-making processes. The shifts over time in relation to how climate change and biological diversity norms were used in the Canadian federal EIA process and then ultimately internalized through incorporation into guideline documents provide support for Koh's theory of transnational legal process, as well as for the conceptualization of EIAs as a pathway for bureaucratic "cognitive reform."[46] Along the same lines, the trajectory of transboundary harm-prevention norms can be understood as evolving from broad principles prohibiting significant transboundary harm toward the acceptance of more precise indicators of when those obligations may be engaged and the substantive limits of the harm principle. For example, the enumeration of specific types of activities or geographic criteria that will trigger EIA obligations serve to reduce state discretion by raising a presumption of significant harm.

The presence of internalized norms provides an indication of broad acceptance of that norm as a basis for justification. As a measurement of effectiveness, it can be said that, because one objective of the EIA process is the legitimation of environmental decision-making, internalization provides evidence of an increased willingness to make environmental decisions in light of accepted environmental principles. The relationship between EIA processes and internalization is not one of linear causality (since internalization will be affected by multiple sources of influence), but, from an institutional design perspective, the presence of internalization points to the efficacy of including EIA commitments in environmental regimes as a means to implement broadly formulated regime principles. The value of EIA commitments in international law is that they provide an avenue for the implementation of international environmental principles that recognizes the normative content of those principles without imposing unacceptable costs on states.

[46] James Boggs, "Procedural v. Substantive in NEPA Law: Cutting the Gordian Knot" (1993) 15 Environmental Professional 25.

This study also points to a number of areas that would benefit from further empirical research. The most pressing issue that arises from this study that could benefit from more rigorous analysis is determining the conditions that improve the ability of EIAs to influence policy outcomes. In connection with transboundary impacts, this study indicates that many of the interactions between states regarding transboundary impacts will occur through government networks. In the case of the Espoo Convention, these connections are subject to greater institutionalization in that contact agencies and informational requirements are specified, but in other cases, such as the Arctic EIA Guidelines, the interactions are subject to informally constituted, but nonetheless explicit, requirements. In still other cases, the interactions arise on an *ad hoc* basis. Looking at specific arrangements for transboundary EIA interactions, the timing of notification, the information made available and the nature of consultation that arises can provide insight into whether the degree of formality impacts policy outcomes. The transnationalism of EIAs suggest that this may be an area where transnational alliances can be formed and used to apply points of external pressure to decision-makers. The emerging role of NGOs in the Espoo and Antarctic Protocol EIA processes is one area that may prove helpful.

Because international EIA commitments rely on domestic processes for implementation, an important question that arises is how different domestic political structures relating to EIAs and the degree of institutionalization of process values within domestic political structures will affect the ability of EIAs to influence policy outcomes. One possible hypothesis arising from liberal IR theory is that countries with closed political systems are less likely to result in the kind of deliberate and reasoned processes that are the key to the functioning of EIAs.[47] Similarly, domestic capabilities may be a further determinant of the success of EIAs. For example, literacy and education levels will impact participation capacity, as will communication infrastructure. Scientific capabilities will affect the extent to which emerging environmental issues can be incorporated into the EIA process. These types of inquiries can lead usefully to a better understanding of the kind of policy adjustments and capacity-building that must be done to successfully use EIA processes to implement international norms.

[47] Robert Keohane has indicated that the degree of liberal democratic accountability mechanisms is likely to be a major condition affecting whether a transnational norm pathway leads to internalization. See Robert Keohane, "When Does International Law Come Home?" (1998) 35 Houston L. Rev. 699 at 711–712.

Along similar lines, greater consideration needs to be given to the role of EIA processes in institutionalizing international environmental norms in developing countries. There is a normative element to this line of research in that this study has identified the possibility that EIAs may be a mechanism that provides developing states and groups within developing states opportunities to consider and elaborate upon international environmental norms in the context of developing state problems and values. Insofar as international environmental law has failed to account for the views of groups underrepresented in formal law-making processes at the international level,[48] EIAs may assist developing states in recapturing international environmental norms.

A final area of inquiry concerns the operation of norms themselves. EIAs are unique institutional arrangements in that they quite deliberately seek to structure dialogue regarding environmental norms. EIA processes would seem to be a fruitful area in which to examine norm dynamics, particularly the conditions under which persuasion and interest-transformation can occur. Institutionalists may also find much of interest in EIA processes. Here, I think that the way in which process requirements can be used to facilitate cooperation between states and transnational actors in EIA processes has larger lessons for international governance. Finally, what makes EIAs particularly interesting is the way in which interest-coordination functions and interest-transformation functions can be combined and be mutually reinforcing. Much of the literature in both international law and international relations speaks to the importance of multiple sources of influence. However, on an abstract level, it is difficult to theorize cogently about processes that involve multiple variables. EIA commitments and processes provide, fittingly, a concrete set of examples of how these differing explanations of actor behavior are combined to produce substantive outcomes. In this regard, EIAs present some methodological advantages in that EIA processes are documented and consistent in their procedural requirements, making shifts in normative content easier to discern.

[48] See Obijiofor Aginam, "Saving the Tortoise, the Turtle, and the Terrapin: The Hegemony of Global Environmentalism and the Marginalization of Third World Approaches to Sustainable Development" in Obiora Okafor and Obijiofor Aginam, eds., *Humanizing Our Global Order: Essays in Honour of Ivan Head* (Toronto: University of Toronto Press, 2003) 12. See also Karin Mickelson, "South, North, International Environmental Law, and International Environmental Lawyers" (2000) 11 YBIEL 52.

8.6 Conclusion: an action-forcing mechanism for international environmental law

International environmental law is not self-activating. Consequently, if the gap between commitment and compliance in international environmental law is to be narrowed, then an integral part of the institutional arrangements designed to address environmental decision-making at transnational and global levels are mechanisms that project environmental norms into deliberations. International EIA commitments address the demand for "action-forcing" mechanisms in international environmental law in a number of important ways. First, EIAs operate across the national/international and public/private divides. In this way, EIAs not only reflect the transnational nature of environmental degradation itself, but also account for the wide scope and variety of persons, and organizations, including states, that are affected by environmental decision-making. To paraphrase Harold Koh, EIAs are a way of "bringing international environmental law home."[49] In bringing international environmental values to bear on domestic decision-making processes, EIAs implement international environmental legal instruments at the domestic level. But the nature of the EIA process is such that neither the participants nor the norms invoked are left unchanged by the process. Unlike formally binding legal processes, the self-regulatory nature of EIA provides opportunities for participants to shape and elaborate on the meaning of environmental norms in light of a set of known circumstances. Because norms in these circumstances are not received passively, but require their active invocation in justificatory interactions, participants can come to identify their own interests with the environmental values of the norms invoked over time.

Secondly, EIAs tend to operate substantively at the level of principles, not precise rules or standards. The structure of international EIA commitments aligns procedural requirements with underlying environmental goals. In this regard, EIAs may gain greater traction as a tool for implementing international law than as a purely domestic mechanism because so many international instruments are drafted in an open-textured manner. This condition points to the particular value of EIA processes in implementing those international environmental agreements where, owing to uncertainty and high sovereignty costs, more precise rules are not forthcoming. In this regard, I would note that EIAs play

[49] Harold Koh, "Bringing International Law Home" (1998) 35 Houston L. Rev. 623.

an important symbolic role in international environmental regimes, in that EIAs affirm the normative character of international environmental principles by providing the means by which international environmental principles can exert influence over policy outcomes.

International EIA commitments are underlain by a basic commitment: that decisions involving public goods such as the environment should be made in a reasoned fashion. A commitment to reason, which lies at the heart of process-oriented approaches to international law, does not separate EIAs from power or politics, but expresses an ethical choice about the kind of politics that states should be engaged in. This is not a universal claim, but rather international EIA commitments identify a set of policy decisions that are most appropriately made with reference to normative criteria.

Appendices

Appendix 1 List of international instruments containing EIA commitments

General environmental principles

Cooperation between States in the Field of the Environment, GA Res. 2995 (XXVII), UNGAOR 27th Sess., Supplement No. 30 (1972), paragraph 2

> Recognizes that co-operation between States in the field of the environment, including co-operation towards the implementation of principles 21 and 22 of the Declaration of the United Nations Conference on the Human Environment, will be effectively achieved if official and public knowledge is provided of the technical data relating to the work to be carried out by States within their national jurisdiction, with a view to avoiding significant harm that may occur in the environment of the adjacent area;

UNEP Principles on Conservation and Harmonious Utilization of Natural Resources Shared by Two or More States, 17 ILM 1094, UN Doc. UNEP/IG.12/2 (1978), Principle 4

> States should make environmental assessments before engaging in any activity with respect to a shared natural resource which may create a risk of significantly affecting the environment of another State or States sharing that resource.
>
> In the present text, the expression "significantly affect" refers to any appreciable effects on a shared natural resource and excludes "de minimis" effects.

World Charter for Nature, GA Res. 37/7, UNGAOR 37th Sess., UN Doc. A/Res/37/7 (1982) 22 ILM 455, sections 11(c) and 16

> 11. Activities which might have an impact on nature shall be controlled, and the best available technologies that minimize significant risks to nature or other adverse effects shall be used; in particular:
>
> (c) Activities which may disturb nature shall be preceded by assessment of their consequences, and environmental impact studies of development projects shall be conducted sufficiently in advance, and

if they are to be undertaken, such activities shall be planned and carried out so as to minimize potential adverse effects;

16. All planning shall include, among its essential elements, the formulation of strategies for the conservation of nature, the establishment of inventories of ecosystems and assessments of the effects on nature of proposed policies and activities; all of these elements shall be disclosed to the public by appropriate means in time to permit effective consultation and participation.

UNEP Goals and Principles of Environmental Impact Assessment, UNEP Res. GC14/25, 14th Sess (1987), endorsed by UNGA Res. 42/184, UNGAOR 42nd Sess., UN Doc. A/Res/42/184 (1987)

[Entire text.]

United Nations Conference on Environment and Development, Rio Declaration, 14 June 1992, 31 ILM 874, UN Doc. A/conf.151/5/Rev.1, Principle 17

Environmental impact assessment, as a national instrument, shall be undertaken for proposed activities that are likely to have a significant adverse impact on the environment and are subject to a decision of a competent national authority.

Association of South Eastern Asian Nations Agreement on the Conservation of Nature and Natural Resources, (1985) 15 EPL 64, Article 14

1. The Contracting Parties undertake that proposals for any activity which may significantly affect the natural environment shall as far as possible be subjected to an assessment of their consequences before they are adopted, and they shall take into consideration the results of this assessment in their decision-making process.

2. In those cases where any such activities are undertaken, the Contracting Parties shall plan and carry them out so as to overcome or minimize any assessed adverse effects and shall monitor such effects with a view to taking remedial action as appropriate.

Transboundary pollution

United Nations Convention on Environmental Impact Assessments in a Transboundary Context, Espoo, 25 February 1991, (1991) 30 ILM 802 (entered into force 14 January 1998)

[Entire text. The text of the Convention is reproduced in Appendix 2 below.]

Protocol on Strategic Environmental Assessment to the Convention on Environmental Impact Assessment in a Transboundary Context, 21 May 2003, UN Doc. ECE/MP/EIA/2003/2 (not yet entered into force)

[Entire text.]

Convention on Access to Information, Public Participation in Decision-Making and Access to Justice in Environmental Matters, Aarhus, 25 June 1998, (1999) 38 ILM 517 (entered into force 30 October 2001), Article 6

[Referring to requirements for notification and public participation in national EIA processes.]

North American Agreement on Environmental Cooperation, 14 September 1993, (1993) 32 ILM 1480 (entered into force 1 January 1994), Articles 2(1)(e) and 10(7)(a)

Article 2

1. Each Party shall, with respect to its territory:
(e) assess, as appropriate, environmental impacts;

Article 10

7. Recognizing the significant bilateral nature of many transboundary environmental issues, the Council shall, with a view to agreement between the Parties pursuant to this Article within three years on obligations, consider and develop recommendations with respect to:

(a) assessing the environmental impact of proposed projects subject to decisions by a competent government authority and likely to cause significant adverse transboundary effects, including a full evaluation of comments provided by other Parties and persons of other Parties;

[See also Commission for Environmental Cooperation, Draft North American Agreement on Transboundary Environmental Impact Assessment, http://cec.org/pubs_info_resources/law_treat_agree/pbl.cfm?varlan=english, entire text]

Marine pollution

United Nations Convention on the Law of the Sea, 18 December 1982, 21 ILM 1261 (entered into force 16 November 1994), Articles 204–206

Article 204 Monitoring of the risks or effects of pollution

1. States shall, consistent with the rights of other States, endeavour, as far as practicable, directly or through the competent international organizations, to observe, measure, evaluate and analyse, by recognized scientific methods, the risks or effects of pollution of the marine environment.

2. In particular, States shall keep under surveillance the effects of any activities which they permit or in which they engage in order to determine whether these activities are likely to pollute the marine environment.

Article 205 Publication of reports

States shall publish reports of the results obtained pursuant to article 204 or provide such reports at appropriate intervals to the competent international organizations, which should make them available to all States.

Article 206 Assessment of potential effects of activities

When States have reasonable grounds for believing that planned activities under their jurisdiction or control may cause substantial pollution of or significant and harmful changes to the marine environment, they shall, as far as practicable, assess the potential effects of such activities on the marine environment and shall communicate reports of the results of such assessments in the manner provided in article 205.

Regional Convention for Cooperation on the Protection of the Marine Environment from Pollution, Kuwait, 23 April 1978, 1140 UNTS 133, (1978) 17 ILM 511 (entered into force 1 July 1979), Article XI

Article XI

a) Each Contracting State shall endeavour to include an assessment of the potential environmental effects in any planning activity entailing projects within its territory, particularly in the coastal areas, which may cause significant risks of pollution in the Sea Area;

b) The Contracting States may, in consultation with the secretariat, develop procedures for dissemination of information of the assessment of the activities referred to in paragraph (a) above;

c) The Contracting States undertake to develop, individually or jointly, technical and other guidelines in accordance with standard scientific practice to assist the planning of their development projects in such a way as to minimize their harmful impact on the marine environment. In this regard international standards may be used where appropriate.

Convention for Co-operation in the Protection and Development of the Marine and Coastal Environment of the West and Central African Region, 23 March 1981, (1981) 20 ILM 746, UN Doc. UNEP/IG.22/7 (entered into force 5 August 1981), Article 13

Article 13

1. As part of their environmental management policies, the Contracting Parties shall develop technical and other guidelines to assist the planning of their development projects in such a way as to minimize their harmful impact on the Convention area.

2. Each Contracting Party shall endeavour to include an assessment of the potential environmental effects in any planning activity entailing projects within its territory, particularly in the coastal areas that may cause

substantial pollution of, or significant and harmful changes to, the Convention area.

3. The Contracting Parties shall, in consultation with the Organization, develop procedures for the dissemination of information concerning the assessment of the activities referred to in paragraph 2 of this article.

Convention for the Protection of the Marine Environment and Coastal Areas of the South-East Pacific, 12 November 1981, (1981) Intl Env. LM Treaties 85 (entered into force 19 May 1986), Article 8

Article 8

1. As part of their environmental management policies, the High Contracting Parties shall develop technical and other guidelines to assist the planning of their development projects in such a way as to minimize their harmful impact in the sphere of application of the Convention.

2. Each High Contracting Party shall endeavour to include an assessment of the potential environmental effects in any planning activity entailing projects within its territory, particularly in the coastal areas, that may cause substantial pollution of, or significant and harmful changes to, the area of application of the Convention.

3. The High Contracting Parties shall, in cooperation with the Executive Secretariat, develop procedures for the dissemination of information concerning the assessment of the activities referred to in paragraph 2 of this article.

Regional Convention for the Conservation of the Red Sea and Gulf of Aden Environment, 14 February 1982, (1982) 9 EPL 56 (entered into force 20 August 1985), Article XI

Article XI

1. Each Contracting Party shall give due consideration to marine environmental effects when planning or executing projects, including an assessment of potential environmental effects, particularly in the coastal areas.

2. The Contracting Parties may, in consultation with the General Secretariat, develop procedures for dissemination of information on the assessment of the activities referred to in paragraph 1 of this article.

3. The Contracting Parties undertake to develop, individually or jointly environmental standards technical and other guidelines in accordance with standard scientific practice to assist the planning and execution of their projects in such a way as to minimize their harmful impact on the marine environment. In this regard international standards may be used where appropriate.

Convention for the Protection and Development of the Marine Environment of the Wider Caribbean Region, 24 March 1983, (1983) 22 ILM 221 (entered into force 11 October 1986),

Article 12

1. As part of their environmental management policies the Contracting Parties undertake to develop technical and other guidelines to assist the planning of their major development projects in such a way as to prevent or minimize harmful impacts on the Convention area.

2. Each Contracting Party shall assess within its capabilities, or ensure the assessment of, the potential effects of such projects on the marine environment, particularly in coastal areas, so that appropriate measures may be taken to prevent any substantial pollution of, or significant and harmful changes to, the Convention area.

3. With respect to the assessments referred to in paragraph 2, each Contracting Party shall, with the assistance of the Organization when requested, develop procedures for the dissemination of information and may, where appropriate, invite other Contracting Parties which may be affected to consult with it and to submit comments.

Convention for the Protection of the Natural Resources and Environment of the South Pacific Region, 25 November 1986, (1987) 26 ILM 38 (entered into force 22 August 1990), Article 16

Article 16

1. The Parties agree to develop and maintain, with the assistance of competent global, regional and subregional organisations as requested, technical guidelines and legislation giving adequate emphasis to environmental and social factors to facilitate balanced development of their natural resources and planning of their major projects which might affect the marine environment in such a way as to prevent or minimise harmful impacts on the Convention Area.

2. Each Party shall, within its capabilities, assess the potential effects of such projects on the marine environment, so that appropriate measures can be taken to prevent any substantial pollution of, or significant and harmful changes within, the Convention Area.

3. With respect to the assessment referred to in paragraph 2, each Party shall, where appropriate, invite:

(a) public comment according to its national procedures;
(b) other Parties that may be affected to consult with it and submit comments. The results of these assessments shall be communicated to the Organisation, which shall make them available to interested Parties.

Convention of the Protection of the Marine Environment of the Baltic Sea Area, (1993) No. 22 Law of the Sea Bulletin 54 (entered into force 17 January 2000), Article 7

Article 7

1. Whenever an environmental impact assessment of a proposed activity that is likely to cause a significant adverse impact on the marine environment of the Baltic Sea Area is required by international law or supra-national regulations applicable to the Contracting Party of origin, that Contracting Party shall notify the Commission and any Contracting Party which may be affected by a transboundary impact on the Baltic Sea Area.

2. The Contracting Party of origin shall enter into consultations with any Contracting Party which is likely to be affected by such transboundary impact, whenever consultations are required by international law or supra-national regulations applicable to the Contracting Party of origin.

3. Where two or more Contracting Parties share transboundary waters within the catchment area of the Baltic Sea, these Parties shall cooperate to ensure that potential impacts on the marine environment of the Baltic Sea Area are fully investigated within the environmental impact assessment referred to in paragraph 1 of this Article. The Contracting Parties concerned shall jointly take appropriate measures in order to prevent and eliminate pollution including cumulative deleterious effects.

Convention on the Protection of the Black Sea Against Pollution, 21 April 1992, (1993) 32 ILM 1101 (entered into force 15 January 1994), Article XV(5)

Article XV

5. When the Contracting Parties have reasonable grounds for believing that activities under their jurisdiction or control may cause substantial pollution or significant and harmful changes to the marine environment of the Black Sea, they shall, before commencing such activities, assess their potential effects on the basis of all relevant information and monitoring data and shall communicate the results of such assessments to the Commission.

Framework Convention for the Protection of the Marine Environment of the Caspian Sea, 4 November 2003, www.caspianenvironment.org/newsite/Convention-FrameworkConventionText.htm (entered into force 12 August 2006), Article 17

Article 17

1. Each Contracting Party shall take all appropriate measures to introduce and apply procedures of environmental impact assessment of any planned activity, that are likely to cause significant adverse effect on the marine environment of the Caspian Sea.

2. Each Contracting Party will take all appropriate measures to disseminate results of environmental impact assessment carried out in accordance with paragraph 1 of this Article, to other Contracting Parties.

3. The Contracting Parties shall co-operate in the development of protocols that determine procedures of environmental impact assessment of the marine environment of the Caspian Sea in transboundary context.

Shared watercourse agreements

United Nations Convention on the Law of the Non-Navigational Uses of International Watercourses, (1997) 36 ILM 719, UN Doc. A/51/869, Res. 51/229 (not yet in force), Article 12

Article 12

Before a watercourse State implements or permits the implementation of planned measures which may have a significant adverse effect upon other watercourse States, it shall provide those States with timely notification thereof. Such notification shall be accompanied by available technical data and information, including the results of any environmental impact assessment, in order to enable the notified States to evaluate the possible effects of the planned measures.

Convention on the Protection and Use of Transboundary Watercourses and Lakes, 17 March 1992, (1992) 31 ILM 1312 (entered into force 6 October 1996), Articles 3(1)(h) and 9(2)(j)

Article 3

1. To prevent, control and reduce transboundary impact, the Parties shall develop, adopt, implement and, as far as possible, render compatible relevant legal, administrative, economic, financial and technical measures, in order to ensure, inter alia, that:

(h) Environmental impact assessment and other means of assessment are applied;

Article 9

2. The agreements or arrangements mentioned in paragraph 1 of this article shall provide for the establishment of joint bodies. The tasks of these joint bodies shall be, inter alia, and without prejudice to relevant existing agreements or arrangements, the following:

(j) To participate in the implementation of environmental impact assessments relating to transboundary waters, in accordance with appropriate international regulations;

Atmospheric pollution

United Framework Convention on Climate Change, 9 May 1992, (1992) 31 ILM 851 (entered into force 21 March 1994), Article 4(1)(f)

Article 4(1)

All Parties, taking into account their common but differentiated responsibilities and their specific national and regional development priorities, objectives and circumstances, shall:

(f) Take climate change considerations into account, to the extent feasible, in their relevant social, economic and environmental policies and actions, and employ appropriate methods, for example impact assessments, formulated and determined nationally, with a view to minimizing adverse effects on the economy, on public health and on the quality of the environment, of projects or measures undertaken by them to mitigate or adapt to climate change;

Agreement between the United States and Canada on Air Quality, 13 March 1991, Can. TS No. 3, (1991) 30 ILM 676 (entered into force 13 March 1991), Article V

Article V

1. Each Party shall, as appropriate and as required by its laws, regulations and policies, assess those proposed actions, activities and projects within the area under its jurisdiction that, if carried out, would be likely to cause significant transboundary air pollution, including consideration of appropriate mitigation measures.

2. Each Party shall notify the other Party concerning a proposed action, activity or project subject to assessment under paragraph 1 as early as practicable in advance of a decision concerning such action, activity or project and shall consult with the other Party at its request in accordance with Article XI.

3. In addition, each Party shall, at the request of the other Party, consult in accordance with Article XI concerning any continuing actions, activities or projects that may be causing significant transboundary air pollution, as well as concerning changes to its laws, regulation or policies that, if carried out, would be likely to affect significantly transboundary air pollution.

4. Consultations pursuant to paragraphs 2 and 3 concerning actions, activities or projects that would be likely to cause or may be causing significant transboundary air pollution shall include consideration of appropriate mitigation measures.

5. Each Party shall, as appropriate, take measures to avoid or mitigate the potential risk posed by actions, activities or projects that would be likely to cause or may be causing significant transboundary air pollution.

6. If either Party becomes aware of an air pollution problem that is of joint concern and requires an immediate response, it shall notify and consult the other Party forthwith.

Conservation of biological diversity

United Nations Convention on Biological Diversity, 5 June 1992, (1992) 31 ILM 818 (entered into force 29 December 1993), Article 14(1)

Article 14

1. Each Contracting Party, as far as possible and as appropriate, shall:

(a) Introduce appropriate procedures requiring environmental impact assessment of its proposed projects that are likely to have significant adverse effects on biological diversity with a view to avoiding or minimizing such effects and, where appropriate, allow for public participation in such procedures;
(b) Introduce appropriate arrangements to ensure that the environmental consequences of its programmes and policies that are likely to have significant adverse impacts on biological diversity are duly taken into account;

Polar ecosystems

Protocol on Environmental Protection to the Antarctic Treaty, 4 October 1991, (1991) 30 ILM 1461 (entered into force 14 January 1998), Article 8 and Annex 1

Article 8

1. Proposed activities referred to in paragraph 2 below shall be subject to the procedures set out in Annex I for prior assessment of the impacts of those activities on the Antarctic environment or on dependent or associated ecosystems according to whether those activities are identified as having:

(a) less than a minor or transitory impact;
(b) a minor or transitory impact; or
(c) more than a minor or transitory impact.

2. Each Party shall ensure that the assessment procedures set out in Annex I are applied in the planning processes leading to decisions about any activities undertaken in the Antarctic Treaty area pursuant to scientific research programs, tourism and all other governmental and non-governmental activities in the Antarctic Treaty area for which advance notice is required under Article VII (5) of the Antarctic Treaty, including associated logistic support activities.

3. The assessment procedures set out in Annex I shall apply to any change in an activity whether the change arises from an increase or decrease in the intensity of an existing activity, from the addition of an activity, the decommissioning of a facility, or otherwise.

4. Where activities are planned jointly by more than one Party, the Parties involved shall nominate one of their number to coordinate the implementation of the environmental impact assessment procedures set out in Annex I.

[The text of Annex I is reproduced in Appendix 3 below.]

1997 Guidelines for Environmental Impact Assessment in the Arctic, http://ceq.eh.doe.gov/nepa/eiaguide.pdf

[Entire text.]

Appendix 2 Convention on Environmental Impact Assessment in a Transboundary Context (Espoo, 1991)

[Note: Two amendments to the Espoo Convention have been adopted by the Parties, but neither have come into force. The first amendment (Amend. 1) was adopted in Decision II/14 of the Meeting of the Parties, *Report of the Second Meeting*, UN Doc. ECE/MP.EIA/4, 7 August 2001. The second amendment (Amend. 2) was adopted in Decision III/7 of the Meeting of the Parties, *Report of the Third Meeting*, UN Doc. ECE/MP.EIA/6, 13 September 2004. The amended text is italicized.]

The Parties to this Convention,

Aware of the interrelationship between economic activities and their environmental consequences,

Affirming the need to ensure environmentally sound and sustainable development,

Determined to enhance international cooperation in assessing environmental impact in particular in a transboundary context,

Mindful of the need and importance to develop anticipatory policies and of preventing, mitigating and monitoring significant adverse environmental impact in general and more specifically in a transboundary context,

Recalling the relevant provisions of the Charter of the United Nations, the Declaration of the Stockholm Conference on the Human Environment, the Final Act of the Conference on Security and Cooperation in Europe (CSCE) and the Concluding Documents of the Madrid and Vienna Meetings of Representatives of the Participating States of the CSCE,

Commending the ongoing activities of States to ensure that, through their national legal and administrative provisions and their national policies, environmental impact assessment is carried out,

Conscious of the need to give explicit consideration to environmental factors at an early stage in the decision-making process by applying environmental impact assessment, at all appropriate administrative levels, as a necessary tool to improve the quality of information presented to decision-makers so that environmentally sound decisions can be made paying careful attention to minimizing significant adverse impact, particularly in a transboundary context,

Mindful of the efforts of international organizations to promote the use of environmental impact assessment both at the national and international levels, and taking into account work on environmental impact assessment carried out under the auspices of the United Nations Economic Commission for Europe, in particular results achieved by the Seminar on Environmental Impact Assessment (September 1987, Warsaw, Poland) as well as noting the Goals and Principles on environmental impact assessment adopted by the Governing Council of the United Nations Environment Programme, and the Ministerial Declaration on Sustainable Development (May 1990, Bergen, Norway),

Have agreed as follows:

Article 1 Definitions

For the purposes of this Convention,

(i) "Parties" means, unless the text otherwise indicates, the Contracting Parties to this Convention;

(ii) "Party of origin" means the Contracting Party or Parties to this Convention under whose jurisdiction a proposed activity is envisaged to take place;

(iii) "Affected Party" means the Contracting Party or Parties to this Convention likely to be affected by the transboundary impact of a proposed activity;

(iv) "Concerned Parties" means the Party of origin and the affected Party of an environmental impact assessment pursuant to this Convention;

(v) "Proposed activity" means any activity or any major change to an activity subject to a decision of a competent authority in accordance with an applicable national procedure;

(vi) "Environmental impact assessment" means a national procedure for evaluating the likely impact of a proposed activity on the environment;

(vii) "Impact" means any effect caused by a proposed activity on the environment including human health and safety, flora, fauna, soil, air, water, climate, landscape and historical monuments or other physical structures or the interaction among these factors; it also includes effects on cultural heritage or socio-economic conditions resulting from alterations to those factors;

(viii) "Transboundary impact" means any impact, not exclusively of a global nature, within an area under the jurisdiction of a Party caused by a proposed activity the physical origin of which is situated wholly or in part within the area under the jurisdiction of another Party;

(ix) "Competent authority" means the national authority or authorities designated by a Party as responsible for performing the tasks covered by this Convention and/or the authority or authorities entrusted by a Party with decision-making powers regarding a proposed activity;

(x) "The Public" means one or more natural or legal persons *and, in accordance with national legislation or practice, their associations, organizations or groups* [Amend 1].

Article 2 General provisions

1. The Parties shall, either individually or jointly, take all appropriate and effective measures to prevent, reduce and control significant adverse transboundary environmental impact from proposed activities.

2. Each Party shall take the necessary legal, administrative or other measures to implement the provisions of this Convention, including, with respect to proposed activities listed in Appendix I that are likely to cause significant adverse transboundary impact, the establishment of an environmental impact assessment procedure that permits public participation and preparation of the environmental impact assessment documentation described in Appendix II.

3. The Party of origin shall ensure that in accordance with the provisions of this Convention an environmental impact assessment is undertaken prior to a decision to authorize or undertake a proposed activity listed in Appendix I that is likely to cause a significant adverse transboundary impact.

4. The Party of origin shall, consistent with the provisions of this Convention, ensure that affected Parties are notified of a proposed activity listed in Appendix I that is likely to cause a significant adverse transboundary impact.

5. Concerned Parties shall, at the initiative of any such Party, enter into discussions on whether one or more proposed activities not listed in Appendix I is or are likely to cause a significant adverse transboundary impact and thus should be treated as if it or they were so listed. Where those Parties so agree, the activity or activities shall be thus treated. General guidance for identifying criteria to determine significant adverse impact is set forth in Appendix III.

6. The Party of origin shall provide, in accordance with the provisions of this Convention, an opportunity to the public in the areas likely to be affected to participate in relevant environmental impact assessment procedures regarding proposed activities and shall ensure that the opportunity provided to the public of the affected Party is equivalent to that provided to the public of the Party of origin.

7. Environmental impact assessments as required by this Convention shall, as a minimum requirement, be undertaken at the project level of the proposed activity. To the extent appropriate, the Parties shall endeavour to apply the principles of environmental impact assessment to policies, plans and programmes.

8. The provisions of this Convention shall not affect the right of Parties to implement national laws, regulations, administrative provisions or accepted legal practices protecting information the supply of which would be prejudicial to industrial and commercial secrecy or national security.

9. The provisions of this Convention shall not affect the right of particular Parties to implement, by bilateral or multilateral agreement where appropriate, more stringent measures than those of this Convention.

10. The provisions of this Convention shall not prejudice any obligations of the Parties under international law with regard to activities having or likely to have a transboundary impact.

11. If the Party of origin intends to carry out a procedure for the purposes of determining the content of the environmental impact assessment documentation, the affected Party should to the extent appropriate be given the opportunity to participate in this procedure [Amend 2].

Article 3 Notification

1. For a proposed activity listed in Appendix I that is likely to cause a significant adverse transboundary impact, the Party of origin shall, for the purposes of ensuring adequate and effective consultations under Article 5, notify any Party which it considers may be an affected Party as early as possible and no later than when informing its own public about that proposed activity.

2. This notification shall contain, *inter alia*:

(a) Information on the proposed activity, including any available information on its possible transboundary impact;

(b) The nature of the possible decision; and

(c) An indication of a reasonable time within which a response under paragraph 3 of this Article is required, taking into account the nature of the proposed activity;

and may include the information set out in paragraph 5 of this Article.

3. The affected Party shall respond to the Party of origin within the time specified in the notification, acknowledging receipt of the notification, and shall indicate whether it intends to participate in the environmental impact assessment procedure.

4. If the affected Party indicates that it does not intend to participate in the environmental impact assessment procedure, or if it does not respond within the time specified in the notification, the provisions in paragraphs 5, 6, 7 and 8 of this Article and in Article 4 will not apply. In such circumstances the right of a Party of origin to determine whether to carry out an environmental impact assessment on the basis of its national law and practice is not prejudiced.

5. Upon receipt of a response from the affected Party indicating its desire to participate in the environmental impact assessment procedure, the Party of origin shall, if it has not already done so, provide to the affected Party:

(a) Relevant information regarding the environmental impact assessment procedure, including an indication of the time schedule for transmittal of comments; and

(b) Relevant information on the proposed activity and its possible significant adverse transboundary impact.

6. An affected Party shall, at the request of the Party of origin, provide the latter with reasonably obtainable information relating to the potentially affected environment under the jurisdiction of the affected Party, where such information is necessary for the preparation of the environmental impact assessment

documentation. The information shall be furnished promptly and, as appropriate, through a joint body where one exists.

7. When a Party considers that it would be affected by a significant adverse transboundary impact of a proposed activity listed in Appendix I, and when no notification has taken place in accordance with paragraph 1 of this Article, the concerned Parties shall, at the request of the affected Party, exchange sufficient information for the purposes of holding discussions on whether there is likely to be a significant adverse transboundary impact. If those Parties agree that there is likely to be a significant adverse transboundary impact, the provisions of this Convention shall apply accordingly. If those Parties cannot agree whether there is likely to be a significant adverse transboundary impact, any such Party may submit that question to an inquiry commission in accordance with the provisions of Appendix IV to advise on the likelihood of significant adverse transboundary impact, unless they agree on another method of settling this question.

8. The concerned Parties shall ensure that the public of the affected Party in the areas likely to be affected be informed of, and be provided with possibilities for making comments or objections on, the proposed activity, and for the transmittal of these comments or objections to the competent authority of the Party of origin, either directly to this authority or, where appropriate, through the Party of origin.

Article 4 Preparation of the environmental impact assessment documentation

1. The environmental impact assessment documentation to be submitted to the competent authority of the Party of origin shall contain, as a minimum, the information described in Appendix II.

2. The Party of origin shall furnish the affected Party, as appropriate through a joint body where one exists, with the environmental impact assessment documentation. The concerned Parties shall arrange for distribution of the documentation to the authorities and the public of the affected Party in the areas likely to be affected and for the submission of comments to the competent authority of the Party of origin, either directly to this authority or, where appropriate, through the Party of origin within a reasonable time before the final decision is taken on the proposed activity.

Article 5 Consultations on the basis of the environmental impact assessment documentation

The Party of origin shall, after completion of the environmental impact assessment documentation, without undue delay enter into consultations with the affected Party concerning, *inter alia*, the potential transboundary impact of the proposed activity and measures to reduce or eliminate its impact. Consultations may relate to:

(a) Possible alternatives to the proposed activity, including the no-action alternative and possible measures to mitigate significant adverse transboundary impact and to monitor the effects of such measures at the expense of the Party of origin;

(b) Other forms of possible mutual assistance in reducing any significant adverse transboundary impact of the proposed activity; and

(c) Any other appropriate matters relating to the proposed activity.

The Parties shall agree, at the commencement of such consultations, on a reasonable time-frame for the duration of the consultation period. Any such consultations may be conducted through an appropriate joint body, where one exists.

Article 6 Final decision

1. The Parties shall ensure that, in the final decision on the proposed activity, due account is taken of the outcome of the environmental impact assessment, including the environmental impact assessment documentation, as well as the comments thereon received pursuant to Article 3, paragraph 8 and Article 4, paragraph 2, and the outcome of the consultations as referred to in Article 5.

2. The Party of origin shall provide to the affected Party the final decision on the proposed activity along with the reasons and considerations on which it was based.

3. If additional information on the significant transboundary impact of a proposed activity, which was not available at the time a decision was made with respect to that activity and which could have materially affected the decision, becomes available to a concerned Party before work on that activity commences, that Party shall immediately inform the other concerned Party or Parties. If one of the concerned Parties so requests, consultations shall be held as to whether the decision needs to be revised.

Article 7 Post-project analysis

1. The concerned Parties, at the request of any such Party, shall determine whether, and if so to what extent, a post-project analysis shall be carried out, taking into account the likely significant adverse transboundary impact of the activity for which an environmental impact assessment has been undertaken pursuant to this Convention. Any post-project analysis undertaken shall include, in particular, the surveillance of the activity and the determination of any adverse transboundary impact. Such surveillance and determination may be undertaken with a view to achieving the objectives listed in Appendix V.

2. When, as a result of post-project analysis, the Party of origin or the affected Party has reasonable grounds for concluding that there is a significant adverse transboundary impact or factors have been discovered which may result in such an impact, it shall immediately inform the other Party. The concerned Parties shall then consult on necessary measures to reduce or eliminate the impact.

Article 8 Bilateral and multilateral co-operation

The Parties may continue existing or enter into new bilateral or multilateral agreements or other arrangements in order to implement their obligations under this Convention *and under any of its protocols to which they are a Party* [Amend. 2]. Such agreements or other arrangements may be based on the elements listed in Appendix VI.

Article 9 Research programmes

The Parties shall give special consideration to the setting up, or intensification of, specific research programmes aimed at:

(a) Improving existing qualitative and quantitative methods for assessing the impacts of proposed activities;

(b) Achieving a better understanding of cause-effect relationships and their role in integrated environmental management;

(c) Analysing and monitoring the efficient implementation of decisions on proposed activities with the intention of minimizing or preventing impacts;

(d) Developing methods to stimulate creative approaches in the search for environmentally sound alternatives to proposed activities, production and consumption patterns;

(e) Developing methodologies for the application of the principles of environmental impact assessment at the macro-economic level.

The results of the programmes listed above shall be exchanged by the Parties.

Article 10 Status of the Appendices

The Appendices attached to this Convention form an integral part of the Convention.

Article 11 Meeting of Parties

1. The Parties shall meet, so far as possible, in connection with the annual sessions of the Senior Advisers to ECE Governments on Environmental and Water Problems. The first meeting of the Parties shall be convened not later than one year after the date of the entry into force of this Convention. Thereafter, meetings of the Parties shall be held at such other times as may be deemed necessary by a meeting of the Parties, or at the written request of any Party, provided that, within six months of the request being communicated to them by the secretariat, it is supported by at least one third of the Parties.

2. The Parties shall keep under continuous review the implementation of this Convention, and, with this purpose in mind, shall:

(a) Review the policies and methodological approaches to environmental impact assessment by the Parties with a view to further improving environmental impact assessment procedures in a transboundary context;

(b) Exchange information regarding experience gained in concluding and implementing bilateral and multilateral agreements or other arrangements regarding the use of environmental impact assessment in a transboundary context to which one or more of the Parties are party;

(c) Seek, where appropriate, the services of competent international bodies and scientific committees in methodological and technical aspects pertinent to the achievement of the purposes of this Convention;

(c) Seek, where appropriate, the services and cooperation of competent bodies having expertise pertinent to the achievement of the purposes of this Convention; [Amend. 2, replacing (c) above]

(d) At their first meeting, consider and by consensus adopt rules of procedure for their meetings;

(e) Consider and, where necessary, adopt proposals for amendments to this Convention;

(f) Consider and undertake any additional action that may be required for the achievement of the purposes of this Convention.

(g) Prepare, where appropriate, protocols to this Convention;

(h) Establish such subsidiary bodies as they consider necessary for the implementation of this Convention. [Amend. 2]

Article 12 Right to vote

1. Each Party to this Convention shall have one vote.

2. Except as provided for in paragraph 1 of this Article, regional economic integration organizations, in matters within their competence, shall exercise their right to vote with a number of votes equal to the number of their member States which are Parties to this Convention. Such organizations shall not exercise their right to vote if their member States exercise theirs, and vice versa.

Article 13 Secretariat

The Executive Secretary of the Economic Commission for Europe shall carry out the following secretariat functions:

(a) The convening and preparing of meetings of the Parties;

(b) The transmission of reports and other information received in accordance with the provisions of this Convention to the Parties; and

(c) The performance of other functions as may be provided for in this Convention or as may be determined by the Parties.

Article 14 Amendments To The Convention

1. Any Party may propose amendments to this Convention.

2. Proposed amendments shall be submitted in writing to the secretariat, which shall communicate them to all Parties. The proposed amendments shall be discussed at the next meeting of the Parties, provided these proposals have been circulated by the secretariat to the Parties at least ninety days in advance.

3. The Parties shall make every effort to reach agreement on any proposed amendment to this Convention by consensus. If all efforts at consensus have been exhausted, and no agreement reached, the amendment shall as a last resort be adopted by a three-fourths majority vote of the Parties present and voting at the meeting.

4. Amendments to this Convention adopted in accordance with paragraph 3 of this Article shall be submitted by the Depositary to all Parties for ratification, approval or acceptance. They shall enter into force for Parties having ratified, approved or accepted them on the ninetieth day after the receipt by the Depositary of notification of their ratification, approval or acceptance by at least three fourths of these Parties. *They shall enter into force for Parties having ratified, approved or accepted them on the ninetieth day after the receipt by the Depositary of notification of their ratification, approval or acceptance by at least three fourths of the number of Parties at the time of their adoption* [Amend. 2, replacing sentence above]. Thereafter they shall enter into force for any other Party on the ninetieth day after that Party deposits its instrument of ratification, approval or acceptance of the amendments.

5. For the purpose of this Article, "Parties present and voting" means Parties present and casting an affirmative or negative vote.

6. The voting procedure set forth in paragraph 3 of this Article is not intended to constitute a precedent for future agreements negotiated within the Economic Commission for Europe.

Article 14 bis Review of compliance

1. The Parties shall review compliance with the provisions of this Convention on the basis of the compliance procedure, as a non-adversarial and assistance-oriented procedure adopted by the Meeting of the Parties. The review shall be based on, but not limited to, regular reporting by the Parties. The Meeting of Parties shall decide on the frequency of regular reporting required by the Parties and the information to be included in those regular reports.

2. The compliance procedure shall be available for application to any protocol adopted under this Convention. [Amend. 2]

Article 15 Settlement of disputes

1. If a dispute arises between two or more Parties about the interpretation or application of this Convention, they shall seek a solution by negotiation or by any other method of dispute settlement acceptable to the parties to the dispute.

2. When signing, ratifying, accepting, approving or acceding to this Convention, or at any time thereafter, a Party may declare in writing to the Depositary that for a dispute not resolved in accordance with paragraph 1 of this Article, it accepts one or both of the following means of dispute settlement as compulsory in relation to any Party accepting the same obligation:

(a) Submission of the dispute to the International Court of Justice;
(b) Arbitration in accordance with the procedure set out in Appendix VII.

3. If the parties to the dispute have accepted both means of dispute settlement referred to in paragraph 2 of this Article, the dispute may be submitted only to the International Court of Justice, unless the parties agree otherwise.

Article 16 Signature

This Convention shall be open for signature at Espoo (Finland) from 25 February to 1 March 1991 and thereafter at United Nations Headquarters in New York until 2 September 1991 by States members of the Economic Commission for Europe as well as States having consultative status with the Economic Commission for Europe pursuant to paragraph 8 of the Economic and Social Council resolution 36 (IV) of 28 March 1947, and by regional economic integration organizations constituted by sovereign States members of the Economic Commission for Europe to which their member States have transferred competence in respect of matters governed by this Convention, including the competence to enter into treaties in respect of these matters.

Article 17 Ratification, acceptance, approval and accession

1. This Convention shall be subject to ratification, acceptance or approval by signatory States and regional economic integration organizations.

2. This Convention shall be open for accession as from 3 September 1991 by the States and organizations referred to in Article 16.

3. *Any other State, not referred to in paragraph 2 of this Article, that is a Member of the United Nations may accede to the Convention upon approval by the Meeting of the Parties. The Meeting of the Parties shall not consider or approve any request for accession by such a State until this paragraph has entered into force for all the States and organizations that were Parties to the Convention on 27 February 2001.* [Amend. 1, paragraphs below renumbered accordingly]

4. The instruments of ratification, acceptance, approval or accession shall be deposited with the Secretary-General of the United Nations, who shall perform the functions of Depositary.

5. Any organization referred to in Article 16 which becomes a Party to this Convention without any of its member States being a Party shall be bound by all the obligations under this Convention. In the case of such organizations, one or more of whose member States is a Party to this Convention, the organization and its member States shall decide on their respective responsibilities for the performance of their obligations under this Convention. In such cases, the organization and the member States shall not be entitled to exercise rights under this Convention concurrently.

6. In their instruments of ratification, acceptance, approval or accession, the regional economic integration organizations referred to in Article 16 shall declare the extent of their competence with respect to the matters governed by this Convention. These organizations shall also inform the Depositary of any relevant modification to the extent of their competence.

7. Any State or organization that ratifies, accepts or approves this Convention shall be deemed simultaneously to ratify, accept or approve the amendment to the Convention set out in decision II/14 taken at the second meeting of the Parties. [Amend. 1]

Article 18 Entry into force

1. This Convention shall enter into force on the ninetieth day after the date of deposit of the sixteenth instrument of ratification, acceptance, approval or accession.

2. For the purposes of paragraph 1 of this Article, any instrument deposited by a regional economic integration organization shall not be counted as additional to those deposited by States members of such an organization.

3. For each State or organization referred to in Article 16 which ratifies, accepts or approves this Convention or accedes thereto after the deposit of the sixteenth instrument of ratification, acceptance, approval or accession, this Convention shall enter into force on the ninetieth day after the date of deposit by such State or organization of its instrument of ratification, acceptance, approval or accession.

Article 19 Withdrawal

At any time after four years from the date on which this Convention has come into force with respect to a Party, that Party may withdraw from this Convention by giving written notification to the Depositary. Any such withdrawal shall take effect on the ninetieth day after the date of its receipt by the Depositary. Any such withdrawal shall not affect the application of Article 3 of this Convention to a proposed activity in respect of which a notification has been made pursuant to Article 3, paragraph 1, or a request has been made pursuant to Article 3, paragraph 7, before such withdrawal took effect.

Article 20 Authentic texts

The original of this Convention, of which the English, French and Russian texts are equally authentic, shall be deposited with the Secretary-General of the United Nations.

IN WITNESS WHEREOF the undersigned, being duly authorized thereto, have signed this Convention.

DONE at Espoo (Finland), this twenty-fifth day of February one thousand nine hundred and ninety-one.

Appendix I List of activities

[Appendix I was revised by Amend. 2. The revised text is not included below.]

1. Crude oil refineries (excluding undertakings manufacturing only lubricants from crude oil) and installations for the gasification and liquefaction of 500 tonnes or more of coal or bituminous shale per day.

2. Thermal power stations and other combustion installations with a heat output of 300 megawatts or more and nuclear power stations and other nuclear reactors (except research installations for the production and conversion of fissionable and fertile materials, whose maximum power does not exceed 1 kilowatt continuous thermal load).

3. Installations solely designed for the production or enrichment of nuclear fuels, for the reprocessing of irradiated nuclear fuels or for the storage, disposal and processing of radioactive waste.

4. Major installations for the initial smelting of cast-iron and steel and for the production of non-ferrous metals.

5. Installations for the extraction of asbestos and for the processing and transformation of asbestos and products containing asbestos: for asbestos-cement products, with an annual production of more than 20,000 tonnes finished product; for friction material, with an annual production of more than 50 tonnes finished product; and for other asbestos utilization of more than 200 tonnes per year.

6. Integrated chemical installations.

7. Construction of motorways, express roads* and lines for long-distance railway traffic and of airports with a basic runway length of 2,100 metres or more.

8. Large-diameter oil and gas pipelines.

9. Trading ports and also inland waterways and ports for inland-waterway traffic which permit the passage of vessels of over 1,350 tonnes.

10. Waste-disposal installations for the incineration, chemical treatment or landfill of toxic and dangerous wastes.

11. Large dams and reservoirs.

12. Groundwater abstraction activities in cases where the annual volume of water to be abstracted amounts to 10 million cubic metres or more.

13. Pulp and paper manufacturing of 200 air-dried metric tonnes or more per day.

14. Major mining, on-site extraction and processing of metal ores or coal.

15. Offshore hydrocarbon production.

16. Major storage facilities for petroleum, petrochemical and chemical products.

17. Deforestation of large areas.

*For the purposes of this Convention:

– "Motorway" means a road specially designed and built for motor traffic, which does not serve properties bordering on it, and which:

(a) Is provided, except at special points or temporarily, with separate carriageways for the two directions of traffic, separated from each other by a dividing strip not intended for traffic or, exceptionally, by other means;

(b) Does not cross at level with any road, railway or tramway track, or footpath; and

(c) Is specially sign-posted as a motorway.

– "Express road" means a road reserved for motor traffic accessible only from interchanges or controlled junctions and on which, in particular, stopping and parking are prohibited on the running carriageway(s).

Appendix II Content of the environmental impact assessment documentation

Information to be included in the environmental impact assessment documentation shall, as a minimum, contain, in accordance with Article 4:

(a) A description of the proposed activity and its purpose;
(b) A description, where appropriate, of reasonable alternatives (for example, locational or technological) to the proposed activity and also the no-action alternative;
(c) A description of the environment likely to be significantly affected by the proposed activity and its alternatives;
(d) A description of the potential environmental impact of the proposed activity and its alternatives and an estimation of its significance;
(e) A description of mitigation measures to keep adverse environmental impact to a minimum;
(f) An explicit indication of predictive methods and underlying assumptions as well as the relevant environmental data used;
(g) An identification of gaps in knowledge and uncertainties encountered in compiling the required information;
(h) Where appropriate, an outline for monitoring and management programmes and any plans for post-project analysis; and
(i) A non-technical summary including a visual presentation as appropriate (maps, graphs, etc.).

Appendix III General criteria to assist in the determination of the environmental significance of activities not listed in Appendix I

1. In considering proposed activities to which Article 2, paragraph 5, applies, the concerned Parties may consider whether the activity is likely to have a significant adverse transboundary impact in particular by virtue of one or more of the following criteria:

(a) *Size*: proposed activities which are large for the type of the activity;
(b) *Location*: proposed activities which are located in or close to an area of special environmental sensitivity or importance (such as wetlands designated under the Ramsar Convention, national parks, nature reserves, sites of special scientific interest, or sites of archaeological, cultural or historical importance); also, proposed activities in locations where the characteristics of proposed development would be likely to have significant effects on the population;
(c) *Effects*: proposed activities with particularly complex and potentially adverse effects, including those giving rise to serious effects on humans or on valued species or organisms, those which threaten the existing or potential use of an affected area and those causing additional loading which cannot be sustained by the carrying capacity of the environment.

2. The concerned Parties shall consider for this purpose proposed activities which are located close to an international frontier as well as more remote proposed activities which could give rise to significant transboundary effects far removed from the site of development.

Appendix IV Inquiry procedure

1. The requesting Party or Parties shall notify the secretariat that it or they submit(s) the question of whether a proposed activity listed in Appendix I is likely to have a significant adverse transboundary impact to an inquiry commission established in accordance with the provisions of this Appendix. This notification shall state the subject-matter of the inquiry. The secretariat shall notify immediately all Parties to this Convention of this submission.

2. The inquiry commission shall consist of three members. Both the requesting party and the other party to the inquiry procedure shall appoint a scientific or technical expert, and the two experts so appointed shall designate by common agreement the third expert, who shall be the president of the inquiry commission. The latter shall not be a national of one of the parties to the inquiry procedure, nor have his or her usual place of residence in the territory of one of these parties, nor be employed by any of them, nor have dealt with the matter in any other capacity.

3. If the president of the inquiry commission has not been designated within two months of the appointment of the second expert, the Executive Secretary of the Economic Commission for Europe shall, at the request of either party, designate the president within a further two-month period.

4. If one of the parties to the inquiry procedure does not appoint an expert within one month of its receipt of the notification by the secretariat, the other party may inform the Executive Secretary of the Economic Commission for Europe, who shall designate the president of the inquiry commission within a further two-month period. Upon designation, the president of the inquiry commission shall request the party which has not appointed an expert to do so within one month. After such a period, the president shall inform the Executive Secretary of the Economic Commission for Europe, who shall make this appointment within a further two-month period.

5. The inquiry commission shall adopt its own rules of procedure.

6. The inquiry commission may take all appropriate measures in order to carry out its functions.

7. The parties to the inquiry procedure shall facilitate the work of the inquiry commission and, in particular, using all means at their disposal, shall:

(a) Provide it with all relevant documents, facilities and information; and

(b) Enable it, where necessary, to call witnesses or experts and receive their evidence.

8. The parties and the experts shall protect the confidentiality of any information they receive in confidence during the work of the inquiry commission.

9. If one of the parties to the inquiry procedure does not appear before the inquiry commission or fails to present its case, the other party may request the inquiry commission to continue the proceedings and to complete its work.

Absence of a party or failure of a party to present its case shall not constitute a bar to the continuation and completion of the work of the inquiry commission.

10. Unless the inquiry commission determines otherwise because of the particular circumstances of the matter, the expenses of the inquiry commission, including the remuneration of its members, shall be borne by the parties to the inquiry procedure in equal shares. The inquiry commission shall keep a record of all its expenses, and shall furnish a final statement thereof to the parties.

11. Any Party having an interest of a factual nature in the subject-matter of the inquiry procedure, and which may be affected by an opinion in the matter, may intervene in the proceedings with the consent of the inquiry commission.

12. The decisions of the inquiry commission on matters of procedure shall be taken by majority vote of its members. The final opinion of the inquiry commission shall reflect the view of the majority of its members and shall include any dissenting view.

13. The inquiry commission shall present its final opinion within two months of the date on which it was established unless it finds it necessary to extend this time limit for a period which should not exceed two months.

14. The final opinion of the inquiry commission shall be based on accepted scientific principles. The final opinion shall be transmitted by the inquiry commission to the parties to the inquiry procedure and to the secretariat.

Appendix V Post-project analysis

Objectives include:

(a) Monitoring compliance with the conditions as set out in the authorization or approval of the activity and the effectiveness of mitigation measures;

(b) Review of an impact for proper management and in order to cope with uncertainties;

(c) Verification of past predictions in order to transfer experience to future activities of the same type.

Appendix VI Elements for bilateral and multilateral co-operation

[The text of Appendix VI is not reproduced here.]

Appendix VII Arbitration

[The text of Appendix VII is not reproduced here.]

Appendix 3 Annex I to the Protocol on Environmental Protection to the Antarctic Treaty

Annex I Environmental impact assessment

Article 1 Preliminary stage

1. The environmental impacts of proposed activities referred to in Article 8 of the Protocol shall, before their commencement, be considered in accordance with appropriate national procedures.

2. If an activity is determined as having less than a minor or transitory impact, the activity may proceed forthwith.

Article 2 Initial Environmental Evaluation

1. Unless it has been determined that an activity will have less than a minor or transitory impact, or unless a Comprehensive Environmental Evaluation is being prepared in accordance with Article 3, an Initial Environmental Evaluation shall be prepared. It shall contain sufficient detail to assess whether a proposed activity may have more than a minor or transitory impact and shall include:

(a) a description of the proposed activity, including its purpose, location, duration and intensity; and

(b) consideration of alternatives to the proposed activity and any impacts that the activity may have, including consideration of cumulative impacts in the light of existing and known planned activities.

2. If an Initial Environmental Evaluation indicates that a proposed activity is likely to have no more than a minor or transitory impact, the activity may proceed, provided that appropriate procedures, which may include monitoring, are put in place to assess and verify the impact of the activity.

Article 3 Comprehensive Environmental Evaluation

1. If an Initial Environmental Evaluation indicates or if it is otherwise determined that a proposed activity is likely to have more than a minor or transitory impact, a Comprehensive Environmental Evaluation shall be prepared.

2. A Comprehensive Environmental Evaluation shall include

(a) a description of the proposed activity including its purpose, location, duration and intensity, and possible alternatives to the activity, including the alternative of not proceeding, and the consequences of those alternatives;
(b) a description of the initial environmental reference state with which predicted changes are to be compared and a prediction of the future environmental reference state in the absence of the proposed activity;
(c) a description of the methods and data used to forecast the impacts of the proposed activity;
(d) estimation of the nature, extent, duration, and intensity of the likely direct impacts of the proposed activity;
(e) consideration of possible indirect or second order impacts of the proposed activity;
(f) consideration of cumulative impacts of the proposed activity in the light of existing activities and other known planned activities;
(g) identification of measures, including monitoring programs, that could be taken to minimise or mitigate impacts of the proposed activity and to detect unforeseen impacts and that could provide early warning of any adverse effects of the activity as well as to deal promptly and effectively with accidents;
(h) identification of unavoidable impacts of the proposed activity;
(i) consideration of the effects of the proposed activity on the conduct of scientific research and on other existing uses and values;
(j) an identification of gaps in knowledge and uncertainties encountered in compiling the information required under this paragraph;
(k) a non-technical summary of the information provided under this paragraph; and
(l) the name and address of the person or organisation which prepared the Comprehensive Environmental Evaluation and the address to which comments thereon should be directed.

3. The draft Comprehensive Environmental Evaluation shall be made publicly available and shall be circulated to all Parties, which shall also make it publicly available, for comment. A period of 90 days shall be allowed for the receipt of comments.

4. The draft Comprehensive Environmental Evaluation shall be forwarded to the Committee at the same time as it is circulated to the Parties, and at least 120 days before the next Antarctic Treaty Consultative Meeting, for consideration as appropriate.

5. No final decision shall be taken to proceed with the proposed activity in the Antarctic Treaty area unless there has been an opportunity for consideration of the draft Comprehensive Environmental Evaluation by the Antarctic Treaty Consultative Meeting on the advice of the Committee, provided that no decision to proceed with a proposed activity shall be delayed through the operation of

this paragraph for longer than 15 months from the date of circulation of the draft Comprehensive Environmental Evaluation.

6. A final Comprehensive Environmental Evaluation shall address and shall include or summarise comments received on the draft Comprehensive Environmental Evaluation. The final Comprehensive Environmental Evaluation, notice of any decisions relating thereto, and any evaluation of the significance of the predicted impacts in relation to the advantages of the proposed activity, shall be circulated to all Parties, which shall also make them publicly available, at least 60 days before the commencement of the proposed activity in the Antarctic Treaty area.

Article 4 Decisions to be based on Comprehensive Environmental Evaluations

Any decision on whether a proposed activity, to which Article 3 applies, should proceed, and, if so, whether in its original or in a modified form, shall be based on the Comprehensive Environmental Evaluation as well as other relevant considerations.

Article 5 Monitoring

1. Procedures shall be put in place, including appropriate monitoring of key environmental indicators, to assess and verify the impact of any activity that proceeds following the completion of a Comprehensive Environmental Evaluation.

2. The procedures referred to in paragraph 1 above and in Article 2 (2) shall be designed to provide a regular and verifiable record of the impacts of the activity in order, inter alia, to:

(a) enable assessments to be made of the extent to which such impacts are consistent with the Protocol; and

(b) provide information useful for minimising or mitigating impacts, and, where appropriate, information on the need for suspension, cancellation or modification of the activity.

Article 6 Circulation of information

1. The following information shall be circulated to the Parties, forwarded to the Committee and made publicly available:

(a) a description of the procedures referred to in Article 1;

(b) an annual list of any Initial Environmental Evaluations prepared in accordance with Article 2 and any decisions taken in consequence thereof;

(c) significant information obtained, and any action taken in consequence thereof, from procedures put in place in accordance with Articles 2 (2) and 5; and

(d) information referred to in Article 3 (6).

2. Any Initial Environmental Evaluation prepared in accordance with Article 2 shall be made available on request.

Article 7 Cases of emergency

1. This Annex shall not apply in cases of emergency relating to the safety of human life or of ships, aircraft or equipment and facilities of high value, or the protection of the environment, which require an activity to be undertaken without completion of the procedures set out in this Annex.

2. Notice of activities undertaken in cases of emergency, which would otherwise have required preparation of a Comprehensive Environmental Evaluation, shall be circulated immediately to all Parties and to the Committee and a full explanation of the activities carried out shall be provided within 90 days of those activities.

Article 8 Amendment or modification

1. This Annex may be amended or modified by a measure adopted in accordance with Article IX (I) of the Antarctic Treaty. Unless the measure specifies otherwise, the amendment or modification shall be deemed to have been approved, and shall become effective, one year after the close of the Antarctic Treaty Consultative Meeting at which it was adopted, unless one or more of the Antarctic Treaty Consultative Parties notifies the Depositary, within that period, that it wishes an extension of that period or that it is unable to approve the measure.

2. Any amendment or modification of this Annex which becomes effective in accordance with paragraph 1 above shall thereafter become effective as to any other Party when notice of approval by it has been received by the Depositary.

Bibliography

Abaza, Hussein, Bisset, Ron, and Sadler, Barry. *Environmental Impact Assessment and Strategic Environmental Assessment: Towards an Integrated Approach* (Nairobi: UNEP, 2004)

Abbott, Kenneth. "Modern International Relations Theory: A Prospectus for International Lawyers" (1989) 14 Yale JIL 335

Abbott, Kenneth, *et al.* "The Concept of Legalization" (2000) 54 Int. Org. 401

Abbott, Kenneth and Snidal, Duncan. "Hard and Soft Law in International Government" (2000) 54 Int. Org. 451

Aginam, Obijiofor. "Saving the Tortoise, the Turtle, and the Terrapin: The Hegemony of Global Environmentalism and the Marginalization of Third World Approaches to Sustainable Development" in Obiora Okafor and Obijiofor Aginam, eds. *Humanizing Our Global Order: Essays in Honour of Ivan Head* (Toronto: University of Toronto Press, 2003) 12

Ahmed, K., Mercier, J., and Verheem, R. "Strategic Environmental Assessment" (2005) Environment Strategy Note No. 14

American Law Institute, *Restatement (Third) of Foreign Relations Law of the United States* (St. Paul, MN: American Law Institute, 1987)

Arend, Anthony. "Do Legal Rules Matter? International Law and International Politics" (1998) 38 Virginia JIL 107

Baber, Walter, and Bartlett, Robert. "Toward Environmental Democracy: Rationality, Reason, and Deliberation" (2001) 11 Kan. J. L. and Pub. Pol'y 35

Bäckstrand, Karin. "Civic Science for Sustainability: Reframing the Role of Experts, Policy-Makers and Citizens in Environmental Governance" (2003) 3 Global Envt'l Politics 24

Barboza, Julio. "Report of the Commission to the General Assembly on the Work of Its Thirty-Eighth Session" in *Yearbook of the International Law Commission, 1982*, vol. 2, Part 2 (New York: United Nations, 1988) 154 (UN Doc. A/CN.4/SER.A/1986/Add.1)

Barnett, Michael, and Finnemore, Martha, *Rules for the World: International Organizations in Global Politics* (Ithaca: Cornell University Press, 2004)

Bartlett, R. V. "Impact Assessment as a Policy Strategy" in R. V. Bartlett, ed., *Policy Through Impact Assessment: Institutionalized Analysis as a Policy Strategy* (Westport, CT: Greenwood Press, 1986) 1

"Rationality and the Logic of the National Environmental Policy Act" (1986) 8 Envt'l Professional 105

"The Rationality and Logic of NEPA Revisited" in Larry Canter and Ray Clark, eds., *Environmental Policy and NEPA: Past, Present and Future* (Boca Raton, FL: St. Lucie Press, 1997) 51

Bartlett, R. V., and Kurian, Priya. "The Theory of Environmental Impact Assessment: Implicit Models of Policy Making" (1999) 27 Policy and Politics 415

Barton, Barry. "Underlying Concepts and Theoretical Issues in Public Participation in Resource Development" in Donald N. Zillman, Alastair R. Lucas and George Pring, eds., *Human Rights in Natural Resource Development: Public Participation in the Sustainable Development of Mining and Energy Resources* (New York: Oxford University Press, 2002) 77

Bastmeijer, Kees, and Roura, Ricardo. "Environmental Impact Assessment in Antarctica" in Kees Bastmeijer and Timo Koivurova, eds., *Theory and Practice of Transboundary Environmental Impact Assessment* (Leiden: Martinus Nijhoff, 2007) 177

Bell, Stuart, and McGillivray, Donald. *Environmental Law* (5th edn, London: Blackstone Press, 2000)

Benvenisti, Eyal. *Sharing Transboundary Resources: International Law and Optimal Resource Use* (New York: Cambridge University Press, 2002)

Bernstein, Steven. *The Compromise of Liberal Environmentalism* (New York: Columbia University Press, 2001)

"International Institutions and the Framing of Domestic Policies: The Kyoto Protocol and Canada's Response to Climate Change" (2002) 35 Policy Science 203

Bilder, Richard. "The Settlement of Disputes in the Field of the International Law of the Environment" (1982) 144 Rec. des Cours 139

Birnie, Patricia, and Boyle, Alan. *International Law and the Environment* (2nd edn, New York: Oxford University Press, 2002)

Bisset, Ronald. "Devising an Effective Environmental Assessment System for a Developing Country: The Case of the Turks and Caicos Islands" in Asit K. Biswas and S. B. C. Agarwala, eds., *Environmental Impact Assessment for Developing Countries* (Boston: Butterworth-Heinemann, 1992) 214

Biswas, Asit K. "Summary and Recommendations" in Asit K. Biswas and S. B. C. Agarwala, eds., *Environmental Impact Assessment for Developing Countries* (Boston: Butterworth-Heinemann, 1992) 235

Bodansky, Daniel. "Customary (And Not So Customary) International Environmental Law" (1995) 3 Indiana J. Global Legal Stud. 105

"The Legitimacy of International Governance: A Coming Challenge for International Environmental Law" (1999) 93 AJIL 596

"Review: Eyal Benvenisti, Sharing Transboundary Resources: International Law and Optimal Resource Use" (2005) 99 AJIL 280

Boggs, James. "Procedural v. Substantive in NEPA Law: Cutting the Gordian Knot" (1993) 15 Envt'l Professional 25

Bonine, John. "Environmental Impact Assessment – Principles Developed" (1987) 17 ELP 5

Boyd, David. *Unnatural Law: Rethinking Canadian Environmental Law and Policy* (Vancouver: UBC Press, 2003)

Boyle, Alan. "State Responsibility and International Liability for Injurious Consequences of Acts Not Prohibited by International Law: A Necessary Distinction?" (1990) 39 ICLQ 1

"The Principle of Co-operation: The Environment" in Vaughan Lowe and Colin Warbrick, eds., *The United Nations and the Principles of International Law* (London: Routledge, 1994) 120

"The Gabcikovo-Nagymaros Case: New Law in Old Bottles" (1997) 8 YBIEL 13

"Codification of International Environmental Law and the International Law Commission: Injurious Consequences Revisited" in Alan Boyle and David Freestone, eds., *International Law and Sustainable Development: Past Achievements and Future Challenges* (New York: Oxford University Press, 1999) 61

"Some Reflections on the Relationship of Treaties and Soft Law" (1999) 48 ICLQ 901

Bregman, Eric, and Jacobson, Arthur. "Environmental Performance Review: Self Regulation in Environmental Law" (1994) 16 Cardozo L. Rev. 465

Brown Weiss, Edith, and Jacobsen, Harold K., eds. "A Symposium on Implementation, Compliance and Effectiveness" (1998) 19 Michigan JIL 303

eds., *Engaging Countries: Strengthening Compliance with International Environmental Accords* (Cambridge, MA: MIT Press, 1998)

Brunnée, Jutta. "Of Sense and Sensibility: Reflections on International Liability Regimes as Tools for Environmental Protection" (2004) 53 ICLQ 351

Brunnée, Jutta, and Toope, Stephen. "Environmental Security and Freshwater Resources: A Case for International Ecosystem Law" (1994) 5 YBIL 41

"Environmental Security and Freshwater Resources: Ecosystem Regime Building" (1997) 91 AJIL 26

"International Law and Constructivism: Elements of an Interactional Theory of International Law" (2000) 39 Columbia J. Transnat'l L. 19

"Interactional International Law" (2001) 3 FORUM 186

The Changing Nile Basin Regime: Does Law Matter?" (2002) 43 Harvard ILJ 105

"Persuasion and Enforcement: Explaining Compliance with International Law" (2002) 13 Finnish YBIL 273

Buzan, Barry. "The Level of Analysis Problem in International Relations Reconsidered" in Ken Booth and Steve Smith, eds., *International Political Theory Today* (London: Polity Press, 1995) 198

Byers, Michael. "Response: Taking the Law Out of International Law: A Critique of the 'Iterative Perspective'" (1997) 38 Harvard ILJ 201

Custom, Power and the Power of Rules: International Relations and Customary International Law (New York: Cambridge University Press, 1999)

Caldwell, Lynton. "Understanding Impact Analysis: Technical Process, Administrative Reform, Policy Principle" in R. V. Bartlett, ed., *Policy Through Impact Assessment: Institutionalized Analysis as a Policy Strategy* (Westport, CT: Greenwood Press, 1989) 6

"Beyond NEPA: Future Significance of the National Environmental Policy Act" (1998) 22 Harvard Envt'l L. Rev. 203

Canadian Environmental Assessment Agency. *Reference Guide: Addressing Cumulative Environmental Effects* (Ottawa: CEAA, 1994), www.ceaa-acee.gc.ca

Reference Guide: Determining Whether a Project Is Likely To Cause Significant Adverse Environmental Effects (Ottawa: CEAA, 1994), www.ceaa-acee.gc.ca

A Guide on Biodiversity and Environmental Assessment (Ottawa: CEAA, 1995), www.ceaa-acee.gc.ca/017/images/CEAA_19E.pdf

Incorporating Climate Change Considerations in Environmental Assessment: General Guidance for Practitioners (Ottawa: CEAA, 2003), www.ceaa-acee.gc.ca

The Cabinet Directive on the Environmental Assessment of Policy, Plan and Program Proposals, www.ceaa-acee.gc.ca/016/index_e.htm

Canadian International Development Agency. "Environmental Assessment at the Canadian International Development Agency," www.acdi-cida.gc.gov.ca

Cash, David, *et al.* "Salience, Credibility, Legitimacy and Boundaries: Linking Research, Assessment and Decision Making" (Cambridge, MA: Kennedy School of Government/Harvard University Faculty Research Working Papers Series, November 2002)

Chayes, Abram. *The Cuban Missile Crisis* (New York: Oxford University Press, 1974)

Chayes, Abram, and Chayes, Antonia. *The New Sovereignty: Compliance with International Regulatory Agreements* (Cambridge, MA: Harvard University Press, 1995)

"On Compliance" (1998) 47 Int. Org. 175

Chayes, Abram, Ehrlich, Thomas, and Lowenfeld, Andreas. *International Legal Process: Materials for an Introductory Course* (New York: Little, Brown and Co., 1968)

Churchill, Robin, and Scott, Joanne. "The MOX Plant Litigation: The First Half-Life" (2004) 53 ICLQ 643

Clark, William, *et al.* "Information as Influence: How Institutions Mediate the Impact of Scientific Assessments on Global Environmental Affairs" (Cambridge, MA: Kennedy School of Government/Harvard University Faculty Research Working Papers Series, November 2002)

Commission for Environmental Cooperation. "Environmental Impact Assessment: Law and Practice in North America" (1999) 3 North American Environmental Law and Policy 1

Connolly, Robert. "The UN Convention on EIA in a Transboundary Context: A Historical Perspective" (1999) 19 Environmental Impact Assessment Review 37

Council on Environmental Quality, *Council on Environmental Quality Guidance on NEPA Analyses for Transboundary Impacts* (Council on Environmental Quality: Washington DC, 1997), http://ceq.eh.doe.gov/nepa/regs/transguide.html

Cover, Robert. "Nomos and Narrative" (1983) 97 Harvard L. Rev. 4

Cullet, Philippe. "Differential Treatment in International Law: Towards a New Paradigm of Inter-State Relations" (1999) 10 EJIL 549

Dalal-Clayton, Barry, and Sadler, Barry, *Strategic Environmental Assessment: A Sourcebook and Reference Guide to International Experience* (London: Earthscan Publications, 2005)

D'Amato, A. *The Concept of Custom in International Law* (Ithaca, NY: Cornell University Press, 1971)

Dernbach, John. "Achieving Sustainable Development: The Centrality and Multiple Facets of Integrated Decisionmaking" (2003) 10 Indiana J. Global Legal Stud. 247

Deutsch, Karl. *Nationalism and Social Communication* (Cambridge, MA: MIT Press, 1953)

Dryzek, J. *Rational Ecology: Environment and Political Economy* (New York: Blackwell, 1987)

Dupuy, Pierre. "Due Diligence in the International Law of Liability" in OECD, *Legal Aspects of Transfrontier Pollution* (Paris: OECD, 1977) 369

Duxbury, Neil. *Patterns of American Jurisprudence* (New York: Oxford University Press, 1995)

Dzidzornu, David. "Environmental Impact Assessment Procedure Through the Conventions" (2001) 10 Eur. Envt'l L. Rev. 15

Ebbeson, Jonas. "The Notion of Public Participation in International Environmental Law" (1998) 8 YBIEL 51

"Innovative Elements and Expected Effectiveness of the 1991 EIA Convention" (1999) 19 Environmental Impact Assessment Review 47

Environment Canada. *Report of the Minister of the Environment on the Five Year Review of the Canadian Environmental Assessment Act*, www.ceaa-acee.gc.ca/013/001/0001/report_e.htm

Eskridge, William Jr., and Frickey, Philip. "An Historical and Critical Introduction to the Legal Process" in Henry Hart, Jr. and Albert Sacks, eds., *The Legal Process: Basic Problems in the Making and Application of Law* (Westbury, NY: Foundation Press, 1994)

Eskridge, William Jr., and Peller, Gary. "The New Public Law Movement: Moderation as a Postmodern Cultural Form" (1991) 89 Michigan L. Rev. 707

Esty, Daniel. "A Term's Limits" (September/October 2001) Foreign Policy 74

Experts Group on Environmental Law of the WCED. *Environmental Protection and Sustainable Development: Legal Principles and Recommendations* (London: Graham & Trotman/Martinus Nijhoff Publishers, 1987)

Ferester, Philip Michael. "Revitalizing the National Environmental Policy Act: Substantive Law Adaptations from NEPA's Progeny" (1992) 16 Harvard Envt'l L. Rev. 207

Finnemore, Martha. "Response: Are Legal Norms Distinctive" (2000) 32 NYU JIL & Pol'y 699

Finnemore, Martha, and Sikkink, Katherine. "International Norm Dynamics and Political Change" (1998) 52 Int. Org. 887

Finnemore, Martha, and Toope, Stephen. "Alternatives to 'Legalization': Richer Views of Law and Politics" (2001) 55 Int. Org. 743

Fowler, H., and de Aguiar, A. "Environmental Impact Assessment in Brazil" (1993) 13 Environmental Impact Assessment Review 169

Franck, Thomas. "Legitimacy in the International System" (1988) 82 AJIL 705

The Power of Legitimacy Among Nations (New York: Oxford University Press, 1990)

Fairness in International Law and Institutions (Oxford: Clarendon Press, 1995)

Frank, David, Hironaka, Ann, and Schofer, Evan. "The Nation-State and the Natural Environment over the Twentieth Century" (2000) 65 Amer. Soc. Rev. 96

Fuller, Lon. "Positivism and Fidelity to Law: A Reply to Professor Hart" (1958) 71 Harvard L. Rev. 630

"The Forms and Limits of Adjudication" (1978) 92 Harvard L. Rev. 353

George, Clive. "Testing for Sustainable Development Through Environmental Assessment" (1999) 19 Environmental Impact Assessment Review 175

Gibson, Robert. "Favouring the Higher Test: Contribution to Sustainability as the Central Criterion for Review and Decisions under the Canadian Environmental Assessment Act" (2000) 10 J. Envt'l L. Prac. 39

Specification of Sustainability-Based Environmental Assessment Decision Criteria and Implications for Determining ''Significance" in Environmental Assessment (Ottawa: CEAA Research and Development Monograph Series, 2000)

Gilpin, Alan. *Environmental Impact Assessment: Cutting Edge for the Twenty-First Century* (Cambridge: Cambridge University Press, 1995)

Goldstein, Judith, *et al.*, eds. "Introduction: Legalization and World Politics" (2000) 54 Int. Org. 385

Gonzalez-Perez, Jeffrey, and Klein, Douglas. "The International Reach of the Environmental Impact Statement Requirement of the National Environmental Policy Act" (1994) 62 Geo. Washington L. Rev. 757

Government of Canada, *Climate Change Plan for Canada* (Ottawa: 2002), www.climatechange.gc.ca/plan_for_canada/index.html

Gray, Kevin. "International Environmental Impact Assessment: Potential for a Multilateral Environmental Agreement" (2000) 11 Colo. J. Int'l Envt'l L. & Pol'y 83

Grieco, Joseph. "Anarchy and the Limits of Cooperation: A Realist Critique of the Newest Liberal Institutionalism" (1988) 42 Int. Org. 485

Gutmann, Amy, and Thompson, Dennis. "Deliberative Democracy Beyond Process" in James Fishkin and Peter Laslett, eds., *Debating Deliberative Democracy* (Malden, MA: Blackwell Publishing, 2003) 31

Guzman, Andrew. "A Compliance-Based Theory of International Law" (2002) 90 California L. Rev. 1823

Haas, Peter. *Saving the Mediterranean: The Politics of International Environmental Protection* (New York: Columbia University Press, 1990)

"Introduction: Epistemic Communities and International Policy Coordination" (1992) 46 Int. Org. 1

Haeuber, Richard. "The World Bank and Environmental Assessment: The Role of Nongovernmental Organizations" (1992) 12 Environmental Impact Assessment Review 331

Handl, Günther. "The Environment: International Rights and Responsibilities" (1980) 74 Proc. Am. Soc. Int'l L. 223

"Environmental Security and Global Change: The Challenge to International Law" (1990) 1 YBIEL 3

Hanqin, Xue. *Transboundary Damage in International Law* (Cambridge: Cambridge University Press, 2003) ch. 5

Hart, H. L. A. "Positivism and the Separation of Law and Morals" (1958) 71 Harvard L. Rev. 593

Hart, Henry Jr., and Sacks, Albert. *The Legal Process: Basic Problems in the Making and Application of Law* (Westbury, NY: Foundation Press, 1994)

Hathaway, Oona. "Between Power and Principle: An Integrated Theory of International Law" (2005) 72 Chicago L. Rev. 469

Henkin, Louis. *How Nations Behave: Law and Foreign Policy* (2nd edn, New York: Columbia University Press, 1979)

Herz, Michael. "Parallel Universes: NEPA Lessons for the New Property" (1993) 93 Columbia L. Rev. 1668

Higgins, Rosalyn. *Problems and Process: International Law and How We Use It* (New York: Clarendon Press, 1994) ch. 1

Hironaka, Anne. "The Globalization of Environmental Protection: The Case of Environmental Impact Assessment" (2002) 43/1 Int'l J. of Comparative Sociology 65

Hironaka, Anne, and Schofer, Evan. "Decoupling in the Environmental Areana: The Case of Environmental Impact Assessments" in Andrew Hoffman, ed., *Organizations, Policy and the Natural Environment: Institutional and Strategic Perspectives* (Palo Alto, CA: Stanford University Press, 2004)

Hobby, Beverly, *et al.*, *Canadian Environmental Assessment Act: An Annotated Guide* (Aurora, Ontario: Canada Law Book Co., 2003)

Holder, Jane. *Environmental Assessment: The Regulation of Decision Making* (New York: Oxford University Press, 2004)

Hurd, Ian. "Legitimacy and Authority in International Politics" (1999) 53 Int. Org. 379

International Association for Impact Assessment. *The Linkages Between Impact Assessment and the Sustainable Development Agenda, and Recommendations for Change: Statements and Policy Briefing for the World Summit on Sustainable Development*, www.iaia.org

International Law Association. "Legal Aspects of the Conservation of the Environment," *Report of the Sixtieth Conference* 157

Irwin, Will. "Impact Assessment – First Session of the Working Group of Experts" (1984) 13 ELP 51

Jacobson, Harold, and Brown Weiss, Edith. "A Framework for Analysis" in Edith Brown Weiss and Harold Jacobsen, eds., *Engaging Countries: Strengthening Compliance with International Environmental Accords* (Cambridge, MA: MIT Press, 1998) 1

Jessup, Philip, *Transnational Law* (New Haven, CT: Yale University Press, 1956)

Kaniaru, Donald, *et al.* "UNEP's Programme of Assistance on National Legislation and Institutions" in Sun Lin and Lal Kurukulasuriya, eds., *UNEP's New Way Forward: Environmental Law and Sustainable Development* (Nairobi: UNEP, 1995) 153

Karkkainen, Bradley. "Toward a Smarter NEPA: Monitoring and Managing Government's Environmental Performance" (2002) 102 Columbia L. Rev. 903

Kennan, George. *American Diplomacy, 1900–1950* (Chicago: University of Chicago Press, 1951)

Kennett, Steven. "The Canadian Environmental Assessment Act's Transboundary Provisions: Trojan Horse or Paper Tiger?" (1995) 5 J. Envt'l L. and Prac. 263

Keohane, Robert. *After Hegemony: Cooperation and Discord in the World Political Economy* (Princeton, NJ: Princeton University Press, 1984)

"International Relations and International Law: Two Optics" (1997) 38 Harvard ILJ 487

"When Does International Law Come Home?" (1998) 35 Houston L. Rev. 699

"Governance in a Partially Globalized World" (2001) 95 Am. Pol. Sci. Rev. 1

Keohane, Robert, and Nye, Joseph. *Power and Interdependence: Politics in a World in Transition* (Boston: Little, Brown & Co., 1977)

"Power and Interdependence Revisited" (1987) 41 Int. Org. 725

Kingsbury, Benedict. "The Concept of Compliance as a Function of Competing Conceptions of International Law" (1998) 19 Michigan JIL 345

Klick, Karen. "The Extraterritorial Reach of NEPA's EIS Requirement after Environmental Defense Fund v. Massey" (1994) 44 Am. U. L. Rev. 291

Knop, Karen. "Here and There: International Law in Domestic Courts" (2000) 32 NYU JIL & Pol'y 501

"Reflections on Thomas Franck, Race and Nationalism (1960): General Principles of Law and Situated Generality" (2003) 35 NYU JIL & Pol'y 437

Knox, John. "A New Approach to Compliance with International Environmental Law: The Submissions Procedure of the NAFTA Environmental Commission" (2001) 28 Ecol. LQ 1

"The Myth and Reality of Transboundary Environmental Impact Assessment" (2002) 96 AJIL 291

"Assessing the Candidates for a Global Treaty on Transboundary Environmental Impact Assessment" (2003) 12 NYU Envt'l LJ 153

Kobus, Dariusz, *et al.* "Comparison and Evaluation of EIA Systems in Countries in Transition" in Ed Bellinger *et al.*, eds., *Environmental Assessment in Countries in Transition* (Budapest: CEU Press, 2000) 157
Koh, Harold. "Transnational Public Law Litigation" (1991) 100 Yale LJ 2347
"Transnational Legal Process" (1996) 75 Nebraska L. Rev. 181
"Why Do Nations Obey International Law" (1997) 106 Yale LJ 2599
"Bringing International Law Home" (1998) 35 Houston L. Rev. 623
"How Is International Human Rights Law Enforced?" (1999) 74 Ind. LJ 1397
Koivurova, Timo. *Environmental Impact Assessment in the Arctic: A Study of International Legal Norms* (Aldershot: Ashgate Publishing, 2002)
Koskenniemi, Martti. "The Politics of International Law" (1990) 1 EJIL 4
"Peaceful Settlement of Environmental Disputes" (1991) 60 Nordic JIL 73
Kovar, Jeffrey. "A Short Guide to the Rio Declaration" (1993) 4 Colorado J. Int'l Envt'l L. & Pol'y 119
Krasner, Stephen. "Structural Causes and Regime Consequences: Regimes as Intervening Variables" (1982) 36 Int. Org. 185
Kratochwil, Friedrich. *Rules, Norms, and Decisions on the Conditions of Practical and Legal Reasoning in International Relations and Domestic Affairs* (New York: Cambridge University Press, 1989)
Lee, N., and George, C., eds., *Environmental Assessment in Developing and Transitional Countries* (Chichester: Wiley Publishers, 2000)
Lee, Rick. *Climate Change and Environmental Assessment* (Ottawa: CEAA Research and Development Monograph Series, 2001)
Leknes, E. "The Roles of EIA in the Decision-Making Process" (2001) 21 Environmental Impact Assessment Review 309
Lessig, Lawrence. "The New Chicago School" (1998) 27 J. Legal Stud. 661
Lowe, Vaughan. "The Politics of Law-Making: Are the Method and Character of Norm Creation Changing?" in Michael Byers, ed., *The Role of Law in International Politics: Essays in International Relations and International Law* (New York: Oxford University Press, 2000) 207
"Sustainable Development and Unsustainable Arguments" in Alan Boyle and David Freestone, eds., *International Law and Sustainable Development: Past Achievements and Future Challenges* (New York: Oxford University Press, 2001) 19
Lynch-Stewart, Pauline. *Using Ecological Standards, Guidelines and Objectives for Determining Significance: An Examination of Existing Information to Support Decisions Involving Wetlands* (Ottawa: CEAA Research and Development Monograph Series, 2000)
MacGarvin, Malcolm. "Science, Precaution, Facts and Values" in T. O'Riordan, J. Cameron and A. Jordan, *Reinterpreting the Precautionary Principle* (London: Cameron May Ltd, 2001) 35
Malanczuk, Peter. *Akehurst's Modern Introduction to International Law* (7th edn, New York: Routledge, 1997)
March, James, and Olsen, Johan. *Rediscovering Institutions: The Organization Basis of Politics* (New York: Free Press, 1989)

"The Institutional Dynamics of International Political Orders" (1998) 52 Int. Org. 943

Marsden, Simon. "SEA and International Law: An Analysis of the Effectiveness of the SEA Protocol to the Espoo Convention, and of the Influence of the SEA Directive and Aarhus Convention on Its Development" (2002) 1 ELNI Rev. 1

McCaffrey, Stephen. *The Law of International Watercourses: Non-Navigational Uses* (New York: Oxford University Press, 2001)

McDorman, T. "Access to Information Under Article 9 of the Ospar Convention (Ireland v. United Kingdom), Final Award" (2004) 98 AJIL 330

Mendelkar, Daniel. *NEPA Law and Litigation* (2nd edn, looseleaf, Deerfield, IL: Clark Boardman Callaghan, 1992)

Michelman, Frank. "Traces of Self-Government" (1986) 100 Harvard L. Rev. 4

Mickelson, Karin. "South, North, International Environmental Law, and International Environmental Lawyers" (2000) 11 YBIEL 52

Mnookin, Robert, and Kornhauser, Lewis. "Bargaining in the Shadow of the Law: The Case of Divorce" (1979) 88 Yale LJ 950

Moravcsik, Andrew. "Taking Preferences Seriously: A Liberal Theory of International Politics" (1997) 51 Int. Org. 513

Mulligan, Shane. "Questioning (the Question of) Legitimacy in IR: A Reply to Jens Steffek" (2004) 10 Eur. J. Int'l Rel. 475

NACEC Secretariat. "Background Paper on Access to Courts and Administrative Agencies in Transboundary Pollution Matters" (2000) 4 North American Environmental Law and Policy 205

Nazari, M. "The Transboundary EIA Convention in the Context of Private Sector Operation Co-financed by an International Financial Institution: Two Case Studies from Azerbaijan and Turkmenistan" (2003) 23 Environmental Impact Assessment Review 441

Nollkaemper, Andre. *The Legal Regime for Transboundary Water Pollution: Between Discretion and Constraint* (Boston: Nijhoff/Graham & Trotman, 1993)

Nordquist, Myron. *United Nations Convention on the Law of the Sea: A Commentary* (Boston: Martinus Nijhoff, 1985)

O'Connell, Mary Ellen. "New International Legal Process" (1999) 93 AJIL 334

OECD, *OECD and the Environment* (Paris: OECD, 1986)

Okowa, Phoebe. "Procedural Obligations in International Environmental Agreements" (1996) 67 BYIL 275

State Responsibility for Transboundary Air Pollution in International Law (New York: Oxford University Press, 2000)

Ostrom, Elinor. *Governing the Commons: The Evolution of Institutions for Collective Action* (Cambridge: Cambridge University Press, 1990)

Paehlke, Robert. *Democracy's Dilemma: Environment, Social Equity, and the Global Economy* (Cambridge, MA: MIT Press, 2003)

Poisner, Jonathan. "A Civic Republican Perspective on the National Environmental Protection Act's Process for Citizen Participation" (1996) 26 Environmental Law 53

Pope, Jenny, Annadale, David and Morrison-Saunders, Angus. "Conceptualising Sustainability Assessment" (2004) 24 Environmental Impact Assessment Review 595

Quentin-Baxter, Robert Q. "Third Report on International Liability for Injurious Consequences Arising out of Acts Not Prohibited by International Law" (UN Doc. A/CN.4/360) in *Yearbook of the International Law Commission 1982*, vol. 2, Part 1 (New York: United Nations, 1984) at 51 (UN Doc. A/CN.4/SER.A/1982/Add.1)

Rao, P. S. "First Report on the Legal Regime for Allocation of Loss in Case of Transboundary Harm Arising Out of Hazardous Activities," UN Doc. A/CN.4/531 (21 March 2003)

Ratner, Steven, and Slaughter, Anne-Marie. "Appraising the Methods of International Law: A Prospectus for Readers" (1999) 93 AJIL 291

"The Method is the Message" (1999) 93 AJIL 410

Raustiala, Kal. "The 'Participatory Revolution' in International Environmental Law" (1997) 21 Harvard Envt'l L. Rev. 537

"The Architecture of International Cooperation: Transnational Networks and the Future of International Law" (2002) 43 Virginia JIL 1

"Form and Substance in International Agreements" [February 2004], http://ssrn.com/abstract=505842

Raustiala, Kal, and Slaughter, Anne-Marie. "International Law, International Relations and Compliance" in Walter Carlsnaes *et al.*, eds., *Handbook of International Relations* (London: Sage Publications, 2001) 538

Roach, Kent. "What's New and Old About the Legal Process" (1997) 47 University of Toronto Law Journal 363

Robinson, Nicholas. "SEQRA's Siblings: Precedents from Little NEPAs in the Sister States" (1982) 46 Albany L. Rev. 1155

"International Trends in Environmental Impact Assessment" (1992) 19 BC Envt'l Aff. L. Rev. 591

Rothwell, Donald. "The Arctic Environmental Protection Strategy and International Environmental Cooperation in the Far North" (1995) 6 YBIEL 65

"Polar Environmental Protection and International Law: The 1991 Antarctic Protocol" (2000) 11 EJIL 591

Rowland, Wade. *The Plot to Save the World* (Toronto: Clarke, Irwin and Co., 1973)

Rubin, Edward. "The New Legal Process, the Synthesis of Discourse, and the Microanalysis of Institutions" (1996) 109 Harvard L. Rev. 1393

Ruggie, John. "Political Structure and Dynamic Density" in John Ruggie, ed., *Constructing the World Polity* (New York: Routledge, 1998) 137

Saarikoski, Heli. "Environmental Impact Assessment (EIA) as Collaborative Learning Process" (2000) 20 Environmental Impact Assessment Review 681

Sachariew, K. "The Definition of Thresholds of Tolerance for Transboundary Environmental Injury Under International Law: Development and Present Status" (1990) 37 Neth. Int'l L. Rev. 193

Sadler, B. *Environmental Assessment in a Changing World: Final Report of the International Study of the Effectiveness of Environmental Assessment* (Ottawa: Canadian Environmental Assessment Agency, 1996)
Sand, Peter. "The Role of Domestic Procedures in Transnational Environmental Disputes" in OECD, *Legal Aspects of Transfrontier Pollution* (Paris: OECD, 1977) 146
Sands, Phillippe. "Sustainable Development: Treaty, Custom and Cross-Fertilization of International Law" in Alan Boyle and David Freestone, eds., *International Law and Sustainable Development: Past Achievements and Future Challenges* (New York: Oxford University Press, 1999) 39
Principles of International Environmental Law (2nd edn, New York: Cambridge University Press, 2003)
Sax, Joseph. "The (Unhappy) Truth About NEPA" (1973) 26 Oklahoma L. Rev. 239
Shelton, Dinah, ed. *Commitment and Compliance: The Role of Non-Binding Norms in the International Legal System* (Oxford: Oxford University Press, 2000)
Sinclair, John, and Diduck, Alan. "Public Involvement in EA in Canada: A Transformative Learning Perspective" (2001) 21 Environmental Impact Assessment Review 113
Slaughter, Anne-Marie. *A New World Order* (Princeton, NJ: Princeton University Press, 2004)
Slaughter, Anne-Marie, Tulumello, Andrew, and Wood, Stepan. "International Law and International Relations Theory: A New Generation of Interdisciplinary Scholarship" (1998) 92 AJIL 367
Slaughter-Burley, Anne-Marie. "International Law and International Relations Theory: A Dual Agenda" (1993) 87 AJIL 205
Sohn, Louis. "The Stockholm Declaration on the Human Environment" (1973) 14 Harvard ILJ 423
Sornarajah, M. "Foreign Investment and International Environmental Law" in Sun Lin and Lal Kurukulasuriya, eds., *UNEP's New Way Forward: Environmental Law and Sustainable Development* (Nairobi: UNEP, 1995) 283
Stewart, Richard B. "The Reformation of American Administrative Law" (1975) 88 Harvard L. Rev. 1669
"A New Generation of Environmental Regulation" (2001) 29 Capital University L. Rev. 21
Summers, R. S. "Naïve Instrumentalism and the Law" in P. M. S. Hacker and Joseph Raz, eds., *Law, Morality and Society* (Oxford: Clarendon Press, 1977) 109
Sunstein, Cass. "In Defense of the Hard Look: Judicial Activism and Administrative Law" (1984) 7 Harvard J. L. & Pub. Pol'y 51
"Social Norms and Social Roles" (1996) 96 Columbia L. Rev. 903
Sur, Serge. *La Coutume Internationale* (Paris: Librairies Techniques, 1990)
Tabb, W. M. "Environmental Impact Assessment in the European Community: Shaping International Norms" (1999) 73 Tulane L. Rev. 923

Taylor, Serge. *Making Bureaucracies Think: The Environmental Impact Statement Strategy of Administrative Reform* (Stanford, CA: Stanford University Press, 1984)

Tesli, Arne, and Husby, Stig Roar. "EIA in a Transboundary Context: Principles and Challenges for a Coordinated Nordic Application of the Espoo Convention" (1999) 19 Environmental Impact Assessment Review 57

Teubner, Gunther. "Substantive and Reflexive Elements in Modern Law" (1983) 17 Law and Soc'y Rev. 239

Toope, Stephen. "Emerging Patterns of Governance and International Law" in Michael Byers, ed., *The Role of Law in International Politics: Essays in International Relations and International Law* (New York: Oxford University Press, 2000) 91

Trebilcock, Michael, and Howse, Robert. *The Regulation of International Trade* (New York: Routledge, 2005)

Tyler, Tom. *Why People Obey the Law* (New Haven, CT: Yale University Press, 1990)

Ulrich, Hans, and d'Oliveira, Jessurun. "The Sandoz Blaze: The Damage and the Public and Private Liabilities" in Francesco Scovazzi and Tullio Francioni, eds., *International Responsibility for Environmental Harm* (London: Graham & Trotman, 1991) 429

United Nations Economic Commission for Europe. *Current Policies, Strategies and Aspects of Environmental Impact Assessment in a Transboundary Context* (New York: United Nations, 1996)

United Nations Environmental Program. *Environmental Impact Assessment Training Resource Manual* (2nd edn, Nairobi: UNEP, 2002)

US Council on Environmental Quality. *Considering Cumulative Impacts Under the National Environmental Policy Act* (Washington DC: Council on Environmental Quality, 1997)

The National Environmental Policy Act: A Study of Its Effectiveness After Twenty-Five Years (Washington DC: Council on Environmental Quality, 1997), http://ceq.eh.doe.gov/nepa/nepa25fn.pdf

Victor, David G., Raustiala, Kal, and Skolnikoff, Eugene, eds. *The Implementation and Effectiveness of International Environmental Commitments* (Cambridge, MA: MIT Press, 1998)

"Introduction and Overview" in David G. Victor, Kal Raustiala and Eugene Skolnikoff, eds., *The Implementation and Effectiveness of International Environmental Commitments* (Cambridge, MA: MIT Press, 1998) 1

Wandesforde-Smith, Geoffrey. "Environmental Impact Assessment, Entrepreneurship, and Policy Change" in R. V. Bartlett, ed., *Policy Through Impact Assessment: Institutionalized Analysis as a Policy Strategy* (Westport, CT: Greenwood Press, 1986) 155

Weiler, Joseph. "The Geology of International Law – Governance, Democracy and Legitimacy" (2004) 64 ZaöRV 547

Weinberg, Philip. "It's Time to Put NEPA Back on Course" (1994) 3 NYU Envt'l LJ 99

Wendt, Alexander. "Anarchy Is What States Make of It: The Social Construction of Power Politics" (1992) 46 Int. Org. 391

Wirth, David. "Teaching and Research in International Environmental Law" (1999) 23 Harvard Envt'l L. Rev. 423

Wood, Christopher. "What NEPA Has Wrought Abroad" in Larry Canter and Ray Clark, eds., *Environmental Policy and NEPA: Past, Present and Future* (Boca Raton, FL: St. Lucie Press, 1997) ch. 7

Environmental Impact Assessment: A Comparative Review (2nd edn, Harlow: Prentice Hall, 2003)

World Bank Group. *Pollution Prevention and Abatement Handbook*, http://lnweb18.worldbank.org/ESSD/envext.nsf/51ByDocName/PollutionPreventionandAbatementHandbook

Strategic Environmental Assessment in World Bank Operations: Experience to Date – Future Potential (Washington DC: World Bank Group, 2002)

World Commission on Environment and Development. *Our Common Future* (New York: Oxford University Press, 1987)

Yeater, Marceil, and Kurukulasuriya, Lal. "Environmental Impact Assessment Legislation in Developing Countries" in Sun Lin and Lal Kurukulasuriya, eds., *UNEP's New Way Forward: Environmental Law and Sustainable Development* (Nairobi: UNEP, 1995) 257

Young, Oran. "Regime Dynamics: The Rise and Fall of International Regimes" (1982) 36 Int. Org. 277

ed., *The Effectiveness of International Environmental Regimes: Causal Connections and Behavioral Mechanisms* (Cambridge, MA: MIT Press, 1999)

The Institutional Dimensions of Environmental Change: Fit, Interplay, and Scale (Cambridge, MA: MIT Press, 2002)

Young, Oran, and Levy, Marc. "The Effectiveness of International Environmental Regimes" in Oran Young, ed., *The Effectiveness of International Environmental Regimes: Causal Connections and Behavioral Mechanisms* (Cambridge, MA: MIT Press, 1999) 1

Index

CAMBRIDGE STUDIES IN INTERNATIONAL AND COMPARATIVE LAW

Books in the series

Humanitarian Occupation Gregory H. Fox

The International Law of Environmental Impact Assessment: Process, Substance and Integration Neil Craik

The Law and Practice of International Territorial Administration: Versailles, Iraq and Beyond Carsten Stahn

United Nations Sanctions and the Rule of Law Jeremy Farrall

National Law in WTO Law Effectiveness and Good Governance in the World Trading System Sharif Bhuiyan

The Threat of Force in International Law Nikolas Stürchler

Indigenous Rights and United Nations Standards Alexandra Xanthaki

International Refugee Law and Socio-Economic Rights Michelle Foster

The Protection of Cultural Property in Armed Conflict Roger O'Keefe

Interpretation and Revision of International Boundary Decisions Kaiyan Homi Kaikobad

Multinationals and Corporate Social Responsibility Limitations and Opportunities in International Law Jennifer A. Zerk

Judiciaries within Europe A Comparative Review John Bell

Law in Times of Crisis Emergency Powers in Theory and Practice Oren Gross and Fionnuala Ní Aoláin

Vessel-Source Marine Pollution The Law and Politics of International Regulation Alan Tan

Enforcing Obligations Erga Omnes *in International Law* Christian J. Tams

Non-Governmental Organisations in International Law Anna-Karin Lindblom

Democracy, Minorities and International Law Steven Wheatley

Prosecuting International Crimes Selectivity and the International Law Regime Robert Cryer

Compensation for Personal Injury in English, German and Italian Law A Comparative Outline Basil Markesinis, Michael Coester, Guido Alpa, Augustus Ullstein

Dispute Settlement in the UN Convention on the Law of the Sea Natalie Klein

The International Protection of Internally Displaced Persons Catherine Phuong

Imperialism, Sovereignty and the Making of International Law Antony Anghie

Necessity, Proportionality and the Use of Force by States Judith Gardam

International Legal Argument in the Permanent Court of International Justice The Rise of the International Judiciary Ole Spiermann

Great Powers and Outlaw States Unequal Sovereigns in the International Legal Order Gerry Simpson

Local Remedies in International Law C. F. Amerasinghe

Reading Humanitarian Intervention Human Rights and the Use of Force in International Law Anne Orford

Conflict of Norms in Public International Law How WTO Law Relates to Other Rules of Law Joost Pauwelyn

Transboundary Damage in International Law Hanqin Xue

European Criminal Procedures Edited by Mireille Delmas-Marty and John Spencer

The Accountability of Armed Opposition Groups in International Law Liesbeth Zegveld

Sharing Transboundary Resources International Law and Optimal Resource Use Eyal Benvenisti

International Human Rights and Humanitarian Law René Provost

Remedies Against International Organisations Karel Wellens

Diversity and Self-Determination in International Law Karen Knop

The Law of Internal Armed Conflict Lindsay Moir

International Commercial Arbitration and African States Practice, Participation and Institutional Development Amazu A. Asouzu

The Enforceability of Promises in European Contract Law James Gordley

International Law in Antiquity David J. Bederman

Money Laundering A New International Law Enforcement Model Guy Stessens

Good Faith in European Contract Law Reinhard Zimmermann and Simon Whittaker

On Civil Procedure J. A. Jolowicz

Trusts A Comparative Study Maurizio Lupoi

The Right to Property in Commonwealth Constitutions Tom Allen

International Organizations Before National Courts August Reinisch

The Changing International Law of High Seas Fisheries Francisco Orrego Vicuña

Trade and the Environment A Comparative Study of EC and US Law Damien Geradin

Unjust Enrichment A Study of Private Law and Public Values Hanoch Dagan

Religious Liberty and International Law in Europe Malcolm D. Evans

Ethics and Authority in International Law Alfred P. Rubin

Sovereignty Over Natural Resources Balancing Rights and Duties Nico Schrijver

The Polar Regions and the Development of International Law Donald R. Rothwell

Fragmentation and the International Relations of Micro-States Self-determination and Statehood Jorri Duursma

Principles of the Institutional Law of International Organizations C. F. Amerasinghe